Inside Microsoft Dynamics Marketing

Mauro Marinilli PhD

CONTENTS AT GLANCE

CHAPTER ONE GETTING STARTED WITH DYNAMICS MARKETING 1

CHAPTER TWO CAMPAIGN AUTOMATION 35

CHAPTER THREE MARKETING EXECUTION 69

CHAPTER FOUR GENERATING AND MANAGING LEADS 95

CHAPTER FIVE EMAIL MARKETING 119

CHAPTER SIX SMS AND ADVANCED EMAIL MARKETING 165

CHAPTER SEVEN HOME PAGE AND ANALYTICS 211

CHAPTER EIGHT ASSETS AND MEDIA 247

CHAPTER NINE PROJECTS 263

CHAPTER TEN BUDGETING 283

CHAPTER ELEVEN CONFIGURING DYNAMICS MARKETING 291

CHAPTER TWELVE DEVELOPER SCENARIOS 319

APPENDIX DYNAMICS MARKETING HISTORY IN PICTURES 329

INDEX 347

INTRODUCTION

Digital marketing is a blooming business, thanks to many, intertwined factors. Among them the digitization of nearly everything that matters to marketers, the ever-increasing marketing budgets, the many digital channels available, the abundance of specialized agencies, and more importantly the demonstrated value marketing practices bring to the business. It does not surprise then that Microsoft (similarly to other large software companies) joined the fold in this space.

Who This Book Is Intended For

This book was written as an agile, yet in-depth introduction to the functionality provided by Dynamics Marketing. It is meant to be used primarily by marketing managers, media buyers, agencies and other marketing professionals in evaluating the capabilities of the product and understanding the details of how Dynamics Marketing would fit their professional practice. It will also be very helpful to power users and IT professionals as a practical guide for getting started with the product, from purchase to user setup to business configuration and daily management.

It will also be useful to Microsoft partners and developers in general to understand what Dynamics Marketing brings to the table from a functional and technical point of view.

ACKNOWLEDGEMENTS

I want to thank the many people who contributed to this book.

This book was written under an intense time pressure and it wouldn't have been possible without the enormous patience of my wife, our family and friends.

I am also very grateful to the people that reviewed the manuscript and spent so much time battling my raucous writing skills. My fascination for long and convoluted sentences, a fanatic dedication to obscure sentence constructions and above all an utterly flamboyant notion of English punctuation. It would have been a much worse book without their precious help.

Finally, heartfelt thanks to all the people that contributed to the product I have the honor of describing in this book. From all the engineers and managers in Copenhagen, Denmark to our team in Seattle to all the other locations (Hyderabad, Pune, Moscow and many more) and especially to that small but tenacious team, for the most part based in Madison Wisconsin, that started it all.

About the Author

Mauro Marinilli got his first computer (a Commodore VIC20) when he was 12. He began publishing computer technical articles for an Italian specialized magazine some years later, where he remained a popular columnist until the 8-bit, listings-driven era was finished. He holds a PhD in CS from the Third University of Rome in applied AI. He has been among the other things a freelance technical author, University researcher and Java developer and consultant, specializing in User Interfaces.

Today Mauro is a Program Manager in Microsoft Dynamics CRM R&D team working on Microsoft Dynamics Marketing. He is responsible for various key functional areas of the product. He has almost a decade of experience in envisioning and building cutting-edge, customer-focused Microsoft Dynamics software. Before joining the Dynamics CRM team, he worked in Dynamics NAV driving various critical areas of the product.

Connect with him at http://lnkd.in/i5EjQn

Stay in Touch

Would you like to provide your feedback for the next releases of the book, receive errata or other low-frequency mailings about this book? Then fill the form at

```
http://bit.ly/1CWiiIr
```

Thanks for your time!

TABLE OF CONTENTS

1 CHAPTER ONE GETTING STARTED WITH DYNAMICS MARKETING 1

1.1 **Introduction** 1
    1.1.1 Dynamics Marketing Supported Internet Browsers 2
    1.1.2 Dynamics Marketing Instances and Dynamics Marketing Application URL 3

1.2 **Getting Started with the User Interface** 3
    1.2.1 Navigation 3
    1.2.2 Forms 7
    1.2.3 Lists 19

1.3 **Main Concepts** 22
    1.3.1 Main Entities at glance 22
    1.3.2 Basic Functionality 23

1.4 **Integration with Other Microsoft Products** 28
    1.4.1 Dynamics CRM 28
    1.4.2 Office 365 28

1.5 **Trial Experience** 32

1.6 **Customer Driven Updates** 33

2 CHAPTER TWO CAMPAIGN AUTOMATION 35

2.1 **Overview** 35

2.2 Main Entities 37
- 2.2.1 Marketing Automation in Dynamics Marketing 39
- 2.2.2 Cross-Campaign Rules 53
- 2.2.3 Advanced Trigger Conditions 55
- 2.2.4 Advanced A/B Testing Setup 55

2.3 Scenarios 57
- 2.3.1 Create a Drip campaign with Campaign Automation 57
- 2.3.2 Anniversary Appreciation Email 60
- 2.3.3 Create a Response Model for a Campaign 61
- 2.3.4 Control Distribution via Cross-Campaign Rules 64

3 CHAPTER THREE MARKETING EXECUTION 69

3.1 Overview 69

3.2 Main Entities 69
- 3.2.1 Campaigns 71
- 3.2.2 Working with Marketing Customers, Vendors and Clients 74
- 3.2.3 Marketing Lists 83
- 3.2.4 Events 85

3.3 Sales Collaborating with Marketing Teams 87

3.4 Scenarios 89
- 3.4.1 Sales People in Dynamics CRM overseeing marketing communications. 89
- 3.4.2 Set Up Events 91
- 3.4.3 Using the Marketing Calendar 93

4 CHAPTER FOUR GENERATING AND MANAGING LEADS 95

4.1 Overview 95
- 4.1.1 An Example 95

4.2 Main Entities 100
- 4.2.1 Managing Leads in Dynamics Marketing 101

4.3 Scenarios 112
- 4.3.1 Create a Landing Page 112
- 4.3.2 Automatically assign a Lead Dynamics Marketing 117

5 CHAPTER FIVE EMAIL MARKETING 119

5.1 Overview 119
5.1.1 Our First Email 119
5.1.2 Some terminology 128
5.1.3 Types of Emails Sent by Dynamics Marketing 129
5.1.4 Purchasing Email Messages 133

5.2 Main Entities 134
5.2.1 Anatomy of an Email Marketing Message 136

5.3 Creating and Editing Emails 141

5.4 Validating and Sending Emails 145
5.4.1 Sending Email Marketing Mailings 146

5.5 What Happens After Sending an Email 148

5.6 Tracking Results 150
5.6.1 Aggregated Numbers - the "Email Performance" Panel 152
5.6.2 Detailed Numbers - the "Contacts" Panel 160

6 CHAPTER SIX SMS AND ADVANCED EMAIL MARKETING 165

6.1 Overview of the SMS Channel 165
6.1.1 Text Messages 167
6.1.2 Text Message Keywords 169
6.1.3 Conclusions 169

6.2 Email Marketing - Overview of the Editing Experience 170
6.2.1 General Concepts 173
6.2.2 Content Blocks 175
6.2.3 Containers 175

6.3 A/B Testing 178

6.4 Adding Dynamic Content to Emails 184
6.4.1 Inserting Recipients' Fields 184
6.4.2 HTML Blocks - Add logic to your emails 186
6.4.3 Dynamic Content in the "From" field 189
6.4.4 Entities in Emails 192

6.5	Sending Emails via API	193
6.6	Creating Traceable Transactional Emails	194
6.6.1	Creating Traceable Transactional Emails	195
6.6.2	Sending Traceable Transactional Emails	199
6.7	External Subscription Center	200
6.8	Contact Permissions Email API	203
6.9	Identify Duplicate Contacts	203
6.10	Troubleshooting Email Delivery	204
6.10.1	Why that email was not sent?	204
6.10.2	Email Marketing Deliverability	207
6.10.3	Emails Marked as Spam	207
6.10.4	Blocked Sender IPs	208
6.11	Advanced Email Configuration	208
6.11.1	Customizing Sending Information	208
6.11.2	Custom SMTP Server	209
6.12	Double Opt-In	209
7	CHAPTER SEVEN HOME PAGE AND ANALYTICS	211
7.1	Overview	211
7.2	Home Page	211
7.3	Dynamics Marketing Social Analytics	215
7.3.1	Setting Up Microsoft Social Listening Integration	220
7.4	Dynamics Marketing External Analytics	221
7.4.1	How to Setup Custom Dynamics Marketing Reports using Power BI	231
7.5	Dynamics Marketing Built-in Reports	235
8	CHAPTER EIGHT ASSETS AND MEDIA	247
8.1	Overview	247

8.2	**Main Entities in this area**	**248**
8.3	**Scenarios**	**249**
8.3.1	Create and Execute a Media Plan	249
8.3.2	Buy Media Associated to a Campaign and Track Results	252
8.3.3	Associate Market and Demographics with Media Buys	256
8.3.4	Use digital asset management to create media content	258

9 CHAPTER NINE PROJECTS ... 263

9.1	**Overview**	**263**
9.2	**Main Entities in this area**	**263**
9.3	**Scenarios**	**265**
9.3.1	Set up External Job requests and track them until completion.	265
9.3.2	Define a Process with Job Templates	269
9.4	**Email Alerts**	**272**
9.4.1	Creating alerts	274
9.5	**Approvals**	**277**
9.5.1	Some Terminology	277
9.5.2	Creating an Approval or Review	278

10 CHAPTER TEN BUDGETING ... 283

10.1	**Overview**	**283**
10.2	**Main Entities**	**284**
10.2.1	Create and Work with Marketing Budgets	286
10.2.2	Account Types	288
10.2.3	Expense Reconciliation	289

11 CHAPTER ELEVEN CONFIGURING DYNAMICS MARKETING ... 291

11.1	**Overview**	**291**
11.2	**Users and security**	**292**
11.2.1	First-time setup	292
11.2.2	User setup	294

11.3	**Integration Settings**	**301**
11.3.1	The Azure Service Bus	301
11.3.2	Configuring the CRM Connector	303
11.4	**Adapting Dynamics Marketing to your Business**	**306**
11.4.1	Custom Contact Fields	306
11.4.2	User Defined Fields	307
11.4.3	Categories	308
11.5	**making your application International**	**310**
11.5.1	Languages	310
11.5.2	Locales and Formats	314
11.5.3	Time Zones	317
11.6	**Technical Setup**	**317**
11.6.1	Communication Options	317

12 CHAPTER TWELVE DEVELOPER SCENARIOS 319

12.1	**Overview for the Developer**	**319**
12.1.1	SDK Services Configuration	321
12.2	**Commercial Emails API**	**324**
12.3	**Traceable Transactional Emails API**	**324**
12.3.1	Sending Transactional Emails via API	324
12.4	**Marketing List Management API**	**325**
12.4.1	Managing Marketing Lists via API	325
12.5	**Scenarios**	**326**
12.5.1	Sending marketing emails from external systems.	326

Conclusions 327

13 APPENDIX DYNAMICS MARKETING HISTORY IN PICTURES 329

INDEX 347

Chapter One
Getting Started with Dynamics Marketing

1.1 Introduction

Dynamics Marketing provides a large amount of functionality for marketers all in one convenient application. Dynamics Marketing is only available as a cloud offering, in one edition: Enterprise.

This includes[1]:

- 5GB storage
- 50K emails per month

Additionally customer can purchase add-on items (to be charged monthly):

- Additional storage[2]
- Additional Email marketing messages[3] (in "packs" of 10K messages per Month)

There are various other ways of obtaining Dynamics Marketing beside the Enterprise Edition.

- There is a trial version of Dynamics Marketing publicly available via Office 365; this is functionally equivalent to an Enterprise edition of the product with a few differences (the most important being that email marketing is throttled at 50 emails per day and that demo data is available).

---

[1] These figures might change over time. See Microsoft product page for the latest details.
[2] Storage includes both file storage (public facing for emails and private for asset management) and the size of the database.
[3] Marketing emails sent via the user interface or configured in campaign automation or via the email API all count to this quota.

- Dynamics CRM Online Enterprise includes Dynamics Marketing Enterprise edition. It is managed centrally via the Office 365 Administration Portal.

FREE OF CHARGE NON-PRODUCTION INSTANCE WHEN YOU PURCHASE 25 OR MORE LICENSES

Dynamics Marketing will automatically provision at no additional cost one extra instance when you purchase 25 or more licenses. The instance is not supposed to be used in production and it is managed in a separate DB under the same Office 365 tenant organization as the main instance, so administrators will need to explicitly add users to this non-production instance. The name of the instance is always "test-" + org name and cannot be changed. Admins will be notified via email of the creation of this additional instance.

1.1.1 Dynamics Marketing Supported Internet Browsers

Dynamics Marketing provides the same browser support matrix of other products of the Office 365 suite. More specifically, all major browsers in their last and penultimate version across main platforms are supported (e.g. IE, Safari, Chrome and FireFox). As of Internet Explorer the product supports all versions from IE 10 through the last, including Edge.

The digital asset management functionality of Dynamics Marketing does not require Silverlight anymore (it was required in previous releases of Dynamics Marketing).

A BROWSER-BASED APPLICATION FOR MANY PLATFORMS

Being a tool for marketing professionals, Dynamics Marketing is designed to work well across different Operating Systems and browsers, including recent versions of Mac and Windows desktops, among others.

1.1.2 Dynamics Marketing Instances and Dynamics Marketing Application URL

The production instance of Dynamics Marketing for an Office 365 tenant *[tenant-name]* is always accessible at:

```
https://[tenant-name].marketing.dynamics.com
```

Note that is *not* possible to rename the instance and that Dynamics Marketing only supports one single production instance per Office 365 tenant (and one single non-production instance, when 25+ licenses are purchased). Extra care needs to be taken when defining the Office 365 tenant name as that will define also the Dynamics Marketing URL.

When employing domains in Office 365 Dynamics Marketing will create the instance using as tenant name the top-level domain of the first domain provided by Office 365.

> **WHO CAN SEE MY DYNAMICS MARKETING URL?**
>
> Understandably so, marketing professionals are very conscious of the image of the company they project to their customers and prospects. They might not like to access Dynamics Marketing with a URL that has a "wrong" tenant name, especially if people outside the company can see that URL (say for example that a student worker was assigned the task of setting up a trial of Dynamics Marketing, but the student worker unwarily used his name as the tenant org name in Office 365). Luckily, by defining carefully your campaigns (essentially hosting landing pages to third-party websites and the like) it is possible to hide the Dynamics Marketing URL to people external to your organization.

1.2 GETTING STARTED WITH THE USER INTERFACE

In this section we will break the ice with the UI of Dynamics Marketing and provide a few convenient insights that also the most seasoned user will find useful. Dynamics Marketing has a consistent UI that, once mastered, will increase your productivity substantially.

1.2.1 Navigation

Reaching the needed page in the product requires mastering a few simple concepts, discussed in this subsection.

A key navigation pattern in Dynamics Marketing is the progression from lists to forms. Typically users find the needed information by filtering, searching or simply parsing list pages, and from there they open the form showing the details of the record at hand. Only one page is open at one time. To have multiple pages opened at once users will need to open Dynamics Marketing in a new browser tab or window.

1.2.1.1 Information Architecture

Dynamics Marketing has pioneered the navigation UI used by other Microsoft products such as Dynamics CRM and Microsoft Social Listening. Such a navigation is available on the top header of the UI by clicking on the Home button:

Figure 1.1 –Dynamics Marketing Navigation UI

Throughout this book we will use a special format to indicate how to navigate to an entity in the system using the navigation control. So for example, to open the list of Jobs from your home page:

```
Home > Projects > Job Management → Jobs
```

You would:

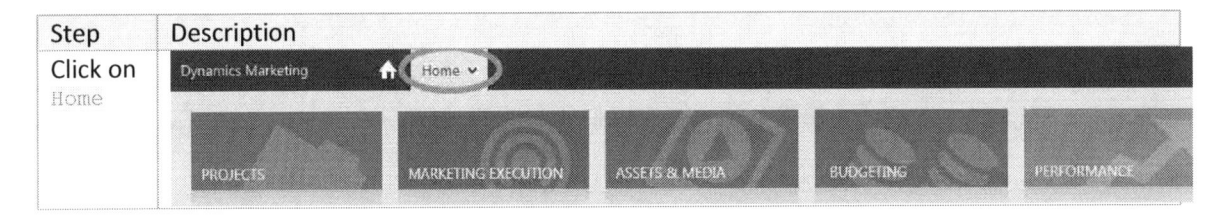

Step	Description
Click on Home	

| Click on Projects | ![Projects screen with PROJECTS tile circled] |

| Click on Jobs | ![Projects screen with Jobs link circled] |

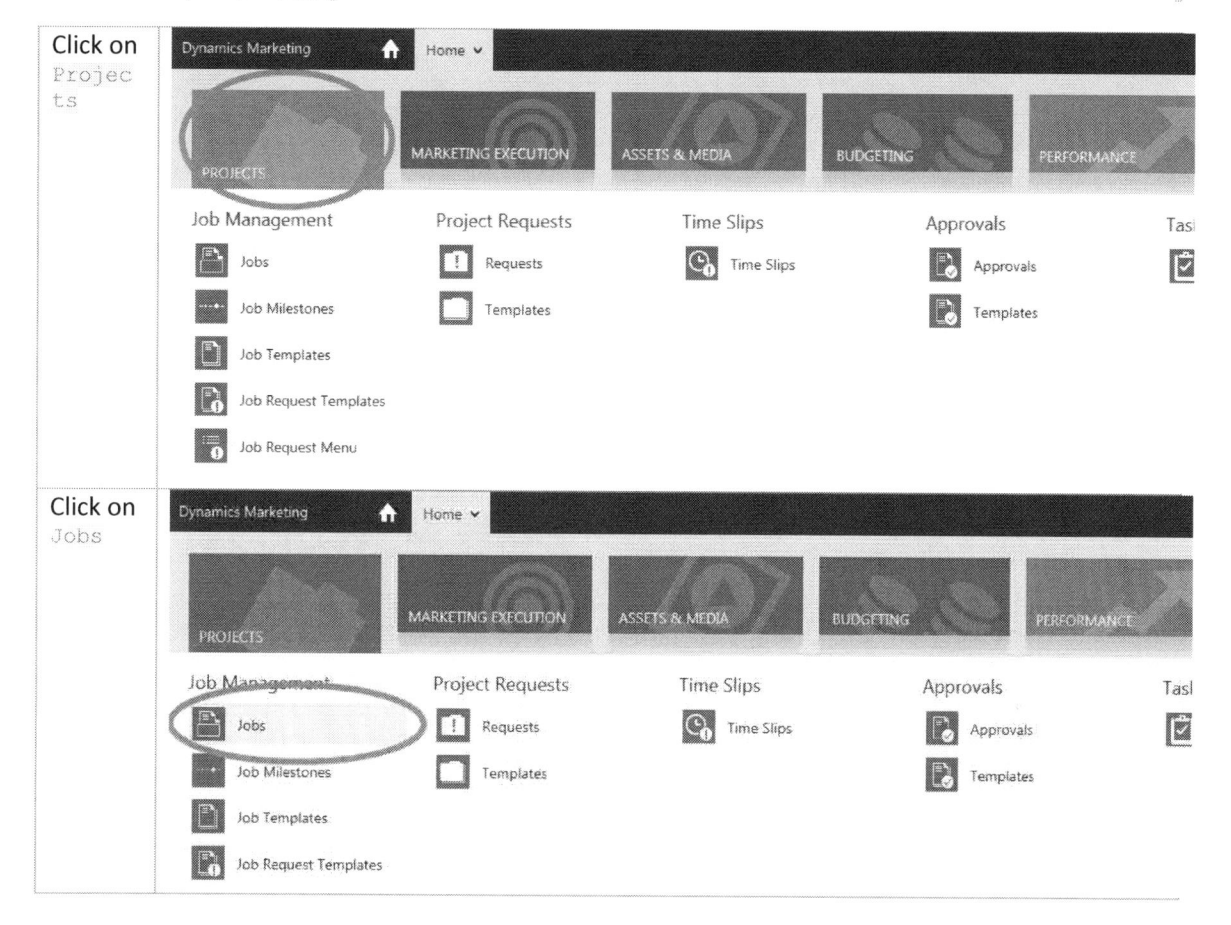

1.2.1.2 Navigating between pages

Dynamics Marketing has a streamlined UI where most navigation from a page to another occurs "in place", i.e. within the current browser tab. Only a few pages are opened in a new window, mostly for productivity reasons. Pages are opened on a Last-In-First-Out stack, and closed accordingly.

At least three actions are usually available at the bottom of each form:

Form Action	Description
Save	The system attempts to save unsaved data to the DB, remaining in the form (no navigation occurs). Any validation error is reported. The unsaved information is not committed to the DB until all validation errors are cleared.
Submit	This action behaves exactly like "Save" with the difference that a navigation is triggered on completion. So if there are no pending

	validation errors the system navigates back to the previously opened page.
Cancel	This action navigates back to the previously opened page without saving any unsaved data. Dynamics Marketing does not warn users navigating away from a form with unsaved data.

A number of forms can have additional actions on top of the standard ones described above. Also, there are a few extensions to these behaviors in a few special forms. These will described in the rest of the book.

1.2.1.3 Navigating to related entities in lists

In some lists, Dynamics Marketing allows users to navigate to a related entity conveniently from the list itself, without the need to open the main entity first. To indicate this capability a small icon is shown while hovering over the link. So from the list of Contacts it is possible to navigate to a new email[4] to that contact by clicking on the email column. This is indicated by a small icon when hovering over the cell.

testemail123@xyzxx.com

Figure 1.2 –Navigating to the email editor

For example when inspecting time slips

```
Home > Projects > Job Management → Time Slips
```

If clicking on a cell of the ID column the system will open the related time slip form, but if clicking on a value in the Company column the related company is opened right away. This is indicated by the hovering-over icon.

In this particular list, this special behavior is also available for the Service column (opening the related Service Item assigned to that time slip) and Contact column (opening the contact form of the person that created the time slip record). Note, the small icons shows while hovering over the various links shown below.

---

[4] These are transactional, "one-to-one emails", not part of the email marketing functionality.

Inside Microsoft Dynamics Marketing

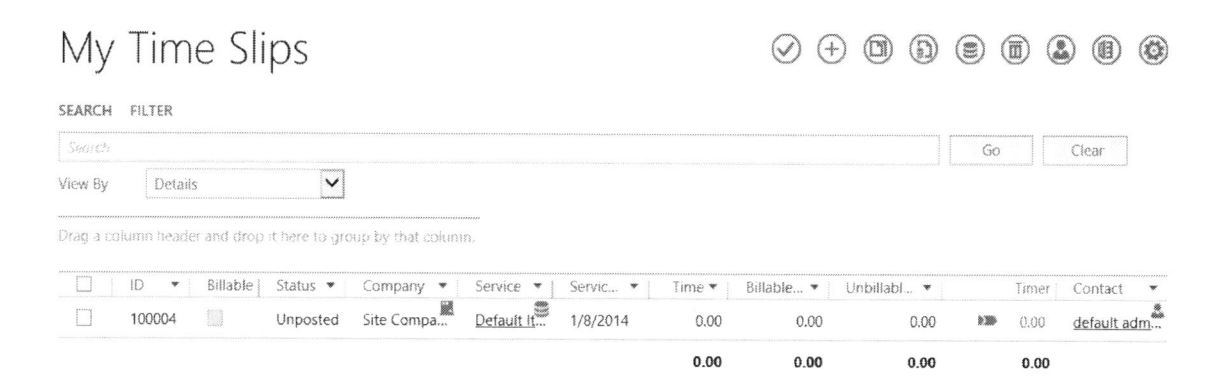

My Time Slips

Figure 1.3 – Navigating to other Entities

Summarizing, when a link is available in a list cell, and there is no additional hover-over icon, the link will open the form for the given entity.

1.2.2   Forms

Forms are pages that provide details for an entity. Depending upon user security permissions, forms can edited.

1.2.2.1   Form Structure

All forms have a header section, then a Related information area, and the submit buttons at the bottom.

See for example the Event form

> Home > Marketing Execution > Event Management → Events

Inside Microsoft Dynamics Marketing

Figure 1.4 – Form Structure

WHEN CREATING A NEW ENTITY ONLY THE HEADER SECTION IS SHOWN

In order to minimize the amount of information needed to create a new record, Dynamics Marketing will not show the Related Information Area. Only after the record has saved successfully will the Related Information Area be displayed.

1.2.2.2 Actions

Actions global to the entity are provided on the top of the form. Hovering over the buttons with the mouse will show you help text about each of the buttons.

For example the Task form:

```
Home > Projects > Tasks → Tasks
```

There are five actions (from left to right):

- Send the content of the task via email
- Add a note
- Add a time slip record to the given task
- Create a Task in response to a Task that has been assigned to you
- Print

Figure 1.5 – Task Form

1.2.2.3 Related Information Area

A powerful UI feature of Dynamics Marketing is the Related Information Area in forms, which allows users to switch to the required related information effortlessly.

For example, let's say we want to define the users that can access a given entity. In fact Dynamics Marketing offers two level of security: the usual, base level is constructed on user privileges for entities and tasks (for example a given user can see but not edit campaigns and email marketing). Dynamics Marketing also provides another level on top of the previous one where the owner of the record can add/remove user access to their record. In order to specify this second level of security, the owner of the record has to select the "Team" panel in the Related Information Area and from there add or remove users as wanted.

Inside Microsoft Dynamics Marketing

For example, to specify people working on a campaign, the Marketing Manager would select the "Team" panel for the given campaign. Campaigns are accessible at:

```
Home > Marketing Execution > Campaign Management → Campaigns
```

From the Campaign record, the user can select the "Team" panel to add or remove user access to their record.

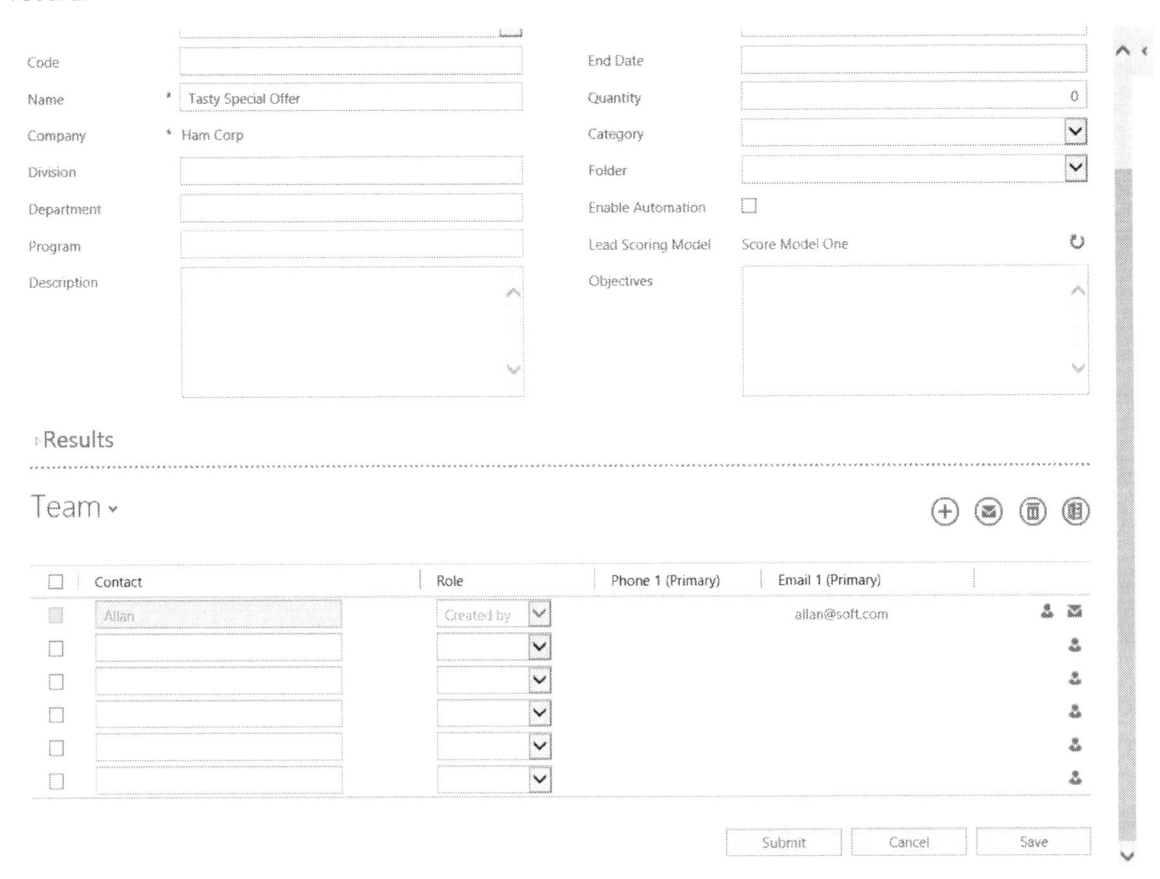

Figure 1.6 –Team Panel

SELECTED PANEL IN FORMS SPANS THE CURRENT USER SESSION

The selected panel (the one users can select from the dropdown list indicating the current pane, by default the first one in alphabetic order) for each entity form is kept in memory for the duration of a user session. After the session is closed (it either expires or the user logs out) the selected panel is reset to the first one. Related information panels available for selection are presented in alphabetical order.

These are the panels that are available in most entities[5] in the system:

- Log – shows tracked changes and events for this entity, if any
- Notes – allows for capturing and viewing generic notes (rich text with pictures) for this entity
- Team – defines the people allowed to access this entity

Other common panels are:

- Approvals – to handle approval workflows i.e. reviewing, routing and approving this entity
- Files – shows the files "attached" to this entity
- Emails – these are "one-on-one" transactional emails (see Chapter 3 "Marketing Execution" for more details) associated to this entity

1.2.2.4 Expandable Panels and Groups

Dynamics Marketing provides progressive disclosure in complex forms to keep visual complexity to a minimum.

In order to minimize the visual complexity some information are only available when expanding a section of the UI. We call these "expandable groups" to differentiate them from usual panels. The only difference is that they are collapsed by default, so you need to know where to find the information.

For instance, the Lead form has three expandable groups each containing important information. They are collapsed by default.

---

[5] Few entities in the system (such as Lodging) have fewer panels than these, while most entities provide more panels than these.

Inside Microsoft Dynamics Marketing

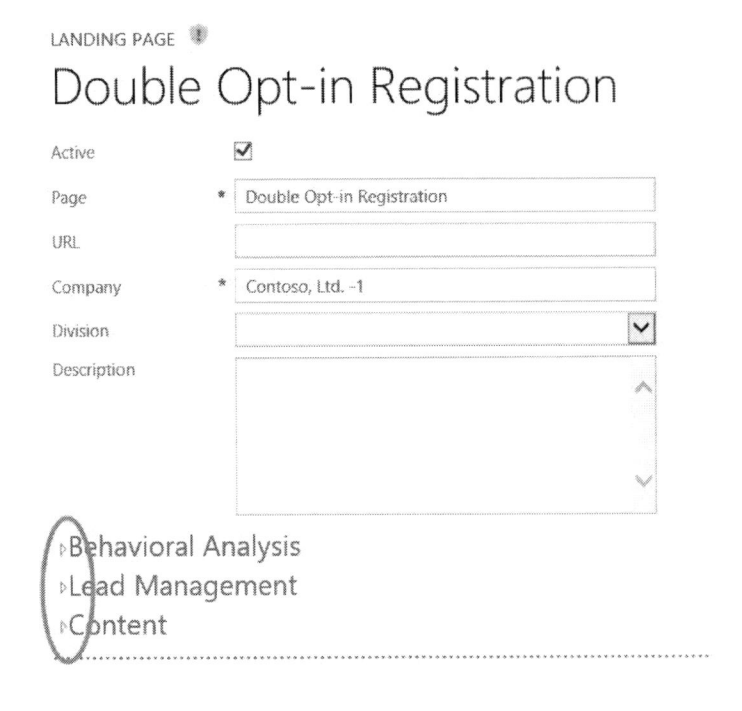

Figure 1.7 –Expandable Panels

The screenshot below shows the way expandable groups work. By clicking on the expandable header the group is shown.

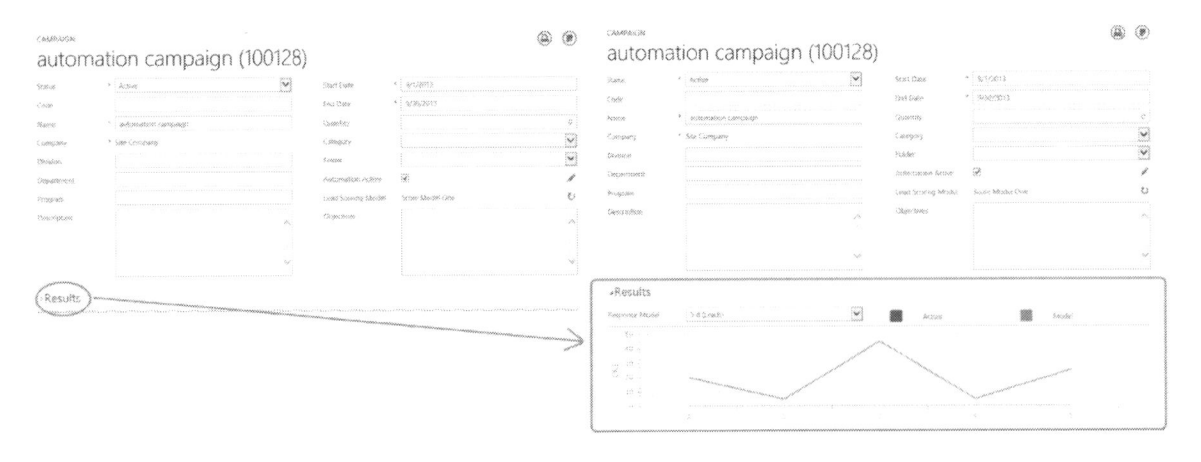

Figure 1.8 –Expandable Panels

To summarize, the following screenshot shows the Details expandable group (A), and the Bookings Related Information panel (B) in the Task form:

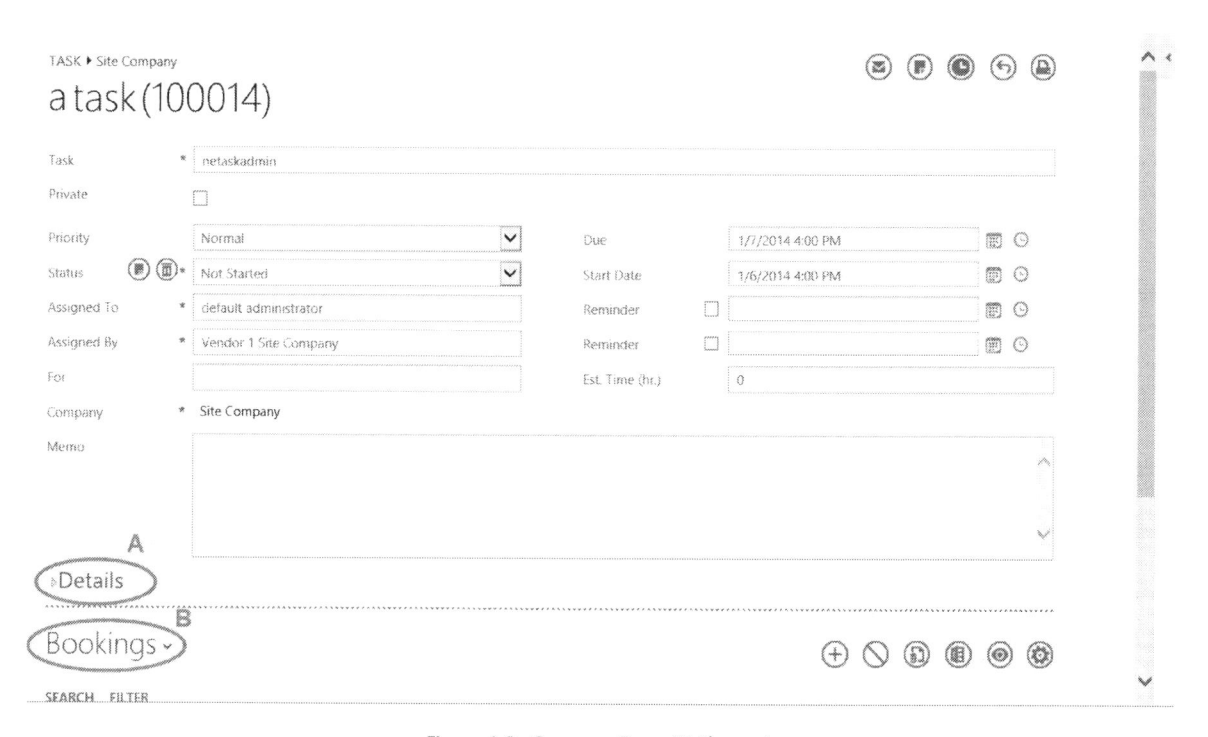

Figure 1.9 –Common Form UI Elements

BE AWARE THAT GROUPS AND RELATED INFORMATION PANELS CAN HAVE THE SAME NAME

Don't get confused by the fact that expandable groups and related information panels can have the same name. They describe different information.

In campaigns for example there is a Result expandable *group* (part of the Campaign form header) and a Result *panel*, selected from the Related Information Panel.

Figure 1.10 – Status Field in Campaign Summary Tab

1.2.2.5 Fields

Finally, in this book, we will refer to single fields available on forms, such as Status in the Campaign form:

Figure 1.10 –Status Field in Campaign Summary Tab

Most of the fields marked as mandatory are indicated with a red star. In some forms mandatory fields are validated only at the time of saving the record (because of some business logic on the form based on user input) so these are mandatory fields but they might not be marked with a red star.

In most fields it is possible to click on the caption to open the related record form (if the field is empty a new entity is created right away and used as a value). So for example, when creating a new Contact I can specify the Company the Contact belongs to. If the company is not in the DB I can create it on the fly by clicking on the Company field caption as shown below.

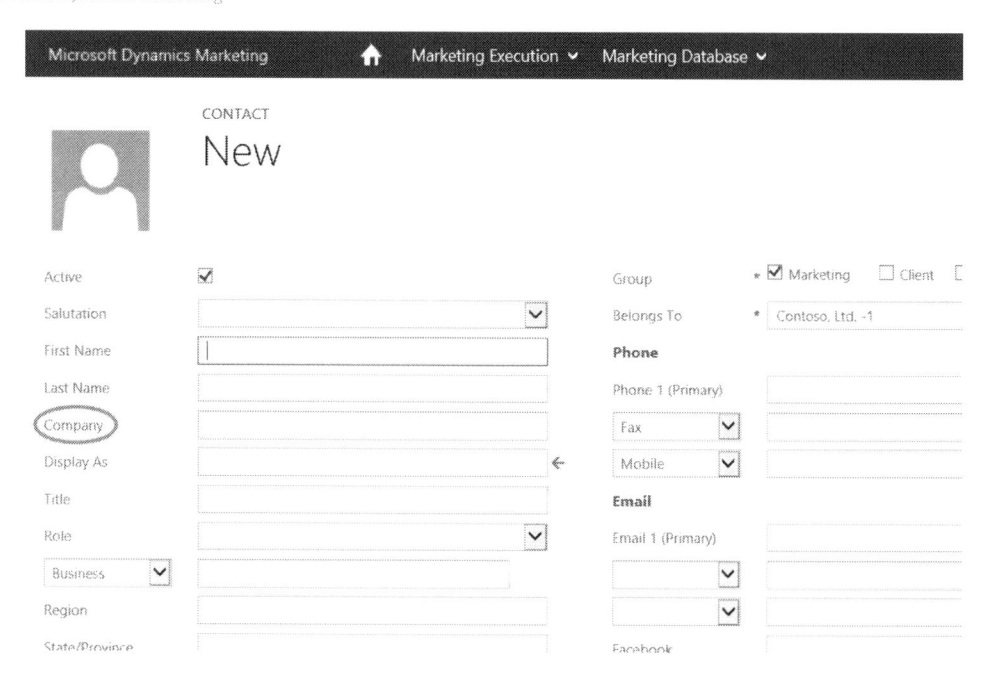

Figure 1.11 –Clicking on Captions

This will prompt the UI to navigate to the form for entering a new Company. When done, clicking on the "Submit" button will bring me back to the Contact form with the value of the company I just created. If a value is already entered in the field clicking on the caption link will navigate to the form for the record itself. So in our previous example, if I click now on the "Company" caption in the Contact form after I entered a company value in the field I will open the Company form for that record.

A number of specialized assist edit buttons are available throughout the application depending upon the entity and the field at hand.

As an example, open the Job form (navigating to the Job list and open an existing Job or create and then save a new record):

```
Home > Projects > Job Management → Jobs
```

Then select the "Item / Service Usage" Related Information panel, as shown below:

Inside Microsoft Dynamics Marketing

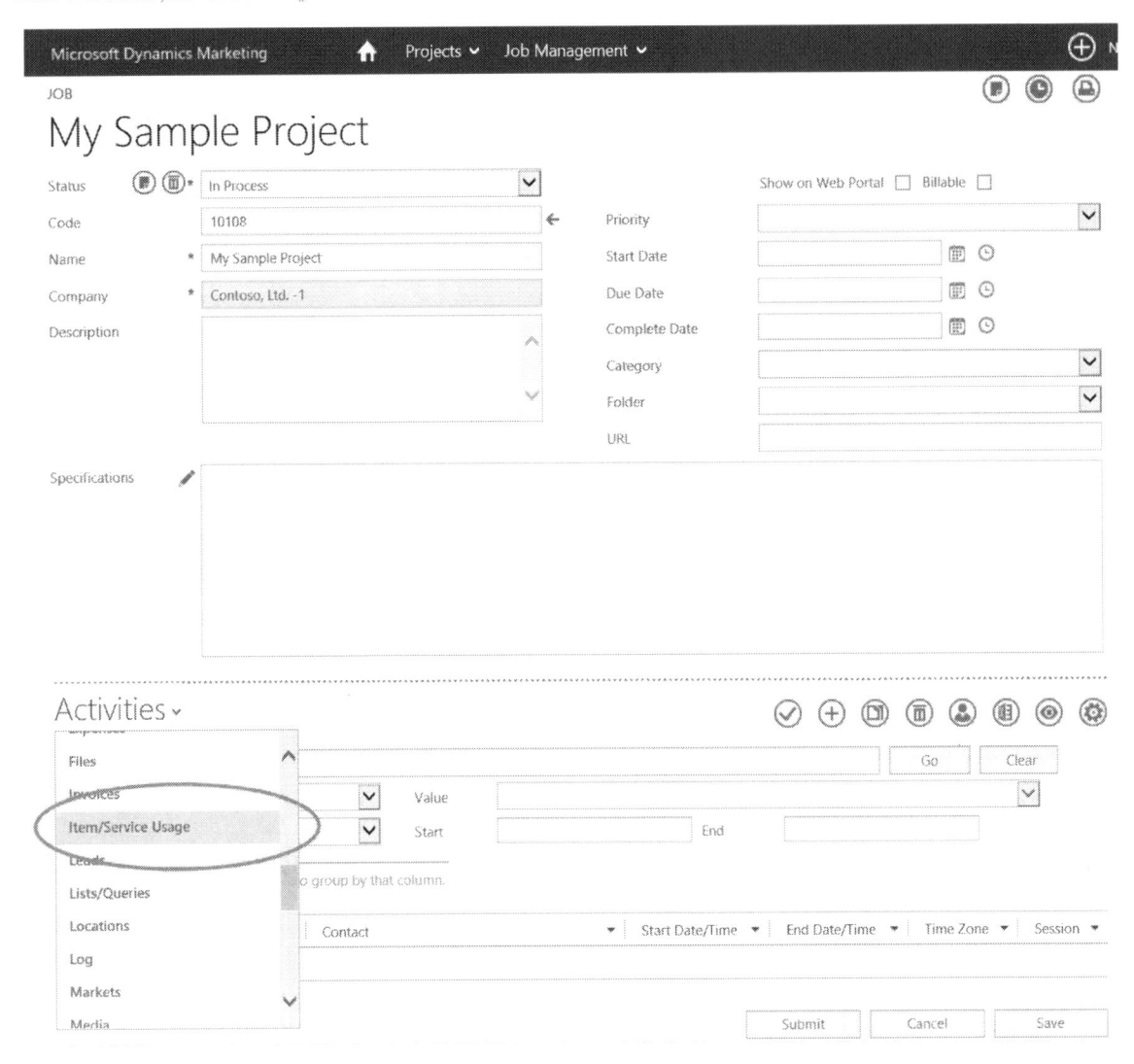

Figure 1.12 –Changing the Related Information Panel

Enter a new Item if no one is available for that Job[6]. Now you can see below an example of an assist edit button for a calculator easing the entering of unit costs in an Item / Service Line form:

---

[6] They can be entered from: Home > Budgeting > Settings > Items / Services.

Inside Microsoft Dynamics Marketing

Figure 1.13 – Example Assist Edit Button

Some fields can be annotated, like for example the Status field in Task forms. The note is visible by hovering over with the mouse on the note icon, as shown below:

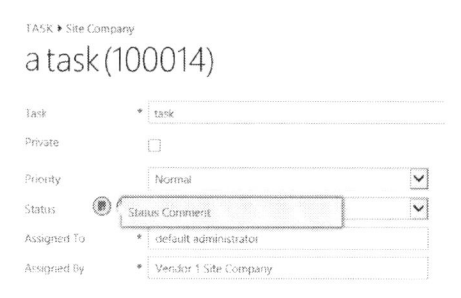

Figure 1.14 – Example Status Comment

1.2.2.5.1 Searching in lookup fields

When you type more than two characters in a lookup field, a dropdown appears showing the results of the text you entered.

Perhaps the single most useful advice in this book concerns the Dynamics Marketing wildcard character in searches. Dynamics Marketing uses two percent sign ("%%") characters to represent the wildcard sign in searches.

While most systems use "*" Dynamics Marketing uses "%%" as the string representing wildcard characters in searches. So by typing "%%" in a lookup field one will get all the values currently available in the DB. Typing combinations of "%%" and text will provide the related result (case-insensitive), as shown in the example below:

Inside Microsoft Dynamics Marketing

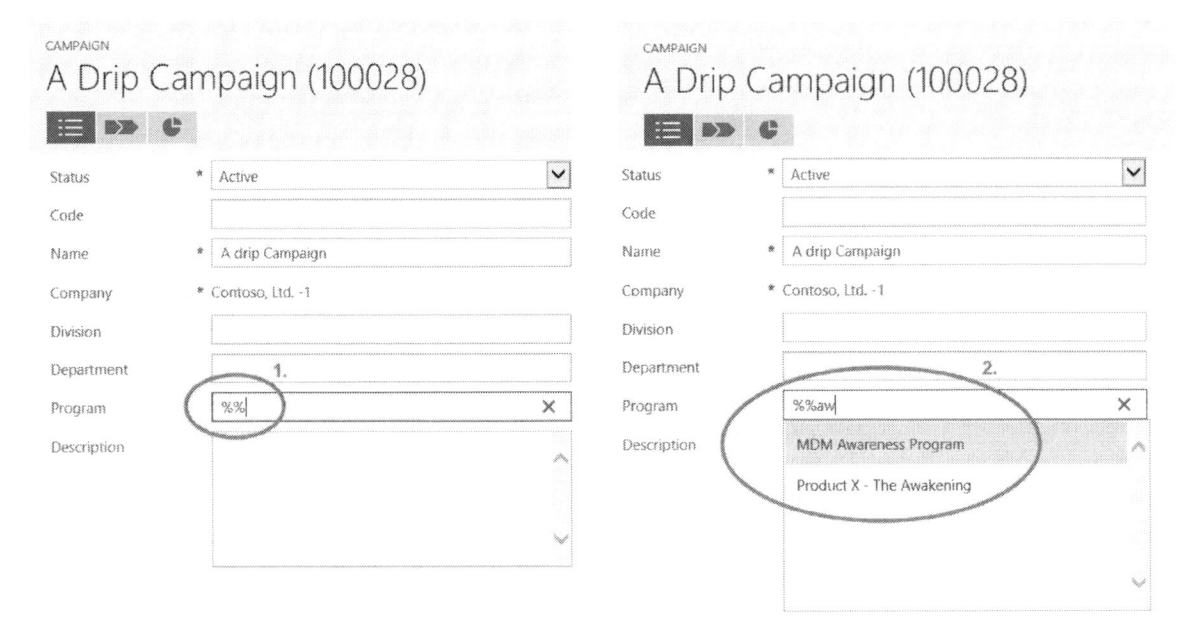

Figure 1.15 –Wildcard Search in Lookup Fields

TABS IN SELECT ENTITIES

Few Entities (Campaign, Email Messages, Approvals and Companies among the others) provide an additional level of navigation in their forms that we call "tabs" or "top-level tabs". See below the two tabs in the Company form.

Tabs are used to switch to other type of information related to the same entity.

1.2.3 Lists

Lists are pages presenting a tabular view of multiple records. In list pages users can filter or search for the data at hand. While the vast majority of lists follow the same behavior, there are a few which provide special functionality (depending on the entity, some of these behaviors are editable cells, special groupings, etc.).

> **YOU CAN PERSONALIZE THE ROWS VISIBLE IN LISTS**
>
> By navigating to User Preferences (the "gear" icon for the Preferences in the Settings menu in the top-right corner of the navigation bar) and editing the "`Items Per Page`" field you can change the number of rows visible in lists throughout the application. This change will only apply to you.
> Keep in mind that loading lists with a large number of rows might impact runtime performance.

1.2.3.1 List Structure

All lists have the same layout: starting from the top they have a filter section, then a grid showing the results taking the remaining of the page.

1.2.3.2 Filtering

On most list pages it is possible to search for some keywords by entering text in the "Search field" and clicking "Go" as shown in the screenshot below.

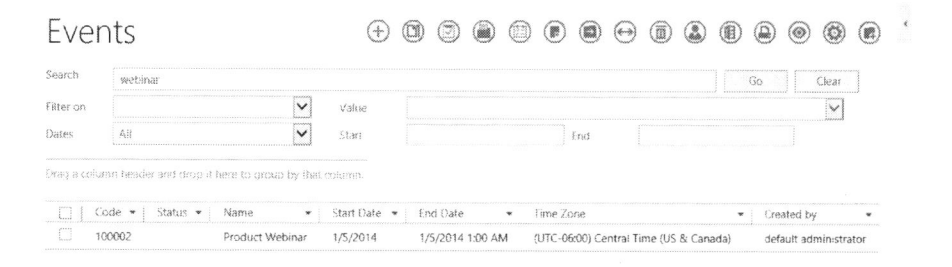

Figure 1.16 – Filtering Example

Inside Microsoft Dynamics Marketing

When available it is possible to set some advanced filtering using the "Filter on", "Value" or "Dates" and "Start", "End" fields and then clicking on "Go".

On most lists, it's also possible to set simple filters using the column header dropdowns, as shown below:

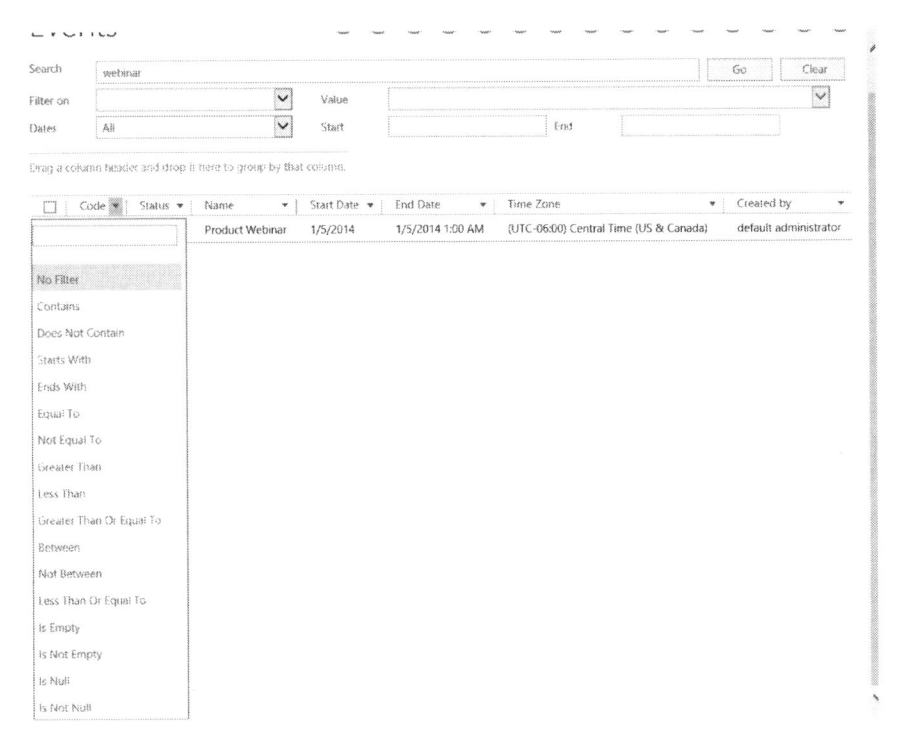

Figure 1.17 –Filtering in Lists

Clicking once will sort the column descending. Clicking a second time will sort the column ascending.

1.2.3.3 Configuring Lists

On some lists it is also possible to "group by" certain fields.

To do this, drag a column header onto the area above the list (with text "Drag a column header and drop it here to group by that column") as shown below:

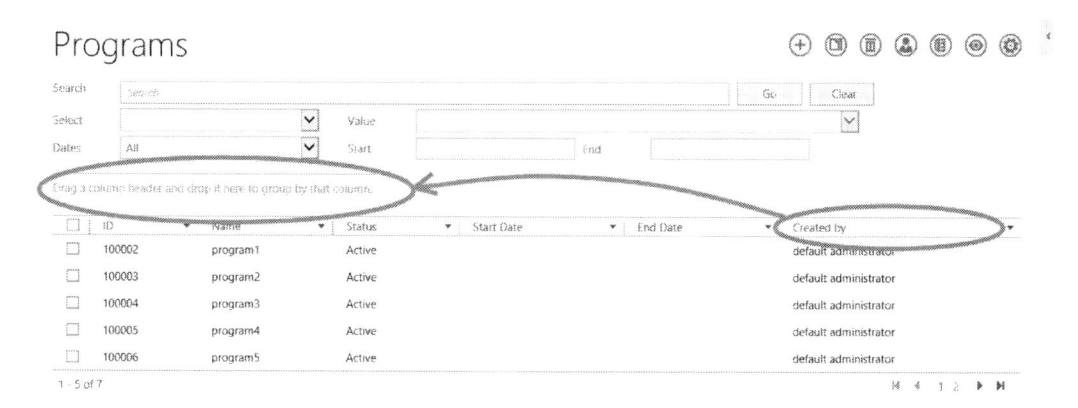

Figure 1.18 – Dragging Columns

Dragging columns to this area will create a pivot view off of the dragged fields.

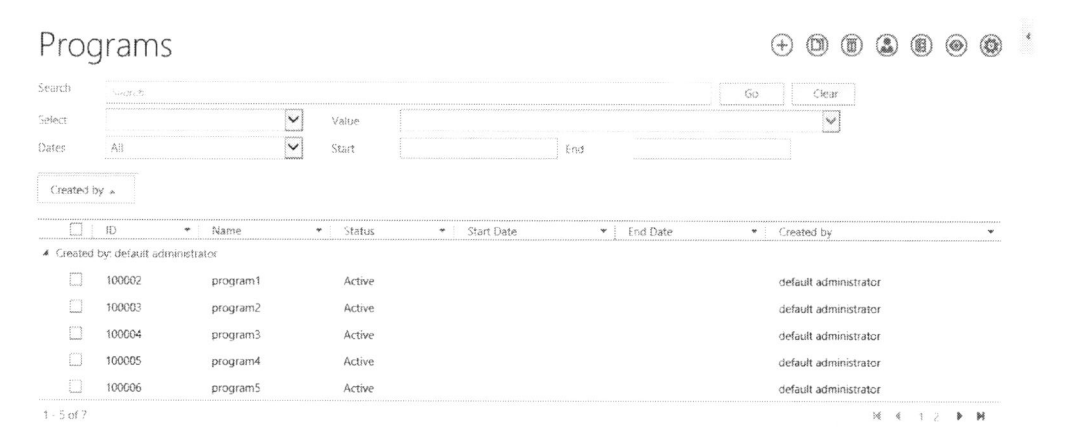

Figure 1.19 – Pivot View in Lists

Of course all the columns of most lists can be configured as needed. By right-clicking on the column header a contextual menu is shown where columns can be customized.

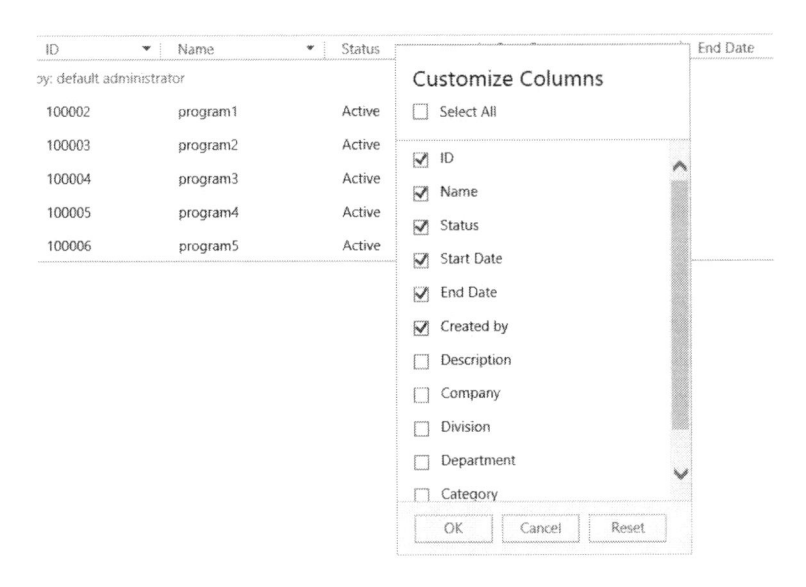

Figure 1.20 –Customizing List Columns

1.3 Main Concepts

1.3.1 Main Entities at glance
Dynamics Marketing is a complex application with hundreds of entities and a wide range of functionality. Let's start getting into the application by focusing on some essential concepts first.

1.3.1.1 People
People are the heart of any Marketing endeavor. Dynamics Marketing represents people as Contacts and / or Users, depending on their business relationship with the customer.

Chapter 3 "Marketing Execution" will provide more details on the way Dynamics Marketing represents people.

1.3.1.2 Companies
In Dynamics Marketing Companies are organizations with which you have business relationships. Dynamics Marketing distinguishes between Marketing Companies (those you market to), Vendor Companies (those that do work for you and from which you purchase Products and Services) and Client Companies (representing clients that can be invoiced for things like Services, Items etc.). And on top of that, your own organization is tracked as a Company too (by default the "Site Company" is the company representing the organization owning and running the system).

Chapter 3 "Marketing Execution" will provide more details on the way Dynamics Marketing represents companies.

1.3.1.3 Tracking Marketing Execution

Marketing databases are the heart of marketing execution.

To break the ice with Marketing Execution in Dynamics Marketing let's start from this essential hierarchy of entities:

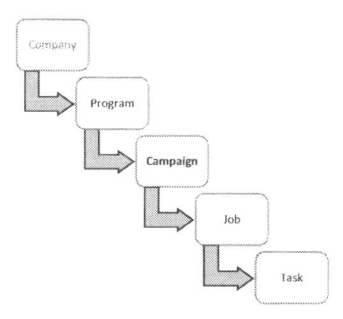

Figure 1.21 –Base Entity Hierarchy

In terms of Marketing Execution, the key entity is Campaign. Campaigns can be organized in Programs (i.e. a Program can be seen essentially as a collection of Campaigns). In turn a Campaign can optionally contain a number of Jobs (representing projects going on with the company related to the given campaign). Finally Jobs are made up of Tasks, assigned to individuals for completion. This hierarchy is not strict, as Campaigns don't need to contain Jobs and Tasks can be created under a Campaign without the need of a parent Job. The system can be configured to enforce a hierarchy between Campaigns and Jobs, but it is not mandatory. Companies are at the top of the hierarchy because all these activities occur under a specific company.

Campaign is a good entity to start exploring Dynamics Marketing entities as it touches most areas in the system. There is an extra step in the basic chain of entities shown above, the possibility of having one or more Events for a Campaign (such as conferences, launch events and so on), and having Jobs associated to such Events. For more on Campaigns and Events see Chapter 3 "Marketing Execution".

1.3.2 Basic Functionality

1.3.2.1 Record Deletion in Dynamics Marketing

Although users can "delete" records if allowed to do so via security permissions, records cannot be permanently removed from the DB. They appear as deleted via the Dynamics Marketing UI but in

Inside Microsoft Dynamics Marketing

reality they are simply marked as "deleted" on the DB. There are few exceptions for this behavior in the product, such as Inventory Use Line Items (which are permanently deleted). If file storage needs to be permanently removed from the system (for instance some old versions of some large media content to allow for more storage) contact Then you can contact Microsoft Support. It is expected that more flexibility will be introduced in a future release to manage file deletions more effectively.

In terms of UI, if enabled via security permissions, users can visualize previously deleted or inactivated items by clicking on the Show Inactive / Deleted action in lists (the one with icon: ◉).

REMOVING SOFT-DELETED FILES

Even though it is not possible to remove DB records it is possible to permanently remove soft-delete files from your file storage, by using the functionality available in:

`Home > Settings > Administration→ File Options`

You can think of this functionality as similar to *"empty your recycle bin"* on the desktop of graphical operating systems like Windows.

1.3.2.2 Record-based Security in Dynamics Marketing

As mentioned previously, Dynamics Marketing provides an additional layer of configurable security where owners of a record can further specify other users allowed to access that record. This is configured by means of the "Team" panel in entity forms.

Administrators and in general users with enough security privileges can override this security limitation and see the records owned (i.e. created) by others in lists. The action "View All / View My" can toggle between showing only those records you own, and all records you have visibility to see via security.

Action Icon	Meaning
👥	You are currently viewing all the records available. To restrict the view only to your items, click on the icon ("View My" action).
👤	You are currently viewing only your records. To view all the items, click on the icon ("View All" action).

Inside Microsoft Dynamics Marketing

Note that in some cases records are created automatically by the system so the only way to access them is to enable viewing them all. An example of this is when the system generates a lead[7]. In this case the system-generated lead is not visible to users in the Leads list until the "View All" action is clicked toggling the view to show all leads available in the DB.

1.3.2.3 Templates

Most entities in Dynamics Marketing allow for the creation of templates, i.e. records that can be reused as blueprint for creation of new records. In Dynamics Marketing, a template is just another record marked with a special flag, so anything that can be saved in a given entity can be saved in a template of that entity too.

Most templates are available under

```
Home > Settings > Administration (Templates)
```

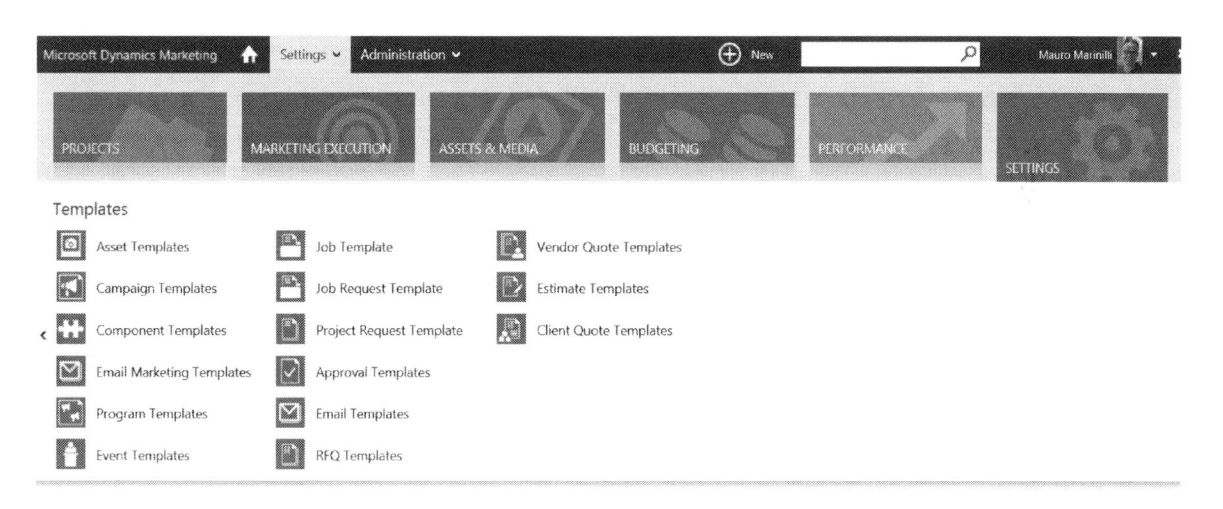

Figure 1.22 –Navigating to Templates

As soon as a template is created for a given entity, creating a new record will display a screen similar to the following:

---

[7] See Chapter Chapter 4 "Generating and Managing Leads" for more details.

Template

Select a template or leave blank to create a new campaign:

Template	
Company *	
Division	

[Submit] [Cancel]

Figure 1.23 –Template Page

Where users are asked whether they want to use a template to seed the creation of the new entity. Anything you specify here (e.g. Company and Division) will override your record with what is specified in the template you choose. If you leave the template dropdown blank the new entity will be created without a template (i.e. with all blank values).

CAMPAIGN TEMPLATES

Campaign templates are more powerful than normal templates in that the Campaign Automation information (if present) is also copied into the new record, along with other useful information to run a campaign.

1.3.2.4 Security Basics

Dynamics Marketing provides a powerful infrastructure for controlling user permissions. Only a few pages are available to all (i.e. via anonymous access) as explained more in detail later in this chapter. All other pages of the application need to be accessed using an authorized User account, as defined in Office 365.

WEB PORTAL USERS

Dynamics Marketing provides a very interesting licensing user type, Web Portal Users.

> These users can be added in unlimited numbers and are currently free-of-charge. They are fully authenticated users (via Office 365) with configurable security privileges that have limited access to some portions of the system. They can be used to give secure, flexible browser-based access to users such as clients, company branches, channel partners, vendors, agencies and so on.

Security can be used to streamline the UI for users that don't need to access some of the functional areas available in the product. Administrators can turn off all the roles related to a certain feature for each user. These users will no longer see that area, avoiding additional training, possible errors, and unnecessary confusion.

We will dig more into the User configuration in Chapter 11 "Configuration".

1.3.2.5   Alerts

Dynamics Marketing provides a rich notification subsystem integrated with various entities. There are two views of alerts in the system. One per contact (you select the non-marketing contact and open the Alerts related information panel) and another global to all alerts in the system, available from the Alert Settings option in the Preferences menu, as shown below.

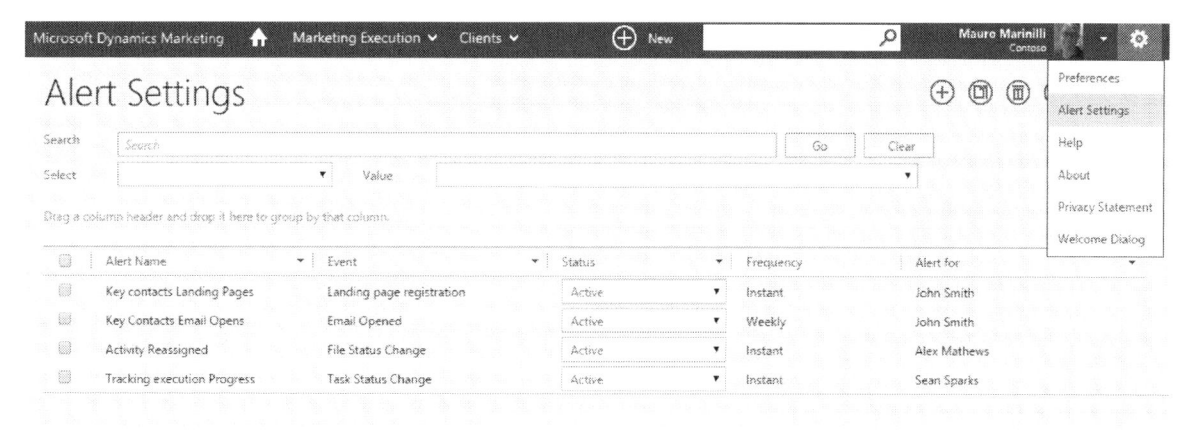

Figure 1.24 –Alert Setting List

We describe the complete list of notifications available in Chapter 5 "Email Marketing" (because alerts are provided via emails).

1.3.2.6   Approval Workflows

Dynamics Marketing provides an approval subsystem integrated with the main system entities.

Reviews and Approvals are quite powerful in Dynamics Marketing and allow for a wide range of customizations, including Templates that capture company's business processes and best practices. The screenshot below shows an example of creating an approval for a new campaign, involving CEO approval, then legal department review and finally publishing for execution:

Figure 1.25 –Approval Request of a new Campaign

1.4 INTEGRATION WITH OTHER MICROSOFT PRODUCTS

Perhaps Dynamics Marketing's most interesting fact lies in the integration of so many aspects of marketing work in one single product, extending also to external systems.

1.4.1 Dynamics CRM

Dynamics Marketing provides a Connector component that makes data integration with Dynamics CRM installations (both on-premises and online) seamless.

Examples of entities that are synchronized with Dynamics CRM are: Campaign, Company, Contact, Lead, Opportunity, and Task.

More technical details on the integration with Dynamics CRM are available in Chapter 11 "Configuration".

1.4.2 Office 365

Dynamics Marketing is part of the Office 365 suite, and as such it provides a standard user interface for business administrators to manage subscriptions (add users, add license seats and manage other O365 subscriptions).

Perhaps the most interesting capability of the Office 365 integration is the Single Sign On that enables seamless integration with other products on Office 365. We will touch the technical aspects related to integrating with other Office 365 in Chapter 12 "Development Scenarios".

> **OFFICE 365 AND DYNAMICS MARKETING -WHO ADMINISTERS WHAT**
>
> A simple rule of thumb might help remembering how administration functionality is split between the two systems. Whenever license changes are involved, log into the Office 365 portal at portal.microsoftonline.com. For all other administration tasks like user security configuration (authorization) or other IT admin tasks log into Dynamics Marketing and navigate to the related page under the Settings area. Similarly to Dynamics CRM, Global and Service Office 365 Administrators automatically become administrators in Dynamics Marketing. See Chapter 11 "Configuration" for more details.

The following screenshot shows the Office 365 portal with a Dynamics Marketing instance being provisioned.

Inside Microsoft Dynamics Marketing

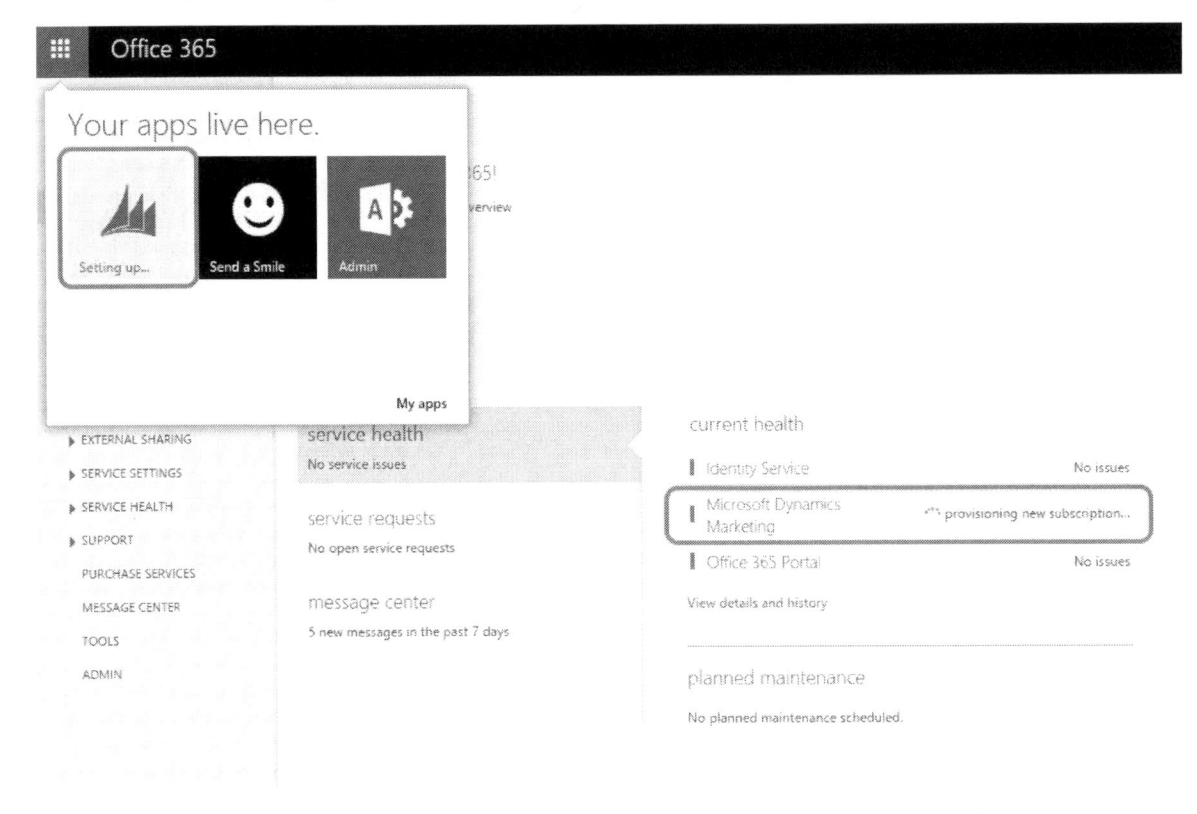

Figure 1.26 –Provisioning a Dynamics Marketing Instance in the Office 365 Portal

When entering information about your tenant organization in the Office 365 Portal remember that Dynamics Marketing will send email notifications (e.g. when the quota of available marketing email messages is reached) to the email address registered in the *"Technical contact email"* field. Keep this value updated in the Office 365 Portal to point to a monitored email address in your organization.

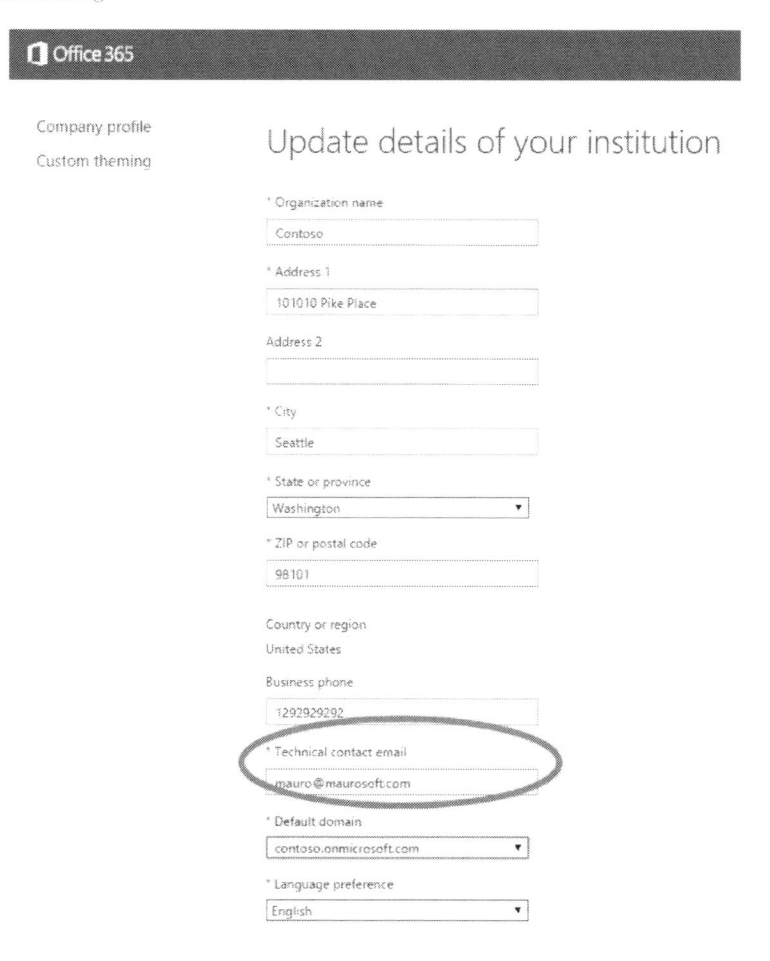

Figure 1.27 – Email Address used for technical notifications

1.4.2.1   Office 365 users are required for most operations

Your vendors and collaborators outside your organization will require an Office 365 user account in order to access Dynamics Marketing, even if only as Web Portal Users. The pages that have anonymous access (i.e. that do not require an Office 365 user login) are:

- Forward to a Friend (opened via a marketing email)
- Landing Pages
- Offers
- Subscription Centers (opened via a marketing email)

- View as a Webpage (opened via a marketing email)

1.5 TRIAL EXPERIENCE

Dynamics Marketing trials are open to the public, so everyone can search online for the Office 365 sign-up page to create a new Dynamics Marketing trial subscription. When opening a trial instance of the first time the *welcome dialog* will show up, allowing users to explore the product and lower the learning curve. The welcome dialog is useful also for demoing the product as it allows to switch roles and home pages with a click without the need to log in with different users.

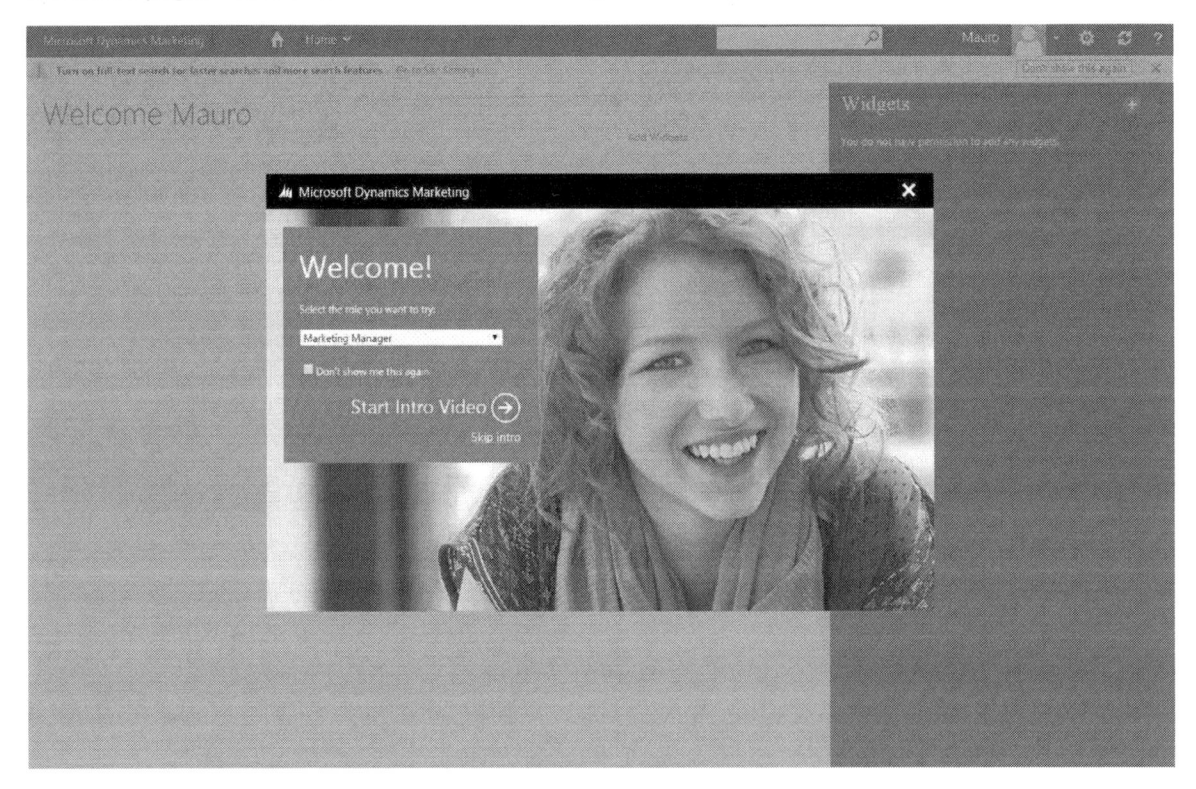

Figure 1.28 –Opening a Trial Instance

Trials provide an additional experience aiming at simplifying as much as possible learning and usage of the product from day one. Here are the main special functionalities for trials:

- *Welcome dialog*, where users can change role and try out different parts of the products. Videos are available to cover the basics of the product so that new users can get up and running right away. Also the home page will change depending upon the selected role.

- *Sample data* is available for users to see some key scenarios out-of-the-box. An important part of the sample data are the reusable email templates.
- *Simplified security*. Admins giving access to other trial user will only need to add new Office 365 users to the Dynamics Marketing trial subscription. They can skip adding a license and set security permissions in Dynamics Marketing for each user. Of course this simplified security is only available in trials. Once the product is purchased these trial security roles are removed and "production" security needs to be configured for all users.

You can always open the welcome dialog at any time in a Dynamics Marketing trial instance by using the preference menu:

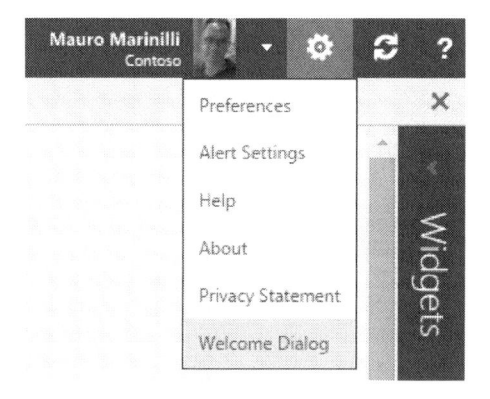

Figure 1.29 –Open the Welcome Dialog

1.6 Customer Driven Updates

Dynamics Marketing major releases need to be approved before they can be applied. Users will be prompted for verifying the scheduled upgrade and for explicit approval. The functionality is very similar to Microsoft Dynamics CRM Customer Driven Upgrades.

CHAPTER TWO
CAMPAIGN AUTOMATION

2.1 OVERVIEW

This chapter describes the Campaign Automation console that enables the definition of complex, multichannel automated campaigns without any code.

As an example of the capabilities of MDM in this area the picture below shows a Campaign Automation model that creates a list of double-opted in contacts to be used in other communications. This model is an application example not a complete implementation of the double opt-in process.

In marketing is key to focus only on those subscribers that really want to hear from you. A typical technique is to send people that signed up for your communications an additional activation email with a link that will activate their subscription. Only those that clicked on the link (hence that have a verified email address) will get added to your list. In our example we call "Opted-In Contacts" this final list. This "sanitized" list of subscribers provides a number of benefits (fewer spam complaints, only managing good email addresses, etc.).

This is a model that implements this scenario in Dynamics Marketing.

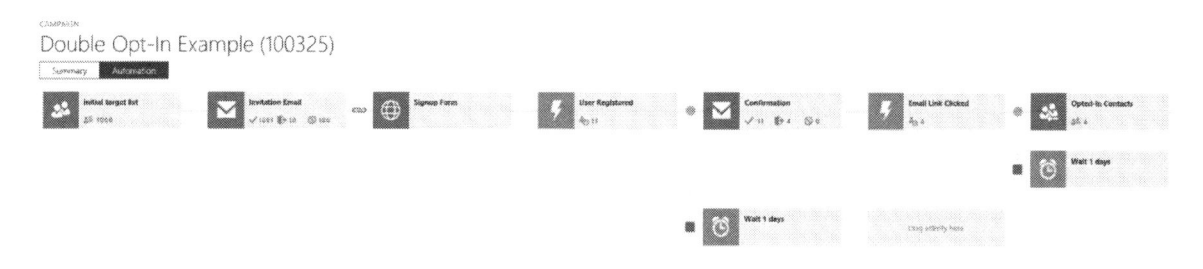

Figure 2.1 –Sample Double Opt-In

Note that full double opt-in is built into the product so marketers don't need to build automated campaigns like this in production. We use it here as an example of a well-known marketing process.

Let's read this Campaign Automation model starting from the left hand side.

Figure 2.2 –First Three Activities in the Double Opt-In Example

We send the "Invitation Email" marketing email (Block 2) to the "initial target list" of Contacts (Block 1). Associated to the email there is a link to a web form (the "Signup Form" Landing Page, Block 3) where recipients are requested to enter the email address they want to use for subscribing with us. Let's see the second half of the model.

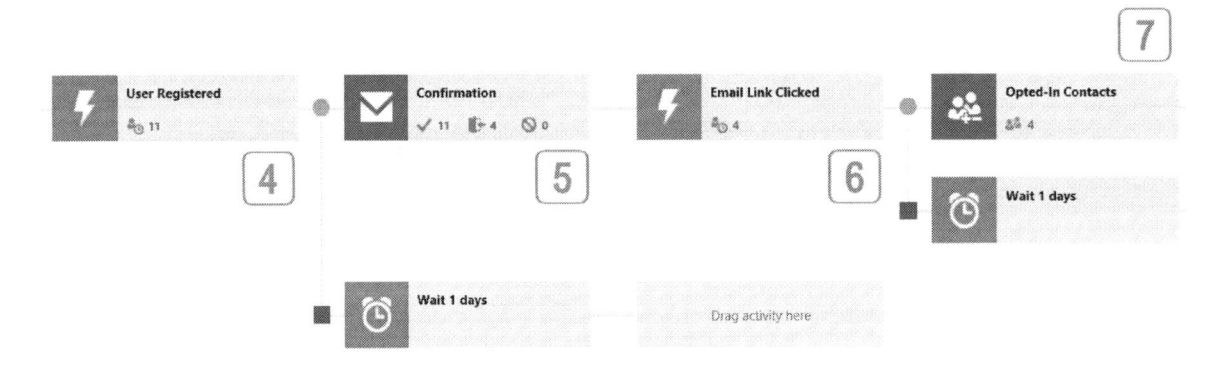

Figure 2.3 –Other Activities in the Double Opt-In Example

All the recipients that subscribed with the "Signup Form" (i.e. that triggered the "User Registered" event, Block 4 in our model) will be sent another email (Block 5, "Confirmation"). At this point all the users that clicked the link in this latter email will be automatically added to the "Opted-In Contacts" list, Block 7.

Note also that, at the same time, this diagram is also indicating the current status, almost in real-time, of customer volumes involved in each branch of the model. So let's go again through the model from the left to the right, now paying attention to the little numbers at the bottom of each block (we will explain them more in detail later in this chapter).

So we start sending an email to one thousand Contacts from our DB[8]. 100 of these emails addresses "hard-bounced" i.e. they were not valid addresses. Perhaps our "initial target list" was old or contained many contacts that we never verified. So far we have 12 recipients that opened the email. Out of these 12 email recipients 11 completed the registration on our "Signup Form" Landing Page. In response to that they all received a "Confirmation" email with the link to activate their subscription. Only four of them have clicked on that link and are now on our "Opted-In Contacts" list.

> **DOUBLE OPT-IN IN DYNAMICS MARKETING**
>
> The example above provides a sample implementation of the double opt-in approach, where a confirmation email is sent to recipients to verify it is actually them. The example above suffers from various issues, like for example the fact that contacts not on the "Opted-In" list might still receive the email (an additional suppression list is required) and the confirmation email must have only one link the activation one. It is provided as an example of a campaign automation model, not a thorough solution to the double opt-in requirements.
>
> Luckily all these issues have been addressed and solved by the integrated double opt-in feature discussed in Chapter 6.

This is just an example of the many possibilities the Campaign Automation console enables. But let's start from the entities implemented in Dynamics Marketing around Campaign Automation.

2.2 Main Entities

We will dig into the details of the Campaign entity in the next chapter. In this chapter we focus on the area more closely related to Marketing Automation.

---

[8] One additional email is due to the "activation" step, i.e. an additional test email.

Entity	Description
Campaigns	The Campaign entity is the hub for all marketing activity and it is described in detail in a following section in this chapter.
Contacts	Contacts represents people.
Cross-Campaign Rules	These rules specify patterns and limitations for the ongoing marketing communication. They are described in detail in a following section in this chapter.
Email Marketing Messages	These are the email marketing messages used in various marketing scenarios. Chapter 5 "Email Marketing" is devoted to such scenarios.
Mobile Text Messages	These are the short text marketing messages sent to mobile phones. Chapter 6 introduces the mobile text channel.
Marketing Lists	These are collections of Contacts used in marketing communications. Dynamics Marketing distinguishes between static lists (when a list of actual contacts is specified) and dynamic lists (where some criteria are specified and contacts are obtained at runtime by querying the DB), the latter being called "Queries". Dynamics Marketing also provides an API for managing lists from an external system, discussed in Chapter 12 "Development Scenarios".
Online Visitors	This entity captures the online activity of internet visitors to the sites tracked by Dynamics Marketing. Visitors are users that Dynamics Marketing cannot (yet) recognize. Once Dynamics Marketing can assign a Visitor record to a known Contact[9] the behavioral data is transferred to the Contact and the Visitor is not updated anymore. Note that there is a lag from the moment of data capture to the actual propagation in Dynamics Marketing.
Social Media	Dynamics Marketing supports integration with Facebook and Twitter.
Websites	These are external web pages that can be tagged (by means of a tracking script generated by Dynamics Marketing) in order to be tracked as part of behavioral data.

HOW DYNAMICS MARKETING TRACKS USER BEHAVIOR

There are essentially five ways user interactions are tracked in Dynamics Marketing for marketing analysis purposes.

- *Redirect URLs*. Dynamics Marketing wraps links in emails and other content with tracking URLs automatically. Users can generate a tracking URL manually for any given link using the Website entity.

- *Tracking scripts*. It is possible to embed JavaScript code in external web pages (i.e.

---

[9] For example when that user opens a marketing email from Dynamics Marketing.

any web page that supports JavaScript) that will track interactions. The Website entity provides this functionality.

- *Landing pages*. When a user interacts with a Landing Page those interactions are tracked in Dynamics Marketing, if configured so.

- *Email Marketing*. Interactions of recipients with an email are tracked in Dynamics Marketing.

- Finally, the user status tracked implicitly in a running campaign automation model.

Dynamics Marketing uses Cookies (when allowed by the end user) to identify users. In order to respect users' privacy settings, Dynamics Marketing only uses http cookies and exclusively stores GUIDs in them.

2.2.1 Marketing Automation in Dynamics Marketing

Dynamics Marketing can automate the execution of personalized multichannel campaigns with millions of contacts, fulfilling the vision of providing scale together with precision, conveniently at marketing professional's fingertips.

The Campaign automation model can be accessed both from the entity form (using the "Automation" button below the Campaign name) and directly from the Campaigns list when a model is defined.

AUTOMATED CAMPAIGNS STATUS AT GLANCE

The Campaign list shows whether there is any campaign automation model and whether is currently running for that record by showing an icon. When the icon is blue the model is running.

Campaigns

SEARCH   FILTER

		ID	Name
☐	▶	100168	A drip Campaign
☐	▶	100167	Another great campaign
☐		100308	Product Launch
☐	▶	100286	Birthday Appreciation
☐	▶	100325	Double Opt-In Example
☐	▶	100297	My Wonderful Campaign
☐		100323	LunaSolar

As a shortcut users can click on the Campaign Automation Status indicator to navigate to the campaign automation model right away.

2.2.1.1 Our first automated campaign

Let's create a simple automated email marketing mailing using a campaign automation model. We start from creating a new Campaign record. When creating a new Campaign with an automation model, the start and end dates are needed.

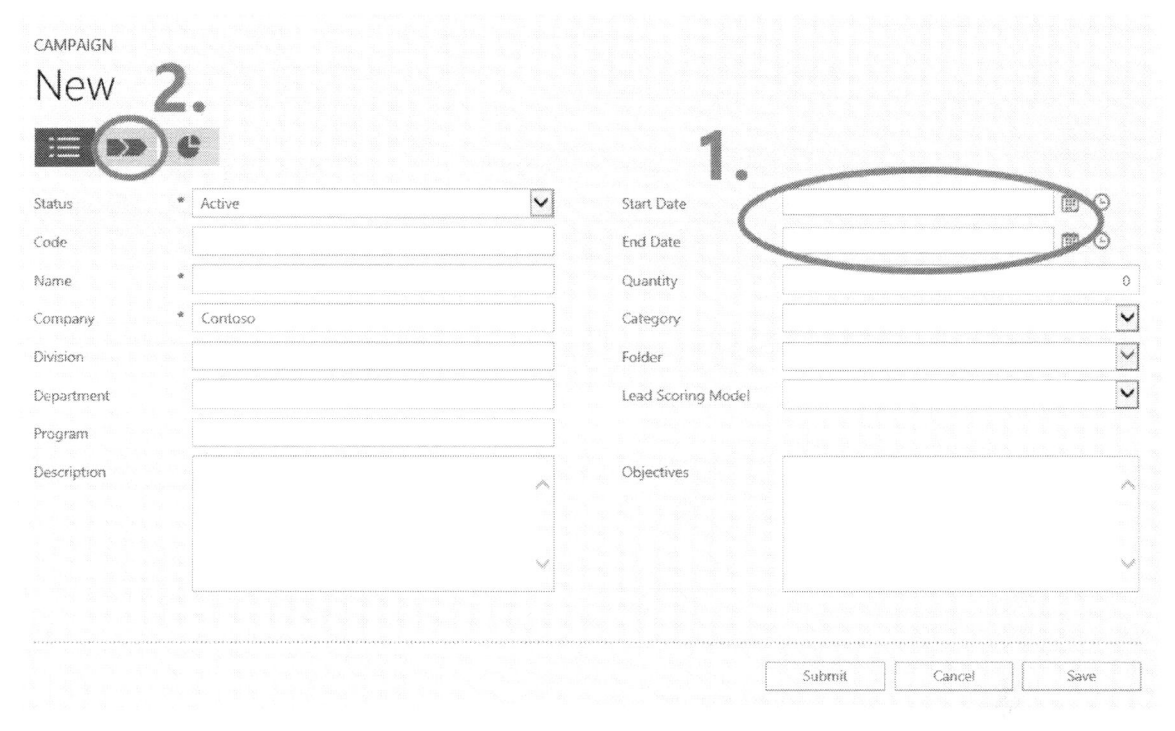

Figure 2.4 –Setting Up an Automated Campaign

When the dates are added and the entity is saved, it is possible to click on the "Automation" button underneath the Campaign name to open the campaign automation model:

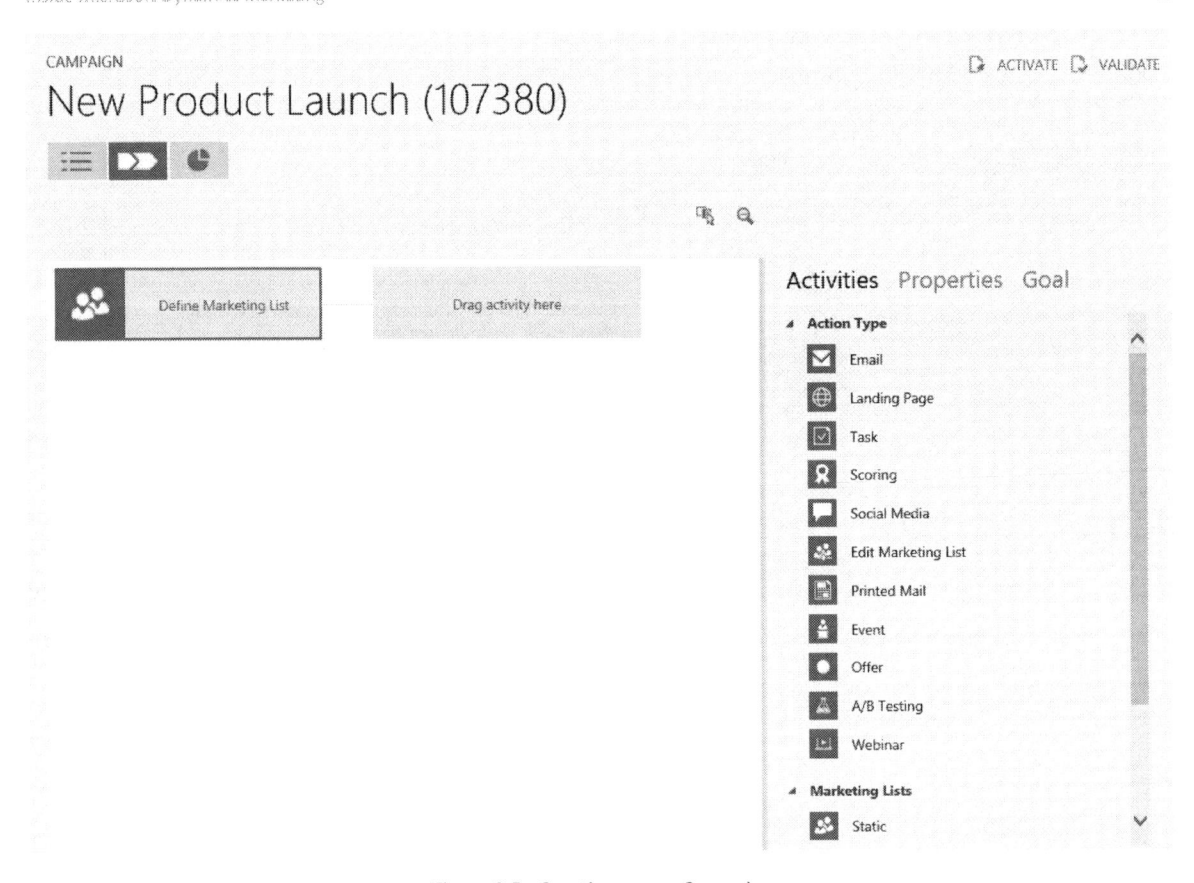

Figure 2.5 – Creating a new Campaign

By dragging the Activities (i.e. the campaign model blocks) from the right hand side area of the screen onto the placeholders in the model editor, it is possible to define your automated campaign.

Let's add a static list and an email activity onto the editor as shown below.

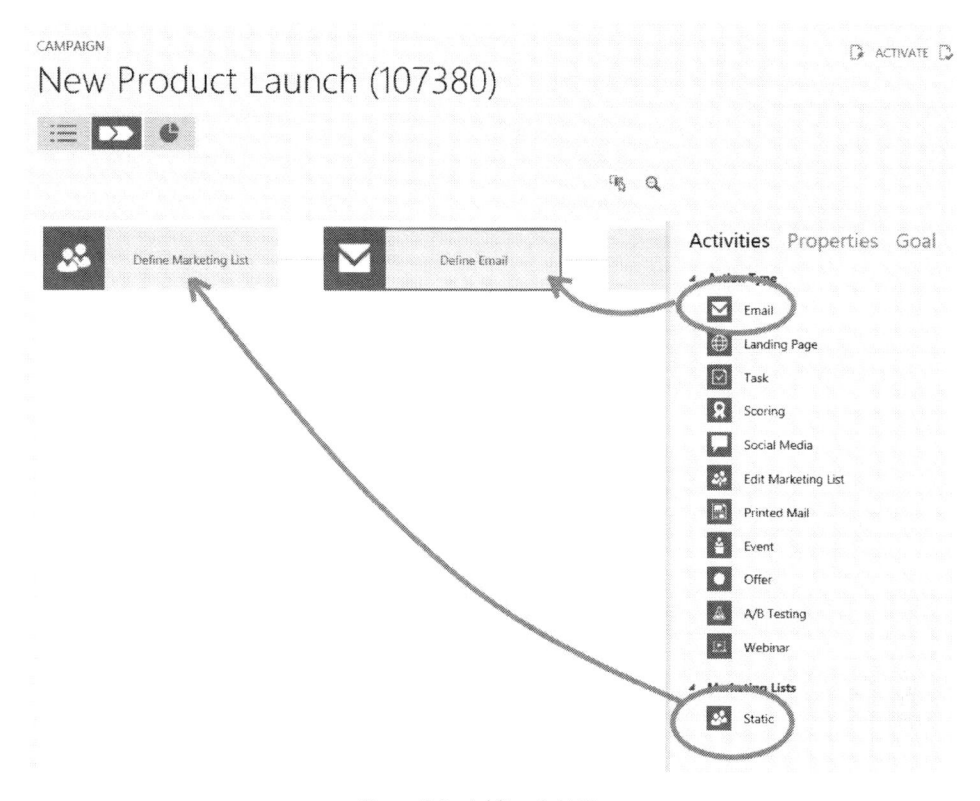

Figure 2.6 –Adding Activities

At this point we can start defining the properties for each activity to complete our campaign model.

We can double-click on each block to open the properties (or alternatively select the block by single-clicking on it, then click on the "Properties" button in the right-hand pane)

Inside Microsoft Dynamics Marketing

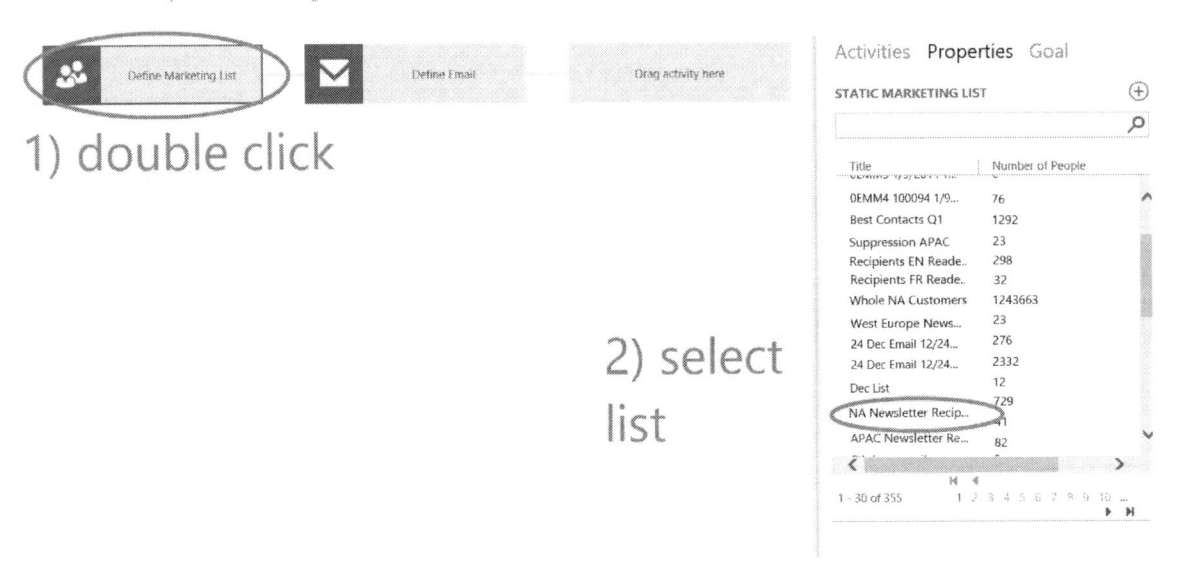

Figure 2.7 –Selecting a List

Now we can see the details of the list and possibly even edit it if needed. By clicking on "Select" the list is selected (this list is now associated to this specific activity block in our designer):

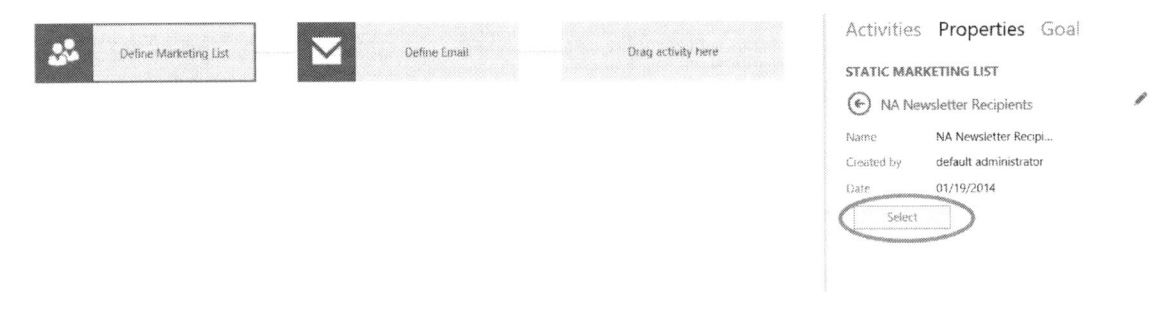

Figure 2.8 –Selecting a List

We now double click on the "Define Email" block and select an existing email. If no email is available in the DB we can create one[10] without leaving the model editor.

---

[10] See Chapter 5 "Email Marketing" on how to create email marketing messages.

When an email message has been selected for the "Define Email" block, our automated campaign is ready to be executed.

We can also validate that the model we entered is correct by clicking the "Validate" action on the top-right corner of the screen:

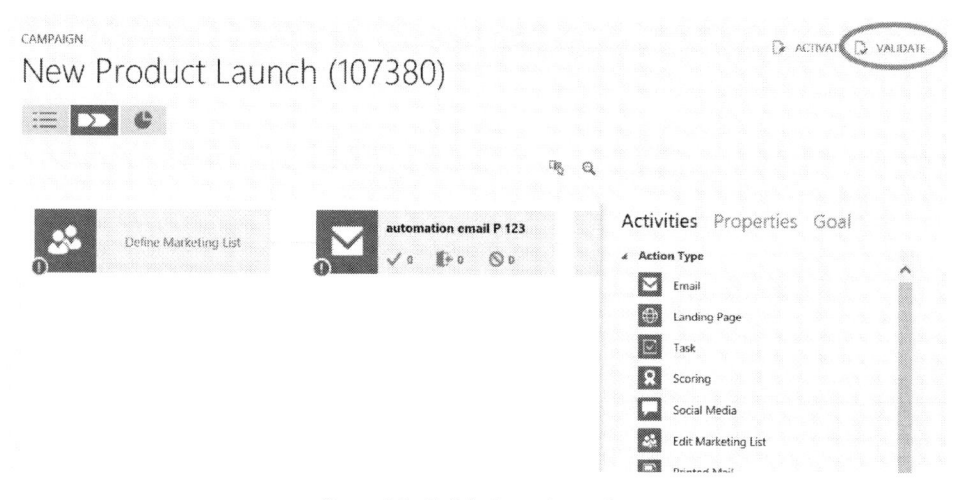

Figure 2.9 –Validating a Campaign

We notice some exclamation points on the invalid blocks. By hovering over them we can see more details about the reason for the invalid configuration. For instance the email message we chose has not been activated, so it is not ready to be sent via an automation model:

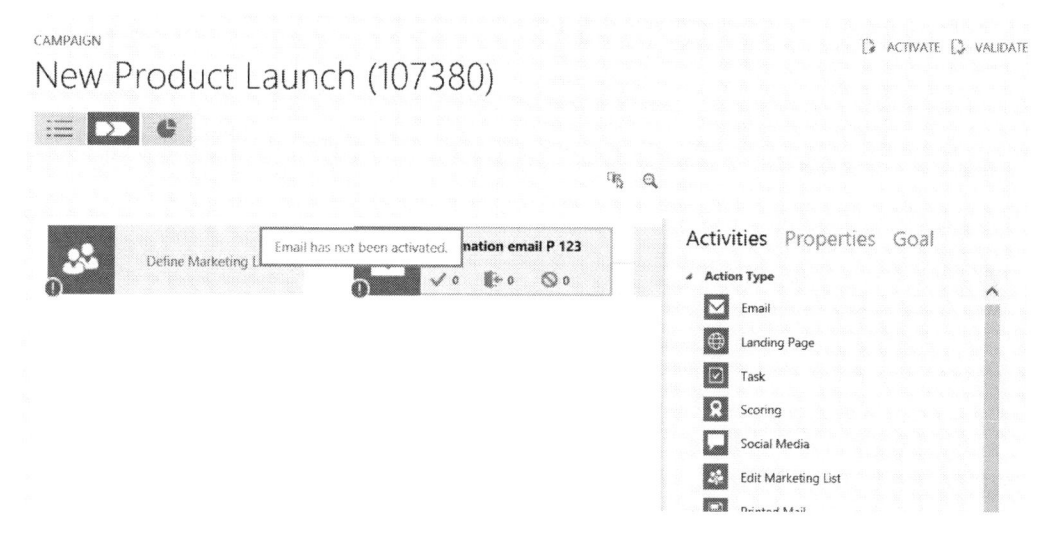

Figure 2.10 –Validation Errors

We need to resolve all the validation issues before we can start the execution of our model. This is achieved by clicking on the Activate button on the top-right corner of the page.

At this point the campaign model is executed and our email marketing mailing gets sent to all our recipients.

> **HOW IT WORKS**
>
> In order to better understand the capabilities of Dynamics Marketing Campaign Automation it is useful to consider the way it works behind the scenes.
>
> Every couple of minutes Dynamics Marketing will "revive" all the active campaign models for a given customer organization, checking for any updates. If no new contacts are detected or there are no other noteworthy events then there are no changes needed and the campaign model is put back to "sleep". If changes are detected (say a new contact has been added to a list or another event described in the model is raised) then the campaign model is run to process these changes.
>
> So Campaign execution performed via Campaign Automation models in Dynamics Marketing is a somewhat iterative process, inherently different from the typical manual execution of a campaign (like an email marketing communication triggered manually for example) where communications are performed at a given time, for all recipients.
>
> Note that both data (say the content of the email used for a drip campaign) and metadata (i.e. the definition of what needs to be done in certain step) can be changed also when the Campaign Model is in execution. Users need to be aware that there is no explicit versioning so changes will not be tracked in different versions of the same Campaign Model. If wanted, users can note down repeated "tweaks" to a running campaign using the Notes panel.

2.2.1.2 The Palette of Available Model Activities

There are three types of model activities, i.e. the building block of a campaign automation model:

- Actions – these blocks perform an action (e.g. sending an email)
- Lists – these are Marketing Lists that are used in the communication. A model always starts with a List.
- Reponses – these blocks provide conditional behavior based on the preceding block. They allow for conditional logic to be used in our models.

Here's a list of all the available model activities in Dynamics Marketing:

Activity (Model Block)	Icon	Description
Email action		Sends an Email Marketing message (having Designation type "Campaign Automation") to the contacts available from the preceding steps of the model.
Landing Page action		Links a Landing page with the preceding model activity. Note that in Dynamics Marketing this relationship has to be specified twice. Once in the email content itself (with a URL pointing to the hosted Landing Page of choice) and a second time by associating the same Landing Page to the email from the campaign model, in order to act upon events associated to that Landing Page in the automation model.
SMS action		Sends an SMS message. See for more details Chapter 6.
Task action		Creates a Task assigned to a specified Contact.
Scoring action		Updates the lead score by running the specified Lead Scoring Model on the Contacts present in that branch of the campaign model.
Social Media action		Posts on Twitter or Facebook.
Edit Marketing List action		Add or remove Contacts from a Marketing List.
Printed Mail action		Send good old printed marketing material via mail. Dynamics Marketing supports integration with third party vendors for this service.
Event action		Register a Contact for an Event.
Offer action		Add an offer. Offers can be created from an Offer Template, the content can be hosted via iFrame on a web page. User behavior regarding the offer consumption is tracked in the Performance panel.
A/B Test action		Add an A/B testing activity. See Chapter 6 "Advanced Email Marketing" for more details on A/B testing.

Webinar action		Add a Webinar (tracked as part of an Event) to the campaign. Webinar are supported using Lync (see Chapter 11 "Configuration" for the configuration details).
Static List		A list of Contacts. Additional contacts added to a Static list are picked up by the automation engine.
Dynamic List		The result of a segmentation query producing a set of Contacts.
Scheduler Response		Add a waiting block for an event to occur / wait for a given amount of time.
Trigger Response		This Response activity provides triggered scheduling based on response to the preceding block.

2.2.1.3 A first Example

The activity that represents conditional behavior is the Trigger Response block. Depending on the preceding block in the model, different events can be captured. Let's see how the Trigger Response activity works with an example.

Imagine we want to launch an offer via email and have an automatic follow-up after one week to those that didn't open the offer.

We start from a blank model adding the Marketing List with the offer recipients and the initial email offer:

Figure 2.11 –Building a Campaign with triggers

At this point we drag a trigger activity after the email block. We notice that a conditional block is added (the green dot being the "true" branch and the red square the "false" outcome). There is also a Scheduler block appended to the "false" branch by default. This is appended automatically for our convenience and can be ignored (left empty) if not needed.

CAMPAIGN
Follow-Up Campaign (107779)

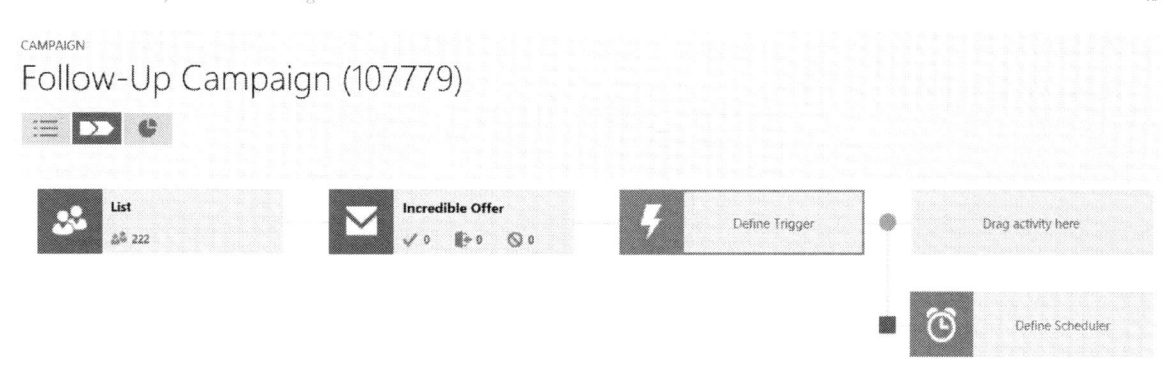

Figure 2.12 –Adding a Trigger Activity

Now we specify the properties of the trigger activity. Email-related events are available because the trigger activity adds more events to choose from depending upon the type of the preceding activity. Next step is to add the reminder email to the "false" branch.

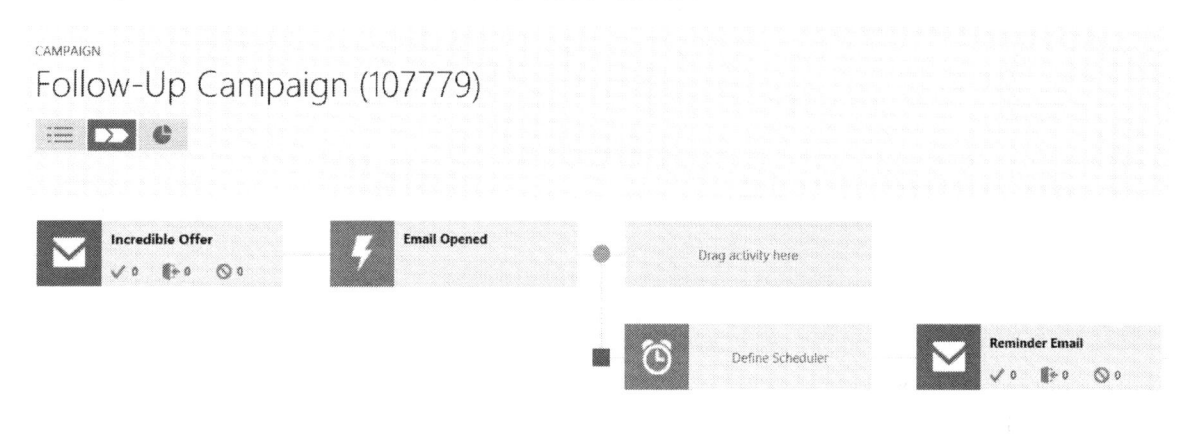

CAMPAIGN
Follow-Up Campaign (107779)

Figure 2.13 –Campaign XX

We define the waiting time in the Schedule activity for specifying the days to wait before sending the reminder email. Note that we leave the "true" branch of the Email Opened trigger block empty as in our small example we don't care what happens when a Contact opens the offer email.

We can read the model above as follows. After an email is sent to all the Contacts in the List, the campaign model will separate the Contacts in two branches, depending whether or not they opened it (i.e. downloaded pictures from the message so that Dynamics Marketing can track them). For those that didn't open the email, a reminder email is sent after one week.

The following table summarizes the main (simple) trigger events based on the activity block preceding the trigger block.

Activity Preceding the trigger	Model	Available triggers for the combination
Email action		- Contact got the email delivered - Contact opened the email - Contact clicked on a link in the email
Landing Page action		- Contact registered on the Landing page - Contact visited the Landing page
Task action		No triggers available for this combination. The block preceding the Task will define the triggers, if any.
Scoring action		No triggers available for this combination. The block preceding the Scoring block will define the triggers, if any.
Social Media action		No triggers available for this combination. The block preceding the Social Media block will define the triggers, if any.
Edit Marketing List action		No triggers available for this combination. The block preceding the Edit List block will define the triggers, if any.
Printed Mail action		No triggers available for this combination. The block preceding the Printed Mail block will define the triggers, if any.
Event action		- Contact attended the Event
SMS action		- Contact got the SMS delivered - the SMS bounced - Contact clicked on a link in the SMS

2.2.1.4 Some things good to know

Before moving on to the next section (we will get more into campaign models with some real-world scenarios later in the chapter) let's see some useful tips when editing campaign models.

CONTEXT MENU

It is possible to use the right Mouse button on a given block to open a context menu with additional actions for the selected block.

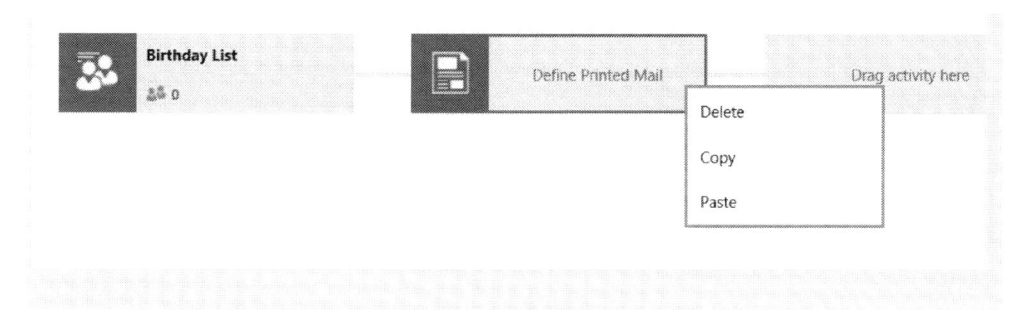

When creating Campaign Templates, if a model is specified, the model will be copied into the new Campaign. This makes reusing complex campaigns very easy.

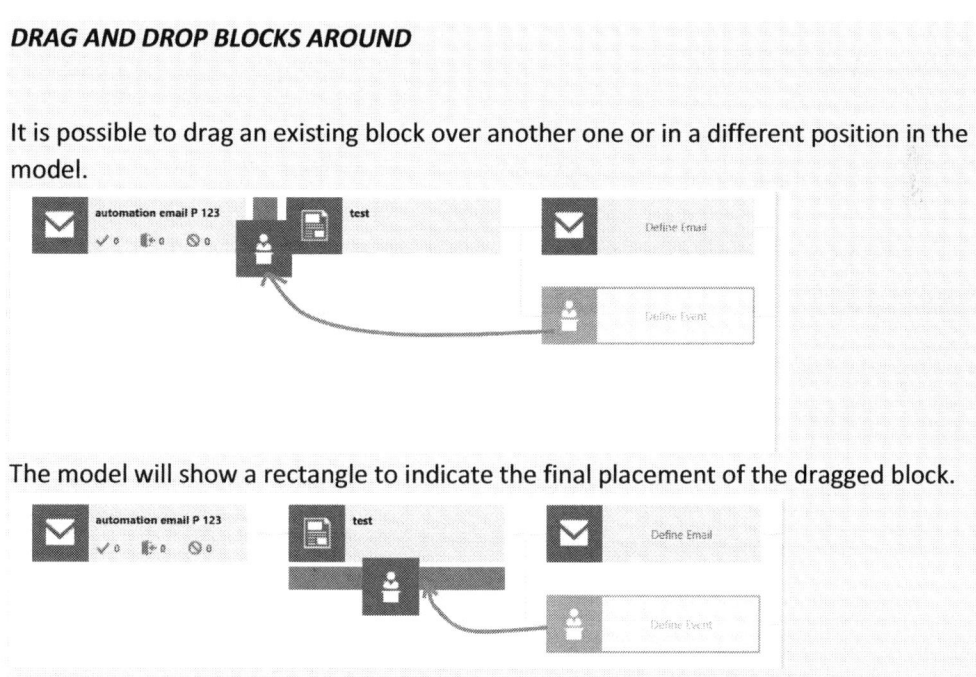

DRAG AND DROP BLOCKS AROUND

It is possible to drag an existing block over another one or in a different position in the model.

The model will show a rectangle to indicate the final placement of the dragged block.

If no placement indicator is shown moving the activity will not succeed.
Blocks can be dropped directly on other blocks. In this case a default behavior depending on the type of blocks will be used.

Inside Microsoft Dynamics Marketing

The Zoom action at the top-right corner allows to show the model in a "compressed" mode in order to have a better overview.

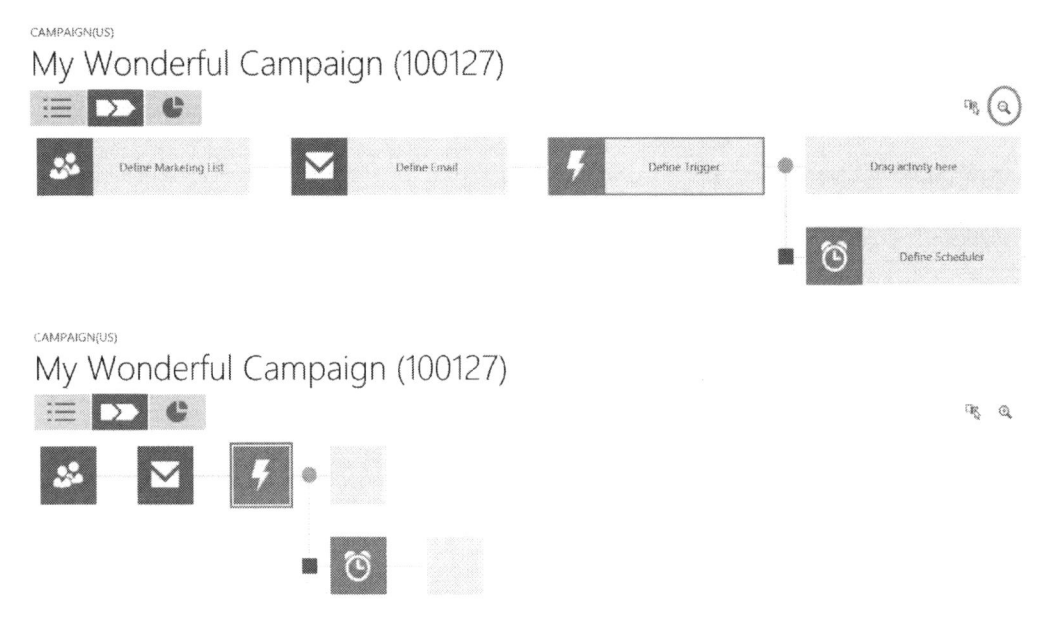

Figure 2.14 –Toggle Zoom Mode

VISIBILITY RULES

Items like emails, landing pages etc. that are used in a campaign automation model need to belong to that Campaign. So if you create an email outside the campaign automation model when you try to the select it from the campaign automation UI you will not see it. The easiest way to simplify the creation of items for a given campaign is to create them while in the campaign automation console UI.

Another thing to keep in mind is the need to activate emails that need to be used in a campaign automation model. Once activated an email is sent to email as a test and at the same time is sealed so it cannot be edited any longer (although in the UI it seems like editing it is possible).

LANDING PAGES CANNOT BE REUSED IN DIFFERENT AUTOMATED CAMPAIGNS

Imagine that exactly the same fields in a landing page needs to be used in different automated campaigns. You might be tempted to prepare one landing page nicely embedded in a web page online, and then reuse the same link and the same landing page for various campaigns. Unfortunately this will not work. For tracking purposes Landing Pages are specific to a Campaign (that is why you can only choose a Landing Page that belongs to that campaign). If you embed a link to Landing Page from another campaign, user Interactions will not be captured.

COMPOSE LISTS BY DRAG AND DROP

It is possible to drag and drop a number of lists together. The model will show them as stacked together:

by clicking on the block all the stacked lists will be shown:

The lists are meant to be added in Union, the "sum" of all members, removing duplicates.

2.2.2 Cross-Campaign Rules

Cross-Campaign Rules are a way to centralize control over the execution of multiple campaigns, possibly created by different people and hence with a lack of centralized overview.

A typical scenario is to have a number of ongoing automated campaigns sending marketing emails. Despite the best efforts to coordinate such campaigns in some cases more emails than anticipated can end up being sent to the same recipient. Users receiving too many marketing emails tend to unsubscribe.

Cross-Campaign Rules are available at

```
Home > Settings > Rules and Models → Cross-Campaign Rules
```

When creating a new rule one can specify the scope (per Program, per Campaign or for all), it must provide the time span the rule stretches across (using the "Duration" field) and the maximum number of emails allowed in that time span, plus the start and end dates the rule will apply.

In the example below any recipient cannot receive more than one marketing email per week.

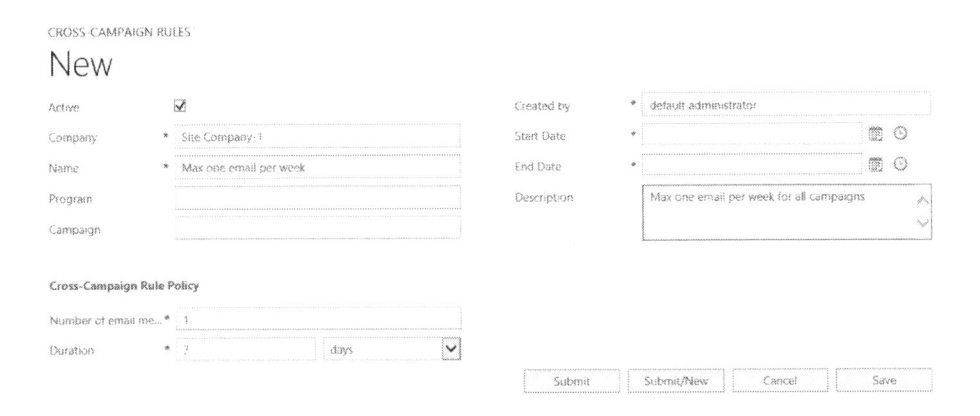

Figure 2.15 – New Cross-Campaign Rule

CROSS-CAMPAIGN RULES ONLY APPLY TO EMAIL MARKETING MESSAGES

Cross-Campaign Rules only control the number of marketing emails, not transactional ones. It is not possible to limit the amount of transactional emails via Cross-Campaign Rules.

We will get more into the details of Cross-Campaigns Rules in a scenario in this chapter.

2.2.3 Advanced Trigger Conditions

All the triggers available in the "Simple" trigger tab can be composed together in the "Advanced" tab to create complex conditions as shown below:

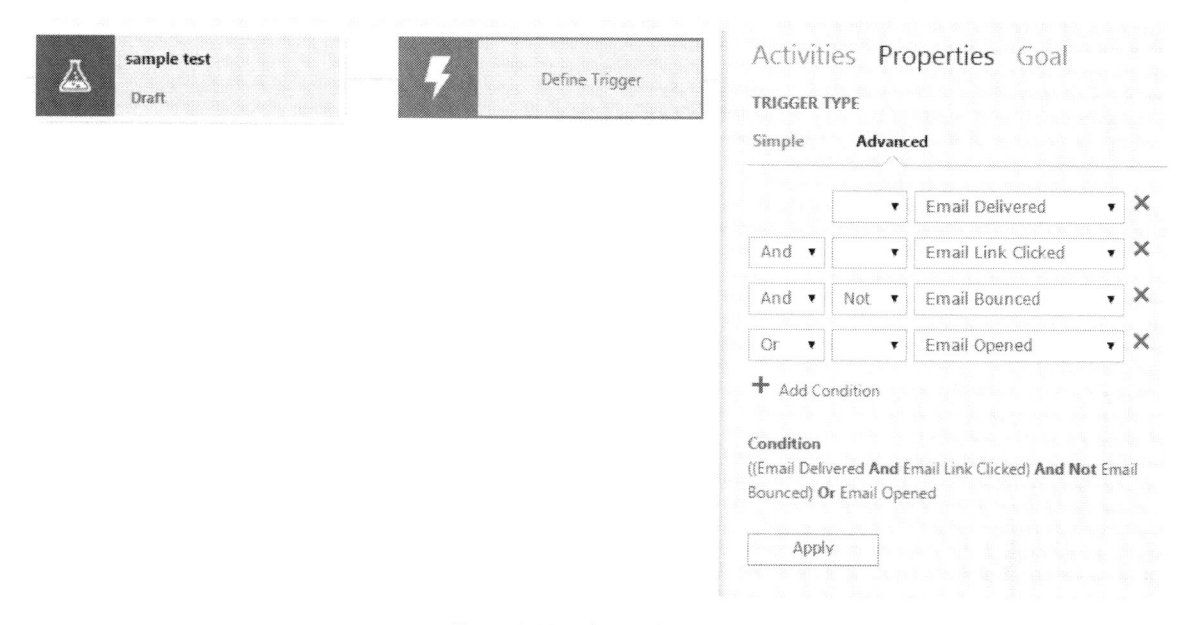

Figure 2.16 –Advanced Triggers

2.2.4 Advanced A/B Testing Setup

When defining A/B tests in the campaign automation editor some additional options are available.

A useful one is the version send time, shown below:

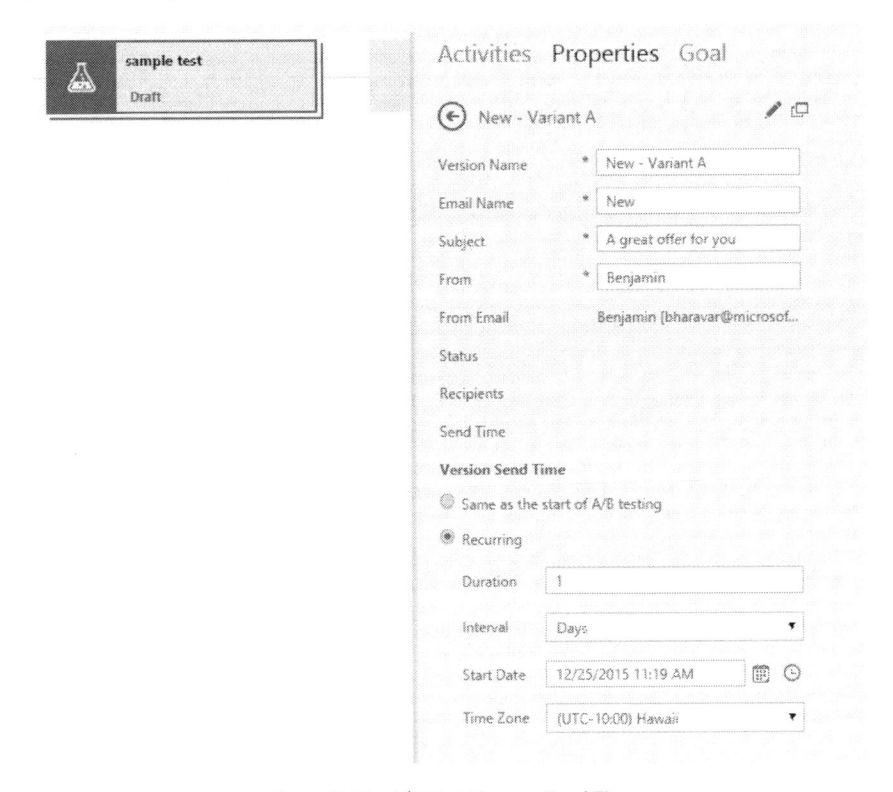

Figure 2.17 –A/B Test Version Send Time

Specify the "Recurring" option for the Version Send Time parameter when you are interested in testing different delivery times. You can experiment with the best time of the day to deliver your emails. This parameter is used in both the testing phase (when both variants are sent) and after the winner is declared. Once the winner is declared the winner email is sent using the same rules specified for the winning variant.

Because of the nature of Campaign Automation models, different contacts move through the workflow at different times. The contacts that come to the A/B testing activity will wait for the next send date as defined in the variant send time setup[11].

So the contacts that are ready to be processed for the A/B testing activity will be sent out at the next date that matches what specified in Recurring option. "Date and time" defines when is the very first date and time we want to send the email. "Duration" and "Interval" define how often we allow the email to be sent.

---

[11] Note of course that none of the contacts will receive the email twice.

Some examples:

- To set up A/B testing of Variant A sent in the morning and Variant B sent in the evening (assuming the starting day is 12/25) we would set up:
    - Variant A: Duration = 1, Interval = Days, Date and time = 12/25 8AM
    - Variant B: Duration = 1, Interval = Days, Date and time = 12/25 8PM

  Variant A will be sent out each day at 8AM starting from 12/25, while Variant B will be sent out each day at 8PM starting from 12/25.

- To set up an A/B testing of Variant A sent on Monday morning and Variant B sent on Friday morning (beginning the first week of calendar year 2015) we should define:
    - Variant A: Duration 1, Interval = Weeks, Date and time = 1/5 9 AM (assuming 1/5/2015 is Monday)
    - Variant B: Duration 1, Interval = Weeks, Date and time = 1/9 9 AM (assuming 1/9/2015 is Friday)

  So Variant A will be sent out each week at 9AM starting from Monday 1/5, Version B will be sent out each week at 9AM starting from Friday 1/9.

So if you are not interested in testing for a delivery time then leave the default option "Same as start of A/B testing". The email is just sent as soon as there are some contacts ready on the A/B testing activity.

2.3 SCENARIOS

Now that we have seen the main functionality available for this area in Dynamics Marketing let's look at some usage examples of the product.

2.3.1 Create a Drip campaign with Campaign Automation

This is the general overview of the entire campaign:

CAMPAIGN
A Drip Campaign (100079)

Figure 2.18 –An Example Drip Campaign

Let's explore the first part in chronological order, which corresponds to beginning from the left in the model.

So we start with a mailing to our entire "initial list", with a call to action to download our product whitepaper. For those that register to our landing page and download the whitepaper we then send an additional invitation after 20 days to read our ebook. For those that didn't accept our invite we wait another 20 days and then send them a target "First Reminder" email.

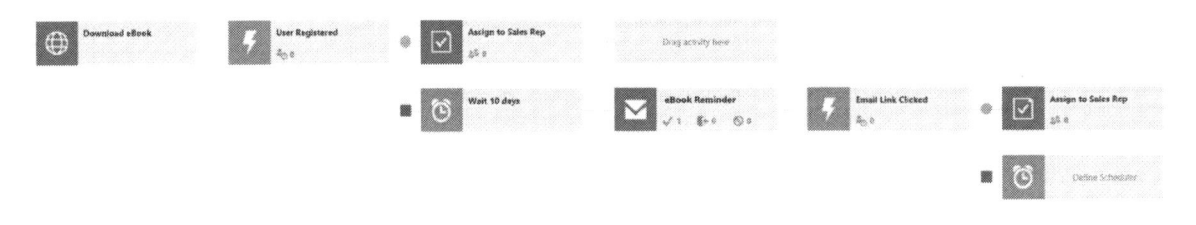

Figure 2.19 –Drip Campaign Example

At this point, for those that downloaded both the ebook and the whitepaper we don't want to waste time and we assign them right away to one of our sales team for direct contact in order to finalize the sale.

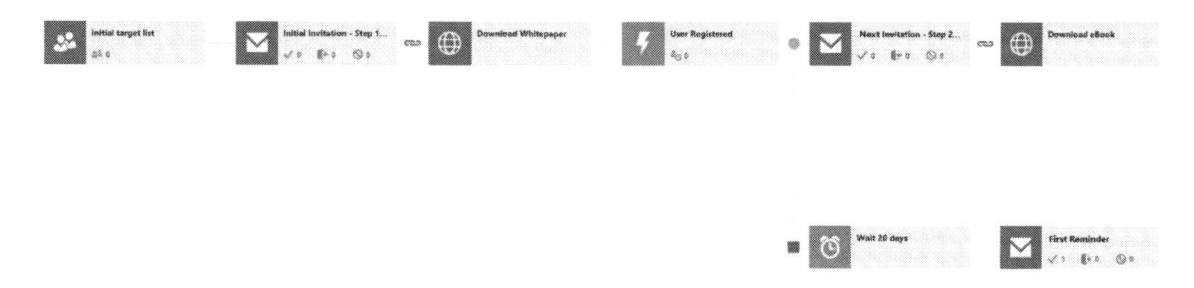

Figure 2.20 –Drip Campaign Example

For those that didn't download the ebook we wait 10 days then we send them a reminder email and those that clicked on the email will be contacted by a sales rep.

Now let's look at the branch modeling the initial email recipients that didn't answer the first call, the one for the whitepaper. For them we will wait 20 days, then if after another 20 days they still didn't register we send them a tailored reminder email.

Figure 2.21 –Drip Campaign Overview

Those that click a link in the email will be assigned to a sales rep. After 10 days, all those that didn't click in a link in the email will be removed permanently from the initial list.

2.3.2 Anniversary Appreciation Email

The following campaign automation model sends a birthday appreciation email to a given segment of the marketing database.

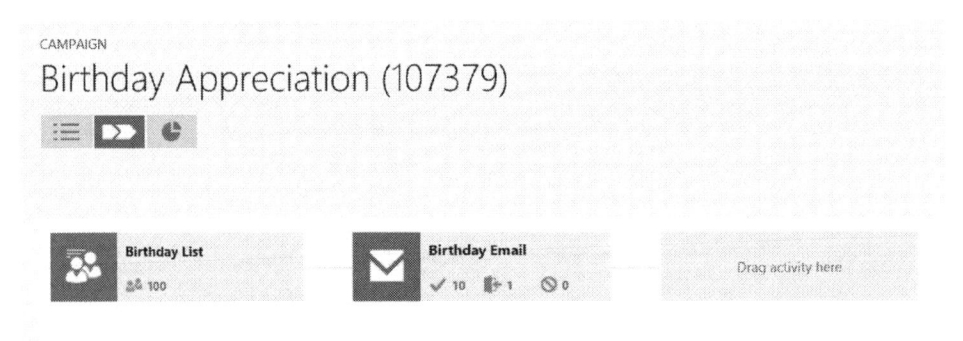

Figure 2.22 –Birthday Appreciation Campaign Example

We customized a User Defined Field (see Chapter 11 "Configuration") to represent a Marketing Contact's birthday. We can then create the following Dynamic List (a List/Query entity of type "Query"). The campaign model shown above will check for any Marketing Contact in our DB that has the "Birthday" field matching our criteria (see the screenshot below) and send them an email.

Birthday List (100 as of 5/10/2014 4:05 PM)

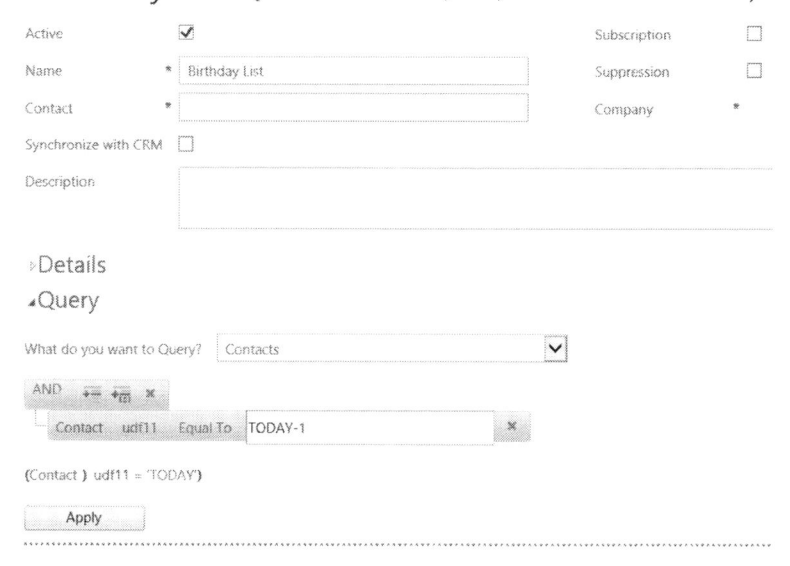

Figure 2.23 – Date Queries

So every marketing contact will get a "Birthday" appreciation email the day before their birthday.

We will see more about creating Queries (i.e. Dynamic Lists) in Chapter 3 "Marketing Execution".

2.3.3   Create a Response Model for a Campaign

A response model defines the expected results for a Campaign. Given that each Campaign has its own aims and goals also response models needs to be flexible and accommodate for various metrics.

The screenshot below shows the various metrics available when defining Response Models in Dynamics Marketing:

Response Model

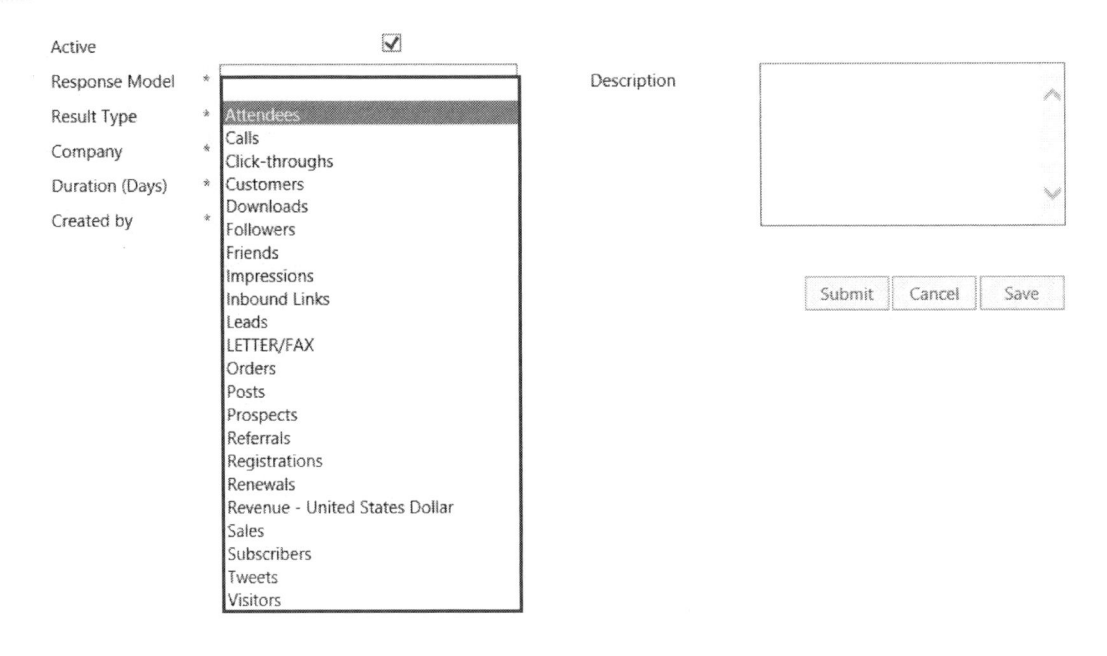

Active	✓	
Response Model *		Description
Result Type *	**Attendees**	
Company *	Calls	
Duration (Days) *	Click-throughs	
Created by *	Customers	
	Downloads	
	Followers	
	Friends	
	Impressions	
	Inbound Links	
	Leads	
	LETTER/FAX	
	Orders	
	Posts	
	Prospects	
	Referrals	
	Registrations	
	Renewals	
	Revenue - United States Dollar	
	Sales	
	Subscribers	
	Tweets	
	Visitors	

[Submit] [Cancel] [Save]

Figure 2.24 –New Response Model

Response Models are available for creation or editing from:

```
Home > Settings > Rules and Models → Response Models
```

They are assigned to a Campaign using the fields in the "Results" expandable group of that Campaign's form.

So our marketing manager is preparing a Campaign for awareness for the launch Event of a new product. Based on her previous experience registrations are a key metric to follow and if everything goes well with the campaign she expects a full house event with a very typical curve based on the reminder sent to the audience and an abrupt closing at the Event date. This is described by the model she defines as shown below:

Response Model

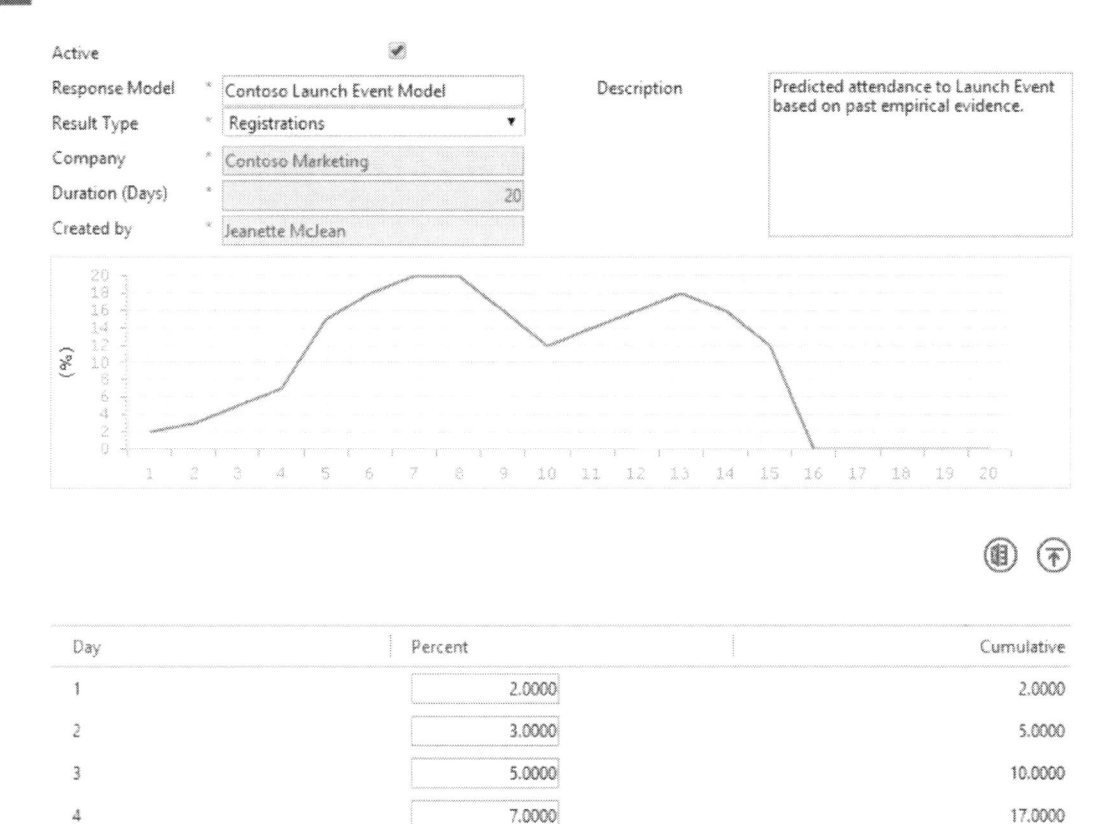

Active	✓		
Response Model	Contoso Launch Event Model	Description	Predicted attendance to Launch Event based on past empirical evidence.
Result Type	Registrations		
Company	Contoso Marketing		
Duration (Days)	20		
Created by	Jeanette McLean		

Day	Percent	Cumulative
1	2.0000	2.0000
2	3.0000	5.0000
3	5.0000	10.0000
4	7.0000	17.0000
5	15.0000	32.0000
6	18.0000	50.0000
7	20.0000	70.0000
8	20.0000	90.0000

Figure 2.25 – Response Model

She assigns the model to the campaign and then monitors the progress of the Campaign against the Response Model she defined[12].

---

[12] While some type of results are automatically tracked by Dynamics Marketing for a campaign other needs to be entered manually.

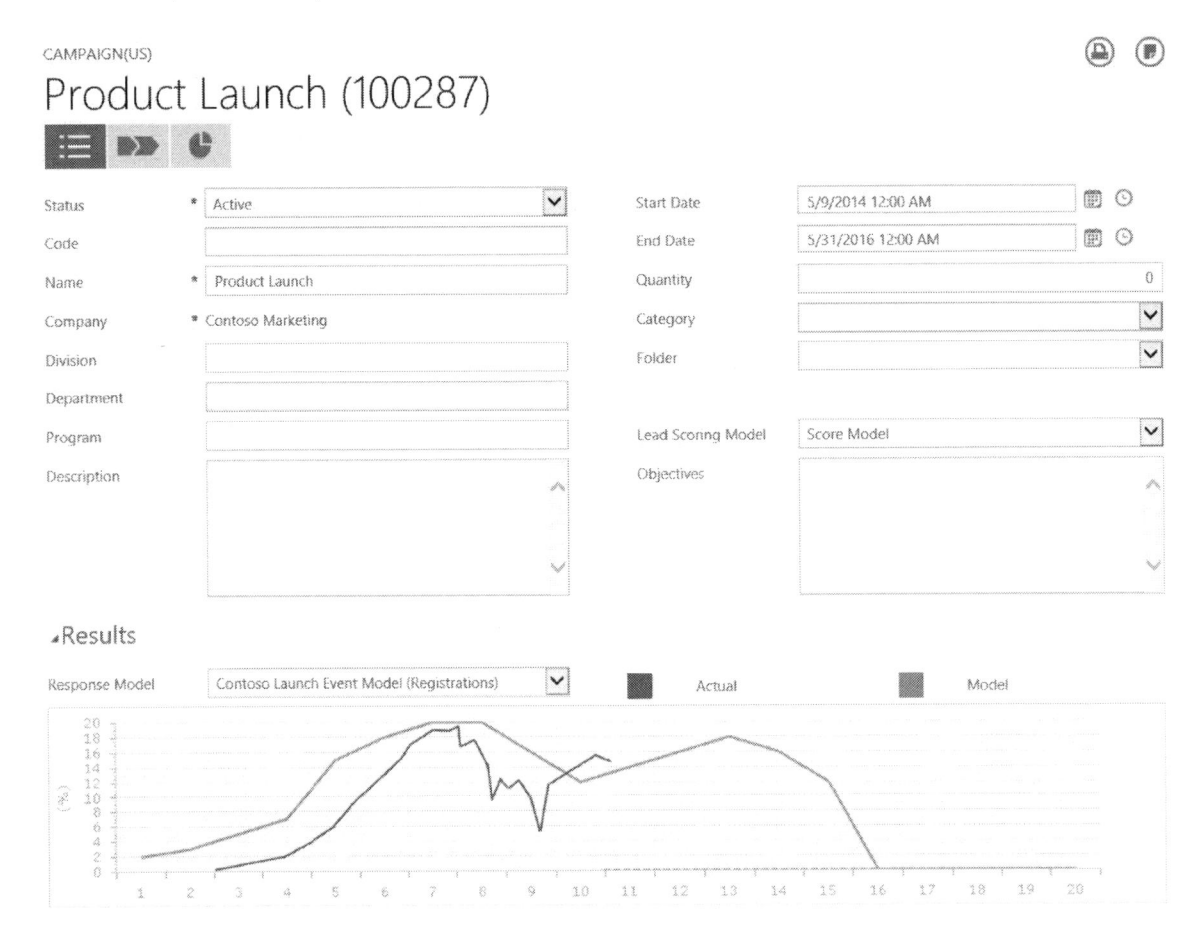

Figure 2.26 – Campaign Results

2.3.4 Control Distribution via Cross-Campaign Rules

The Marketing Manager has many automated campaigns running at the same time and a policy from his manager dictates that a user cannot be contacted more than twice in a month.

The Marketing Manager sets the following rule in the system:

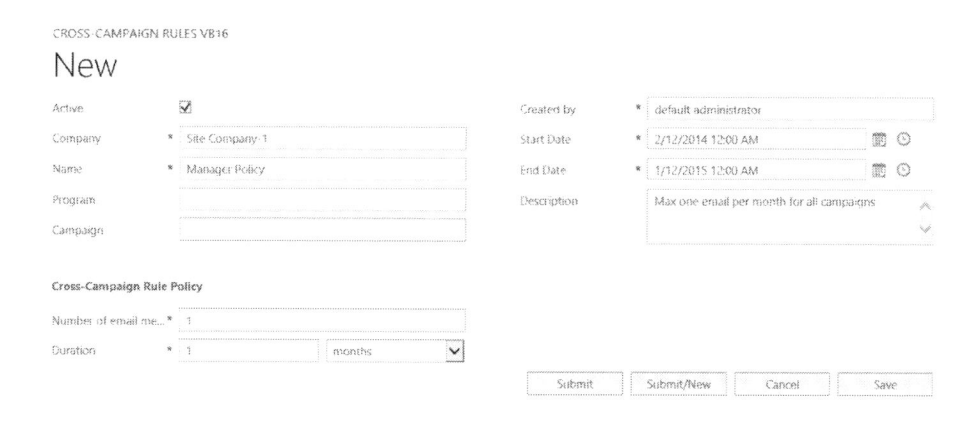

Figure 2.27 –Cross-Campaign Rule Definition

Emails are being sent by Dynamics Marketing in various ways (automated campaigns and manual sends by marketing people) and when a limit is reached for a rule, the additional marketing emails are not sent. The Manager can easily see the emails that were blocked by going into the Summary group of the Performance panel of the Email Marketing Message:

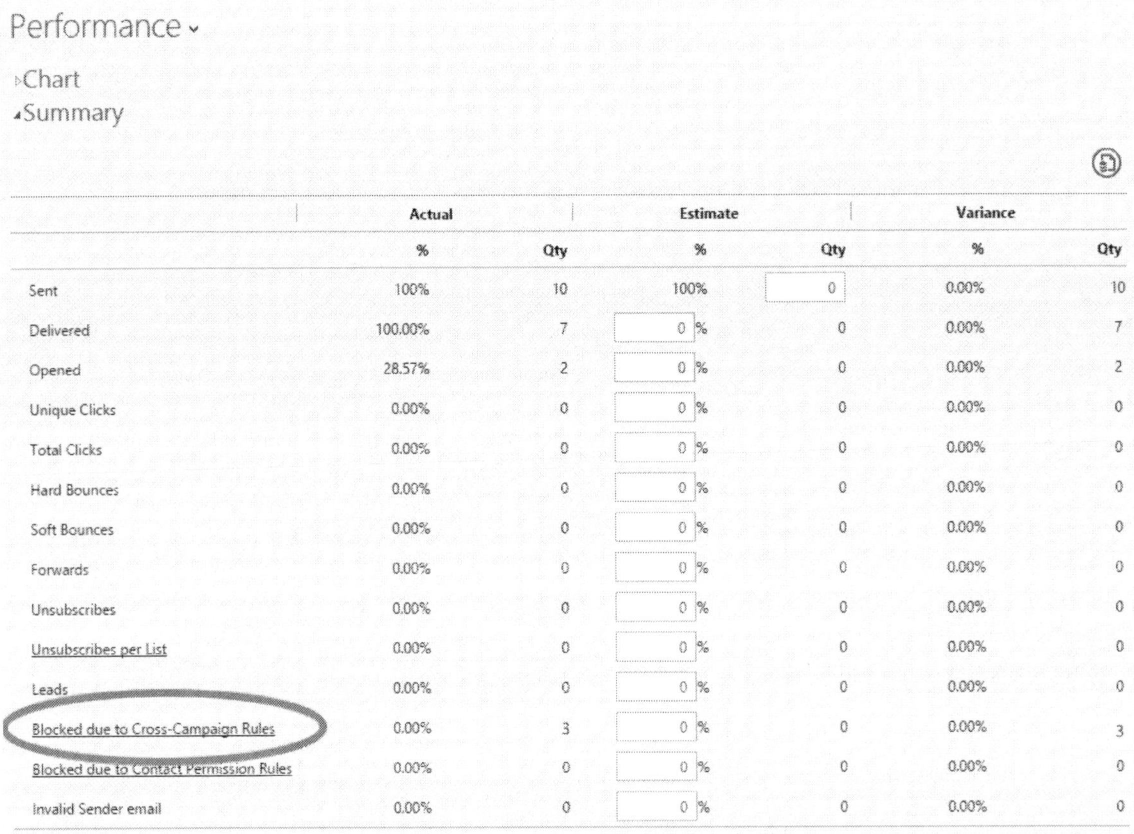

Performance

▷ Chart
▲ Summary

	Actual		Estimate		Variance	
	%	Qty	%	Qty	%	Qty
Sent	100%	10	100%	0	0.00%	10
Delivered	100.00%	7	0 %	0	0.00%	7
Opened	28.57%	2	0 %	0	0.00%	2
Unique Clicks	0.00%	0	0 %	0	0.00%	0
Total Clicks	0.00%	0	0 %	0	0.00%	0
Hard Bounces	0.00%	0	0 %	0	0.00%	0
Soft Bounces	0.00%	0	0 %	0	0.00%	0
Forwards	0.00%	0	0 %	0	0.00%	0
Unsubscribes	0.00%	0	0 %	0	0.00%	0
Unsubscribes per List	0.00%	0	0 %	0	0.00%	0
Leads	0.00%	0	0 %	0	0.00%	0
Blocked due to Cross-Campaign Rules	0.00%	3	0 %	0	0.00%	3
Blocked due to Contact Permission Rules	0.00%	0	0 %	0	0.00%	0
Invalid Sender email	0.00%	0	0 %	0	0.00%	0

Figure 2.28 –Cross-Campaign Rules

To inspect the messages that have been blocked, click on "Blocked due to Cross-Campaign Rules" in the screen above to see the list of recipients that were actually blocked for this mailing:

RECIPIENTS BLOCKED DUE TO CROSS-CAMPAIGN RULES

Appreciation Email

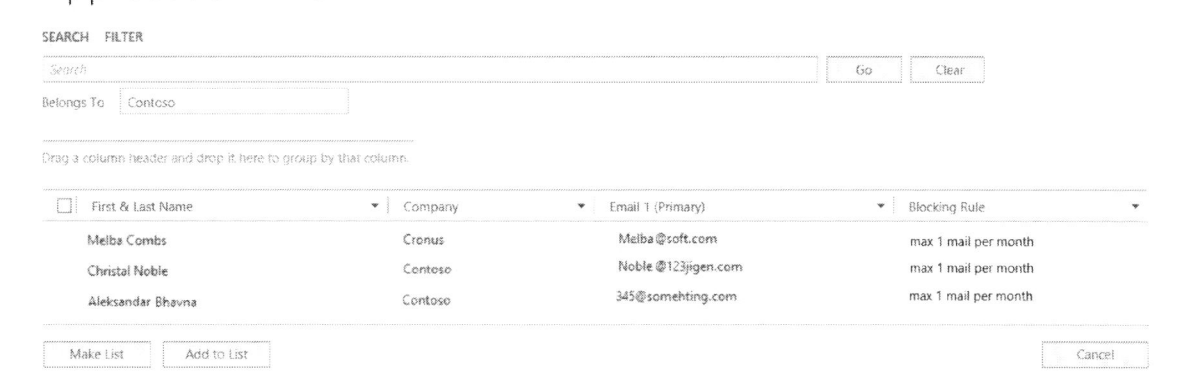

First & Last Name	Company	Email 1 (Primary)	Blocking Rule
Melba Combs	Cronus	Melba@soft.com	max 1 mail per month
Christal Noble	Contoso	Noble@123jigen.com	max 1 mail per month
Aleksandar Bhavna	Contoso	345@somehting.com	max 1 mail per month

Figure 2.29 – Recipients Blocked Because of Cross-Campaign Rules

CREATE A LIST FROM BLOCKED EMAIL MARKETING MESSAGES

It is possible to copy the Contacts that have been blocked into an existing or a new Marketing List for future use.

It is also possible to see all the email sent to a particular Contact by seeing the Status field in the "Email Mktg" panel for a given Contact and by expanding one of the emails with Status "Blocked due to Rule" is possible to see which rules applied.

CHAPTER THREE
MARKETING EXECUTION

3.1 OVERVIEW

This chapter describes the beating heart of a marketing organization using Dynamics Marketing – the Marketing Execution area. Roughly speaking Marketing Execution is comprised of two somewhat distinct areas. The first area is about the assembly of traditional Marketing Resource Management-oriented entities. The second area is about the digital marketing aspects that were covered in the previous chapter. In this chapter we focus on the first area and we will learn how to create in-person marketing events like trade shows, or performing transactions like pay vendors or bill customers, etc.

3.2 MAIN ENTITIES

The Campaign entity is the heart of most marketing operations, but Marketing Execution in Dynamics Marketing is not limited to it. While we will dig into the details of Campaigns in the next section let's see an overview of the main entities in this area first.

Entity	Description
Activities	These are calendar items representing calendar-related interactions.
Attendance	Event Attendance is used to track Contacts who are invited to Events, representing whether they attended the Event or not.
Campaigns	The Campaign entity is the hub for all marketing activity and it is described in detail in a following section in this chapter.
Companies	Companies are organization your business interacts with. Dynamics Marketing distinguishes between Marketing Companies (those you market to), Vendor Companies (those that do work for you and from which you purchase Products and Services) and Client Companies (representing clients that can be invoiced for Services, Items etc.). And on top of that, your own organization is tracked as a Company too (usually the "Site Company").

Entity	Description
Activities	These are calendar items representing calendar-related interactions.
Attendance	Event Attendance is used to track Contacts who are invited to Events, representing whether they attended the Event or not.
Campaigns	The Campaign entity is the hub for all marketing activity and it is described in detail in a following section in this chapter.
Contacts	Contacts represents people, including people you work with or you want to market to etc. Later in this chapter we will dig into the various flavors of contacts represented in Dynamics Marketing.
Contracts	These entities can be used to record business contracts in the sytem.
Cross-Campaign Rules	These rules specify patterns and limitations for the ongoing marketing communication. They are described in detail in a following section in this chapter.
Email Marketing Messages	These are the email marketing messages used in various marketing scenarios. Chapter 5 "Email Marketing" is devoted to such scenarios.
Equipment	Equipment entities are used for tracking equipment employed in meetings, conferences, trade shows, demonstrations and events.
Events	These are "physical" marketing events such as product launches, trade shows and the like. This area is described in detail in a following section in this chapter.
Fulfilment	Fulfillment in Dynamics Marketing refers to the sending of 'physical' mail to prospects and clients.
Leads	These are potential customers generated and managed by Dynamics Marketing as part of the marketing process. Chapter 4 "Generating and Managing Leads" is devoted entirely to explore this important area of the product.
Lodging	Lodging provides functionality related to tracking accommodations for event attendees (guests) and staff.
Marketing Calendar	The marketing calendar displays activities, tasks, jobs, campaigns, etc. for a given time interval.
Marketing Lists	These are collections of Contacts used in marketing communications. Dynamics Marketing distinguishes between static lists (when a list of actual contact is specified) and dynamic lists (where some criteria are specified and contacts are obtained at runtime querying the DB), the latter being called "Queries".
Marketing Plans	These are similar to Media Plans but targeting marketing activity.
Online Visitors	This entity captures the online activity of internet visitors to the sites tracked by Dynamics Marketing. These are unique users that could not be associated yet to a Contact in Dynamics Marketing. Once Dynamics Marketing manages to make this association (e.g. when a Contact interacts with an Dynamics Marketing marketing email) the behavioral data for the Visitor is copied into the corresponding Contact and the Visitor record is not updated anymore.

Entity	Description
Activities	These are calendar items representing calendar-related interactions.
Attendance	Event Attendance is used to track Contacts who are invited to Events, representing whether they attended the Event or not.
Campaigns	The Campaign entity is the hub for all marketing activity and it is described in detail in a following section in this chapter.
	Note that it might take a few hours from the time a user visits a monitored web page on the Internet until the data is tracked in this entity.
Opportunities	These are typically used by Sales/Business Development users to track potential business opportunities. Dynamics Marketing allows the seamless data integration with Dynamics CRM Opportunities.
Programs	The main use of Programs is as aggregation of campaigns. They are used to organize several campaigns, events and jobs together in order to roll up marketing data, results and financial data (budgets, costs and revenues).
Redirecting URLs	When we want to track the access to some external links using Dynamics Marketing we can enter them as Redirecting URLs. Any link created directly by Dynamics Marketing is already tracked (specifically for: Landing Pages, Email Marketing messages, Lead Management, Subscription Center, and "Forward to a Friend"), so only external third-party links will need a Redirecting URL.
Registration	This entity captures information related to Contacts attending Events.
Social Media	Dynamics Marketing supports integration with Facebook and Twitter.
Sponsorship	Used in setting up Events, this entity captures sponsorships and booth rentals by event participants and exhibitors.
Staffing	This entity captures the activities of Event staff and speakers.
Travel	This area provides functionality for defining travel itineraries for Contacts. This area uses entities such as Lodging, Itineraries, Transportation etc.
Vendors	These are Companies from which your organization purchases Products and Services.
Venues	Venues represents the physical places where Events are held (e.g. conference centers, exhibit halls, hotels, stadiums and resorts). Venues can have facilities tracking events and sessions that take place in them.
Websites	These are external web pages that can be tagged (by means of a tracking script generated by Dynamics Marketing) in order to be tracked as part of behavioral data.

3.2.1 Campaigns

Marketing professionals traditionally organize their efforts in "campaigns" with the underlying focus on reaching out to potential or existing customers. Modern campaigns have grown into complex and powerful instruments that span across budgeting, project management, multichannel execution, sophisticated reporting and more. Dynamics Marketing enables marketing professionals to manage sophisticated campaigns the way they envision them.

The Campaign list is available at:

```
Home > Marketing Execution > Campaign Management → Campaigns
```

3.2.1.1 Related Information

The Campaign entity is a hub for many processes going on in the Marketing area. The following table describes all the entities available as "related information" for a given Campaign. Most related entities can be associated manually to a campaign, unless specified otherwise.

Related information	
Activities	All the activities (simple calendar-related events) associated to the campaign.
Advertisements	Any advertisement (e.g. display advertisements, direct mailings, banners, Radio and TV commercials, billboards, etc.) associated to the campaign.
Analysis	This provides a quick summary of important financial figures for the campaign.
Approvals	Any approval in any state for this campaign.
Bookings	Any Media Bookings (used for clients to reserve Media Inventory until the Booking is invoiced) for this campaign.
Brands	Product Brands associated to this campaign. It is possible to specify an allocation ratio (default is 100%).
Brief	Text content with a given type (Objectives, goals, target audience, etc.) associated to the campaign to summarize its purpose or some of its aspects.
Budgets	All the budget worksheets associated to the campaign.
Channels	All the channels associated to the campaign. A channel is used to represent the distribution channels used to market and sell products. It is possible to specify an allocation ratio (default is 100%).
Client Quotes	All quotes associated to the campaign.
Components	All components associated to the campaign.
Contacts	Contacts cannot be associated manually to a campaign.
Details	Text sections detailing any area of interest for the campaign, also the section title can be defined ("Item" field).
Email	One-to-one transactional emails associated to this campaign.

Related information	
Email Mktg	Email Marketing Messages (both editing and sent ones) associated to the campaign.
Email Performance	The aggregated Email Marketing performance results of all the sent Email Marketing messages for this campaign.
Estimates	Estimates associated to a campaign.
Events	Events associated to a campaign.
Expenses	Expenses associated to a campaign.
Files	Files associated to a campaign.
Invoices	Invoices associated to a campaign.
Item/Service Usage	Items associated to a campaign. These cannot be associated manually to a campaign.
Jobs	Jobs associated to a campaign.
Landing Pages	All landing pages associated to a campaign.
Leads	All leads generated by this campaign.
Lists/Queries	All Lists associated to a campaign.
Locations	All locations associated to the campaign. It is possible to specify an allocation ratio (default is 100%).
Log	Log lines associated to a campaign. These lines cannot be associated manually to a campaign.
Markets	Market segments (associated with media use) related to a campaign.
Media	The media orders (those you order from vendors), media expenses and media invoices associated to the campaign.
Media Plans	Media plans associated to the campaign.
Merge/Purge	Merge/Purge associated to the campaign. Text values for each category.
Notes	The notes associated with the campaign.
Offers	The offers associated with the campaign.
Phone #s	The phone numbers associated with the campaign.
Products/Services	Products and Services associated with the campaign. It is possible to specify an allocation ratio (default is 100%).
Purchase Orders	All the Purchase Order associated with the campaign.
Requests	All the Project Requests associated with the campaign. Note that these are different than Job Requests. Project Requests are more articulated than Job Requests in that they are placed in a queue where they can be reviewed or assigned for review. After review and approval, a mix of Task, Job, Campaign, Event or Program can be created as wanted.
Results	The Marketing Performance Measurement associated to the campaign.
RFQs	All the requests for quote associated with the campaign.
Sales Orders	The sales orders associated with the campaign.
Social Media	The social media messages associated with the campaign.

Related information	
Source Codes	The source codes associated with the campaign.
Tasks	The tasks associated with the campaign.
Team	The users that are working on the campaign.
Time Slips	Time Slips associated with the campaign.
Vendor Quotes	The vendor quotes associated with the campaign.

SIMPLIFIED UI FOR LARGE DATABASES

Dynamics Marketing supports marketing DBs with millions of records. In order to provide a smoother UI experience, search and other UI functionality are simplified when your DB is greater than 250 thousands records.

3.2.2   Working with Marketing Customers, Vendors and Clients

Dynamics Marketing provides a wide range of entities and functionality for managing marketing clients (companies and their employees our organization markets to), normal clients (companies and their employees our organization works for, in order to invoice them for Product or Services) and vendors (companies and their employees we acquire Services and Products from).

3.2.2.1   Companies

Contacts are associated with a number of undertakings such as Projects they are assigned to, transactions in which they are involved, assigned Tasks and so on. All this information is aggregated by Dynamics Marketing at the level of the Company they belong to so that a holistic view of the activity going on for a given client organization is easily available. The following table lists the Related Information panels available for Marketing Companies.

Related information	
Activities	All the Activities (simple calendar-related events) associated to the Company.
Bookings	Any Media Bookings (used for clients to reserve Media Inventory until the Booking is invoiced) for this Company.
Client Quotes	All quotes associated to the Company.

Related information	
Contacts	All Contacts associated to the Company via the "Company" field in the Contact form.
Contracts	This entity represents the legal contracts, if captured in the system.
Details	Default values for Company-related information are gathered here.
Emails	One-to-one transactional emails sent by Contact associated to this Company.
Estimates	Estimates associated to this Company.
Files	Files associated to this Company
Invoices	Invoices associated to the Company
Item / Service Usage	Items associated to a Company.
Leads	All leads generated that are associated to this Company. Leads are used to represent customer interest.
Log	Any log lines associated to this Company.
Media Usage	The usage of media for this Campaign.
Notes	The notes associated with the Company
Opportunities	Captures possible Opportunities related to this Campaign.
Payments	The Marketing Performance Measurement associated to the Company
Results	
Sales Orders	The sales orders associated with the Company.
SMS	Mobile Text Messages.
Teams	Users working on the Company

The "Belongs to" field is used to represent complex organization setups. We will describe how this field is used in real scenarios together with other fields in a later section of this chapter.

3.2.2.1.1 The "Group" field

Companies are grouped in different types depending upon the Group field. There are three checkboxes that define different combinations.

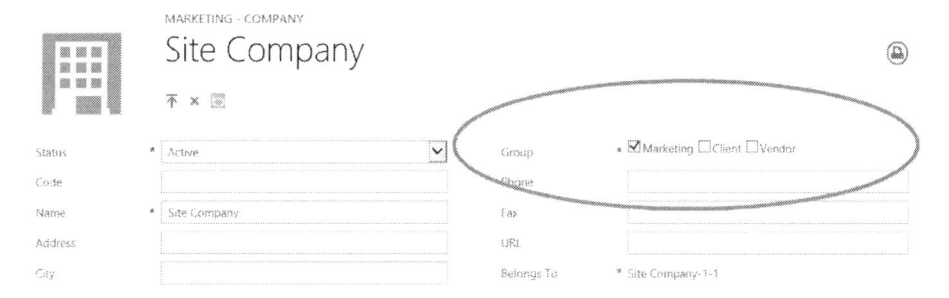

Figure 3.1 –Type of Contacts

This table shows the available combinations of groups for Companies.

Company Checkboxes Selected for the "Group" field	Description
Marketing	These are the companies that are the target of our marketing activity on behalf of our clients. Note that Dynamics Marketing doesn't allow for a Marketing company to also be a client or a vendor company at the same time.
Client	These are the client companies we work for.
Vendor	These are the vendor companies we get services and items from.
Client and Vendor	These are companies with who we work and at the same time we also request services and products from.
(None)	This is equivalent to define the Company as a "Staff" Company, i.e. a Company that works for you but you don't need to track business interactions that you would have with a Vendor Company.

The "Company" field in a Contact represents the Company the Contact works for.

> **CHANGING "GROUP" FOR AN EXISTING COMPANY OR CONTACT**
>
> if you change a "Marketing" Company to "Client" and/or "Vendor" Dynamics Marketing will create a copy of the Company to preserve previous references in the database.

3.2.2.2 Modeling Complex Organizational Scenarios with Dynamics Marketing Companies

Let's start from the simplest setup. Imagine Dynamics Marketing is used in a marketing department part of an organization. All the marketing activities are on behalf of the organization. Dynamics Marketing represents this simple setup by means of just one Company (usually the default one is called the "Site Company"). This company represents the organization that purchased Dynamics Marketing and uses it for its own marketing activities.

Let's now get a step further, looking at an agency that runs the marketing activities on behalf of one single client. Dynamics Marketing represents this client as a Client Company. Depending on the kind of markets they work in, they would need also to represent the organizations they market to, on behalf of their client. Such organizations are represented in Dynamics Marketing as Marketing Companies. And let's add another piece of the puzzle, the vendors our marketing agency will get services or products from. Such vendors are represented as Vendor Companies.

So we have a marketing agency that works with a number of external vendors (they might provide things like printing services, creative content, merchandise, etc.) on behalf of one client. Such a client has a number of target organizations (i.e. the Marketing Companies) that they market to. Of course very few agencies work with one single client only. Most agencies work with a number of clients at the same time. This poses a small issue, as the approach we described so far tracks the Company people work with, but not the related Client Company. Dynamics Marketing provides the "Belongs to" field to represent this additional property. So Marketing Companies have an additional field ("Belongs to") representing the Client Company the agency (Site Company) is working for. Note that this field cannot changed once the Company is created.

3.2.2.3 Contacts

Contacts follow the same structure of Companies described in the previous subsection, with minor differences. We discuss them here as part of the Company entity for completeness.

Contacts have an extra "Staff" option in the Group field. This option is used for people working for (or on behalf of) your organization.

The following table reports the available combinations of the "Group" field for Contacts.

Contact Checkboxes Selected for the "Group" field	Description
Marketing	Dynamics Marketing allows to specify as a separate group Contact which belong to Companies you are marketing to. You use this option to keep Contacts separate for each Client Company, when your organization uses Databases that belong to your Clients. Also your Sales people can add prospects as "Marketing" Contacts to keep them separate from Clients, Vendors and Staff. These Contacts need to specify the parent Company by means of the "Belongs To" field.

Contact Checkboxes Selected for the "Group" field	Description
Client	These Contacts work for one of your Client Companies (i.e., one of the Companies that service through Dynamics Marketing). Typically your coworkers (registered in Dynamics Marketing as "Staff" Contacts) work together with Client Contacts.
Vendor	These are Contacts of Vendor Companies, i.e. Companies that do work for you and from who you purchase Products and Services.
Staff	These Contacts work for your organization, although not necessarily as employees.
Client and Vendor	In some cases the same Company that you work for can provide Services or Products to your own organization. This arrangement is useful when financial transactions are needed to and from the same organization.
Client, Staff and Vendor	In some cases you can be providing services to your own organization and people working for your organization can provide you with Services that you want to formally account for and trace using Dynamics Marketing. This might sound convoluted but by using this setup you can invoice or issue orders to your own company without resorting to complex workarounds and have Dynamics Marketing taking care of all the details.
Staff and Vendor	With this setup you can provide Services or Products to your own organization. For example imagine you want to track transactions related to the production of media by a branch of your own organization.
Client and Staff	Use this option when you need to have your own Company behaving as a Client to yourself (i.e. bill yourself for Product or Services and keep track of these transactions as part of your budgeting).
(None)	Dynamics Marketing allows leaving all groups unselected for a Contact.

STAFF CONTACTS ARE COMING FROM OFFICE 365

While you can still create a Staff Contact manually in Dynamics Marketing, most of them will be coming automatically from the Office 365 organization your administrator has set up. Dynamics Marketing will create automatically a User and a Staff Contact for each user created in Office 365 (and update changed fields accordingly[13]). This could come handy, say for sending a newsletter to all your employees. A dynamic list will gather all your employees (all Staff Contacts that are Active) for your newsletter.

A handy functionality available for marketing contacts is the Marketing Engagement view, providing a complete overview of some relevant marketing information for that contact.

Figure 3.2 – Contact Marketing Engagement

This is the marketing engagement view for a brand new contact, just registered on one of our landing pages:

---

[13] Fields propagated from Office 365 are shown as read-only in Dynamics Marketing.

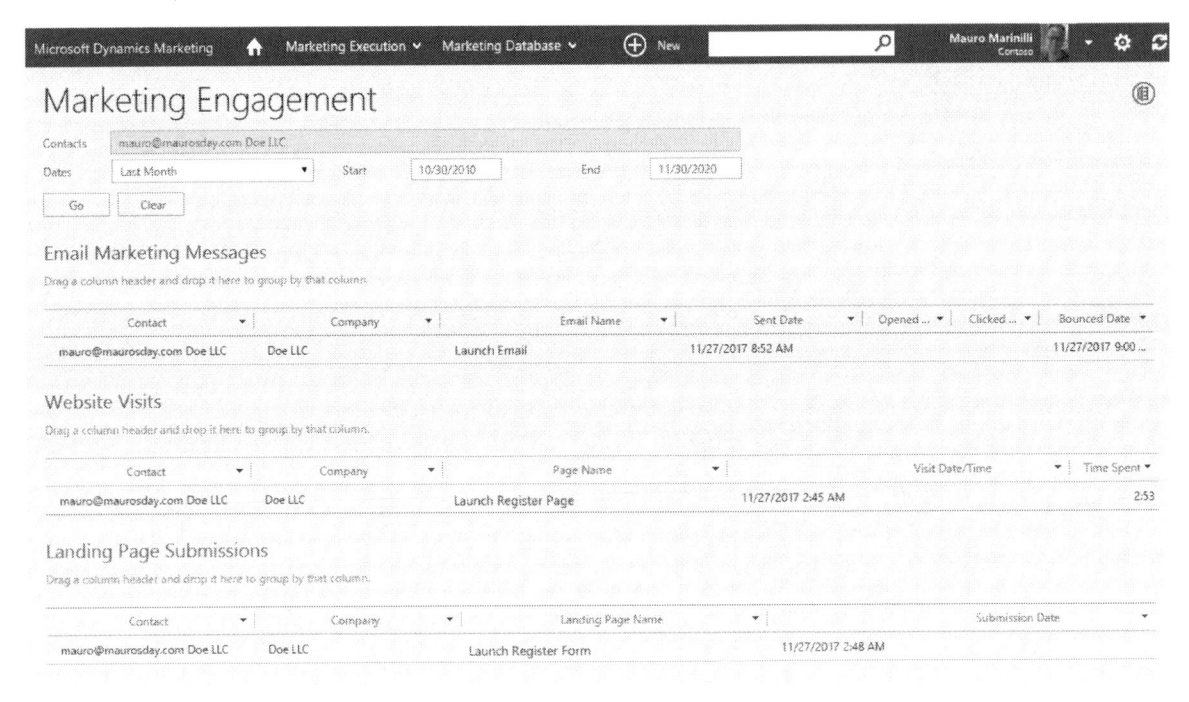

Figure 3.3 – Marketing Engagement Page

3.2.2.4 When a Contact is considered unique

Depending upon how a Contact enters Dynamics Marketing the criteria for its uniqueness can be different. When a contact is considered unique it will not be created anew but the latest details will update the existing one in the DB.

How the Contact enters Dynamics Marketing	Criteria for uniqueness
Manual input via UI	No specific criteria in Dynamics Marketing, i.e. it is always considered "new" regardless of the value of the fields entered in the UI.
Import file via UI	When first name, last name, email and "Belongs to" company are the same as another contact in the DB the new contact is not added to the system (the import will mark the record as "skipped" in the import report). Note that this criteria does not apply to the contacts in the import file itself, so if there are two exact lines in the import file they will create two separate contacts.
Landing page	When first name, last name, email and "Belongs to" company are the same as another Contact in the DB that records gets updated and no new Contact is created.
CRM Connector	No specific criteria in Dynamics Marketing.
API	Same as landing pages.

3.2.2.5 Companies' Divisions and Departments

For large organizations or where an additional level of granularity is required Dynamics Marketing allows for a two-level subdivision hierarchy. Companies can be broken down into Divisions and these further down in Departments.

Divisions are optional parts of a Company where one Company can have many Divisions but a Division can only have one Company. Once you associate a Contact or Task or Invoice etc. to a Division you cannot change the association. Organizations that only have one main office / hub or with tightly coupled small subsidiaries, won't use Divisions.

Divisions are available under

    Home > Settings > My Company → Divisions

Departments are parts of one Division. Many Departments can belong to a single Division. In turn Departments can only belong to one Division. They are available from the Departments panel of the Division form. Departments are available under

    Home > Settings > My Company → Departments

So how would you use Departments then? Imagine you want to upload a File related to your Creative Production department for your North America division of your Company. By uploading the file for that Department the file will appear under the File tabs of the parent Division, and in turn will appear for the Company the Division belongs to. This "roll up" mechanism applies to all the entities available as Related Information for the Department entity.

The Related Information panels available for a Department are:

- Approvals
- Bookings
- Budgets
- Campaigns
- Client Quotes
- Email
- Events
- Expenses
- Files
- Invoices
- Jobs
- Log
- Notes
- Programs
- Purchase Orders
- Requests
- Sales Orders
- SMS
- Tasks
- Team
- Time Slips
- Vendor Quotes

3.2.2.6 Locations

Dynamics Marketing supports the notion of Location (i.e. a geographical annotation of an item related to a marketing activity).

Locations are available under

```
Home > Settings > My Company -> Locations
```

One Company can have many Locations. Likewise, a Division can have many Locations too. Locations can be grouped into Regions and the same Location can belong to multiple Regions.

These are the entities available as Related Information for a Location:

- Approvals
- Bookings
- Budgets
- Campaigns
- Client Quotes
- Email
- Expenses
- Files
- Invoices
- Jobs
- Log
- Notes
- Programs
- Purchase Orders
- Regions
- Requests
- Results
- Sales Orders
- Team
- Vendor Quotes

3.2.3 Marketing Lists

Dynamics Marketing provides functionality for grouping contacts for marketing purposes. While most of the time you will be concerned with Marketing Contacts, Dynamics Marketing allows the creation of lists of any type of Contacts.

Marketing Lists are used in Campaign Automation models, Email Marketing mailings and in various other areas of the product.

Marketing Lists are available under

```
Home > Marketing Execution > Marketing Lists → Marketing Lists
```

Then creating a new List users are prompted with the type (more options shown depending upon your configuration):

Type

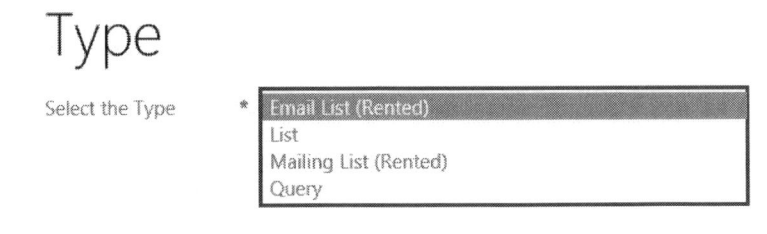

Select the Type * | Email List (Rented)
                   List
                   Mailing List (Rented)
                   Query

Figure 3.4 –Type of Marketing List

In the following subsections we will go through each type in detail.

3.2.3.1 Static Lists
These are "static" collections of Contacts, i.e. contacts are added or removed one by one manually[14].

3.2.3.2 Dynamic Lists (Queries)
These are "dynamic" collections of Contacts obtained by filtering at a given time the database according to some criteria we call the "query". The query is run when needed. For email marketing messages sent manually the query is run once, at the time of sending. For email marketing messages run via automation the query is run constantly as long as the campaign is active.

3.2.3.3 Email Lists (Rented)
There are list of contacts used for email marketing purposes. While Dynamics Marketing supports importing such lists we strongly discourage users to add purchased lists to your Email Marketing campaign, as that is the first reason for poor deliverability.

These lists are available from Media Outlets.

3.2.3.4 Mailing Lists (Rented)
These lists are used for the delivering of promotional content using printed material.

Most users will use the first two types only.

---

[14] Static lists can also maintained by an external system via an API described in Chapter 12 "Development Scenarios".

3.2.4 Events

Dynamics Marketing provides functionality for managing marketing initiatives that take place at a specific venue or location. With Events you can track trade shows, special marketing events, conferences, meetings, etc.

Events are available under

> Home > Marketing Execution > Event Management → Events

Similarly to other functional areas, Dynamics Marketing provides a rich set of capabilities for managing detailed information related to events. One can start with tracking the planning and initial documentation (using Brief, Notes and Files) handling budgeting aspects and overall final costs. Managing all the Event Staff or the participants, including their Travel Itineraries and creating a detailed Schedule. Handling the various Facilities involved with the Event is also possible, as well as managing all the equipment, brochures, and other materials you might for the Event. Jobs and Tasks can be associated to an Event to track all the work performed for the Event, or attach Media Plans or handle shipments associated with events, equipment and materials.

Related information	
Advertisements	Any advertisement (e.g. display advertisements, direct mailings, banners, Radio and TV commercials, billboards, etc.) associated with the event.
Analysis	This provides a quick summary of important financial figures for the event.
Approvals	Any approval in any state for this event.
Attendance	The attendance (Contacts) for the event.
Bookings	Any Media Bookings (used for clients to reserve Media Inventory until the Booking is invoiced) for this event.
Brands	Product Brands associated to this event. It is possible to specify an allocation ratio (default is 100%).
Brief	Text content with a given type (Objectives, goals, target audience, etc.) associated to the event to summarize its intent, planning or some of its aspects.
Budgets	All the budget worksheets associated to the event.
Channels	All the channels associated to this event.
Client Quotes	All quotes associated to the event.
Email	One-to-one transactional emails associated to this event.
Email Marketing	Email Marketing Messages (both editing and sent ones) associated to the event.

Related information	
Equipment Requests	Track requests for equipment from your speakers with this entity.
Estimates	Estimates associated to the event.
Events	Events associated to the event.
Expenses	Expenses associated to the event.
Files	Files associated to the event.
Invoices	Invoices associated to the event.
Functions	This is used for track seating at functions (round tables, meals, buffets, etc.).
Item/Service Usage	Items associated to the event. These cannot be associated manually.
Jobs	Jobs associated to the event.
Leads	All leads generated by this event.
Lists/Queries	All Lists associated to this event.
Locations	All locations associated to the event. It is possible to specify an allocation ratio (default is 100%).
Lodging	Lodging captures details about the accommodation of the various participants (things like room number, check-in and check-out dates etc.).
Log	Log lines associated to a campaign. These lines cannot be associated manually to a event.
Media	The media orders (those you order from vendors), media expenses and media invoices associated to the event.
Media Plans	Media plans associated to the event.
Notes	The notes associated with the event.
Performance	These are the email marketing statistics of all the mailings associated to this Event.
Products/Services	Products and Services associated with the event. It is possible to specify an allocation ratio (default is 100%).
Purchase Orders	All the Purchase Orders associated with the event.
Registration	The details related to registering users to an Event.
Registration Setup	This captures the details related to the setting up of a registration scheme for an Event.
Requests	All the Project Requests associated with the event (these are different than Job Requests).
Results	The Results associated to the event.
RFQs	All the requests for quotes associated with the event.
Sales Orders	The sales orders associated with the event.
Sessions	Sessions make up the overall schedule for an Event. Things like the place (Venue) and the time are defined in a Session.

Related information	
Shipping	Most non-trivial Events will require shipments to the venue (merchandise, direct rentals and so on).
Social Media	The social media messages associated with the event, if any.
Sponsorship	Sponsorships comprises a number of Items and can be booked, reserved etc. The Type category can be used to tag sponsorships as needed (e.g. "Platinum", "Bronze" etc.) without resorting to a User-Defined Field.
Source Codes	The source codes associated with the event.
Staff Info	These are Notes (rich formatted text) attached to an Item for people working on the Event organization and execution.
Staff/Speakers	These are calendar activities assigned to participants and organizers.
Tasks	The tasks associated with the event.
Team	The users that are working on the event. As with other entities this list provides data visibility rules within Dynamics Marketing.
Time Slips	Time Slips associated with the event.
Travel	This entity captures traveling information for a Contact participating in an Event. Things like the destination, reminders, and related entities such as Accommodations and Transportation plus the usual ones like Emails (i.e. the plain transactional emails exchanged for this travel journey), any attached Files, Logs and Notes.
Vendor Quotes	The vendor quotes associated with the event.

Webinars are meant to be "virtual events" part of an even instance. See Chapter 2 "Campaign Automation" for more details on webinars and how they are used in Campaign Automation models.

3.3 SALES COLLABORATING WITH MARKETING TEAMS

Given the large volumes of marketing communication and the fast pace of execution typical of many companies, at times sales people might be disconnected from the marketing communications going on, even for their own accounts and contacts. This is not a problem with Dynamics Marketing, thanks to the Seller Portal. The portal is available under the Marketing Contact List:

```
Home > Marketing Execution > Marketing Database → Marketing Contacts
```

Inside Microsoft Dynamics Marketing

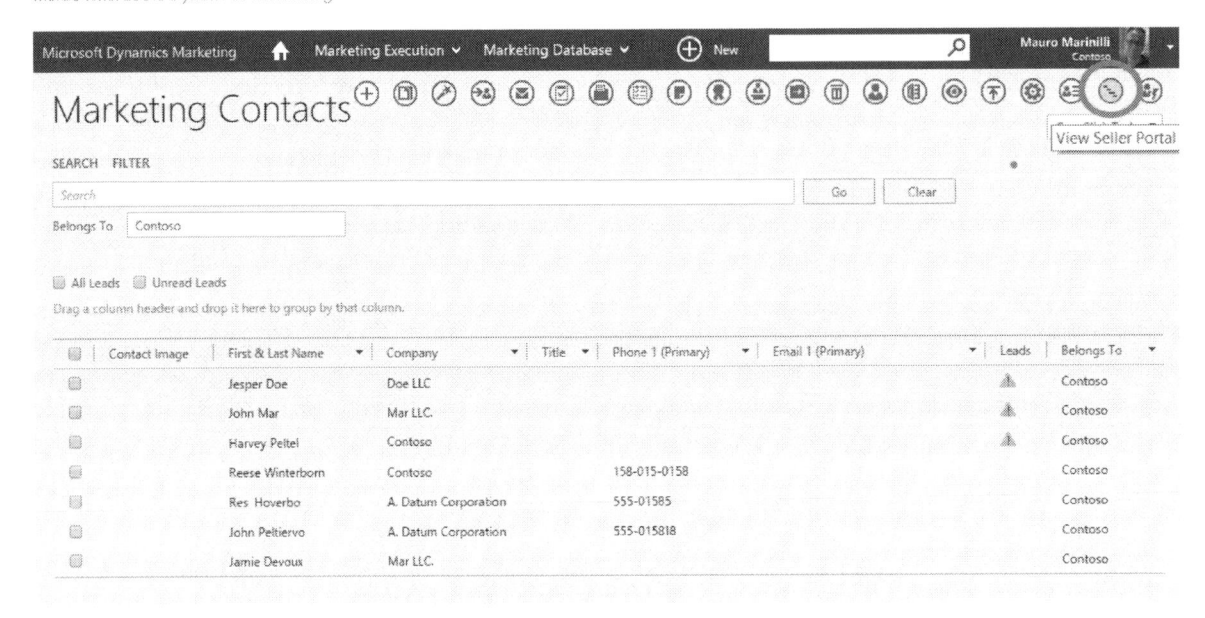

Figure 3.5 –Opening the Seller Portal

The Seller portal is available both for Contacts and Companies. Using the portal is not only possible to have a complete overview of the entire marketing communication to the selected contacts or companies but it is also possible to control what is being sent (if security permissions allow). An example of the marketing activities involving one contact is shown below. We will see how the portal can be used from Dynamics CRM later in this chapter.

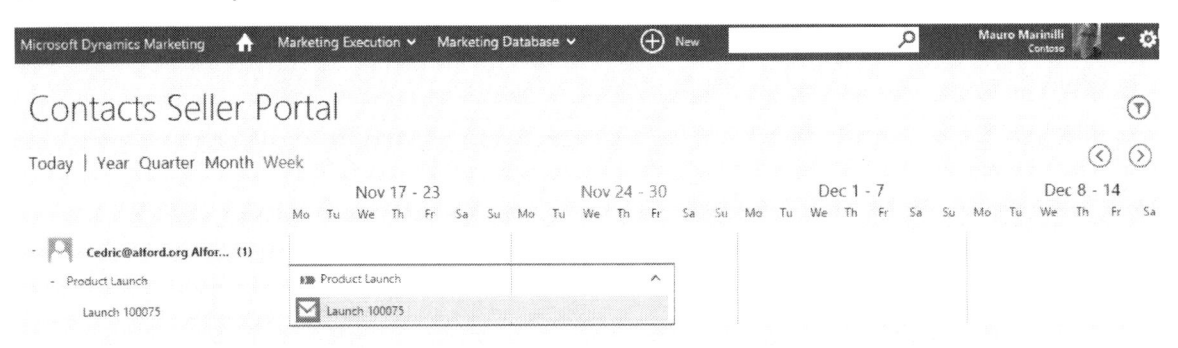

Figure 3.6 –Marketing Communication to a Contact

Inside Microsoft Dynamics Marketing

3.4 SCENARIOS

Now that we have seen the main functionality available for this area in Dynamics Marketing, let's look at some usage examples of the product.

3.4.1 Sales People in Dynamics CRM overseeing marketing communications.

A sales person using Dynamics CRM wants to see the latest marketing communication going to two accounts she owns. She opens Dynamics CRM, selects the accounts of interests and opens the Marketing Portal as shown below:

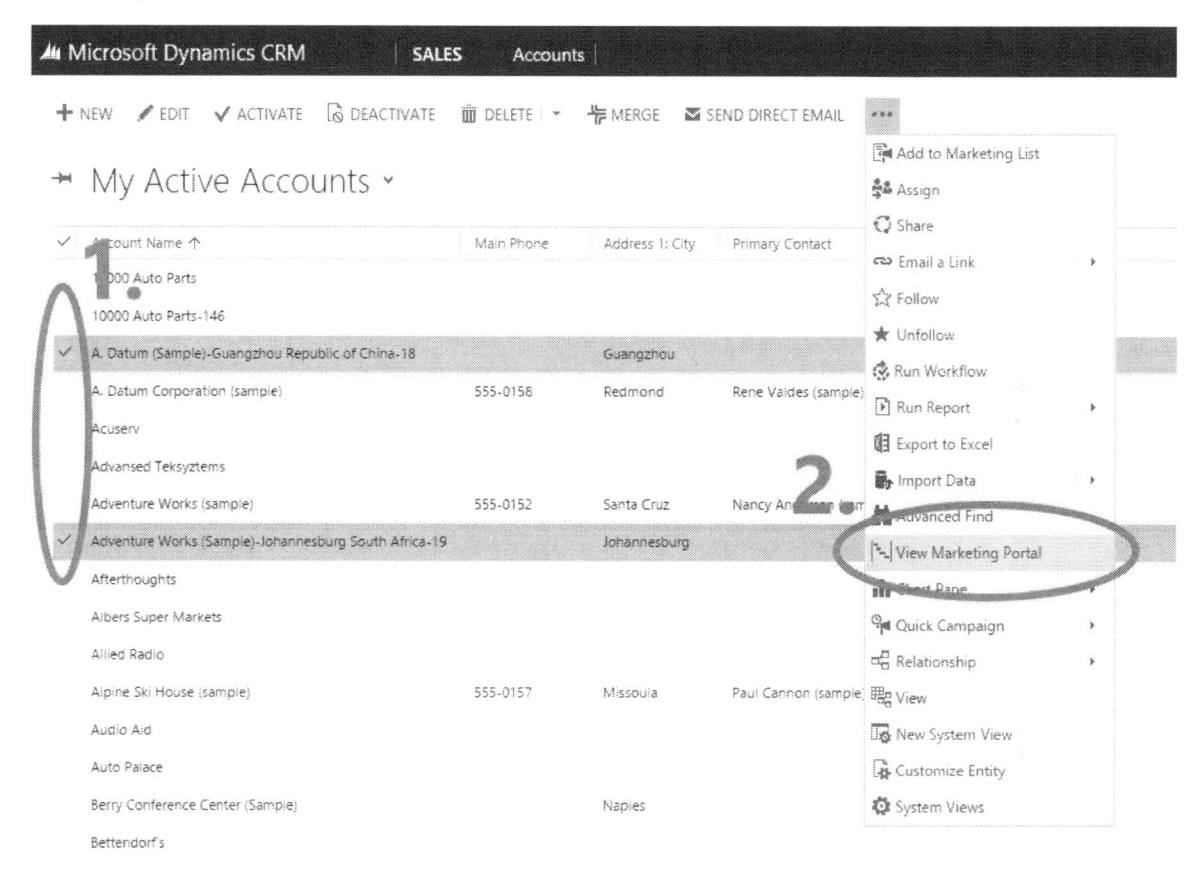

Figure 3.7 –Controlling Marketing Activity for some Accounts in Dynamics CRM

This will open up Dynamics Marketing in a new browser tab (even if the sales person does not have access to Dynamics Marketing[15]):

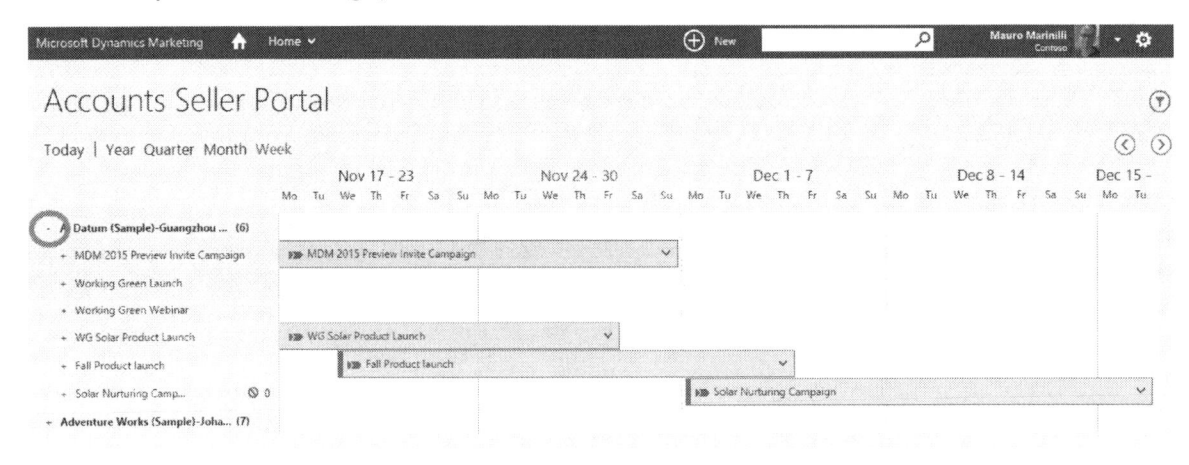

Figure 3.8 –Marketing Communications for a Dynamics CRM Account

Now she can expand the account (represented in Dynamics Marketing as a company and synchronized via the CRM Connector) and see all the marketing activities going on. She can of course change the time range (to see future or past activities) and add additional filtering etc.

Now she wants to dig into a particular campaign, so she expands that and inspects all the marketing messaging going on as part of that campaign with her company of interest.

---

[15] Only a "light" Seller Portal licensing is required, not a full Dynamics Marketing license.

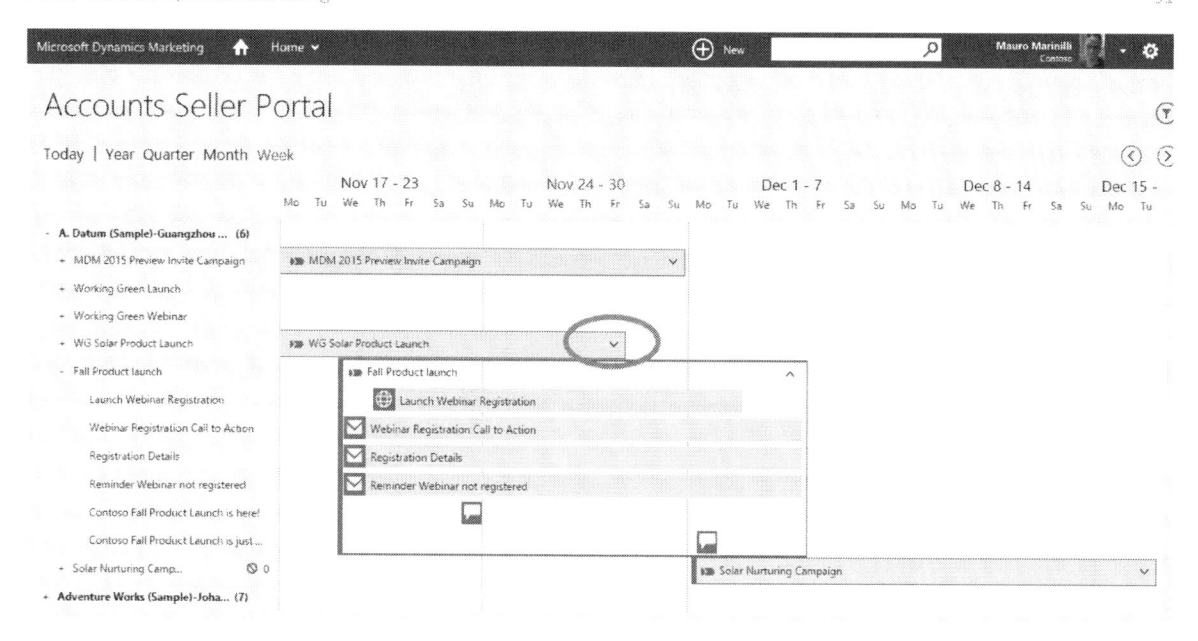

Figure 3.9 –Details of Marketing Communications

From here she can drill into each and every message that will open contextually to the portal so she can inspect all the details of what is going on. If she is not happy with some communication she can block it directly from the portal or get in touch with the marketing people for clarifications.

> **GETTING IN TOUCH WITH A CLICK**
>
> Dynamics Marketing provides "one-click call" functionality using Lync or Skype so that it is straightforward to get in touch with our colleagues or contacts using these technologies. See Chapter 11 "Configuration" for more details.

3.4.2 Set Up Events
Events are available under

```
Home > Marketing Execution > Event Management → Events
```

From here a marketing manager can set up complex promotional events in Dynamics Marketing. For example a product launch can be registered in Dynamics Marketing, including the allocated budget and all the main details of its organization.

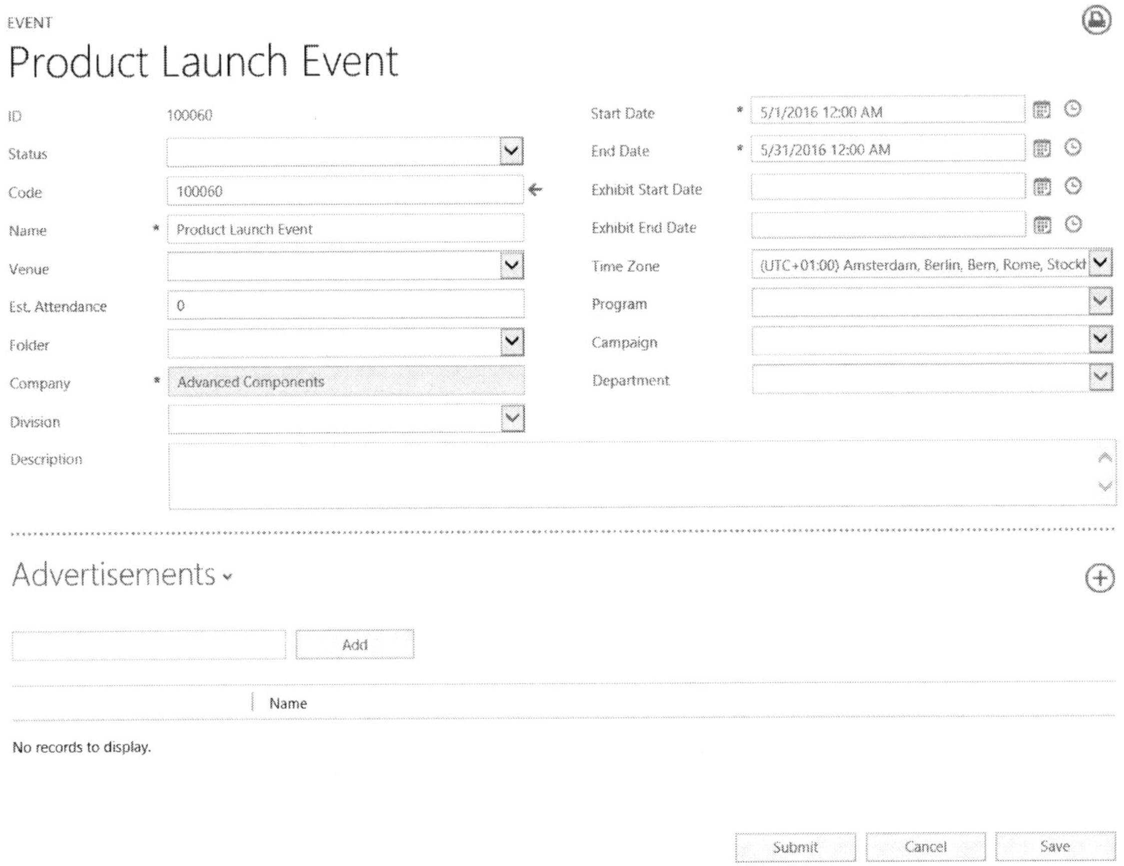

EVENT
Product Launch Event

ID	100060	Start Date	* 5/1/2016 12:00 AM	
Status		End Date	* 5/31/2016 12:00 AM	
Code	100060	Exhibit Start Date		
Name	* Product Launch Event	Exhibit End Date		
Venue		Time Zone	(UTC+01:00) Amsterdam, Berlin, Bern, Rome, Stockh	
Est. Attendance	0	Program		
Folder		Campaign		
Company	* Advanced Components	Department		
Division				
Description				

Advertisements

Name

No records to display.

[Submit] [Cancel] [Save]

Figure 3.10 – Event Example

The following screen shows the registration of attendees for the event:

Inside Microsoft Dynamics Marketing

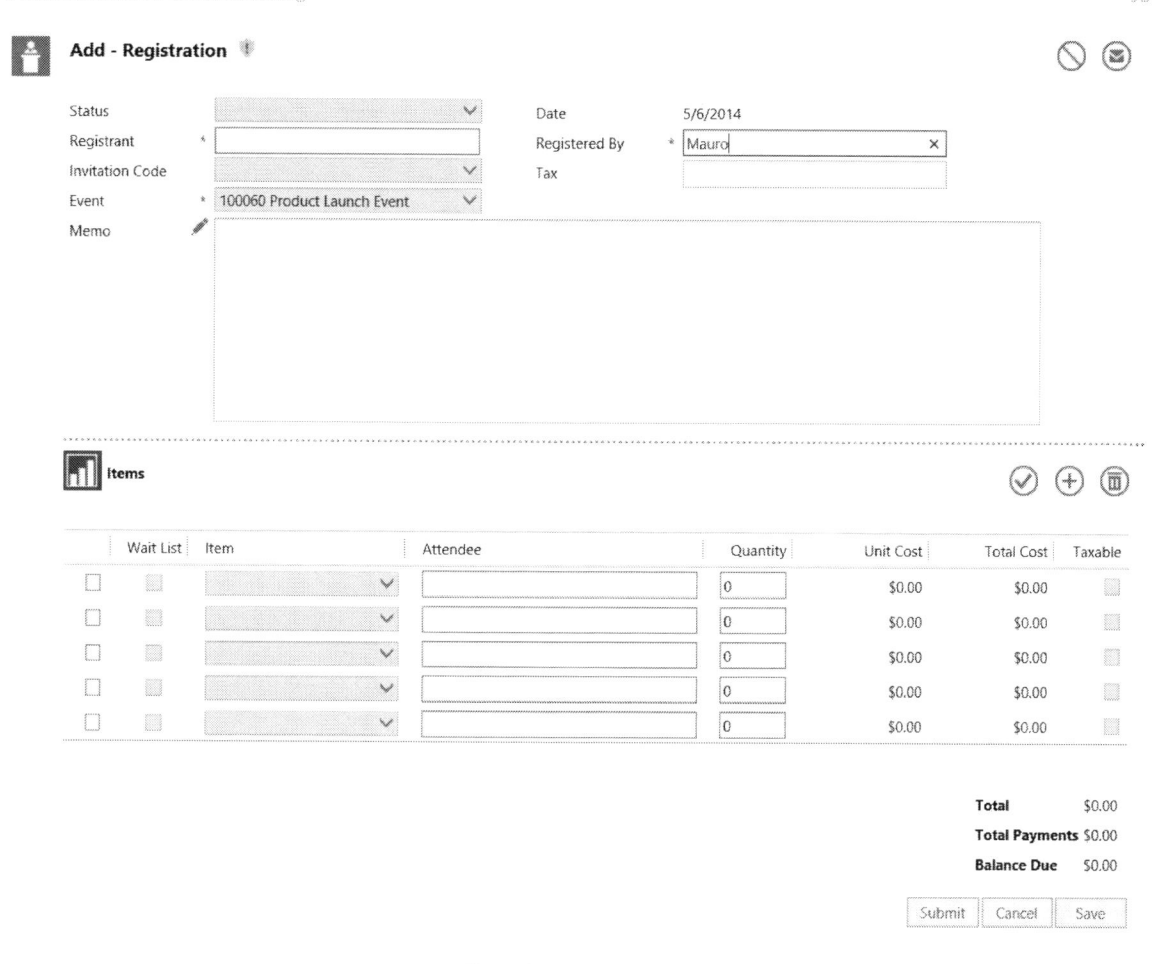

Figure 3.11 –Event Setup

3.4.3 Using the Marketing Calendar

Dynamics Marketing provides a convenient calendar functionality that shows all the marketing activities going on in a given period of time. The Marketing Calendar is available at:

      Home > Marketing Execution > Calendar → Calendar

See below for an example.

Inside Microsoft Dynamics Marketing

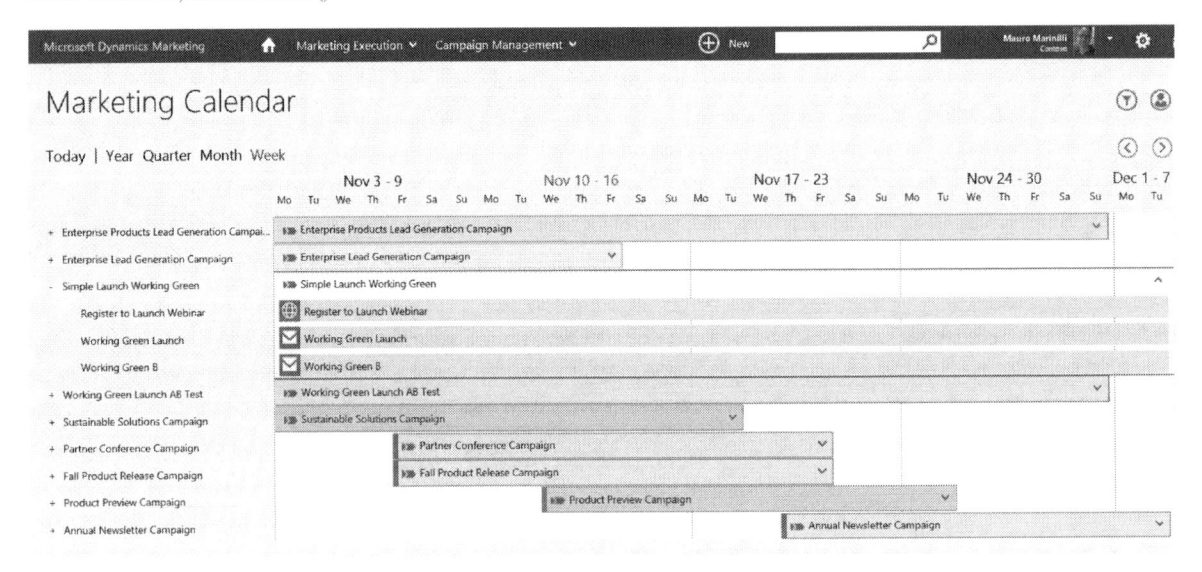

Figure 3.12 – Marketing Calendar

CHAPTER FOUR
GENERATING AND MANAGING LEADS

4.1 OVERVIEW

The creation of customer interest is a key task for the Marketing function in an organization. In Dynamics Marketing such customer interest and the Marketing Contacts that are generated and refined over time as part of this process are captured in the Lead entity, representing the history of customer interactions and all related information including the likelihood to generate a sale. Dynamics Marketing provides a flexible toolset that can be tailored to a wide range of organizations and business contexts. Whether your organization works in the B2B (Business-to-Business) space[16] or in the B2C space Dynamics Marketing can accommodate your needs efficiently.

Usually the Marketing department in an organization is responsible for Lead generation, while pursuing and closing promising Leads usually falls onto the Sales department. Dynamics Marketing provides a close integration with Dynamics CRM that makes this process across departments and software tools seamless and efficient. In this scenario not only Leads generated in Dynamics Marketing are readily available in Dynamics CRM but also the outcome of each Sales operation is promptly reflected in Dynamics Marketing. Few products on the market today can provide such a seamless integration between Sales and Marketing as Dynamics CRM and Dynamics Marketing provide[17].

4.1.1 An Example
Let's break the ice with an example. Imagine our organization works in the B2B space –say it sells components for large-scale renewable energy power plants, for instance. Our market are installers and other specialized engineering companies, from small companies to large industrial conglomerates

---

[16] In B2B the products and services of the organization are marketed to other businesses. B2B sales processes take longer than business-to-consumer relationships. B2B sales decision making may take place at more than one level, possibly including many stakeholders.

[17] For more details on how to set up the data integration with Dynamics CRM see Chapter 11 "Configuration".

working on large scale projects. The sales cycles are usually long (six months and more) involving various people from prospect companies.

We created a specific Program in Dynamics Marketing to track the launch of our new breakthrough high-efficiency transfer components. As part of this Program we are running multiple Campaigns.

We designed an Inbound Campaign to provide whitepapers, infographics and multimedia content for our new products[18]. Not only we defined all the content and web pages for prospects to interact with, we also prepared a dedicated Lead Scoring Model to accurately assess Leads based on users online behavior and demographics data. Only the most promising leads should be passed onto the Sales team. Our sales team uses Dynamics CRM.

Let's follow the journey of one of these prospects, from its creation through the sales cycle concluding with how the Return on Marketing Investment (ROMI) can be attributed at the end of the campaign.

A technical manager working for a prospect customer receives our promotional email[19]. He is interested in our offer so he opens the link and registers on our Landing Page. A new Lead is then generated in Dynamics Marketing and already scored based on the automatic lead scoring model we defined.

---

[18] The entire process, from the asset creation (including the Landing Pages that will allow downloads of the content) to the budgeting and execution has been managed entirely in Dynamics Marketing.

[19] See Chapter 5 "Email Marketing" for more details on marketing emails.

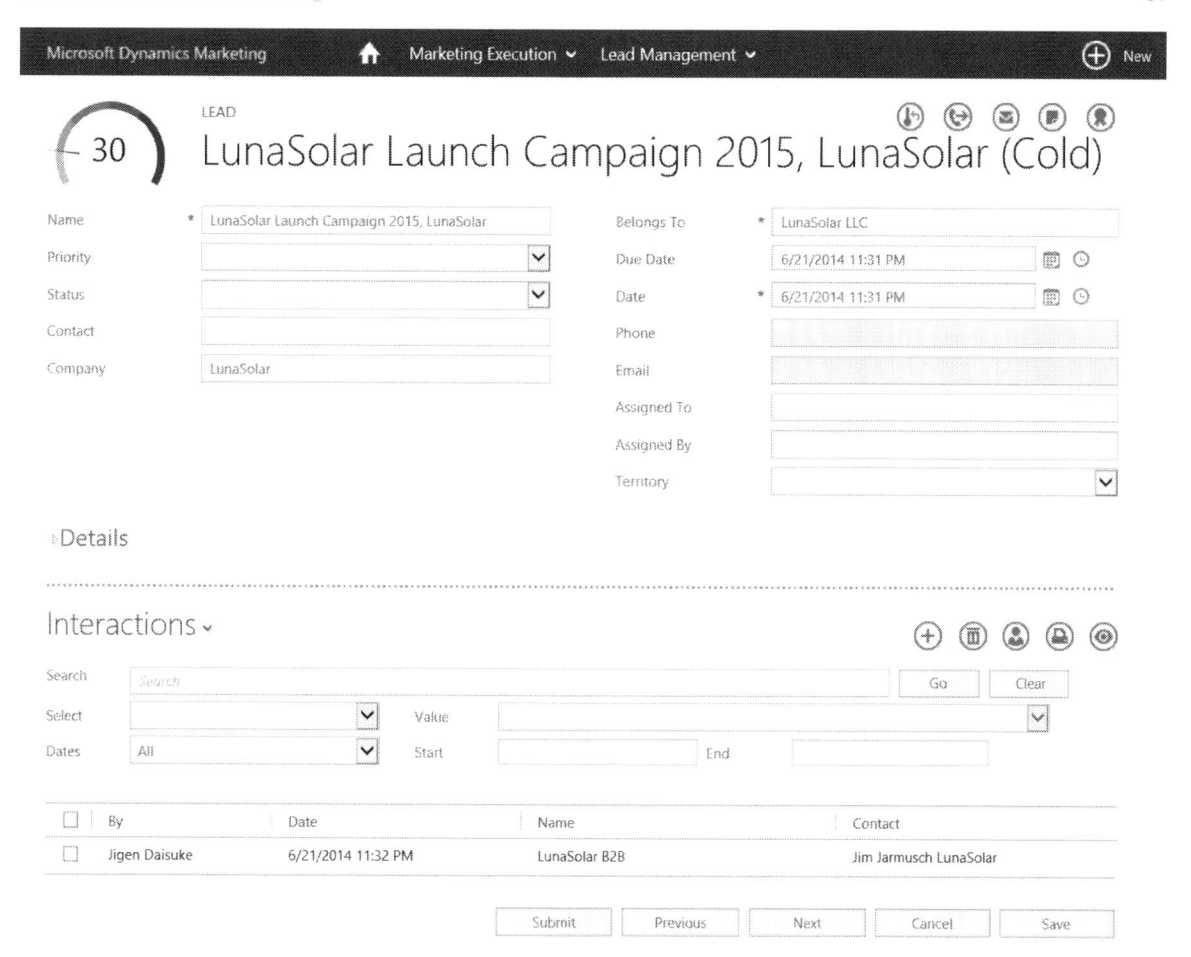

Figure 4.1 –Lead Form

By selecting the Interactions panel a Marketing Manager can see that this Lead was originated from responding to a promotional email. The manager can dig into the details of that Lead Management Interaction, if needed.

Sometime later, another contact working for the same company appears on our radar again by downloading a whitepaper via an Dynamics Marketing Landing Page[20]. This event is tracked back in Dynamics Marketing and the new score for the prospect increases.

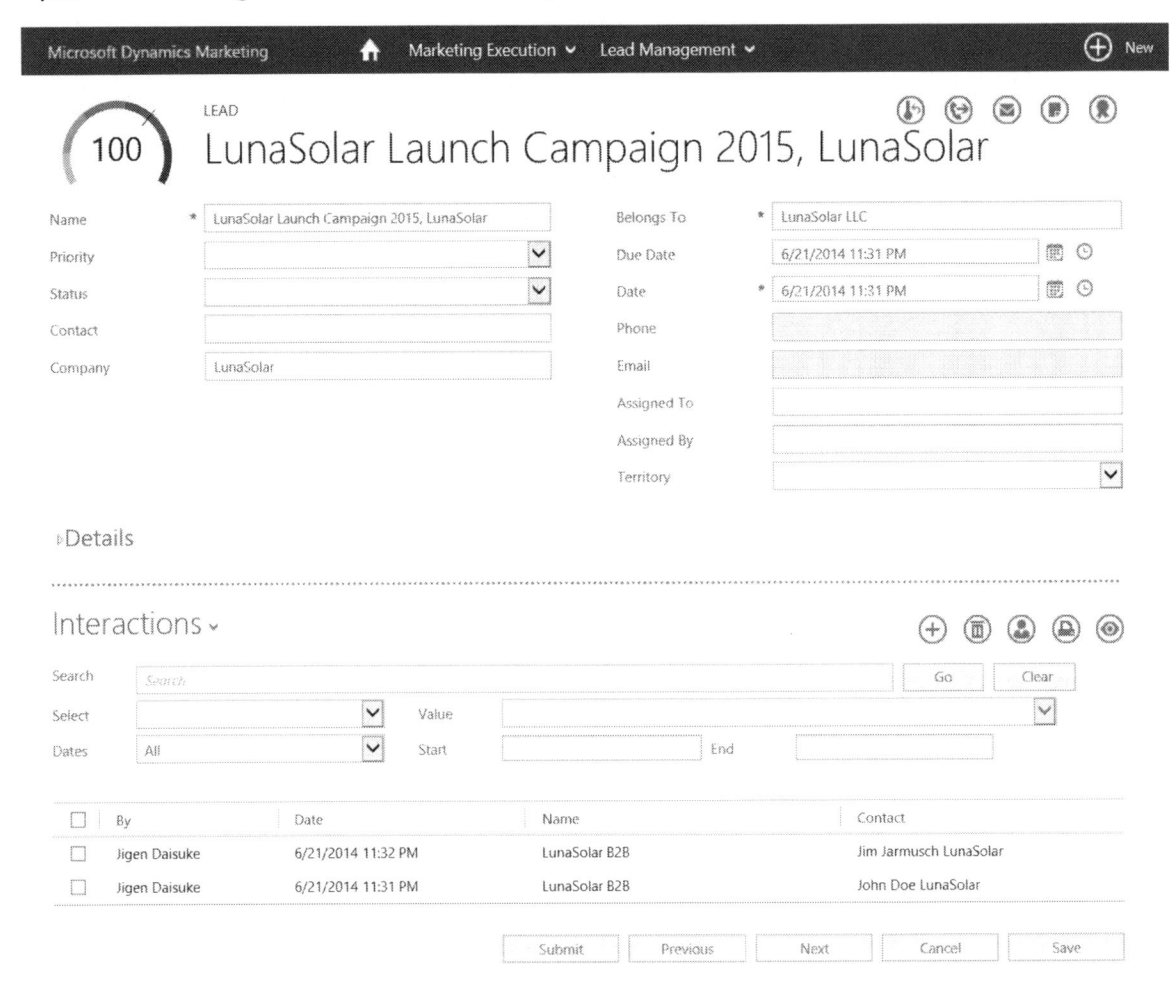

Figure 4.2 –Type of Contacts

---

[20] For example this could be driven by a drip campaign, as described in Chapter 2 "Campaign Automation".

More interactions from users of the prospect company happen over time to the point that the Lead is now automatically scored as "Sales Ready". We can track with scoring rules the time spent by prospects looking at our pricing web page for example, or other behavior that we think is revealing of interest in our product and industry.

Because of being now marked as "Sales Ready" this lead is automatically copied into Dynamics CRM where a sales person is assigned to it following up with the prospect.

It turns out that the prospect was indeed considering the sale at that point in time (and considering other competitors too) but our sales rep managed to close the deal for the company.

After the deal is closed in Dynamics CRM that information is passed back into Dynamics Marketing automatically[21] and the Marketing Manager can see in Dynamics Marketing an update in the overall Return on Marketing Investment (ROMI) from the variation in the Budget vs. Actual in the Budget Worksheet.

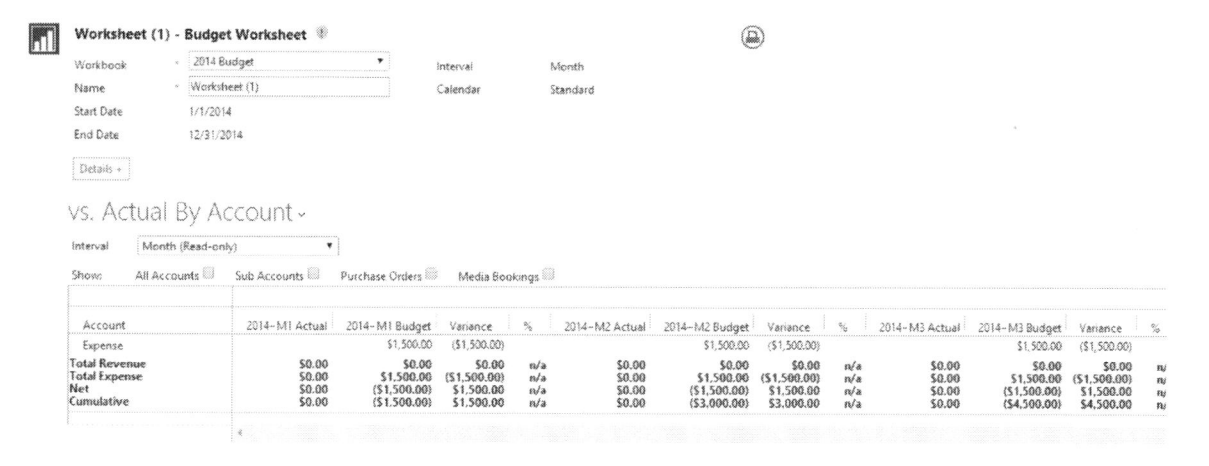

Figure 4.3 –Budget Worksheet

In this brief example we have seen how the various pieces of the Dynamics offering working together in a real-world scenario for a B2B company.

---

[21] All the data transfer is provided automatically by the Dynamics Marketing CRM Connector.

Let's now dig more into the details of Lead Management in Dynamics Marketing. As usual we start from exploring the feature area in the rest of this section, while digging into the main entities details in the next section and finally concluding the chapter with some sample scenarios.

4.2 MAIN ENTITIES

These are the main entities revolving around Lead Management.

Entity	Description
Marketing Companies	These are Companies we market to. See for more information Chapter 3 "Marketing Execution".
Marketing Contacts	These are Contacts within the Marketing Companies we market to. See for more information Chapter 3 "Marketing Execution".
Lead Interactions	Dynamics Marketing tracks the various events that connected one or more prospects (represented as Contacts) to a Lead, like for example a person viewing the pricing web page or downloading a particular document from the organization website. Interactions can also be entered manually (for instance a Sales Person makes a significant contact like performing an online demo, etc.).
Landing Pages	These are web forms collecting prospect data. Dynamics Marketing can automatically generate a Lead when a user fills in one of these. Dynamics Marketing
Leads	Leads represent potential sales (of either an individual or organization). The Lead entity represents
Lead Assignment Rules	After a Lead has been scored it can be assigned to the proper person in the organization (more specifically the "Assigned To" and optionally other values such as "Status", "Territory" or "Priority" will get updated). After the rule is applied based on defined Criteria the Lead will be shown as "unread" (i.e. displayed in a bold font).
Lead Scoring Model	A Lead Scoring Model is composed of Rules that changes the Lead score according to some trigger condition. Depending upon the defined scope of the model, the model is used for scoring a lead (all its rules are run against the Lead and the final score aggregated accordingly)-
Marketing Lists	These are collections of Contacts used in marketing communications.
Opportunities	Usually the most promising Leads generated by Dynamics Marketing become Opportunities, and hopefully many of them will in turn become successful sales. Note that Dynamics Marketing integrates seamlessly with Dynamics CRM so that Opportunities created in Dynamics Marketing can be closed in Dynamics CRM.
Opportunity Metrics	This page shows statistics about Opportunities (number of Opportunities by owner). Also of interest is the Opportunities Forecasts page showing the total amount (i.e. the sum of all Opportunities' total amounts) per owner.

4.2.1 Managing Leads in Dynamics Marketing

Leads are available from:

> Home > Marketing Execution > Lead Management → Leads

> **MANAGING LEADS MANUALLY**
>
> Although Dynamics Marketing provides a number of automations and models to process Leads automatically it also provides various actions to handled Leads manually, from the user interface. It is possible among the other things to mass-update a number of fields in a selection of Leads at once, reach out to them easily via email, import and export them and so on.

Before digging into the functionality provided by Dynamics Marketing in this area let's take a step back and see the overall picture and how Dynamics Marketing fits into it.

4.2.1.1 Lead Lifecycle in Dynamics Marketing

Dynamics Marketing Lead Management accommodates a large number of sales pipeline models and organizations.

The following table provides a summary of the main steps in managing leads with Dynamics Marketing.

	Step	How to implement the step in Dynamics Marketing
1	Eliciting Leads	Set up Landing Pages, EM messages, manual data entry and automated campaigns in order to create Leads in the system.
2	Assessing Leads	Set up automatic lead scoring rules to clearly indicate which level of maturity a given lead is at throughout the sales process.
3	Assigning a promising Lead to a Sales Rep	Leads are often assigned to a sales rep for follow up. The sales rep reaches out to the Lead Contact and attempts to close a sale. A Lead may also be added to a list or rescored via campaign automation for additional marketing at this time.
	Promote suitable Leads to Opportunities	Dynamics Marketing allows for the conversion of suitable Leads into Opportunities. Simpler and less structured Sales and Marketing organizations might not require this step.
4	Closing unpromising Leads	Leads that are not qualified and don't have the potential to mature through nurturing should be removed from consideration for future marketing efforts.

IMPORTING LEADS

Dynamics Marketing allows users to import Leads manually (using the "Import" action in the Leads list page). The format of the input file must be comma-separated (csv) entries. If a Company or a Contact cannot be found in the DB they are created on the fly for the newly imported Leads.

Leads can also entered from an external system using Dynamics Marketing API.

4.2.1.2 Automatically Scoring Leads

You can set up Lead Scoring Models in Dynamics Marketing that can automatically assign a score to Leads.

Lead Scoring Models are available from:

    Home > Settings > Rules and Models → Lead Scoring Models

This is how the form appears in Dynamics Marketing:

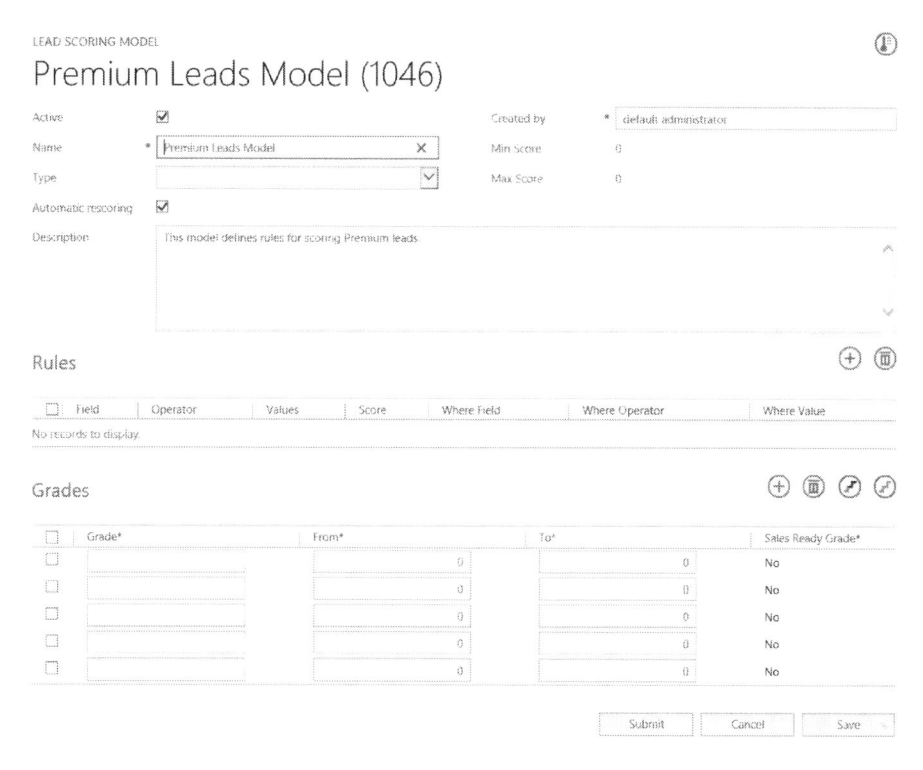

Figure 4.4 –Lead Scoring Model

Models need to have a scope defined, i.e. to which Leads the Lead Scoring Model should be applied. Dynamics Marketing is quite flexible in terms of how to define this association, enabling a wide range of business processes, as we will see later in this chapter. The scope of a Lead Scoring Model in Dynamics Marketing can be: per a specific Campaign (all Leads generated by Campaign 100069 will use this model for instance), per a specific Program (that is, a set of Campaigns) or simply for all your Campaigns. The scope for a Lead Scoring Model is defined using the "Lead Scoring Model" field in the related entity (i.e. in Programs or single Campaigns).

Once a Lead Scoring Model is in place lead scoring can be triggered manually ("Score" or "Rescore"[22] action in both the Leads list and form pages, from the Campaign's Leads panel or directly from the Lead Scoring Model) or performed automatically by the system. Dynamics Marketing automatically triggers scoring in the following cases:

- When a Lead is created via a Landing Page.

---

[22] Once a lead is manually scored it cannot be rescored again if the user does not have a Lead Scoring User Role.

- When manually imported into Dynamics Marketing.

FROM VISITOR TO LEAD

Dynamics Marketing tracks the behavior of anonymous users (users not yet associated to a Contact) visiting tracked web pages (i.e. registered as Websites in Dynamics Marketing) and assigning them a Visitor ID[23]. These visits can be seen in the Visitor list.

Dynamics Marketing can associate a Contact to that anonymous visitor in two cases. When the user registers on a Landing Page (which has a Website associated to it and it is enabled for creating Interactions) or when the user opens one Dynamics Marketing marketing email. Once the user's Contact is associated to a Visitor ID all past visits in the Visitors list are now associated to the Contact. These visits can be used for lead scoring as well (by creating rules about website visits).

For example imagine we collected a Contact at a trade show and this Contact afterwards went to our website, registered and then also downloaded a whitepaper about our product. At each interaction Dynamics Marketing will update the scoring according to chosen model. This is how that Lead will appear in Dynamics Marketing:

---

[23] By means of a browser-specific cookie. Such cookies last 2 years from creation.

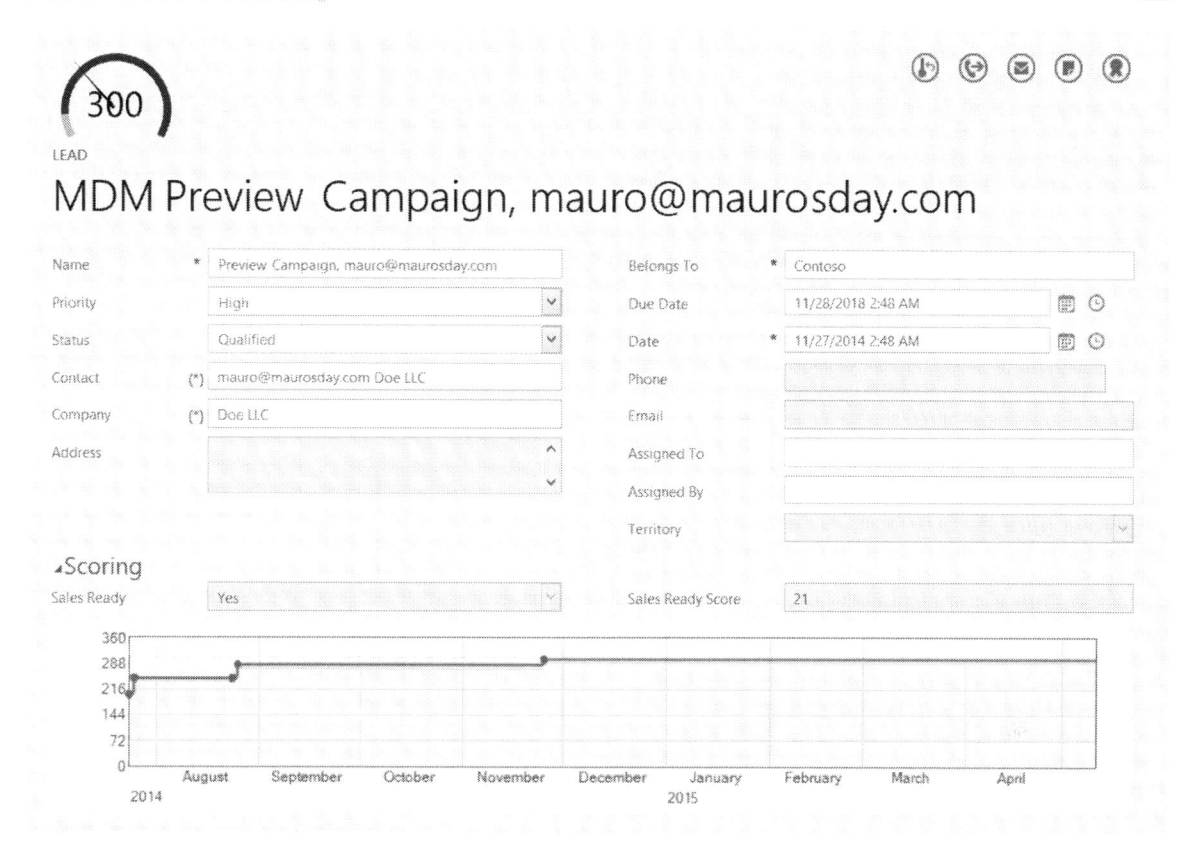

Figure 4.5 –An Example Lead

LEAD LOG PANEL

The complete history of all the meaningful events occurred to a Lead in Dynamics Marketing since its creation in the system is shown in the "Log" panel, under the Related Information menu in the Lead form.

4.2.1.3 Define your Leads Strategy in Dynamics Marketing

Let's see in details the options available to setup your Lead creation and management policies in Dynamics Marketing.

In the Company entity is possible to define the details for managing Leads belonging to that Company.

Figure 4.6 –Lead Management Options

The three fields in the Lead Management expandable group above are used as follows:

- Creation Strategy: this field specifies how Leads should be created and where they will belong to.
    o Per Campaign: all interactions of a prospect contact or company will be aggregated under one lead per campaign for the prospect contact or company. Lead scoring and behavioral analysis are made per campaign.
    o Per Program: all interactions of a prospect contact or company will be aggregated under one lead per program for the prospect contact or company. Leading scoring and behavioral analysis are made per marketing program.
    o Per Client / Site: all interactions of a prospect contact or company will be aggregated under one lead per marketing client or the site company for the prospect contact or company. Lead scoring and behavioral analysis are made per client or site company.
- Creation Scope: this option specifies how Interactions should be rolled up into Leads.
    o Per Prospect Contact: all prospect interactions will be converted into one separate lead for the prospect contact based on the marketing strategy defined in the Creation Strategy field.

    o Per Prospect Company: all prospect interactions will be converted into one separate lead for the prospect company based on the marketing strategy defined in the Creation Strategy field.
- Scoring Model: which Lead Scoring Model should be used (given the rules described below).

By combining the various options provided by the Creation Strategy and Creation Scope fields is possible to adapt Dynamics Marketing to your industry characteristics and business requirements. The following table provides some more details on how the various combinations can be used.

Creation Strategy	Creation Scope Where to create a Lead (and aggregate all prospect Interactions under)	
	Per Prospect Contact	Per Prospect Company
Per Campaign	All interactions of a prospect Contact will be aggregated under one Lead per Campaign.	All interactions of a prospect Company will be aggregated under one Lead per Campaign.
Per Program	All interactions of a prospect Contact will be aggregated under one Lead per Program.	All interactions of a prospect Company will be aggregated under one Lead per Program.
Per Client	All interactions of a prospect Contact will be aggregated under one Lead per marketing client (or the site company) for the prospect Contact.	All interactions of a prospect Company will be aggregated under one Lead per marketing client (or the site company) for the prospect Company.

4.2.1.4 Retrieving the Right Lead Scoring Model

This section clarifies the subtleties of assigning a scoring model for leads or campaigns.

Dynamics Marketing will retrieve the Lead Scoring Model of a Lead in the following way:

- If the Lead has a Campaign specified, Dynamics Marketing will use the scoring model from the campaign

- If the Lead does not have a campaign specified but has a program defined, Dynamics Marketing will use the scoring model from the Program

- If the Lead does not have neither a Campaign or a Program specified, Dynamics Marketing will use the scoring model from the "Belongs To" Company.

In turn Dynamics Marketing will use the Lead scoring Model of a Campaign in the following way:

- If the Campaign has a Lead Scoring Model specified, Dynamics Marketing will use the scoring model from the Campaign

- If the Campaign does not have a lead scoring model specified but has a Program with a model specified, Dynamics Marketing will use the scoring model from the Program

- If the Campaign does not have a lead scoring model specified and there is no Program / or the Program does not have a Lead Scoring Model defined, then Dynamics Marketing will use the scoring model from the Company.

4.2.1.5   Define your Leads Scoring Rules

Lead Scoring Rules are the juice of a Lead Scoring Model. They define the criteria that trigger changes in the score for a given Lead. They can be added or edited from the Lead Scoring Model form.

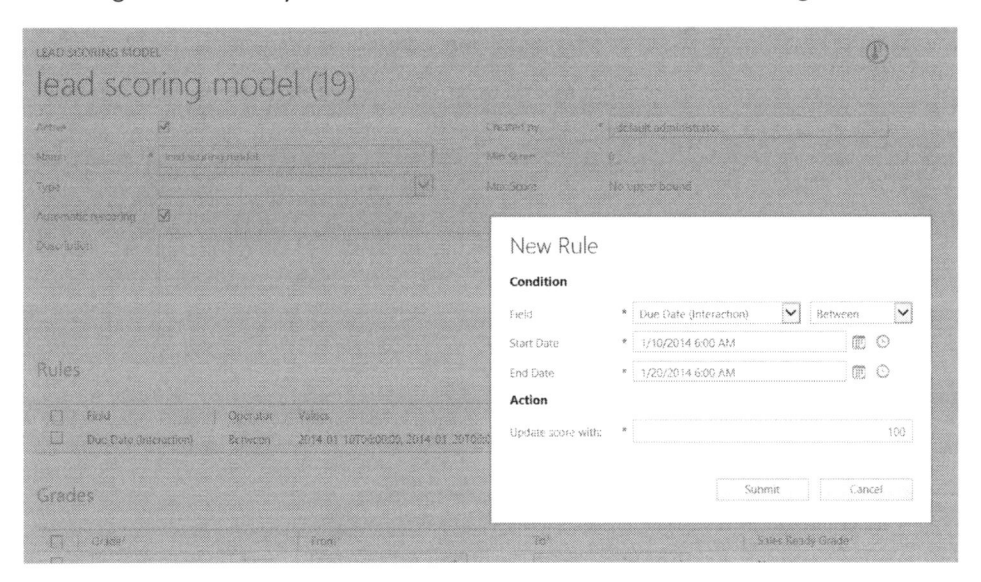

Figure 4.7 –New Lead Scoring Rule

It is possible to specify Start and End dates for each Rule.

The table below shows all the Fields available for constructing Lead Scoring Rules. Depending on the field data type different operators are available. Some fields will provide custom properties for more elaborated criteria, such as for example the "Web Site" option. In the screenshot below an example rule is created for this field that increases a Lead's score of 50 points if a prospect visited the "Pricing Site" Web Site for more than 3 and less than 50 minutes.

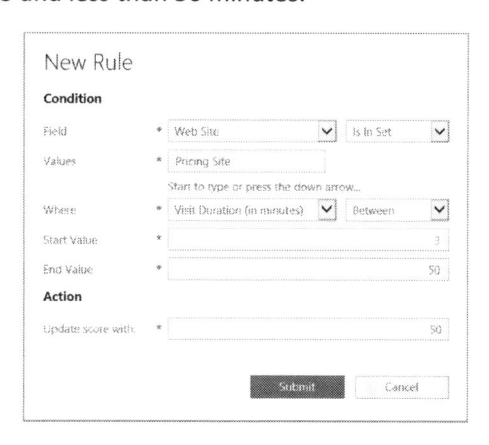

Figure 4.8 –Example Rule

Condition Field	Meaning
Campaign (Interaction)	The Campaign the Interaction belongs to.
Campaign (Lead)	The Campaign the Lead belongs to
Description	The Description field.
Due Date (Interaction)	The Due Date on a newly created Interaction.
Due Date (Lead)	The Due Date on a newly created Lead.
Email	The Email field for the Lead. If the Lead has been created via a Landing Page this is the value entered by the user.
Email Message	The Email Message
Landing Page	The Landing Pages the Lead has been generated from. You can specify whether this rule should apply at each new submission or for all.
Name (Interaction)	The name of the Interaction.
Name (Lead)	The name of the Lead.
Phone	The phone of the Lead.
Priority (Interaction)	The priority of the Interaction.
Priority (Lead)	The priority of the Lead.
Program (Interaction)	The Program the Interaction belongs to.
Program (Lead)	The Program the Lead belongs to.

Condition Field	Meaning
Campaign (Interaction)	The Campaign the Interaction belongs to.
Campaign (Lead)	The Campaign the Lead belongs to
Description	The Description field.
Due Date (Interaction)	The Due Date on a newly created Interaction.
Due Date (Lead)	The Due Date on a newly created Lead.
Email	The Email field for the Lead. If the Lead has been created via a Landing Page this is the value entered by the user.
Search Engine	The Search Engine field specified.
Source Code	The Source Code field specified.
Status	The Status field specified.
Type	The Type field specified.
Web Site	The MDM Web Site the Contact has visited. It is possible to define criteria based upon: duration of visit (seconds or minutes); number of distinct visits; total unique pages visited; simple visit (i.e. the rule applies for each distinct visit).

This list does not include user defined fields that can be enabled for this functionality. If not entirely renamed such fields will typically appear as "User <ID>" followed by the data type represented.

> **DEPRECIATION RULES**
>
> "Recency", a parameter measuring how fresh is our relationship with the prospect is one of the most powerful indicators of the overall quality of a lead.
> Dynamics Marketing allows for the creation of "depreciation" rules that diminish the overall lead score over time. So if the score is not increased by new interactions it will slowly go down, representing the fact that the lead is progressively losing interest.

4.2.1.6 "Lead Interactions"

All the Interactions tracked for a Lead can be found under the "Interactions" panel in the Lead form.

In Dynamics Marketing an Interaction represents an expression of user interest relevant to our digital marketing efforts. Something that can impact the score Dynamics Marketing keeps for a given Lead. Examples of interactions as tracked by Dynamics Marketing are filling in a landing page, clicking on a link in a marketing email, etc.

A Lead does not require to have Interactions at all. Similarly, a Lead does not require to be related to website visits in order to be scored for a given Website visit. So only the data in the Lead record will affect its scoring, independently of whether it has or not interactions.

If the Lead is associated to a Contact, the automated scoring will be based on the websites specified by the scoring rule, (i.e. reading the visit tracking information existing in the system for that website, so without the need of Interactions records). If the Lead is associated to a company, Dynamics Marketing will accumulate the visit tracking info for each of the contacts belonging to the company (for the Website specified in the scoring rule) and then apply the rule.

4.2.1.7 "Sales Ready" Leads in Dynamics Marketing

Dynamics Marketing also allows to specify ranges of score values that can be used to qualify succinctly the "goodness" of a lead, i.e. how close the Lead is to be ready for the sales team to pick it up. It is possible also to define the "sales ready grade", to mark a Lead as ready for sales[24].

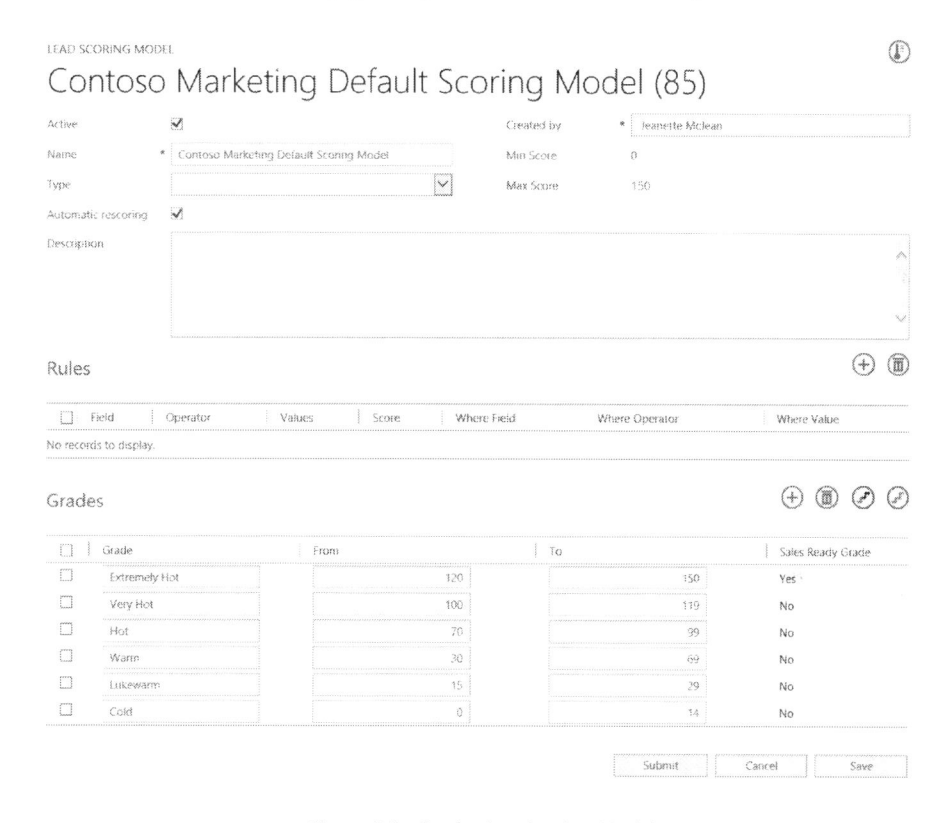

Figure 4.9 –Grades in a Scoring Model

---

[24] When Dynamics Marketing is used in conjunction with Dynamics CRM with a CRM Connector configured for synchronizing Leads, records scored with a "Sales Ready" grade in Dynamics Marketing are then automatically copied over to Dynamics CRM.

MARK A LEAD AS READ / UNREAD

For convenience Dynamics Marketing allows users to mark Leads as "read / unread" directly in the Leads list by clicking on the column with the "arrows" icon, as shown below.

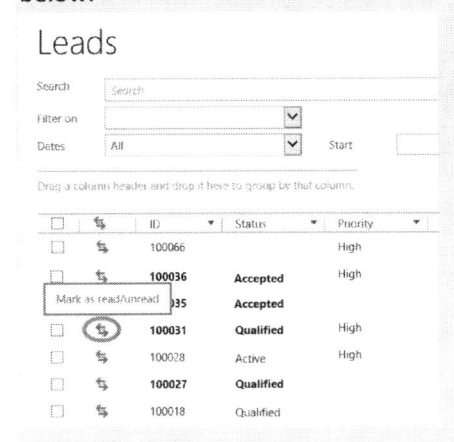

Unread Leads are shown in bold. Toggling "Read / Unread" Leads is also available from the list toolbar. By selecting multiple lines and invoking the action from the toolbar is possible to mark many Leads at once.

Now that we have completed our overview of the main entities in this area let's look at some scenarios of interest.

4.3 Scenarios

Landing Pages are an important part of Lead generation in Dynamics Marketing. Our first scenario is about creating a simple landing page that can be used also in automated campaigns.

4.3.1 Create a Landing Page

A Marketing Manager wants to set up a new Landing Page for their new offering. She has a clear idea of the type of information she wants to capture from online visitors, all she is left to do is to set this up in Dynamics Marketing.

She creates a new Landing Page for people downloading the new ebook:

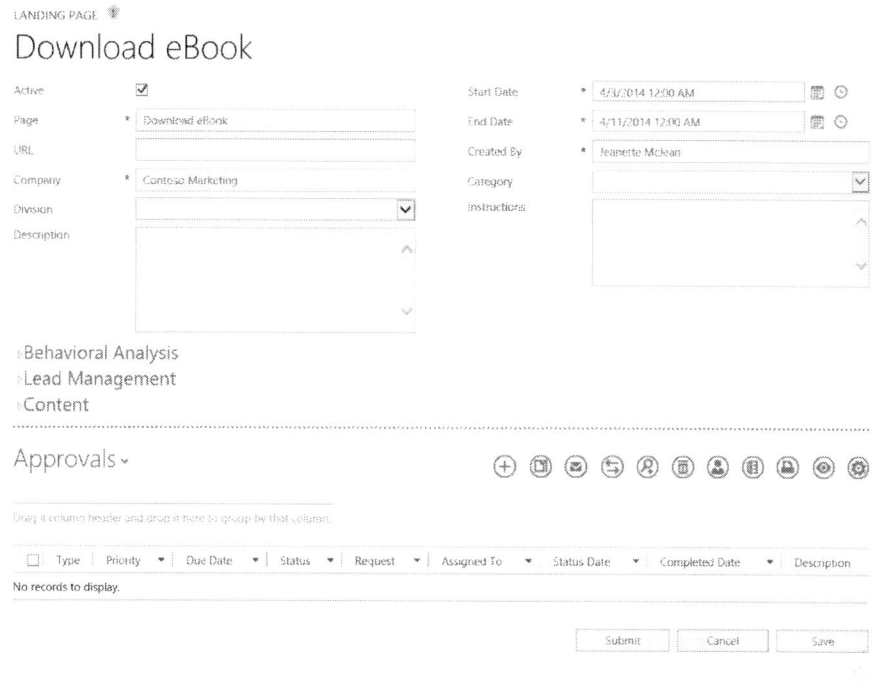

Figure 4.10 –Type of Contacts

Now she sets up in Dynamics Marketing the model she has in mind.

She expands the "Lead Management" group and selects the checkbox for generating a new Lead associated to when the form is filled in online. She then enters a Website for this page[25]. The scope and the strategy are shown here only as a reminder because these are set elsewhere as we discussed previously. She also specifies the priority of the newly created Lead.

---

[25] Note that without enabling the generation of Interactions a Landing Page is not actionable. In other words Dynamics Marketing will not track it. By selecting the "Generating Leads" checkbox Interactions are created in the system. By selecting an existing Website the system is able to also track user visits and their durations.

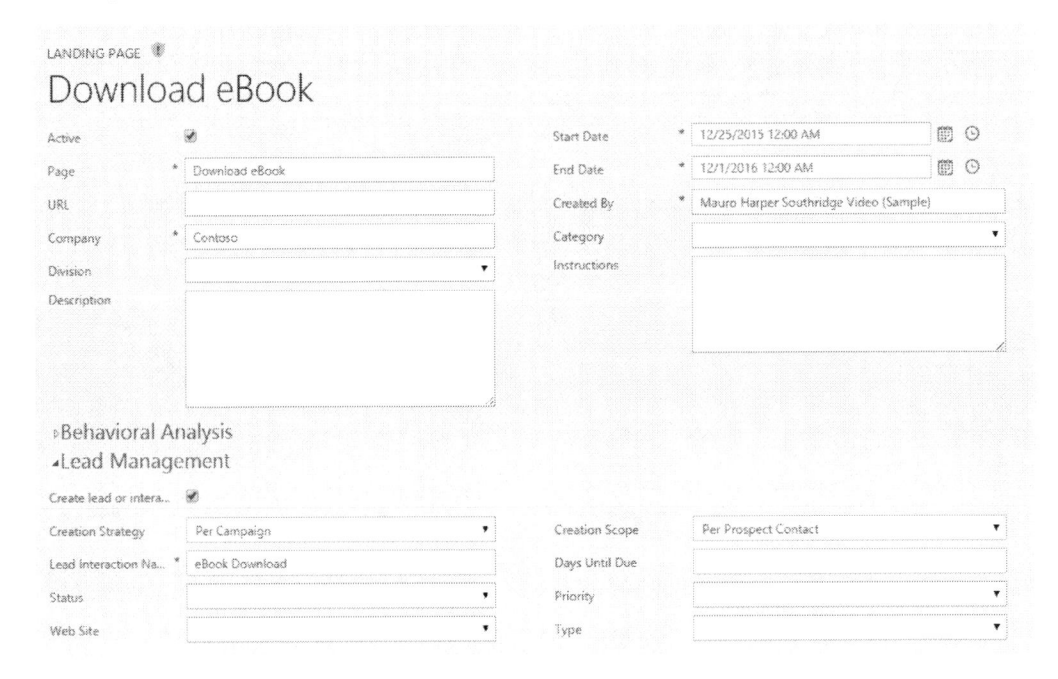

Figure 4.11 –Lead Management in Landing Pages

Her next step is to define the actual content of the page.

She only needs an English version of the page so she doesn't add additional versions and starts editing the English version of the form.

LANDING PAGE
Download eBook

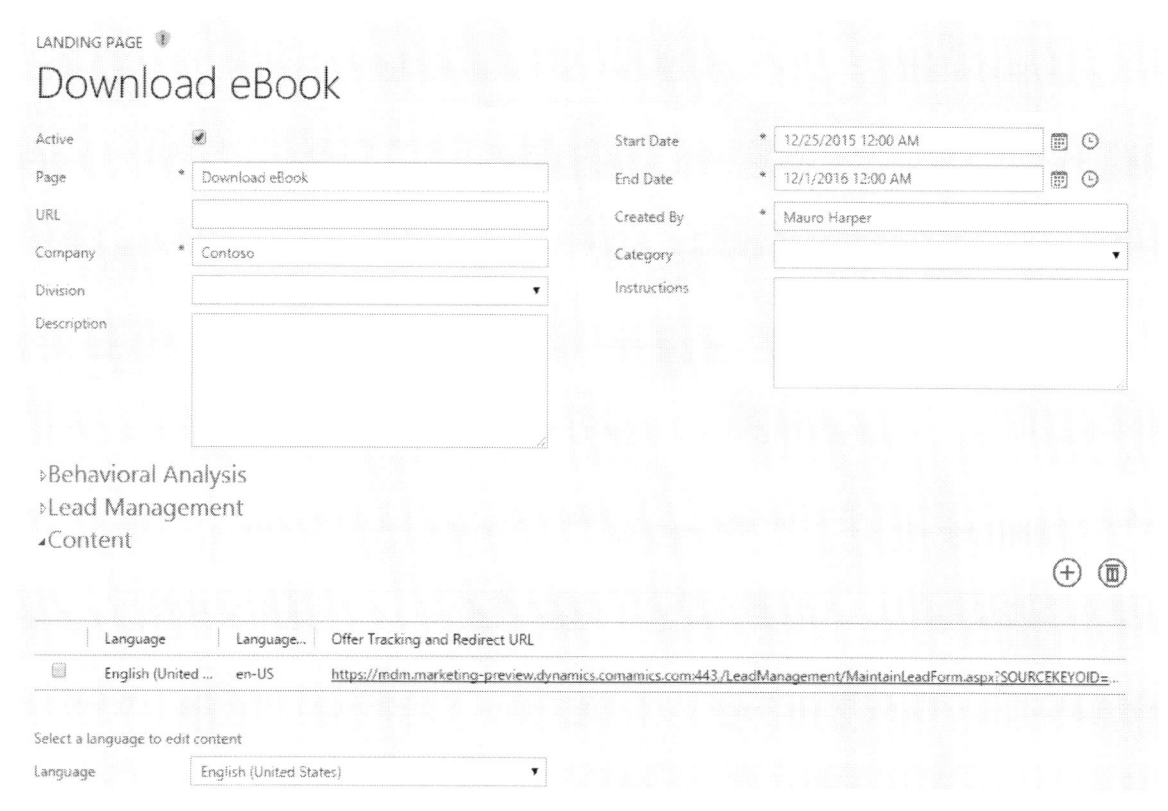

Active	✓		Start Date	* 12/25/2015 12:00 AM
Page	* Download eBook		End Date	* 12/1/2016 12:00 AM
URL			Created By	* Mauro Harper
Company	* Contoso		Category	
Division			Instructions	
Description				

▷ Behavioral Analysis
▷ Lead Management
▲ Content

	Language	Language...	Offer Tracking and Redirect URL
☐	English (United...	en-US	https://mdm.marketing-preview.dynamics.comamics.com:443/LeadManagement/MaintainLeadForm.aspx?SOURCEKEYOID=...

Select a language to edit content
Language: English (United States)

Figure 4.12 – Example Landing Page

She will leave the technical details (visual branding, HTML details etc.) to a colleague. She is interested in setting up the business requirements for the lead capturing via this Landing Page, so she expands the "Form Details" expandable group.

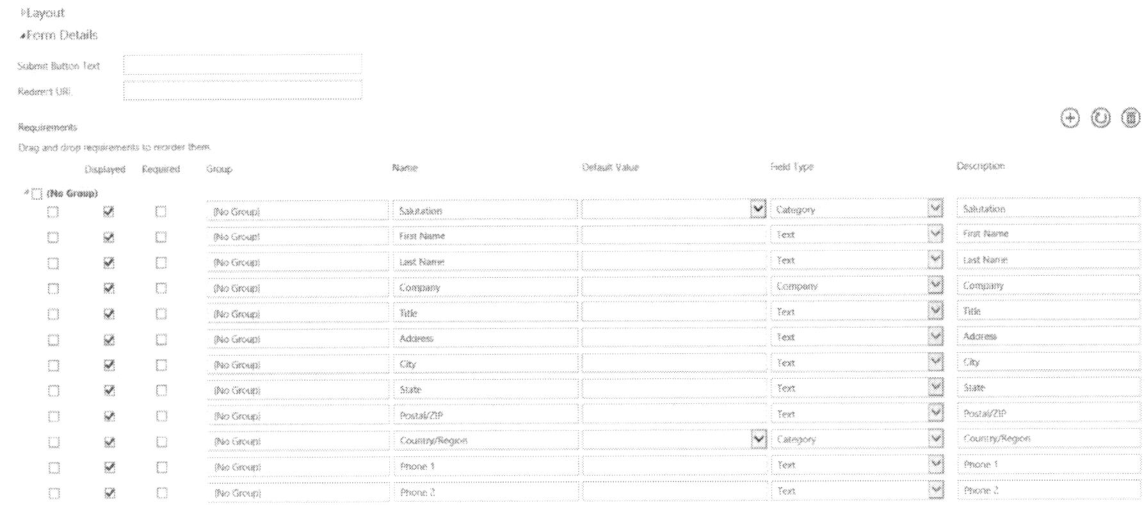

Figure 4.13 – Landing Page Fields

Here she selects the fields she wants to have on the Landing Page specifying whether or not they must be filled in and other details (default values, the type, etc.)

She can preview the structure of the resulting page (with the exclusion of applied HTML styles and other branding) by clicking on the link beside the language in the Content expandable panel.

> **IFRAME URL COLUMN**
>
> The links in the iframe column can be embedded in the hosting web pages as iframes. Moreover they provide a fully functional page for internal test. So by clicking on them users can fully test the functionality of their Landing Page without the need of embedding it in a web page.

Note that in Dynamics Marketing it is not possible to control the number of columns the fields will be displayed in.

> **CONFIRMATION EMAIL**
>
> It is possible to automatically send an email every time a Landing Page is filled in by a visitor by selecting the details in the "Confirmation" expandable group.

At this point her work is done and the page can be already published online. A technical person can polish the visual appearance of the page using the Layout options in the page and by creating an HTML page on the company website that hosts (via an iFrame) the landing page and style it accordingly.

Similarly to many other Dynamics Marketing entities also Landing Pages can be sent through a customizable review and approval process before being approved and deployed as part of a campaign.

A Landing Page in Dynamics Marketing has the following related entities:

- Approvals
- Emails
- Leads
- Log
- Notes
- Results

4.3.2   Automatically assign a Lead Dynamics Marketing

Dynamics Marketing also provides functionality for automatic lead assignment rules available from:

`Home > Settings > Rules and Models → Lead Assignment Rules`

These rules allow to assign a lead matching a given set of criteria to a sales person.

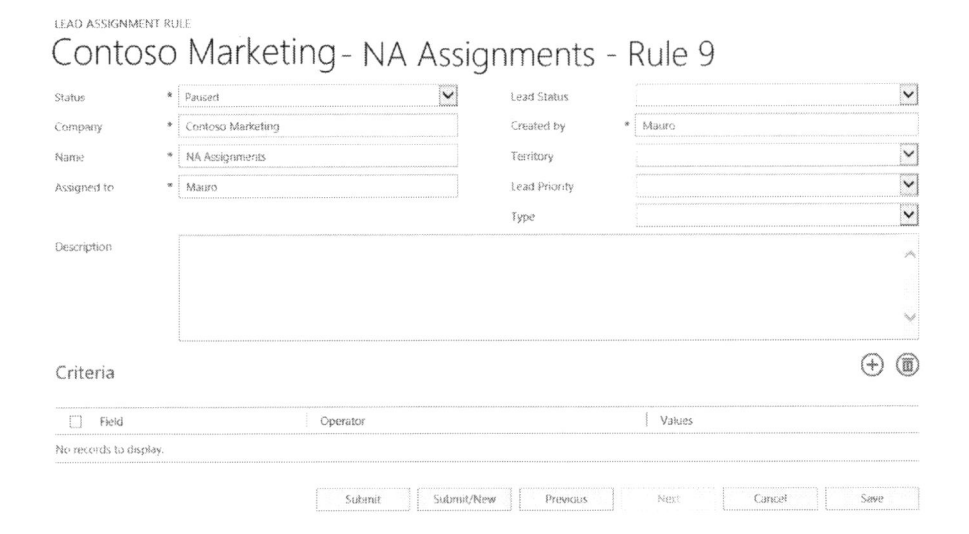

Figure 4.14 –Lead Assignment Rules

Not only you can specify a Contact to assign the Lead to, you can also define the Territory, priority and more useful information when the rule is triggered based on the chosen criteria.

CHAPTER FIVE
EMAIL MARKETING

5.1 OVERVIEW

Among other things Dynamics Marketing packs a full-fledged, enterprise level Email Service Provider (ESP) facility, ready to use for marketing professionals of all trades and expertise. Dynamics Marketing enables customers to send millions of emails per day, in various flavors and with various levels of control. Dynamics Marketing is a very convenient, well rounded one-stop solution for your email marketing needs, from the easiest setup to the most advanced ones (employing custom domains and other advanced technical configurations). In this chapter we focus on the essential scenarios while leaving the most advanced ones for the next.

5.1.1 Our First Email

Let's get started exploring this area by creating and sending our first email. We will use the sample email templates provided with a trial version of Dynamics Marketing.

The first step is to activate the template so that we can use it for our new email.

We open the list of email marketing templates by navigating to:

```
Home > Marketing Execution > Email Marketing→ Templates
```

The list appears empty, because the templates are created by another user (a demo user) and are inactive by default. So all we need to do is to click on the button to show all records (not just those created by the current user) and the button to show the inactive records:

Inside Microsoft Dynamics Marketing

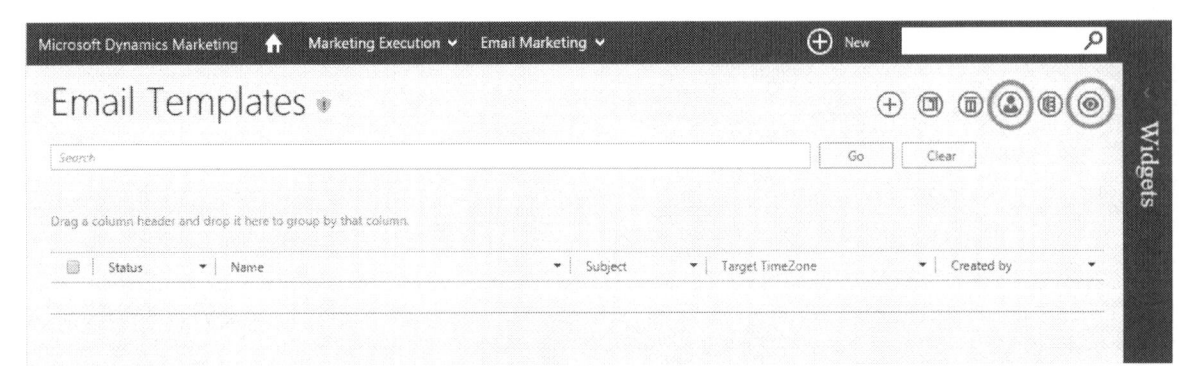

Figure 5.1 –Showing Sample Email Templates

Now the list will show all the sample templates (all sample templates are inactive on a default trial DB). Let's choose one and activate it so that we can use it for our email message.

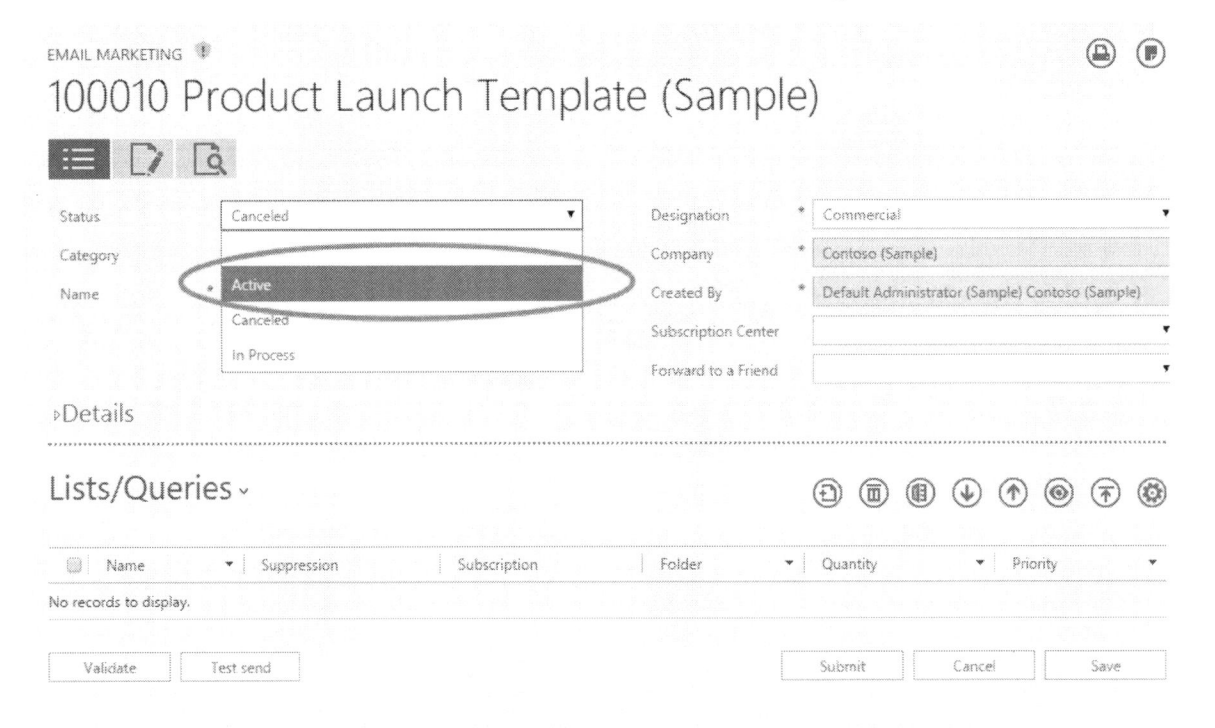

Figure 5.2 –Activating a Sample Email Template

After saving the template we can now use it for a new email.

Let's navigate to the list of email marketing messages:

```
Home > Marketing Execution > Email Marketing→ Templates
```

Then clicking on "+" to create a new message, choosing the template we just activated:

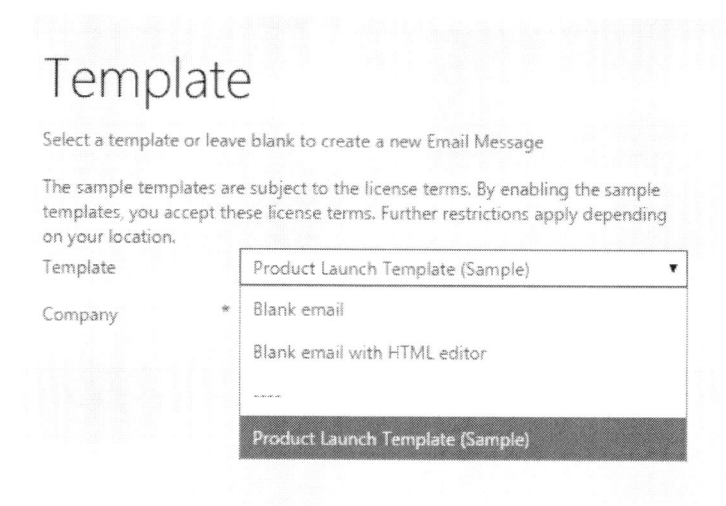

Figure 5.3 –Choosing a Sample Email Template

Now our new email (using the sample template) is ready. It is a good idea to change the default name to something more meaningful like "My first email". We choose a subscription center (for simplicity we can choose the sample one).

At this point we are ready for the content. Let's click on the "Edit Content" button to switch to editing the email content.

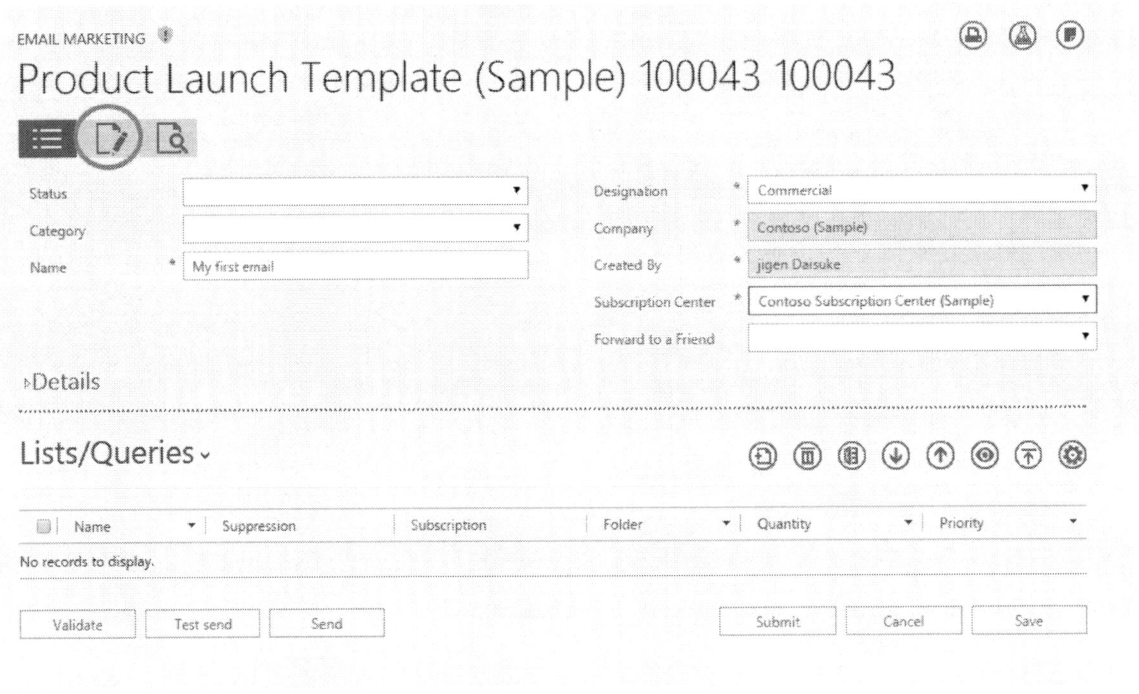

Figure 5.4 –Editing the New Email

Let's fix the email content to our liking, for example by changing the text in one of the blocks, by clicking on the block and then editing its content in the right-hand side panel.

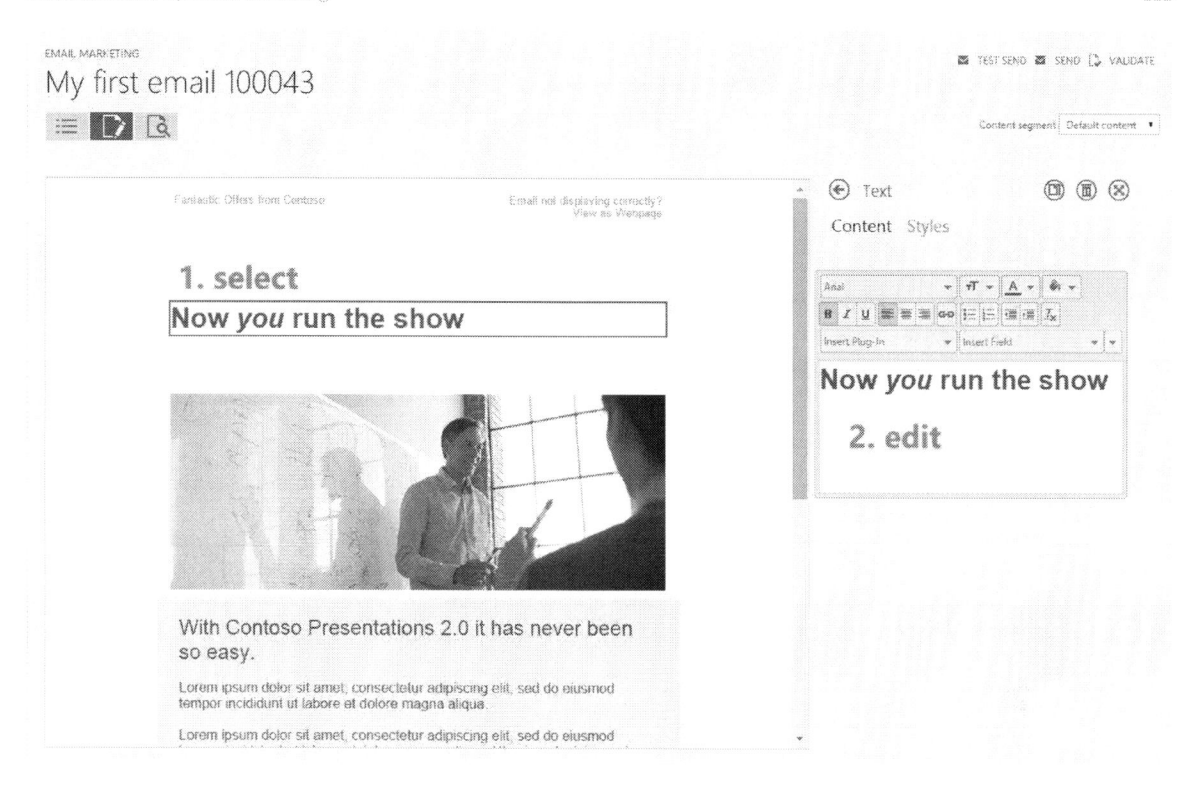

Figure 5.5 –Choosing a Sample Email Template

We can also change the selected block's styles by clicking on "Styles".

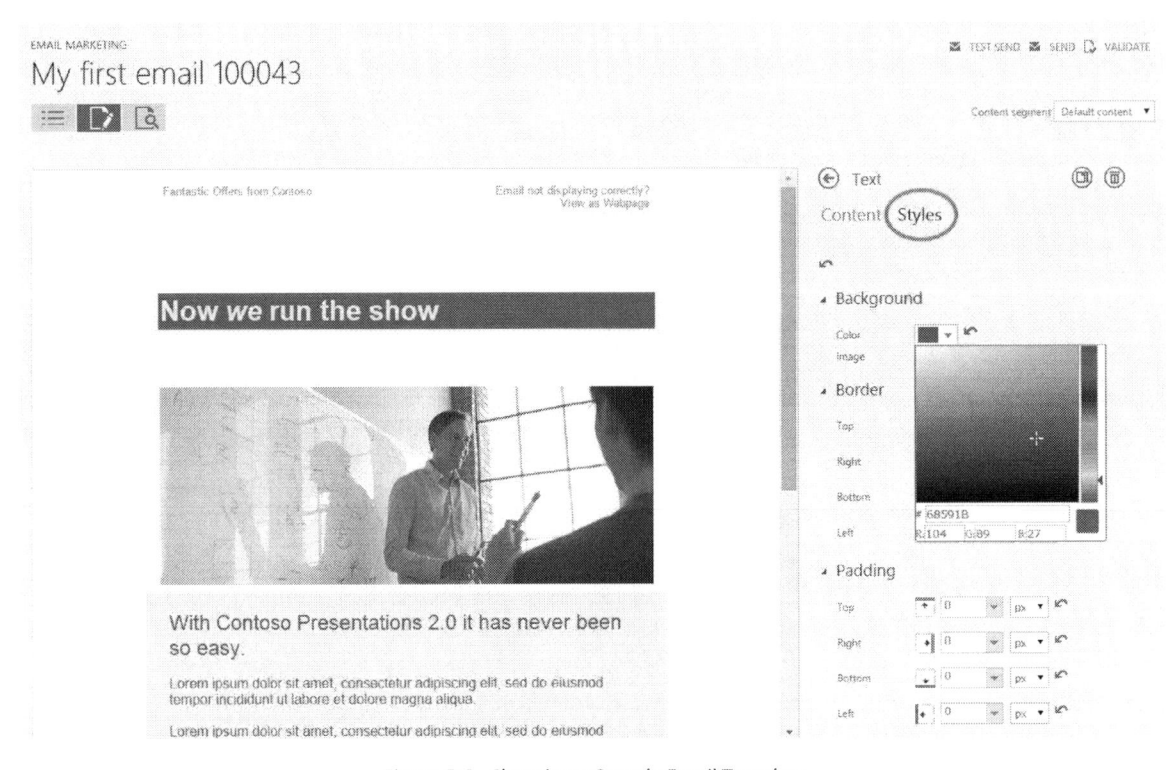

Figure 5.6 –Choosing a Sample Email Template

When done we can see how the email will look like on different form factors by clicking on the "Preview" button.

EMAIL MARKETING
My first email 100043

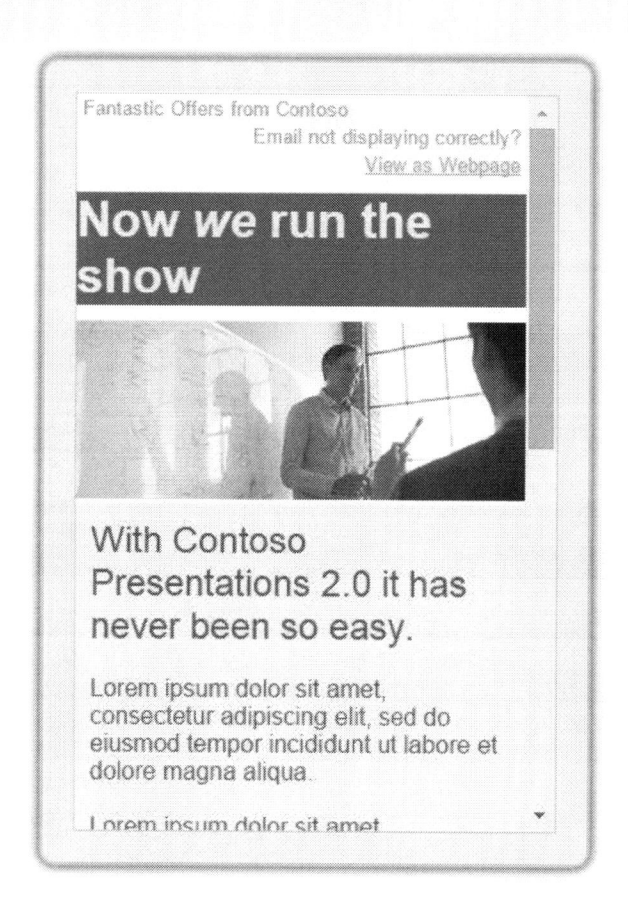

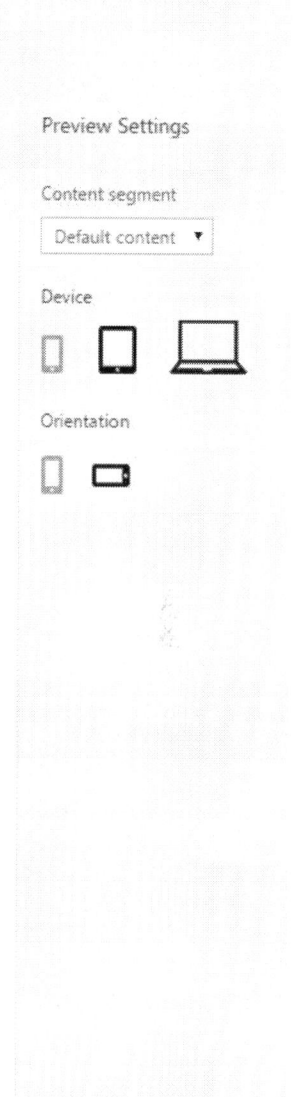

Figure 5.7 – Previewing an Email

For simplicity we will send our first email to ourselves as a test, by clicking the "Test Send" button in the top-right corner. The system will validate the email to see if everything is OK before sending it out. The Validation dialog will give us a summary:

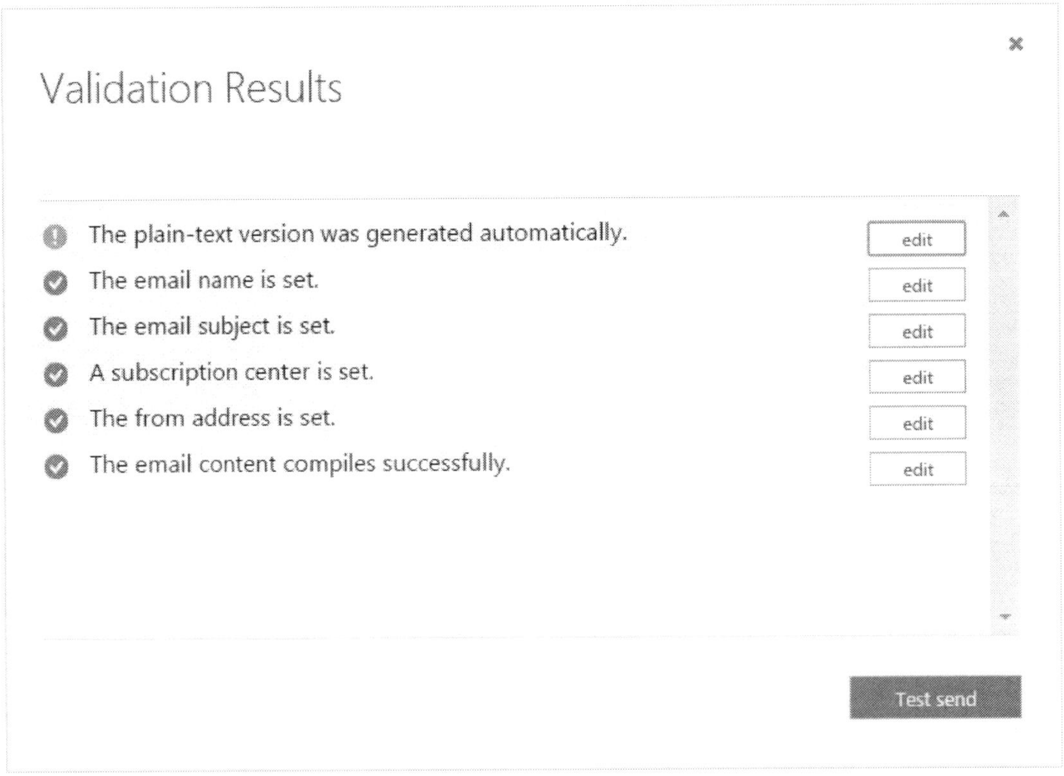

Validation Results

- ⚠ The plain-text version was generated automatically. [edit]
- ✓ The email name is set. [edit]
- ✓ The email subject is set. [edit]
- ✓ A subscription center is set. [edit]
- ✓ The from address is set. [edit]
- ✓ The email content compiles successfully. [edit]

[Test send]

Figure 5.8 –Ready to Send Our First Email

We have only one warning (no errors) about the system notifying us that the plain-text version was generated automatically from the HTML text. If we want we can change that by clicking on "Edit", or change in a similar way the other items, like for example the email subject. But we are eager to see our first Dynamics Marketing marketing email in our inbox, so we click "Test send" in the dialog.

This will open the following dialog where existing marketing lists, contacts and even plain email addresses can be entered. We enter an email address as shown below:

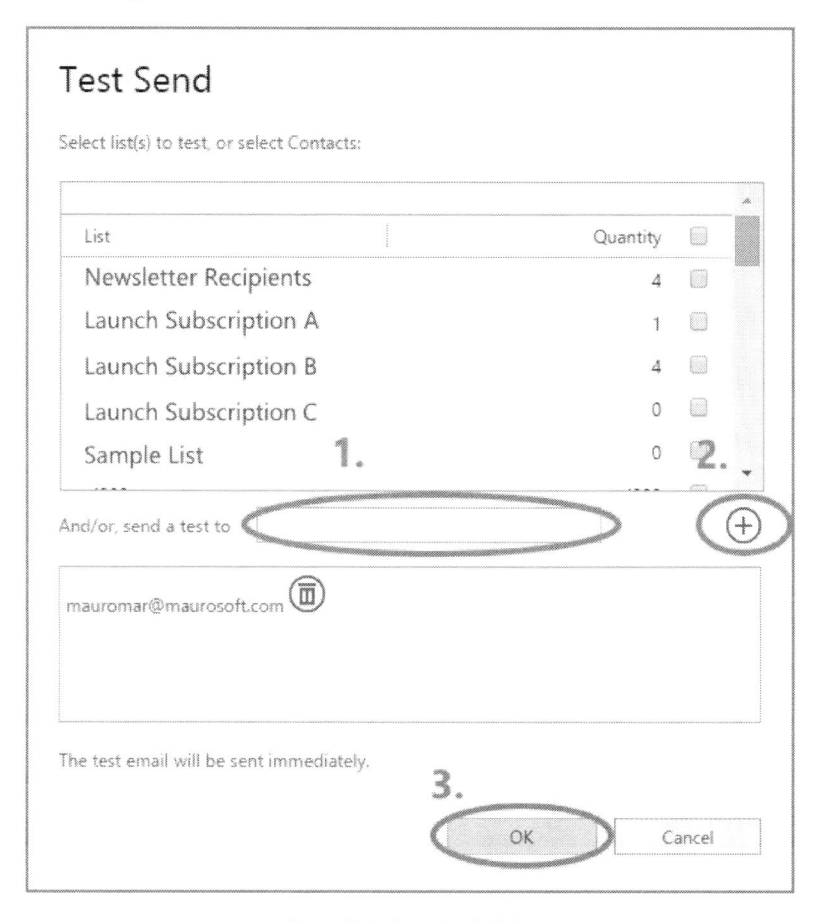

Figure 5.9 –Test Send Dialog

When clicking OK the email message is sent to our test email address.

This little walkthrough showed how easy it is to create and send marketing emails with Dynamics Marketing. Also, one of the nice features of the content block email editor is that it allows marketing professionals to focus primarily on their content. The system will take care of generating the right HTML that will render nicely on a vast array of devices and emails clients[26], rendered using adaptive layout and the latest technologies when available. We will dig into the details of the email editor in the next chapter.

---

[26] Among them: Outlook desktop and Outlook.com, Apple Mail, Gmail, Yahoo, AOL, Lotus Notes and many others on many desktop and mobile devices.

5.1.2 Some terminology

Before digging into the details of crafting Email Marketing messages with Dynamics Marketing let's spend a minute looking at the various terms and concepts. We will use the term email "message" to indicate a record in the DB representing the information of an email message, including all the needed fields (To, CC etc.) not just the mere content.

We will use the terms "mailings" or "communication" to indicate a batch of Email Marketing messages sent together as part of one marketing action or an "email marketing blast". Although most of what we will discuss in this chapter is also available from within the Campaign Automation Console, our focus here will be mainly on manual messages.

A draft message is a message that has not been sent yet. Already-sent and yet-to-be-sent (draft) messages are represented by the same entity and available from the same list and form pages so users need to pay attention to the Status field to tell them apart.

> **EMAIL MARKETING TEMPLATES IN DYNAMICS MARKETING**
>
> As mentioned in Chapter 1 "Overview" Dynamics Marketing has a special implementation of entity templates, which are exactly like normal entities but flagged as "templates" so that they appear in a separate list in the UI.
> Regarding Email Marketing Templates they are located under:
>
> ```
> Home > Marketing Execution > Email Marketing→ Email Marketing
> Templates
> ```
>
> An Email Marketing Template is exactly like a usual Email Marketing message with the main difference that it cannot be sent, and it is meant to be used as a blueprint to create prepopulated new Email Marketing messages. There will be no direct link between the original template and the actual message created from it after creation.

With the term "dynamic content" we refer to special content that is customized for each recipient. For example the text Contact.Name get instantiated to "John", personalized to the value of the "Name" field for the given recipient. We will see examples of this functionality later in this chapter. Dynamics

Marketing provides three types of ways of customizing an email for each recipient: adding single personalized fields (e.g. the recipient's first name), list or segment-based adaptation (having different variations of a mailing depending on the list the recipient is in). The most advanced option allows the use of Razor [27] syntax for fully controlling the customized content.

> **WHICH EMAIL ADDRESS IS USED TO SEND EMAILS IN DYNAMICS MARKETING**
>
> The Contact entity is the only entity used for sending all types of emails available in Dynamics Marketing:
>
> `Home > Marketing Execution > Marketing Database → Marketing Contacts`
>
> The field on the Contact used to send emails is the "Email 1 (Primary)" field. Every time we use Contacts to send emails in Dynamics Marketing, the primary email address field is used.

5.1.3   Types of Emails Sent by Dynamics Marketing

It should not come as a surprise that Dynamics Marketing can send emails of various types to accommodate different user needs and scenarios. Let's start with a list of all the email types available in Dynamics Marketing, then we will dig into the capabilities of each type.

---

[27] See: http://www.microsoft.com/web/category/razor for news on this technology.

Type	Description
| Email Marketing via Campaign Automation | Campaign automation is accessible from the Campaign entity at<br><br>```
Home > Marketing Execution > Campaign
Management→ Campaigns
```<br><br>The actual email messages are the same as the Manual Email Marketing ones described below. |
| Manual Email Marketing | This is about sending Email Marketing mailings manually via the UI. Users create their email message, set up the various recipient lists, send out the mailings by clicking on the "Send" button all by using the Email Message form at<br><br>```
Home > Marketing Execution > Email Marketing→
Email Marketing Messages
```<br><br>It is also possible to send marketing email messages via API as well. |
| Traceable Transactional Emails | These are transactional emails with all the power of traditional email marketing messages (i.e. traceability, dynamic content etc.). Imagine a utility company that sends your monthly bills as emails using this functionality. It is not an Email Marketing communication because you have an ongoing business relationship with them, so you cannot "unsubscribe" from your monthly bill emails unless you cancel the subscription or change the delivery preferences. At the same time the email is personalized with your data, visually pleasant and fully traceable, virtually indistinguishable from an Email Marketing communication. Of course from time to time the same company can contact you about their latest offer and other promotional material (with your consent) –they will use normal Email Marketing communication for those emails.
These type of emails have also another useful characteristic. The ability to use a data "blob" to be used by the email content as described later in this chapter in more detail.
As of Dynamics Marketing these emails can only be sent via a dedicated external API. |
| Plain Transactional Emails | These are "One-on-one" emails sent via Dynamics Marketing, from a user to another user (or more). Every entity that has an Email panel provides the capability of sending a plain email to other contacts with some information related to the entity. For example users will mail expenses or purchase orders to their customers using this functionality. |

Type	Description
Email Marketing via Campaign Automation	Campaign automation is accessible from the Campaign entity at `Home > Marketing Execution > Campaign Management→ Campaigns` The actual email messages are the same as the Manual Email Marketing ones described below.
Manual Email Marketing	This is about sending Email Marketing mailings manually via the UI. Users create their email message, set up the various recipient lists, send out the mailings by clicking on the "Send" button all by using the Email Message form at `Home > Marketing Execution > Email Marketing→ Email Marketing Messages` It is also possible to send marketing email messages via API as well.
Manual Email Marketing test-send	These are test emails (sent to test a communication before issuing a mailing) that are slightly different than normal email marketing messages.
A/B Test via Campaign Automation	A/B tests can be executed from within an automated campaign, as discussed in the chapter.
A/B Test via Manual Send	This is about sending Email Marketing A/B Tests manually via the UI. A/B Test will be discussed in the next chapter.
Notification Emails sent by Dynamics Marketing	These are "plain transactional emails" sent automatically by Dynamics Marketing to users as notification, triggered by some business-related event. See Chapter 11 "Configuration" for more details on how to set these up. For example when a Task assigned to you is overdue or and approval that involves you is completed Dynamics Marketing sends you one of these emails. Note that Dynamics Marketing will send also technical notification emails to administrators in some particular cases.

Now that we are a bit more familiar with each email type (see the Scenarios section of this and next chapter for more use cases on each type) let's see what they do for us and how they differ:

Capability in Dynamics Marketing	Email Marketing via Campaign Automation *	Manual Email Marketing *	Traceable transactional emails	Plain transactional emails	Manual Email Marketing test-send	Notification emails sent by Dynamics Marketing
Can send via external API	✗	✓	✓	✗	✗	✗
Can send manually via UI	✗	✓	✗	✓	✓	✗
Has dynamic content	✓	✓	✓	✗	✗	✗
Can have dynamic data (XML blob)	✗	✗	✓	✗	✗	✗
Can have rich text & pictures	✓	✓	✓	✓	✓	✗
Recipients-Traceable (Performance panel)	✓	✓	✓	✗	✗	✗
Always / never has Subscription center link	✓	✓	✗	✗	✓	✗
Can be sent to a List/Query	✓	✓	✗	✗	✓	✗
Can have CC, BCC	✗	✗	✗	✓	✓	✗
Can have multiple recipients in To, CC, BCC	✗	✗	✗	✓	✓	✗
Can have attachments	✗	✗	✗	✓	✗	✗
Consumed in EM packs (billed)	✓	✓	✓	✗	✓	✗
Has highest deliverability	✗	✗	✓	✓	✗	✓
Same Message can be sent again and again	✓	✗	✓	✗	✓	✗

(*) including A/B Testing.

Don't worry if some of these capabilities are not entirely clear at this point, we will dig more into the details in the rest of this chapter.

USING THE RIGHT TYPE OF EMAIL HAS LEGAL IMPLICATIONS

The email types discussed are not just important from a technical point of view, they also have legal repercussions if misused.

For instance using a Traceable Transactional email for a marketing communication is illegal in most jurisdictions (following US' CAN SPAM, the EU's Directive on Privacy and Electronic Communications etc.) because recipients cannot unsubscribe from it.

Dynamics Marketing provides various checks and controls to prevent illegal usage (like requiring a Subscription Center for emails and so on), but the ultimate responsibility of using the tool in the most appropriate way rests in the user's hands. Yours!

5.1.4 Purchasing Email Messages

Every subscription includes credits for 50 thousand emails per month, comprising email marketing and traceable transactional emails. Customers that need more can purchase additional email messages (in "packs" of 10000 each) available as Office 365 Add-ons to the subscription, renewed every month. The total quota of email messages expires at the end of every month without carry-ons of unused messages. So every first calendar day of the month the same amount of messages is available for sending (that is 50000 if your subscription has not purchased any Add-Ons email packs). An Office 365 administrator can change the monthly add-ons as wanted. Changes will be effective the next month.

A warning is shown when you are reaching your monthly quota. When you reach that quota and past a small tolerance threshold the system will delay sending the messages attempting to queue them until the quota is restored at the beginning of the month. A notification email will be sent to the administrator notifying the mailings that were delayed because of missing credit.

You don't get charged extra when you go beyond your monthly quota. Your emails that go beyond the monthly quota will be delayed until your quota is available again.

The daily quota is more restrictive in that when you go beyond your daily quota emails are not sent (they are queued) and a notification email is sent to the administrator.

The amount of available messages is visible in the Email Marketing Message list, both the daily and the monthly quotas[28]:

---

[28] "Scheduled" in the screenshot below refers to the number of emails currently scheduled to be sent in the future. This number might be approximated due to campaign automation real-time adjustments.

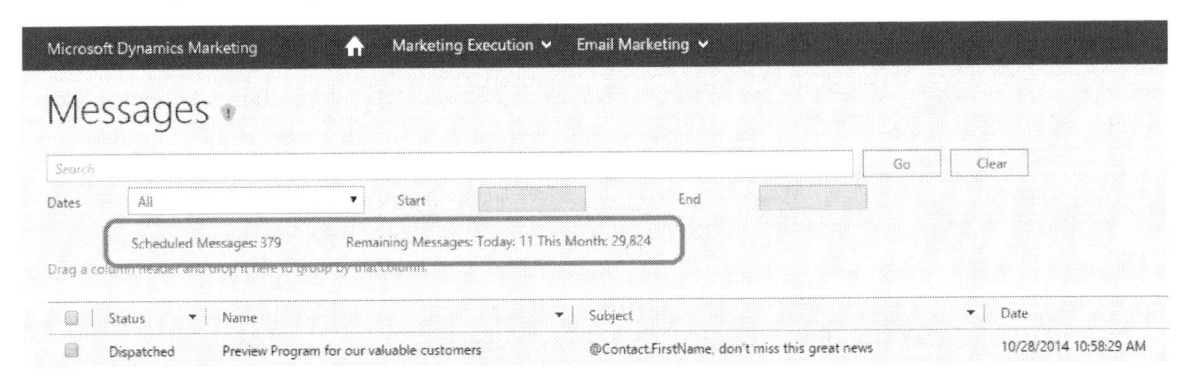

Figure 5.10 –Email Quotas are shown in the Email Messages List

For paid subscriptions the daily quota is half your monthly quota. That means in a day you cannot send more than half of all the emails you can send in a month. Emails exceeding the daily quota will be queued for execution the day after. For Trials the quota is 50 emails per day.

As shown in the previous sections, not all the type of emails sent by Dynamics Marketing are charged.

> **"FORWARD TO A FRIEND" EMAILS ARE NOT BILLED**
>
> Dynamics Marketing provides the ability of adding "forward to a friend" links in Email Marketing messages that enable recipients of the marketing message to forward it to some other email address. These forwarded emails are not billed.

5.2 MAIN ENTITIES

Starting the journey of mastering Dynamics Marketing Email Marketing capabilities will require getting familiar with the following entities.

Entity	Description
Email Marketing Message	These messages are used for the following types of emails described previously: - Email Marketing messages via Campaign Automation - Manual Email Marketing messages - Traceable Transactional Email messages - Manual Email Marketing test-send These messages are available under: `Home > Marketing Execution > Email Marketing → Email Marketing Messages`
Email Messages	These are the "plain" Transactional Email Messages, sent manually via the Dynamics Marketing UI from a user to one or more another recipients, without using marketing lists. These are located under: `Home > Projects > Emails → Emails`
Marketing Lists	These are collection of Contacts. Dynamics Marketing distinguish between two *main* types of lists: static ones (a mere list of contacts) and dynamic ones, also known as Queries as they are equivalent to SQL queries over Contact attributes. Both types can be used to "feed" an Email Marketing mailing. Marketing Lists are available under: `Home > Marketing Execution > Marketing Lists → Marketing Lists` On top of the two basic types mentioned before you can also create rented lists. So in total these are all the possible types of Marketing Lists (if enabled): - Email List (Rented). - List: (also known as "static list") a collection of Contacts. - Mailing List (Rented). - Query: (also known as "dynamic list") a SQL query retrieving a set of Contacts based on the DB data at the moment of the execution of the query.

Plug-ins	Plug-ins are snippet of text that can be inserted in the content of an email message. They can be configured to provide a wide range of capabilities.
	While demo data provide some "sample" plug-ins these should not be used in production, because of legal implications.
	A correct Sender Address is needed in emails in many legislations so it is important not to use the sample one.

5.2.1 Anatomy of an Email Marketing Message

Let's dig into the Dynamics Marketing UI to understand the various options available for Email Marketing messages. As seen in our first example the email message form is available under:

```
Home > Marketing Execution > Email Marketing→ Email Marketing
Messages
```

This page provides three tabs or views:

- Summary where all the usual entity record is available,
- Designer –where the email content is edited,
- Preview –showing a preview of the email for different form factors

Every time we switch Tab, any pending change to our email is saved.

These three tabs are accessible using the buttons under the email name:

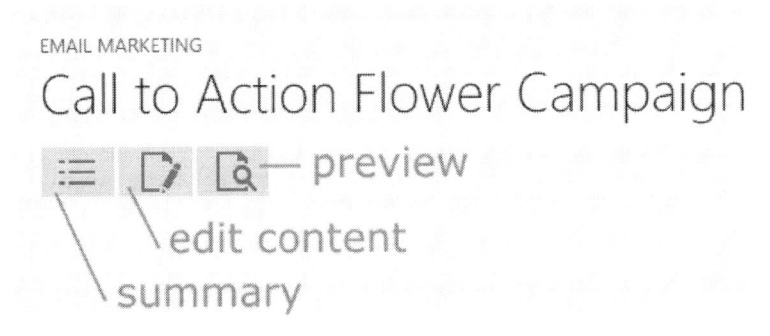

EMAIL MARKETING
Call to Action Flower Campaign
≡ 🗋 🔍 — preview
 \\ \\edit content
  \\summary

Figure 5.11 –The three views of an email message

The Summary is where all the data is available, similarly to other Dynamics Marketing entities:

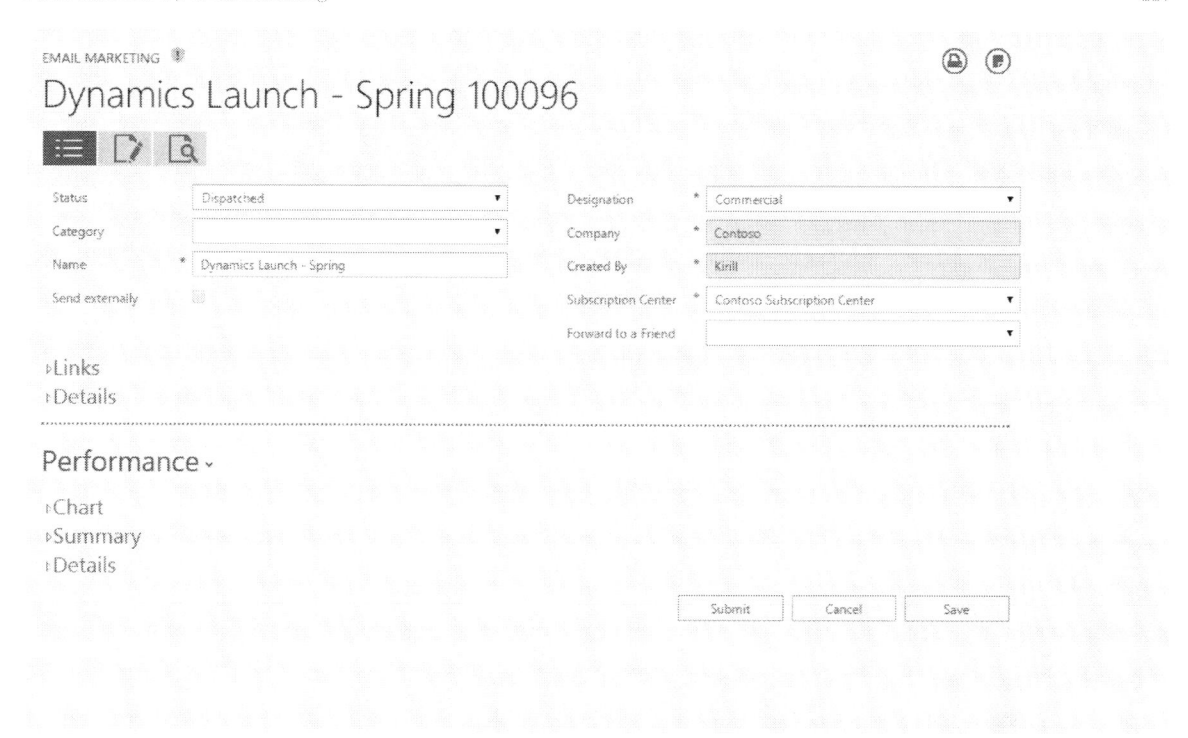

Figure 5.12 –Summary Tab

The Designer tab is where all the email content editing is performed, as discussed later there are two types of editor that can be shown in the Designer tab, the drag and drop editor we have seen already and another one for advanced users that allows for coding HTML emails. In the following screenshot the content block editor is shown.

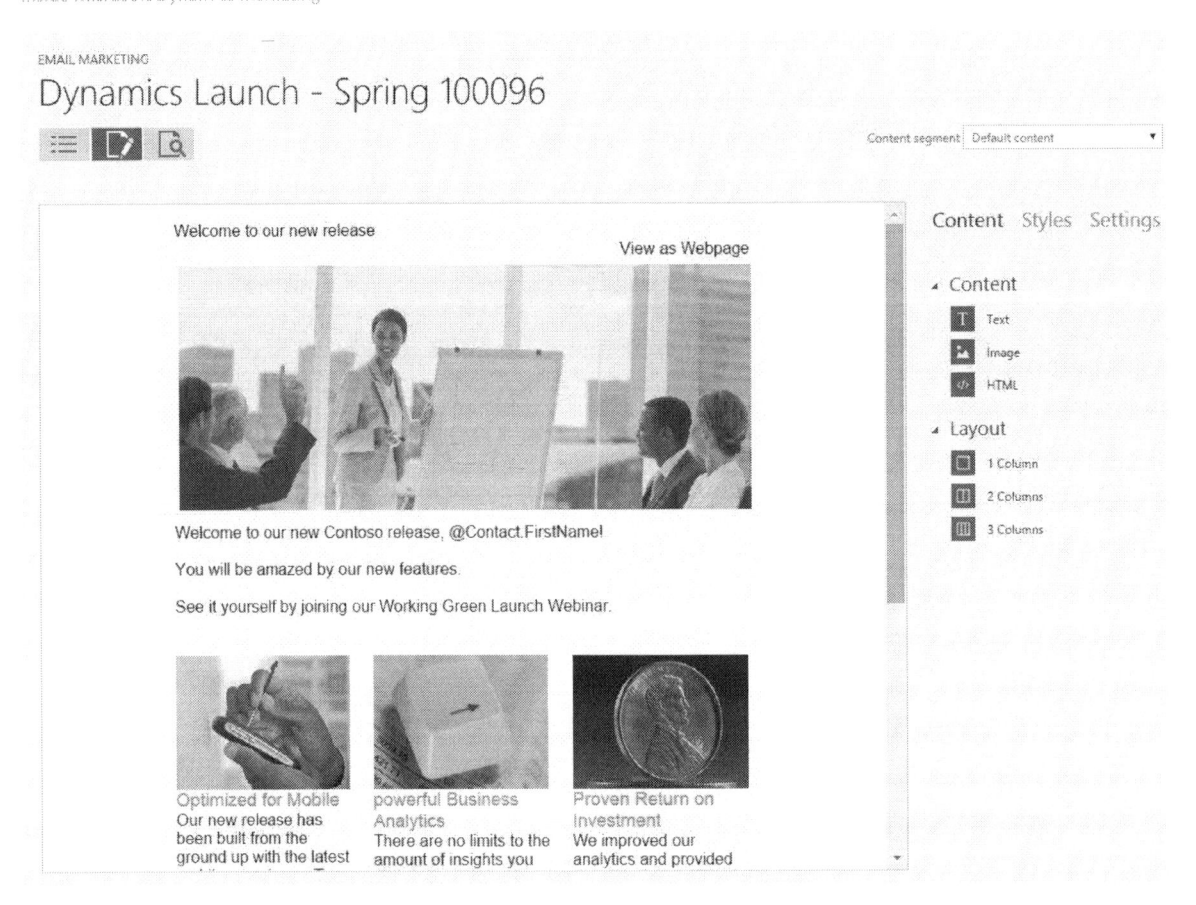

Figure 5.13 –Designer Tab

Finally, the preview tab shows the email preview for different screen sizes:

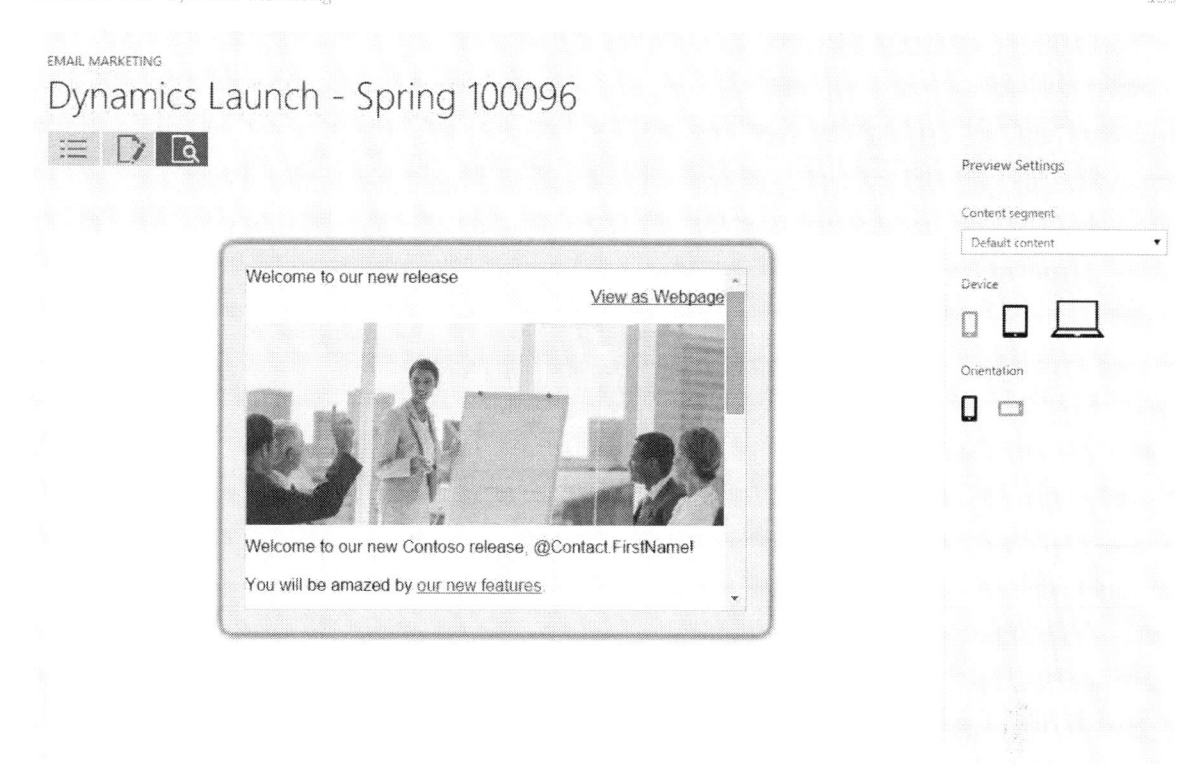

Figure 5.14 –Preview Tab

Here is a list of the main fields in the Summary Tab:

Field or Button	Description
Status	The two options "Active" and "In Process" are used for approval and both values will allow the email to be sent. When the email is sent manually the status is changed to "Dispatched". When an email message is activated as part of a Campaign Automation model, its status changes to "Active". Later in this chapter we will cover all the possible values for this field that are useful to understand how Dynamics Marketing is handling the message.
Priority	This value is used in the actual email priority field.
Name	The name chosen for this Email Message. Used for internal purposes.
Designation	The Campaign Automation engine will only use emails that have Designation "Campaign Automation" –such type of emails require an extra "activation" step which can be used to substitute the manual "test" that can be performed on the other types of email messages. Likewise, email messages with Designation "A/B Testing" are used for A/B testing. The other two values (Commercial and Transaction) are essentially equivalent.
Company	This is the company this email refers to.
Created By	The author of this email. By default is the Contact associated to the current User.
Send Externally	This checkbox will mark the message to be sent via the external API. Once this is saved it cannot be changed anymore, as special functionality will be enabled for this message based on this choice. Once this is selected the message will be controlled via the dedicated API that can pass along data blob for richer content. In Dynamics Marketing this option is the only way to send Traceable Transactional Emails. See next chapter for more details.
Subscription Center	A Subscription Center is mandatory in order for users to be able to unsubscribe from a subscription list or from all the communication with the company. It is required to select one and use it in the body of the email message in order to send it. It is possible to control the subscription lists that are shown in a subscription center to a given marketing contact.
Forward to a Friend	This field allows to select one of the "forward to a friend" plug-ins available in the DB.

HANDLING MULTIPLE CONTACTS WITH THE SAME EMAIL ADDRESS

Dynamics Marketing supports multiple Contacts with the same email address, which means among the other things:
- if a Contact "unsubscribes all" from his Subscription Center, it remains unsubscribed even if the same email address is added again in another Contact for the customer org.

- multiple Contacts sharing the same email address can be used in a mailing. If this is not desired, users need to take care of their Contact DB explicitly in order to avoid multiple Contacts sharing the same email address.

5.3 CREATING AND EDITING EMAILS

Dynamics Marketing provides two alternative editors for creating emails. These are accessible from the Template page as shown below:

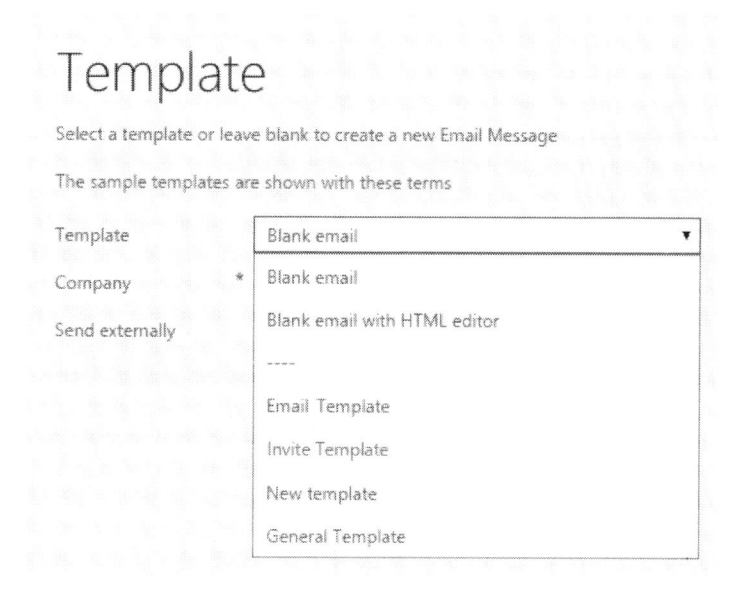

Figure 5.15 – Choosing the Email Editor and Template

The Template dropdown provides two standard options followed by the list of email templates available on the DB. The first two options are:

- *Blank email* – this option will create a new email using the content block editor without any content.
- *Blank email with HTML editor* – this will create a blank HTML email using the HTML editor.

Inside Microsoft Dynamics Marketing

We are already familiar with the first option (the block editor) so let's have a closer look at the second choice, using the HTML editor. When choosing this option the Summary tab will still look the same but when editing the content (clicking on the icon below):

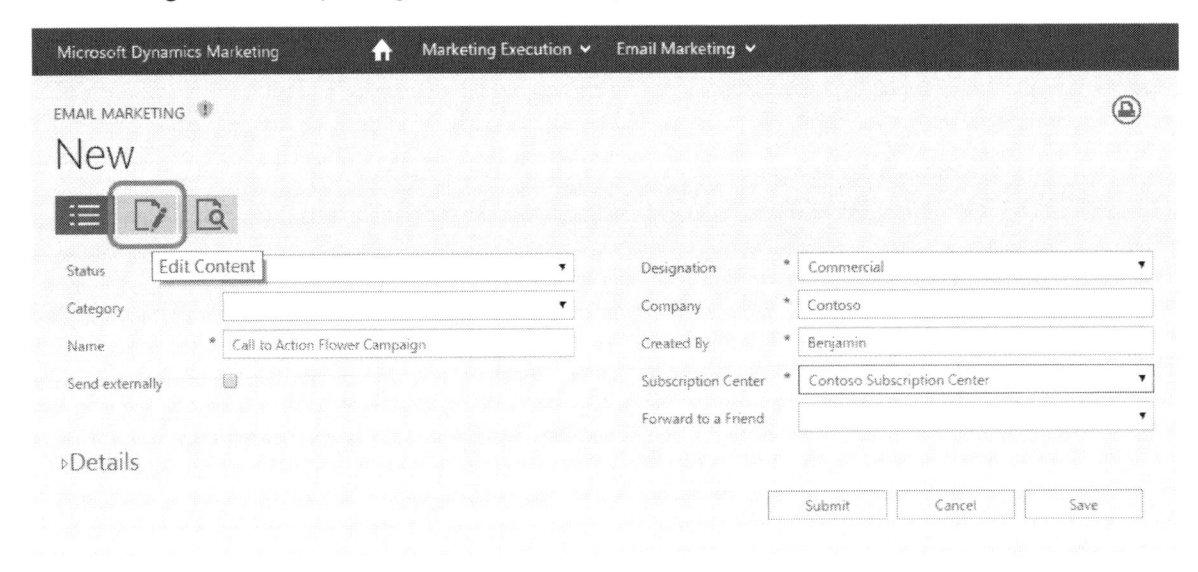

Figure 5.16 –Editing the Content of an Email Message

The HTML editor is used, where user can directly enter HTML code:

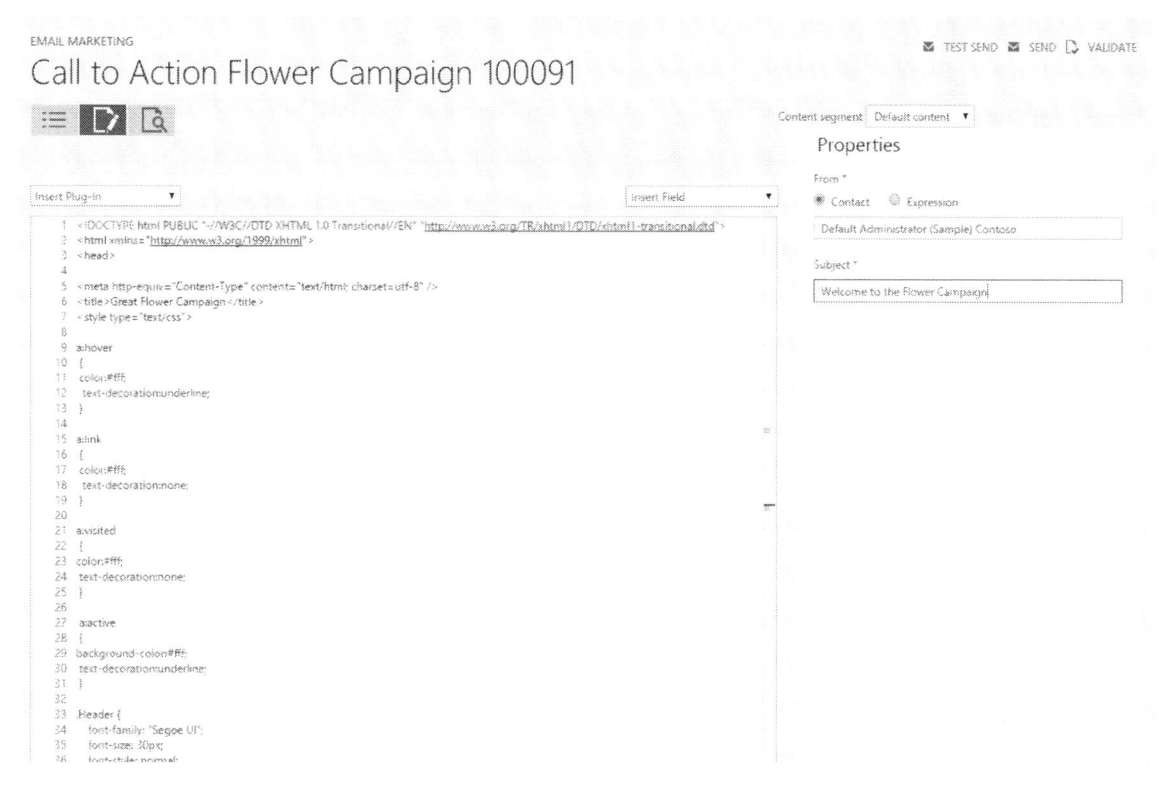

Figure 5.17 – The HTML Editor

EMAILS ARE OPENED WITH THE SAME EDITOR THAT CREATED THEM

When you create initially an email or a template with one editor, that same editor will be used when you edit that email again or will reuse that template.

The HTML editor provides full control over the content of the email that will be sent. It requires email HTML skills and it is a great option for advanced technical users and specialized vendors.

SEGMENT-BASED ADAPTATION

Some reader might have noticed a dropdown available in the top-right corner (with caption "Content Segment") both in the Designer and Preview tabs and in the validation dialog is used to show different variants of the email based on segments (Marketing Lists) the recipient contact belongs to.

This dropdown is populated with the Lists selected for this email (i.e. the Lists added in the Lists/Queries panel). Changing the value in this field also changes the email content. This way it is possible to write different content for each different list. The priority value in the Lists/Queries panel in the Summary tab determines which list will win in case of the same contact belonging to two or more Lists. More on the usage of this dropdown in the next chapter.

5.4 Validating and Sending Emails

Before sending an email the system will validate it to make sure meets all Dynamics Marketing requirements. The validation action can be performed also separately so users can validate an email while they are building it.

The validation step will control for:

- A valid email address in the From field,
- A subject line,
- A list of recipients (for manual emails),
- All Razor code used, if any, will compile correctly,
- A sender address and subscription center plug-ins are used in the email content (this has legal implications)
- A plain-text version of the email is entered,
- And various other information (non-empty email content, internal name etc.)

An "Edit" button is available beside each item so that users can fix the issues or even change the value of a correct item just before sending the email.

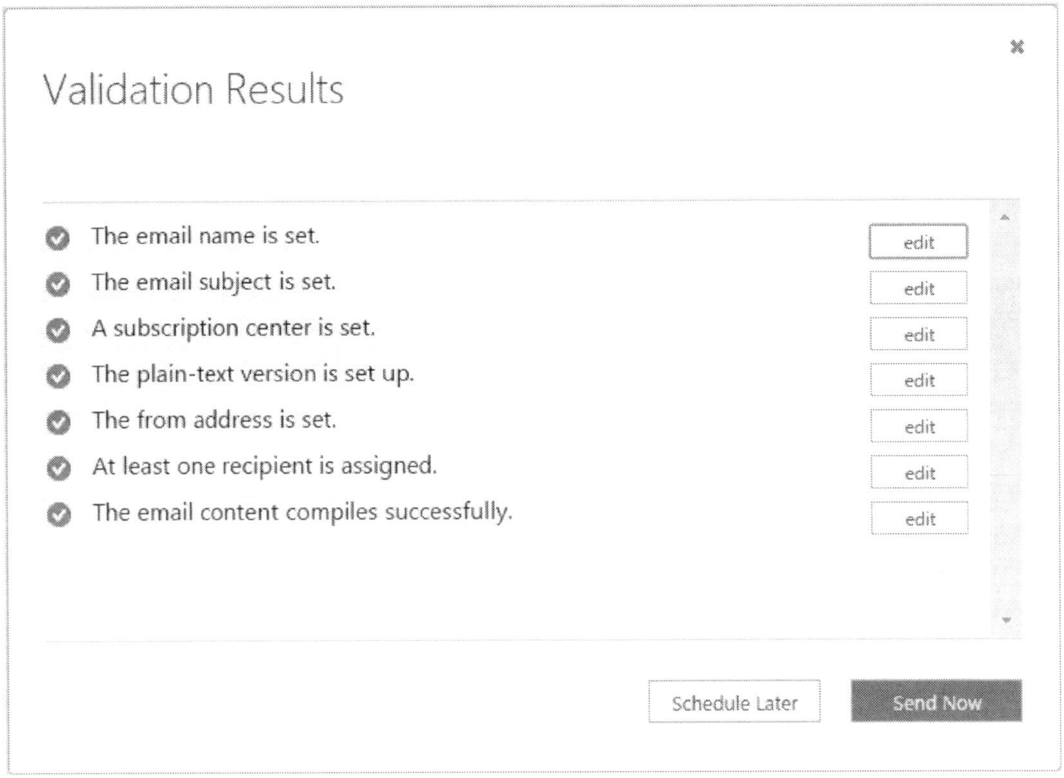

Figure 5.18 –A valid Email Ready to be Sent

5.4.1 Sending Email Marketing Mailings

Let's imagine that a marketing manager prepares a newsletter to be sent manually to a list of recipients.

Our marketing manager already has an Email Marketing Template to use for her newsletter. She creates a new Email Marketing Message based on her template in Dynamics Marketing.

She tweaks some details on the message as she prefers. When ready with the content she can move on to select the Marketing Lists for the email recipients.

From here she can add an existing list to this mailing by clicking on the "Add" action in the List/Queries panel.

Marketing Lists are added as a union of all the contacts, if they are not added as Suppression lists. Contacts from Suppression Lists are instead removed from the final list of recipients. Marketing Lists marked as "subscription lists" will be shown in the Subscription Center page allowing recipients to unsubscribe to each list separately.

PRIORITIES IN MARKETING LISTS

In Dynamics Marketing sections of an email can be adapted based on the Marketing List the Contact belongs to. A priority value is used to decide which Marketing List is used for content adaptation when the same Contact belongs to more than one Marketing List. For more information on dynamic content in Dynamics Marketing see the related scenario in next chapter.

Once the lists are defined and everything else is ready, it is time to send out the mailing.

REQUIRED INFORMATION BEFORE SENDING AN EMAIL MARKETING MESSAGE

Dynamics Marketing requires some information to be defined before sending out an email marketing message. The trickiest one to figure out at first are the Subscription Center and the Sender Address. Both of them are plug-ins that must be present in the email content (in all its variations). They must be created beforehand in the DB and then used in an email content.
When validating the email the system will provide default values where possible, to simplify the required data entering. For instance the plain text version of the email (which is needed for ensuring high deliverability rates) is generated automatically by the system based on the HTML version.

In general it would take a couple of minutes to get a mailing delivered, although many things would affect this time, depending upon current server load, number of recipients in the mailing type of emails used (for example sending to a very large number of email addresses from a single ESP might lower down the overall delivery time because of server-side throttling) etc.

HIGH PROPRITY EMAIL MARKETING MESSAGES

> Dynamics Marketing supports sending emails with high priority (Importance "high"). This capability must be used very sparingly as it might be interpreted as spamming activity, thus impacting negatively the deliverability of future emails.

Summarizing, mailings are sent by Dynamics Marketing depending on user request (whether to be sent immediately or as a schedule send) and on server load.

5.5 What Happens After Sending an Email

Dynamics Marketing provides a complex and scalable infrastructure to send large volumes of emails efficiently. Let's get familiar with some of the details of this process.

> ***TRACKING WHEN A MESSAGE IS SENT***
>
> When an email is sent manually the Status field will change and the time the email was sent is shown in the title caption for the email message.
>
> Things are a bit more complex in case of emails sent automatically such as those sent via Campaign Automation or A/B Testing, because a single mailing can be automatically broken down into smaller groups of emails sent over a given period of time. Email Activation time (when the activation email is sent) is shown. The Contacts panel provides timestamps or each recipient.

Sometime after the mailing has been sent the results start coming in. Recipients might open an email[29], click on one of the links in the email, and so on. Dynamics Marketing keeps track of all these actions and shows the statistics right in the Email Message form, in the "Performance" panel. If multiple mailings are added to a Campaign, Dynamics Marketing can show the aggregated results using the "Email Performance" panel in the Campaign form. Aggregated results are also available per Marketing List, from within the List entity.

A Dynamics Marketing user can track the aggregated results gathered so far per each mailing by opening the Email Marketing message and select the "Performance" panel. Under this panel we have three expandable groups showing precious information for analyzing the results of the mailing.

The Status field in the Summary Tab provides information about where an email message is in the pipeline. For emails used in Campaign Automation the Status will be "Active".

---

[29] Email Marketing messages tracks email opening by the number of recipients that download the email pictures.

STATUS OF AN EMAIL MARKETING MESSAGE SENT MANUALLY

The Status field indicates the stage a mailing is going through once has been "sent" by the user. The value "Queuing" for example is indicating that the mailing is about to be prepared for the external delivery. It does not denote that the email has been already dispatched to email service providers.

Another way to understand when a mailing has been dispatched to the Internet (i.e. to external email service providers that are taking care of delivering it over time) users can select the "Contacts" panel and inspect the available results. If there are no contacts shown it means the message is still being processed internally by Dynamics Marketing. If there are some Contacts shown (for example some hard bounces are reported) then it means the mailing has been dispatched to the Internet already, at least for some of the recipients.

The "Status" field in an email message shows the status of a mailing once it has been sent. This is the sequence of status values when a mailing is sent:

1. Queueing. The mailing is being queued onto Dynamics Marketing specialized cloud service.

2. Queued. Dynamics Marketing specialized cloud service accepted the mailing and it will process it soon.

3. Processing. Dynamics Marketing specialized cloud service is now processing the mailing (i.e. running personalization and any other operation before sending it out)

4. Sending. Dynamics Marketing specialized cloud service is finally sending emails to the Internet

5. Dispatched. The mailing has been "sent to the Internet". This does not guarantee delivery though. The emails have left Microsoft servers and have been "released to the wild".

Note that some of these states usually last for a very short period of time while others typically take longer to progress.

Finally there are a few other "exceptional" states like "Failed" which should not happen in production.

5.6 TRACKING RESULTS

Dynamics Marketing provides a number of metrics and KPIs for analyzing the results of our email marketing efforts, available from the Summary Tab.

We can divide these reports in two groups. Those that show aggregated results (i.e. results global to the entire mailing, like the total number of people that opened the email so far) and those showing the detailed results, i.e. what every single contact did with that email.

The first group of results, about aggregated KPIs, are available under the "Email Performance" Related Information panel:

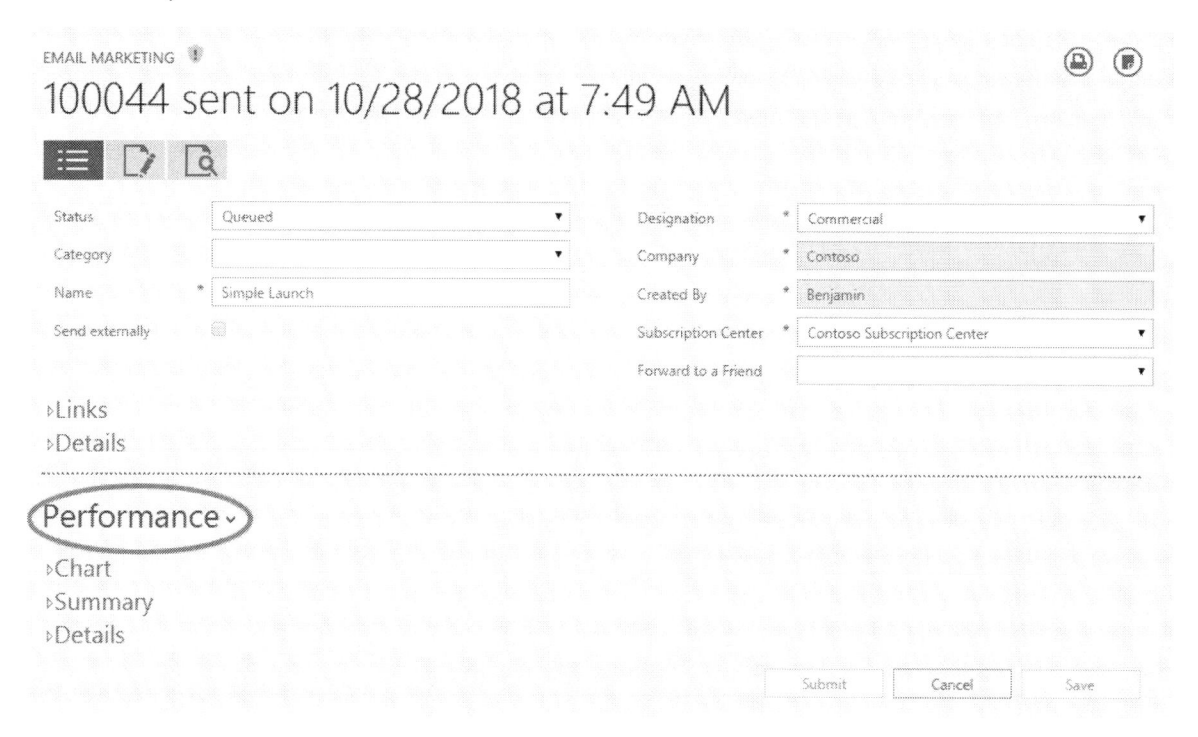

Figure 5.19 –Performance Panel

The second group of results, those for every contact are available under the "Contacts" Related Information panel:

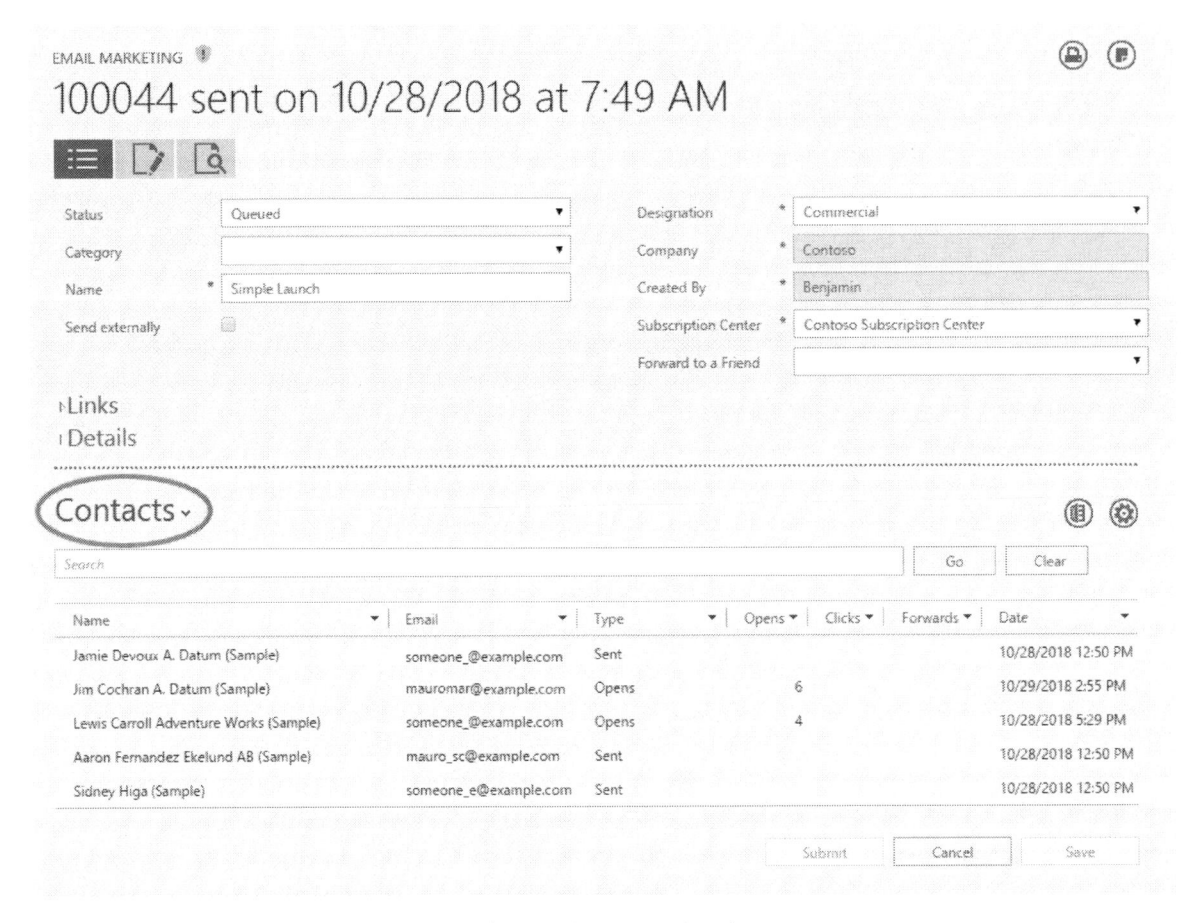

Figure 5.20 –Contacts Panel

Detailed results can also be obtained by using the "Email Tracking Results" OData feed.

The remaining of the chapter will explore the details of each option.

5.6.1 Aggregated Numbers - the "Email Performance" Panel

The Email Performance panel shows a number of KPIs to users organized in three expandable panels, showing information about the mailing in progressive order of complexity (simpler views are shown first):

- Chart – this provides a visual overview of the main KPIs for this mailing
- Summary – this shows all the main aggregated KPIs for this mailing
- Details – this provides detailed aggregated information about the mailing in four views:
    - Internet Service Provider
    - Link
    - List
    - Performance over Time

The screenshot in the next page shows the UI with these three panels expanded.

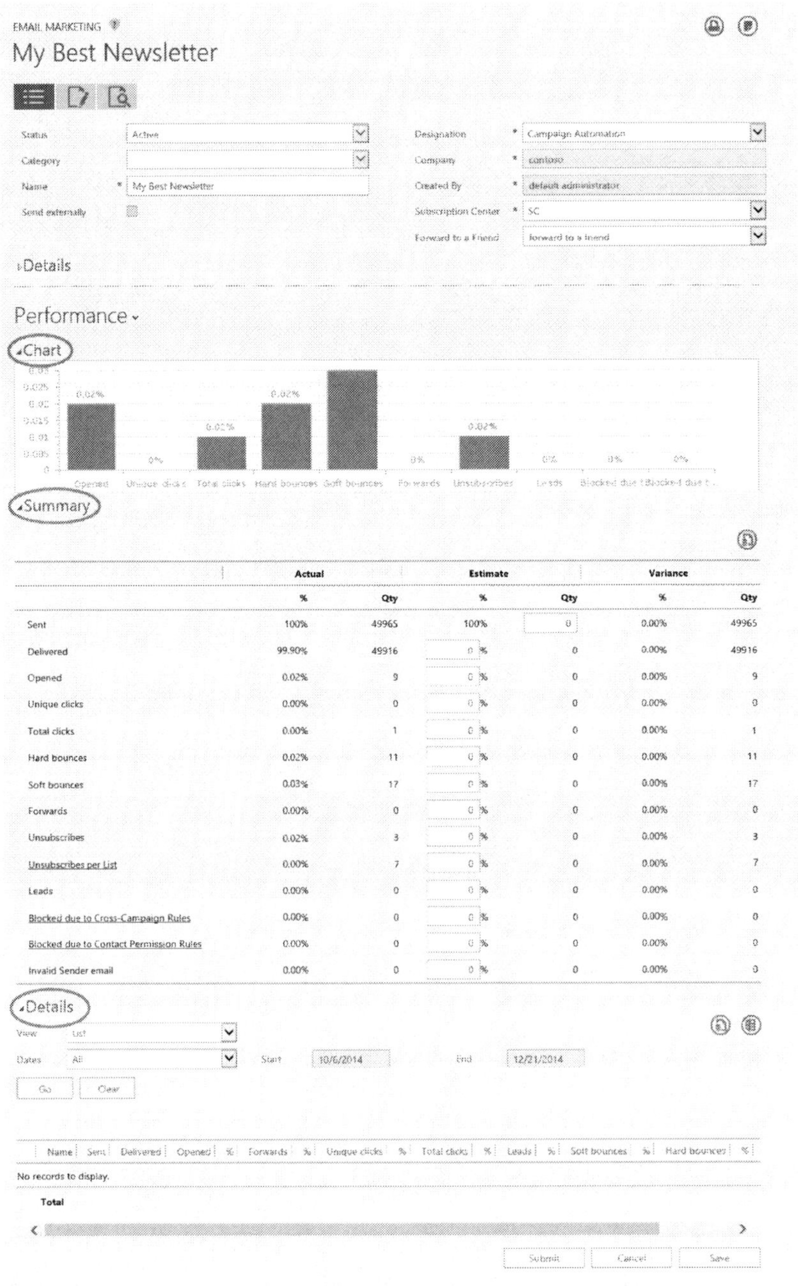

Figure 5.21 –Performance Panel

Let's look at these various panels, starting from the Chart.

5.6.1.1 Email Performance - Chart
The Email performance chart provides an overview of the main KPIs for the message.

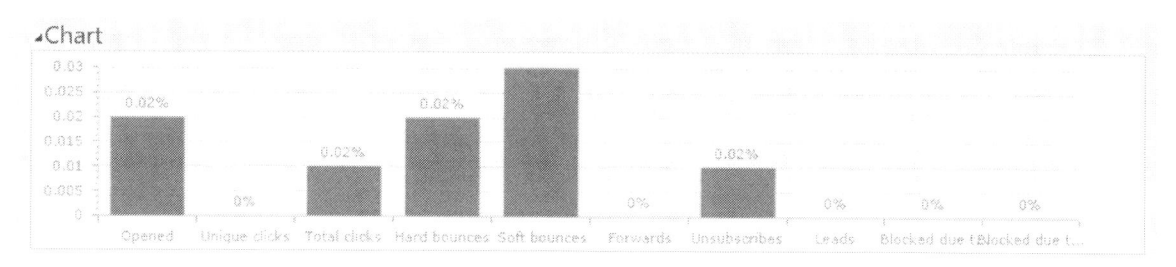

Figure 5.22 –Performance Chart

This chart provides a visual overview on the most important indicators (both discrete count values and percentages):

- Opened emails. Counting the number of times an email recipient downloads the images for the email.
- Unique clicks. The unique amount of clicks in the links contained in the email.
- Total clicks. The total amount of clicks.
- Hard bounces. Emails with a permanently flawed email address. These could be due also to email addresses blacklisted because of "spam" activity.
- Soft bounces. These are temporary failures to deliver an email. A full inbox, a connection issue or even an Internet Service Provide blocking temporarily our mailing could all be classified as "soft bounces".
- Forwards. Emails that have been forwarded by a recipient to one or more "friends". If the forward to a friend plug-in has not be employed this figure will always be zero.
- Unsubscribes. Number of recipients that unsubscribed (both from one or more subscription lists and from all lists).
- Leads. The number of leads generated from all the recipients.
- Blocked due to Cross-Campaign rules. The emails that were not sent if some Cross-Campaign rules did prevent sending them.
- Blocked due to Contact Permission Rules. The emails that were not sent due to the Contact Permission setup (described in the next chapter).

5.6.1.2 Email Performance - Summary

This view provides information similar to the one shown visually in the Chart area:

▲Summary

	Actual		Estimate		Variance	
	%	Qty	%	Qty	%	Qty
Sent	100%	49965	100%	0	0.00%	49965
Delivered	99.90%	49916	0 %	0	0.00%	49916
Opened	0.02%	9	0 %	0	0.00%	9
Unique clicks	0.00%	0	0 %	0	0.00%	0
Total clicks	0.00%	1	0 %	0	0.00%	1
Hard bounces	0.02%	11	0 %	0	0.00%	11
Soft bounces	0.03%	17	0 %	0	0.00%	17
Forwards	0.00%	0	0 %	0	0.00%	0
Unsubscribes	0.02%	3	0 %	0	0.00%	3
Unsubscribes per List	0.00%	7	0 %	0	0.00%	7
Leads	0.00%	0	0 %	0	0.00%	0
Blocked due to Cross-Campaign Rules	0.00%	0	0 %	0	0.00%	0
Blocked due to Contact Permission Rules	0.00%	0	0 %	0	0.00%	0
Invalid Sender email	0.00%	0	0 %	0	0.00%	0

Figure 5.23 –Summary Expandable Panel

By entering the quantity field and possibly the various % estimates, it is possible to calculate the variance values.

CLICKABLE LINES

The first column of some rows in the Summary panel can be clicked to drill more into the details of that particular information. These additional lists and the information they provide will be discussed more in detail in the next chapter.

More in detail:

- **Sent**
  The total number of emails that were initially part of the mailing and were sent
- **Delivered**
  The total number of emails that were delivered
- **Opened**
  The unique opens (number of recipients that downloaded pictures in their email)
- **Unique Clicks**
  The unique clicks (number of recipients that clicked at least one link in their email)
- **Total Clicks**
  Total clicks
- **Hard Bounces**
  Number of recipients that had a permanently flawed email address.
- **Soft Bounces**
  Number of recipients that had been declared "soft bounces". Dynamics Marketing attempts to send the message a number of times in a number of hours before declaring an email address as "soft bounced"[30].
- **Forwards**
  Number of unique forwards (when the forward to a friend plug-in is used in the email)
- **Unsubscribes**
  Unique unsubscribes for that mailing
- **Unsubscribes per List**
  These are the number of recipients' unsubscribes for each list employed in a manual mailing (not used in campaign automation). So if a recipient clicks "unsubscribes all" in her Subscription Center and she was in three lists, all of them in this mailing then the "Unsubscribes per List" will be 3 and the "Unsubscribes" will be one.
- **Leads**
  Unique Leads generated via this mailing
- Blocked due to Cross-Campaign Rules
  The number of emails that were not sent because of some cross-campaign rule. If cross-campaign rules are not used then this will always be zero.
- **Blocked due to Contact Permission Rules**
  The number of emails that were not sent because of contact permission. If the contact permission API (described in next chapter) is not used then this number will always be zero.
- **Invalid Sender email**

---

[30] Note also that if an email hits 5 soft bounces in 180 days then it becomes permanently blocked similar to a hard bounce.

This is the number of emails that could not be sent because the "From" address specified as an expression was not a valid email address. In order to ensure high deliverability rates and delivering high quality messages Dynamics Marketing will not send emails with malformed "From" address values. If expressions (built using Dynamic content as described in the next chapter) are not used this line will be zero.

5.6.1.3   Email Performance - Details

The Details panel provides four views with different data:

"Internet Service Provider" shows a view per domain of the various statistics.

- "Link" provides statistics about the URLs contained in the email message (excluding plug-ins and other "system" links in the email). The CTR (Click Through Rate) and # clicks are provided for each URL.
- "List" provides aggregated statistics over the Marketing Lists used for the mailing.
- "Performance Over Time" shows global statistics over time, with a configurable time interval. This view provides the details of what happened to the email message after it was sent.

See a screenshot of the "Performance Over Time" view below.

Details

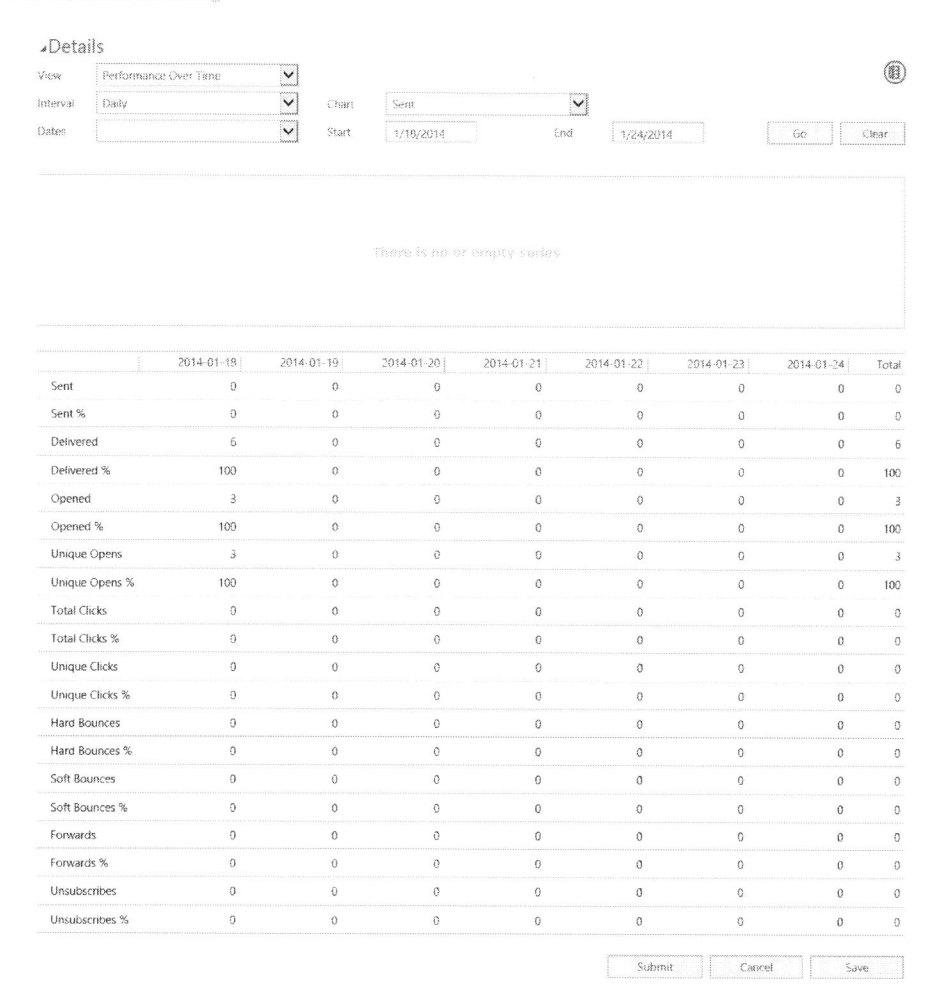

	2014-01-18	2014-01-19	2014-01-20	2014-01-21	2014-01-22	2014-01-23	2014-01-24	Total
Sent	0	0	0	0	0	0	0	0
Sent %	0	0	0	0	0	0	0	0
Delivered	6	0	0	0	0	0	0	6
Delivered %	100	0	0	0	0	0	0	100
Opened	3	0	0	0	0	0	0	3
Opened %	100	0	0	0	0	0	0	100
Unique Opens	3	0	0	0	0	0	0	3
Unique Opens %	100	0	0	0	0	0	0	100
Total Clicks	0	0	0	0	0	0	0	0
Total Clicks %	0	0	0	0	0	0	0	0
Unique Clicks	0	0	0	0	0	0	0	0
Unique Clicks %	0	0	0	0	0	0	0	0
Hard Bounces	0	0	0	0	0	0	0	0
Hard Bounces %	0	0	0	0	0	0	0	0
Soft Bounces	0	0	0	0	0	0	0	0
Soft Bounces %	0	0	0	0	0	0	0	0
Forwards	0	0	0	0	0	0	0	0
Forwards %	0	0	0	0	0	0	0	0
Unsubscribes	0	0	0	0	0	0	0	0
Unsubscribes %	0	0	0	0	0	0	0	0

Figure 5.24 –Performance – Details View

5.6.1.4 Email Performance – Additional Performance Figures

Dynamics Marketing allows for exporting your detailed results to standard CSV files that can be opened for example with Excel. The screenshot below shows where the action is located in the UI.

Inside Microsoft Dynamics Marketing

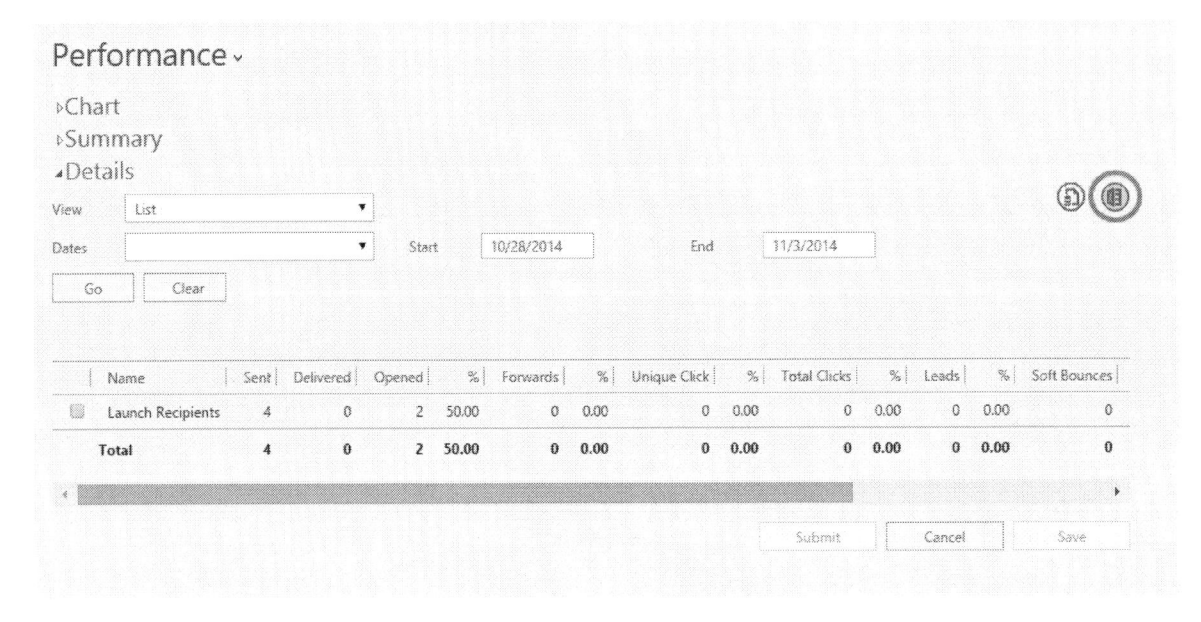

Figure 5.25 –Performance – Export to Excel

5.6.2 Detailed Numbers - the "Contacts" Panel

The "Contacts" panel provides information about each recipient contact and the latest action performed, the time it occurred and its details.

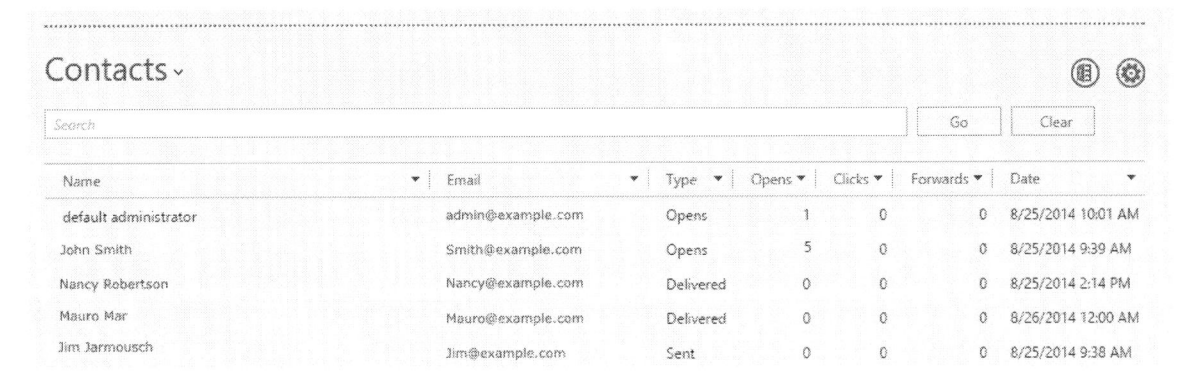

Figure 5.26 –Contacts Panel

More details are available when clicking on a contact.

> **ONLY THE FIRST 30 CONTACTS ARE SHOWN IN THE UI**
>
> Only the first 30 lines of Contacts are shown in the Contacts Panel. In order to visualize all the contacts from the UI users can use the export to Excel functionality, or tap into

the OData feed. Typically a mailing to 50K recipients would generate a file of about 10 MB or less.

The Type column in particular shows the type of the latest action tracked by the system. The main values for the Type field used in marketing emails are shown in the following table.

Caption in List (English)	Value when exported (xlsx)	Meaning
Clicks	[CLICK]	Number of clicks in the email performed by the Contact.
Delivered	[DELIVERED]	The email has been delivered to the ESP.
Hard Bounce	[HARD BOUNCE]	The email address had some permanent flaws and it resulted in a Hard Bounce. This email address is then removed from the Primary Email field for that contact (to avoid reusing it in the future), but it is still shown in the "Email" column in this view.
Leads	[LEADS]	Whether a Lead was generated for this Contact.
Soft Bounce	[SOFT BOUNCE]	
Render	[RENDER]	The Contact opened the email and downloaded its pictures.
Sent	[SENT]	The email has be dispatched on the Internet by Dynamics Marketing, and no other result is available yet.
Invalid Sender Address	[INVALID SENDER ADDRESS]	The "From" was populated using an expression that resulted in an invalid email address, so that email was not sent. You can see the aggregate figures for these emails in the Summary area of the Performance panel.

5.6.2.1 Navigating Email Marketing Figures

Note also that the email marketing messages sent to a contact are available in the "Email Marketing" panel for that Contact form, including also traceable transactional emails. So for example these are all the emails ever sent to this Contact in our DB:

Figure 5.27 –Marketing Emails Sent to a Contact

Similarly, one can also see aggregated views of all email marketing messages sent related to other entities. So all the mailings having a given Marketing List can be seen from the "Email Marketing" panel in the list form:

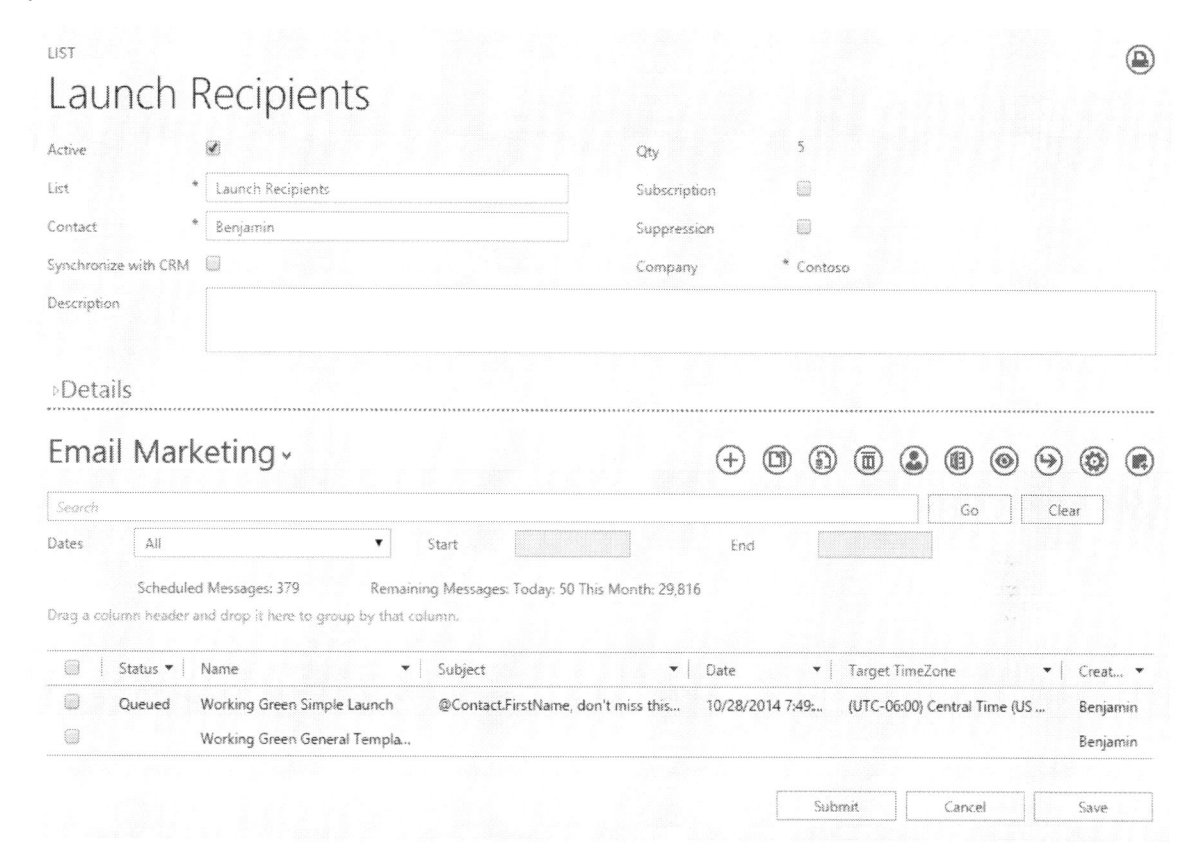

Figure 5.28 – Marketing Emails Associated to a Marketing List

Rollup also works for emails, recipient contacts and other data on Campaigns (all email marketing messages sent as part of a Campaign) and Programs (all emails for all Campaigns under a Program):

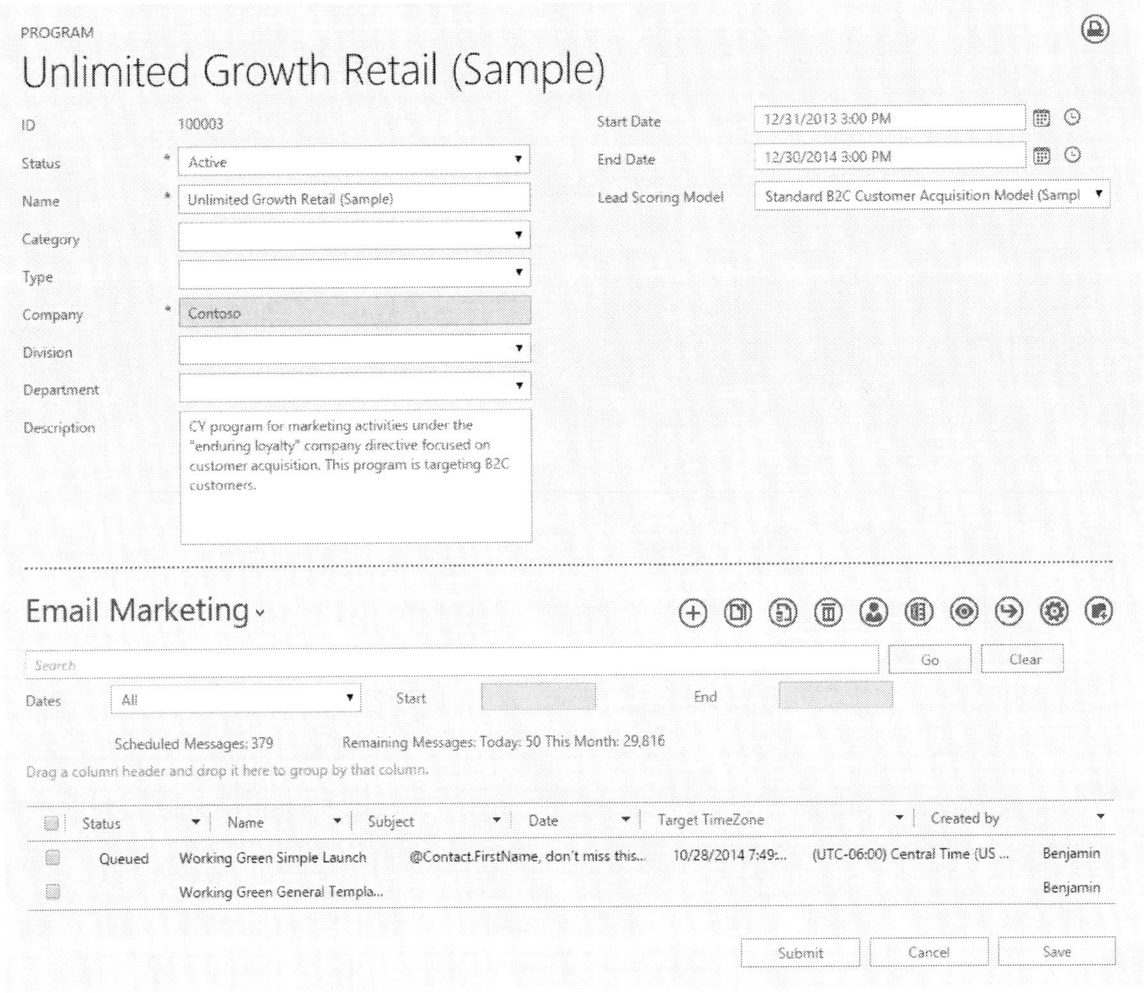

PROGRAM
Unlimited Growth Retail (Sample)

ID	100003		Start Date	12/31/2013 3:00 PM
Status	* Active		End Date	12/30/2014 3:00 PM
Name	* Unlimited Growth Retail (Sample)		Lead Scoring Model	Standard B2C Customer Acquisition Model (Sampl
Category				
Type				
Company	* Contoso			
Division				
Department				
Description	CY program for marketing activities under the "enduring loyalty" company directive focused on customer acquisition. This program is targeting B2C customers.			

Email Marketing

Scheduled Messages: 379   Remaining Messages: Today: 50 This Month: 29,816

Drag a column header and drop it here to group by that column.

	Status	Name	Subject	Date	Target TimeZone	Created by
☐	Queued	Working Green Simple Launch	@Contact.FirstName, don't miss this...	10/28/2014 7:49:...	(UTC-06:00) Central Time (US ...	Benjamin
☐		Working Green General Templa...				Benjamin

[Submit] [Cancel] [Save]

Figure 5.29 –All Marketing Emails Associated to a Program

Chapter Six
SMS and Advanced Email Marketing

In this chapter we explore more in depth some of the email marketing functionality seen in the previous chapter and we introduce briefly the SMS channel.

6.1 Overview of the SMS Channel

Dynamics Marketing also provides an outbound channel for mobile text messaging, also known as SMS (short message service). While the SMS/text message channel it is nicely integrated with the rest of Dynamics Marketing UI and concepts (from the integration in campaign automation from the UI and concepts of the text messages and related entities) there are some distinctive behaviors that need to be called out explicitly.

The SMS messaging entities are available under:

```
Home > Marketing Execution > SMS Marketing
```

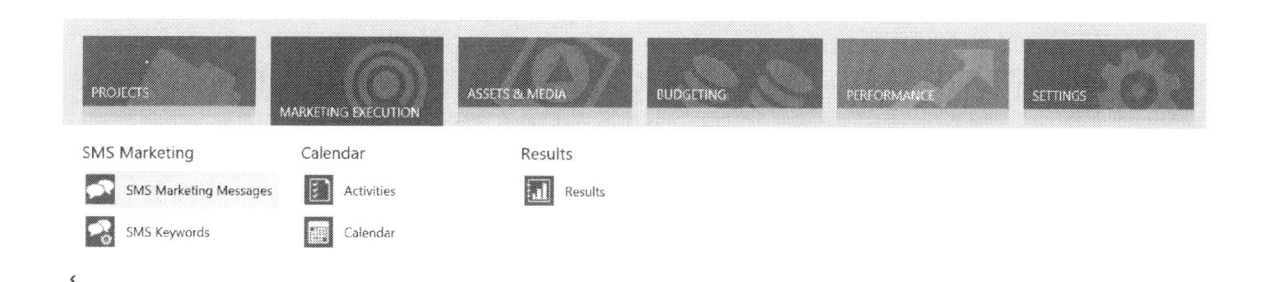

Figure 6.1 – SMS Marketing

SHORT CODES

A short code is a special phone number to which contacts will send text messages. Some countries (like the United States and Canada) require each marketing organization to have a dedicated short code, while other countries allow different marketing organizations to share the same short code.

Similarly to email marketing, SMS marketing is strictly regulated in most countries and regions. For this reasons Dynamics Marketing provides some built-in functionality aimed at aligning with these rules. Also similarly to email marketing, though, is ultimately the marketer's responsibility to comply with the law.

The main regulatory concepts specific to marketing text messages are:

- *SMS-centric operations*. It should be possible to perform all operations (sign up, unsubscribe, etc.) by means of SMS messages. These text messages work like commands (containing specific *keywords*) sent to the short code representing the marketing organization. This is different than the email marketing channel for example, where support for web pages (and access to a web browser) is expected for things like accessing the subscription center to unsubscribe, etc. This way it will be possible to market consistently to worldwide customers that have access only to the SMS channel.
- *Strict opt-in*. In most countries marketing organizations are only permitted to send marketing SMS messages to contacts that have provided an explicit consent. The flow is thought to be started by the marketing contact, who must send an SMS message containing a specific keyword. Double opt-in, as required in some jurisdictions, demands the contact to reply a second time to a confirmation message. Luckily Dynamics Marketing supports both double and single opt-in. This has a subtle effect on sending marketing text message with Dynamics Marketing, as they appear as being "filtered" against the opt-in list. So if a marketer attempts to send a text message to a contact that didn't know explicitly opted-in, the message will not be sent.

- *Opt-out process*. Instructions for opting out are usually included in the confirmation message to the opt-in. Dynamics Marketing handles opt-out keywords to make this process simple and reliable.
- *Confirmation message*. The first message that Dynamics Marketing sends to a freshly opted-in contact is called the confirmation message. Many countries regulate the content of these messages to help ensure that recipients are well informed. Typical confirmation messages include the service name and description, messaging frequency, the available commands (usually the opt-out, help keywords) a reference to terms and conditions, and a statement of rates and data charges that apply. Dynamics Marketing supports also "help" requests by sending an SMS with the appropriate keyword supported in different languages.
- *Traceability*. Dynamics Marketing provides support for managing opt-in and keeping a detailed record of opt-ins and opt-outs, helping marketers ensure that marketing messages are only sent to contacts that complied with the country opt-in regulations. These records can be audited as needed.

6.1.1 Text Messages

Similarly to emails, SMS are organized in messages, where plug-ins and dynamic content can be used. Also the Performance related information panel for SMS messages is organized in the same way as email messages.

The Text Message form is available at:

```
Home > Marketing Execution > SMS Marketing → SMS Marketing Message
```

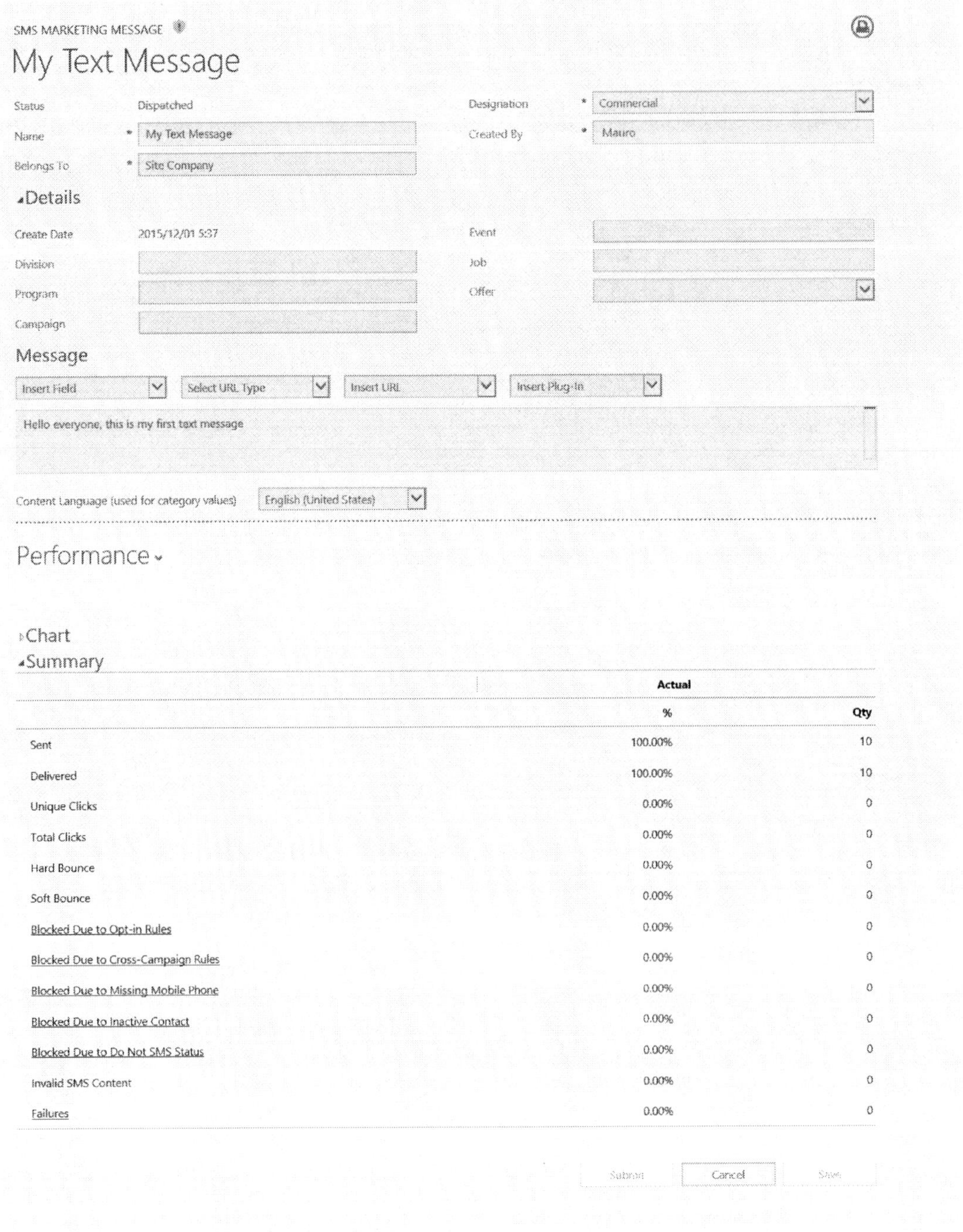

Figure 6.2 – SMS Message Form

A NOTE ON PRIVACY AND SECURITY OF SMS MESSAGES

SMS marketing messages pass through several third-party networks and third-party service providers, also different for each geographic location. As a result, the Microsoft privacy policies and standards cannot be fully enforced.
So information like Recipients' telephone numbers and the text message's content might be visible to the third parties involved in delivering it.

6.1.2 Text Message Keywords

Each text message keyword is related to a company or campaign, and must be included by contacts in a text message when opting-in. Each keyword must be associated with an opt-in confirmation message, an opt-out keyword, and an opt-out confirmation message.

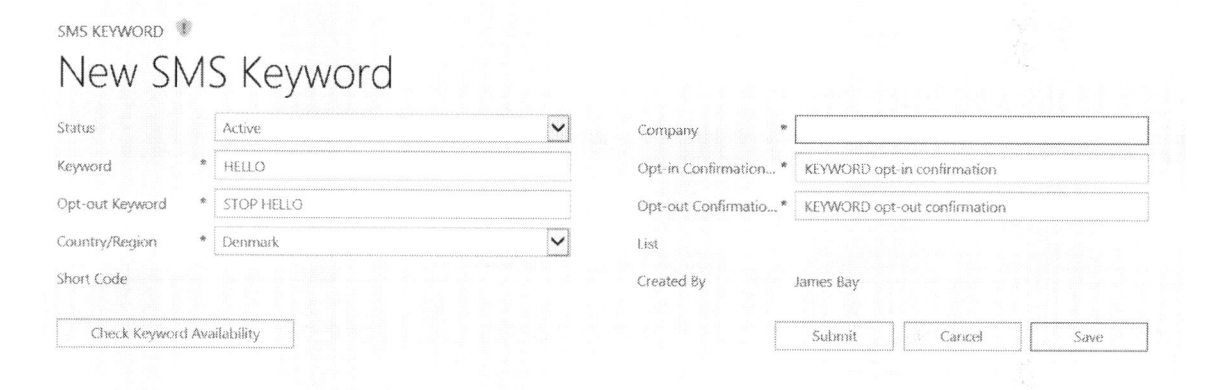

Figure 6.3 – SMS Keyword Form

6.1.3 Conclusions

Given the UI similarities with other outbound channels such as email marketing, the SMS channel is straightforward to use in Dynamics Marketing, but a few caveats we outlined above.

> **SMS AVAILABILITY IN YOUR COUNTRY**
>
> SMS marketing messages depends upon third-party providers and as such it might not yet be active for your country. Please refer to the online product documentation for the latest list of available countries.

This concludes our brief introduction to SMS marketing. In the rest of this chapter we will have a deeper look at email marketing functionality.

6.2 Email Marketing - Overview of the Editing Experience

Let's start from an overview of the content block editor. This editor enables marketers to create professional-looking marketing emails in any Unicode language that render nicely across a wide range of email clients and devices. Marketers don't need to know about HTML coding; the email code is generated automatically using the latest adaptive layout technology on the email clients that support it.

The editor UI can be thought as divided in two areas, the content area on the left and the details about the selected item on the right hand side.

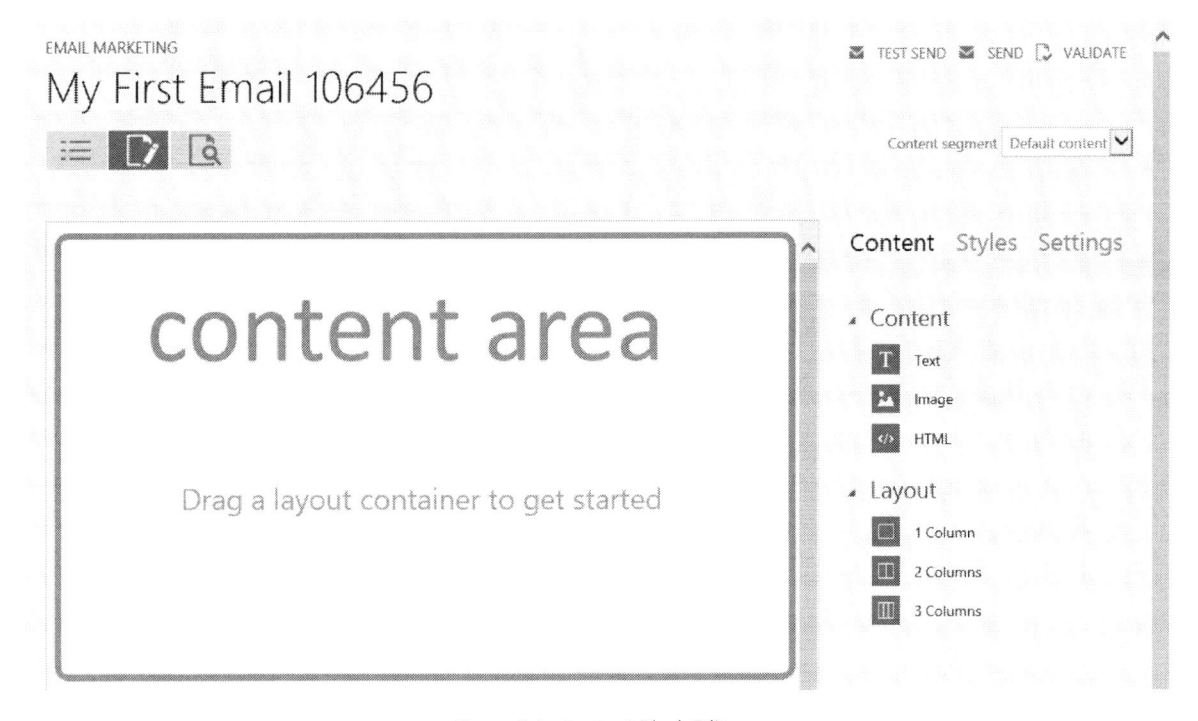

Figure 6.4 – Content Block Editor

In turn the details of the selected item come in multiple tabs. Each item can have a content or a styles tab.

When no selection is shown the editor is selecting the entire email, so that the styles below are the styles for the entire email.

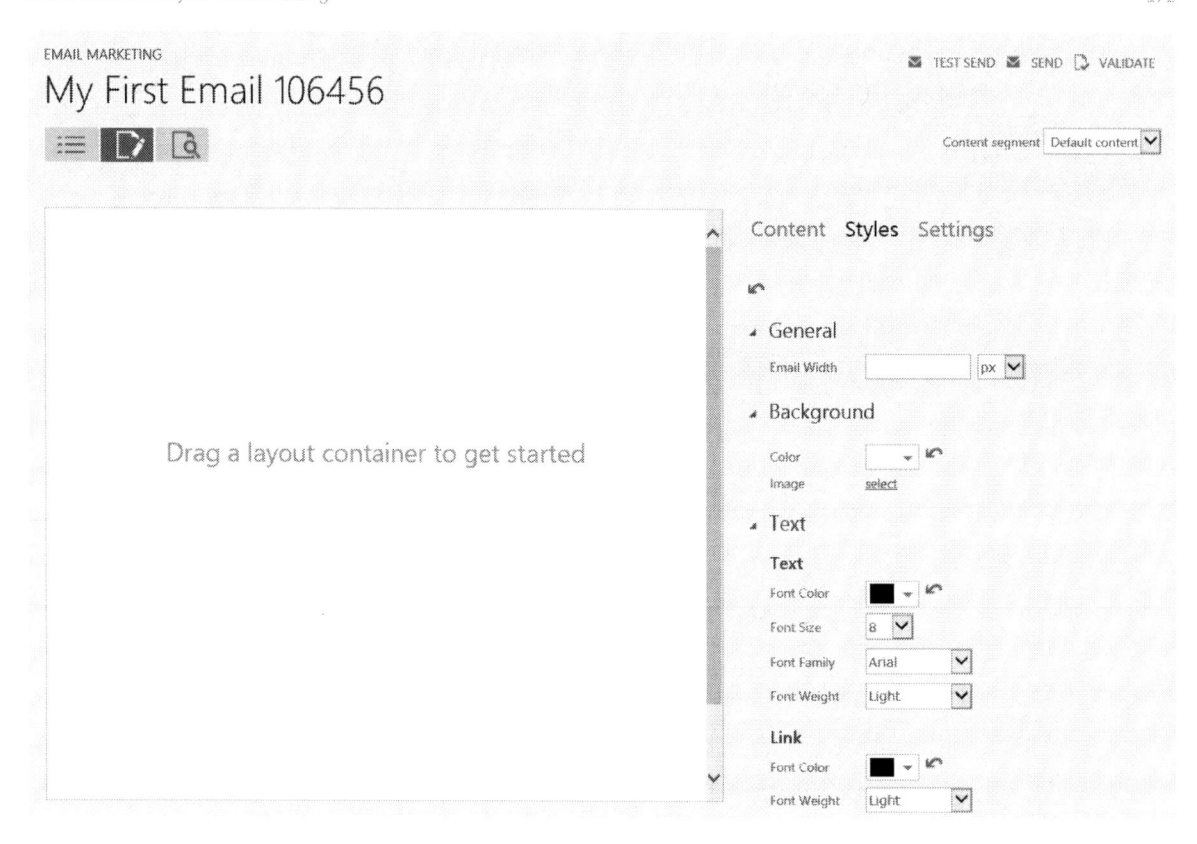

Figure 6.5 –Email Styles

Note that the email subject and from address are available from the Settings tab for the entire email:

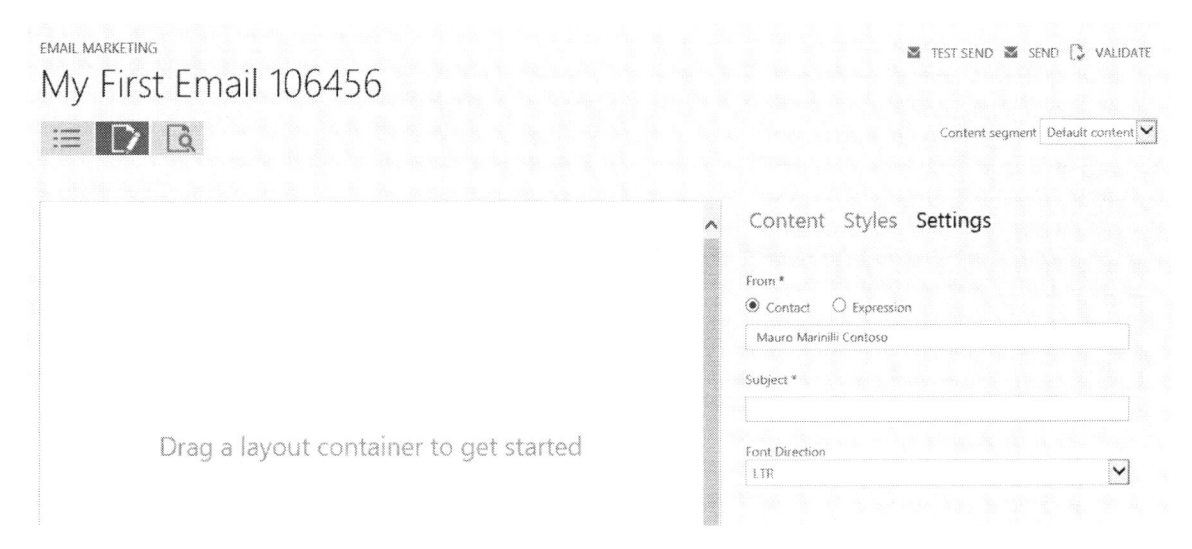

Figure 6.6 –Email Setting Tab

Also from this tab is possible to change the text direction so that emails can be written in any language, including right-to-left ones.

> **STYLES THAT ARE NOT SPECIFIED ARE "INHERITED" FROM THE CONTAINING ITEM**
>
> When some style property for a content block is specified then it will override the same property defined in the containing column. If that property is not specified the system will attempt to use the property from the container the column belongs to. If that is not specified it will attempt to use the property for the entire email.

6.2.1 General Concepts

The content of an email is broken into content blocks. Blocks are added to columns in a container. It is not possible to add a container into another container or a block into another block.

In order to simplify the selection of the various blocks, containers and columns, the editor expands their borders so that hovering hover with the mouse makes it easy to understand what will be selected[31].

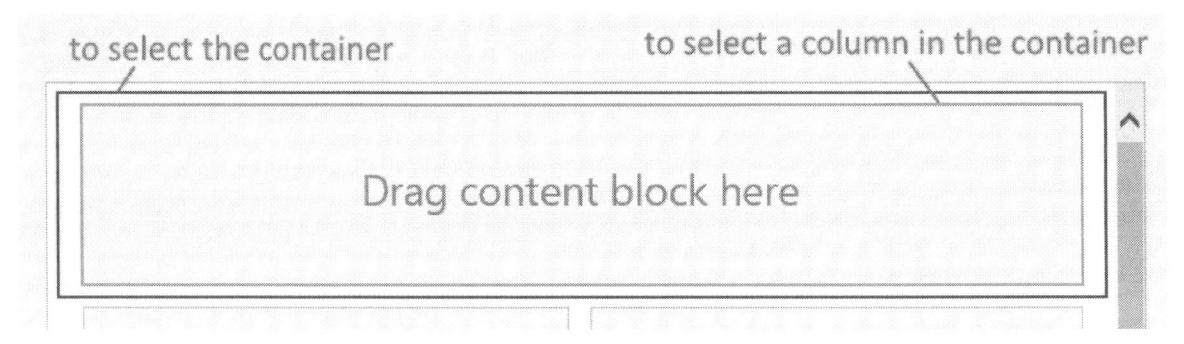

Figure 6.7 –Select Columns in a Container

When clicking on a block, column or container in the content area the details are shown in the right-hand side panel.

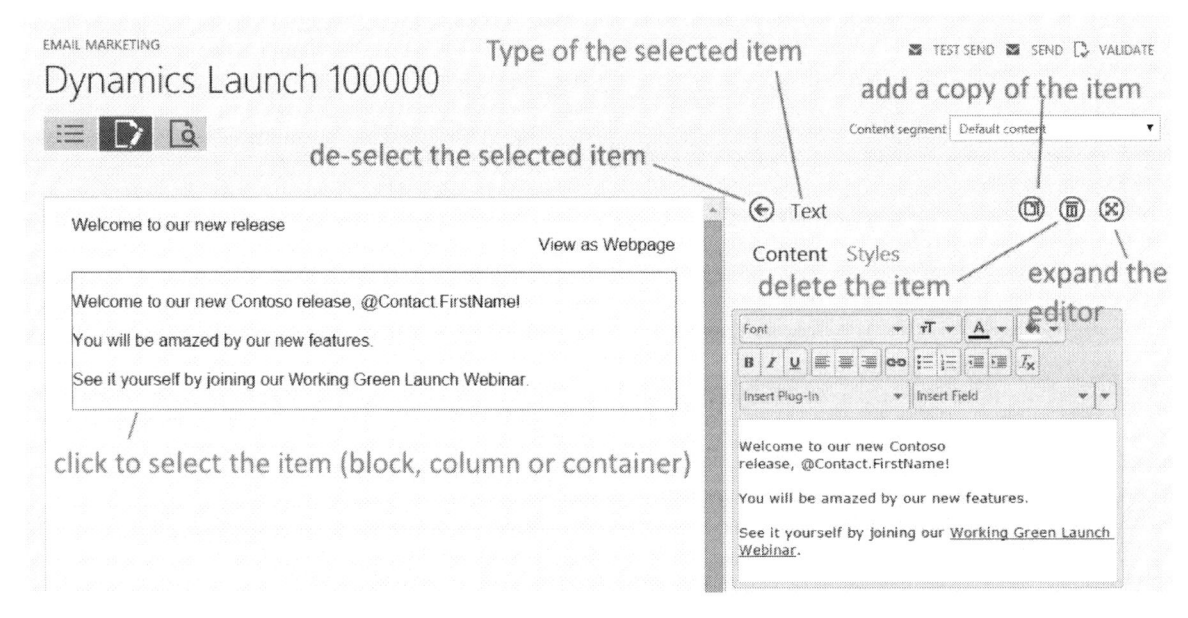

Figure 6.8 –Select items

---

[31] Notice how the Preview does not show such "expanded" borders.

When trying to select an item just hover over with the mouse in the content area and click to see on the right-hand side panel what has been selected.

6.2.2 Content Blocks

There are three types of content blocks:

- *Text*. These blocks represent formatted text with links. It is not possible to embed pictures wrapped with text.
- *Image*. These are used for adding pictures, both from Dynamics Marketing media library or from an external URL.
- *HTML*. These blocks are for HTML or Razor code[32].

6.2.3 Containers

There are three types of containers, depending on the number of columns. Columns in containers always have equal width. It is not possible to assign custom widths to columns. The picture below shows the three types of containers (the most complex layout possible is with three columns) when dragged on an empty email.

---

[32] Note that you can add Razor code to any "normal" text block by using the "@{}" syntax. HTML blocks keep your email more structured and organized when it comes to Razor code but they are not strictly needed.

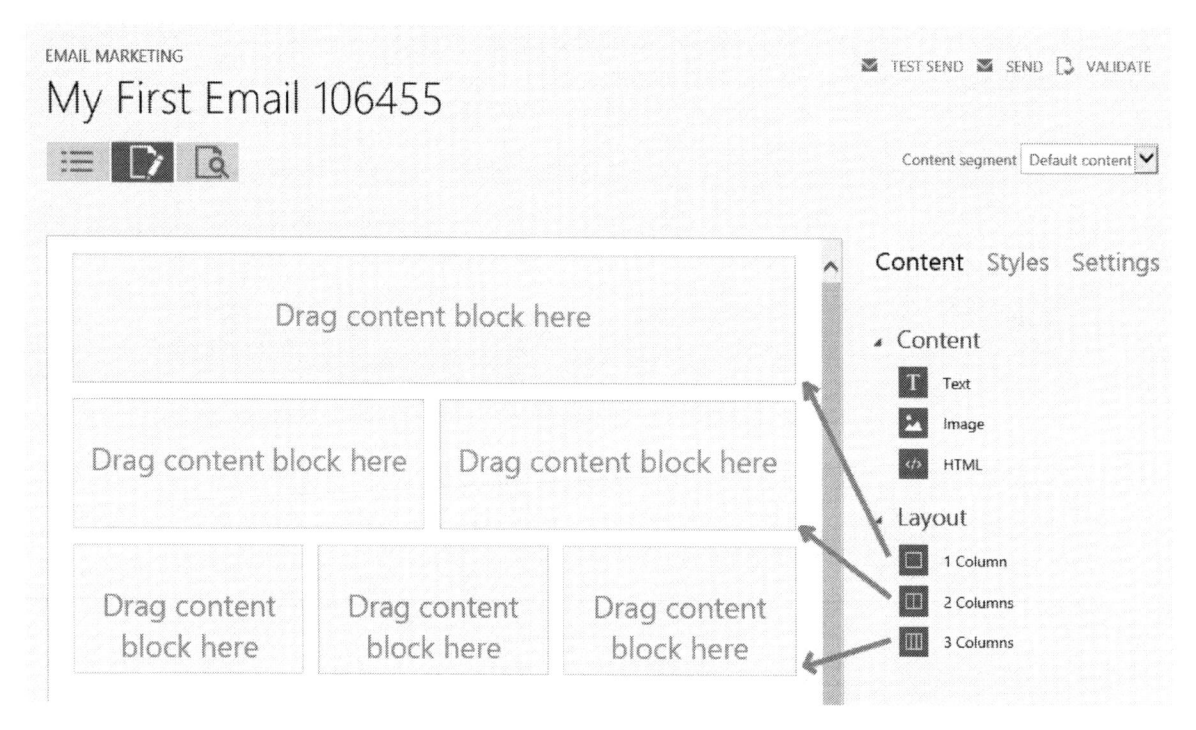

Figure 6.9 –Different Containers

6.2.3.1   Example of using containers: creating a text-only "button"

A typical scenario for marketing emails is to provide a clear, prominent call-to action button in an email. Having the button as text makes it easier to use when pictures are not downloaded.

One way to implement this is to use a three-column container and place a text block in the center column. Columns will keep an equal width even when empty so we will get a one-third width, center-aligned button as show below:

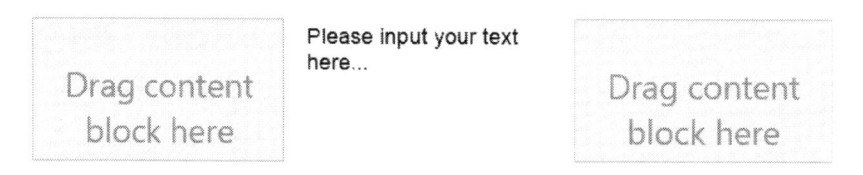

Figure 6.10 –Call to action button

Now let's style our text block to our liking by clicking on the "Styles" tab for the text block.

For example changing the block background color as shown below:

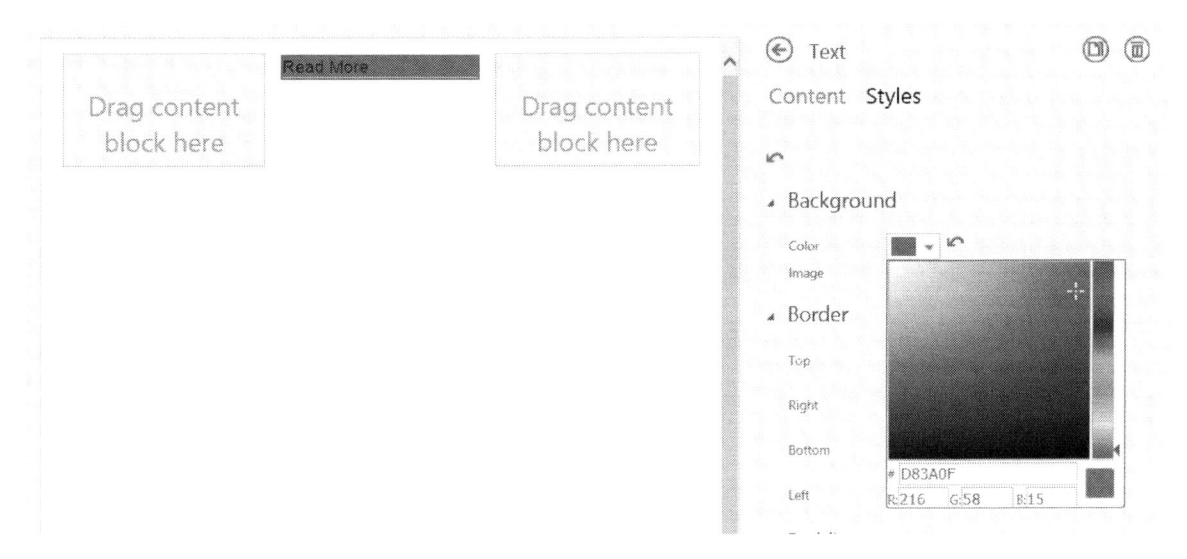

Figure 6.11 –Background color on a text block

And adding some padding and / or border to the block etc. Then we can style the text as well as shown below.

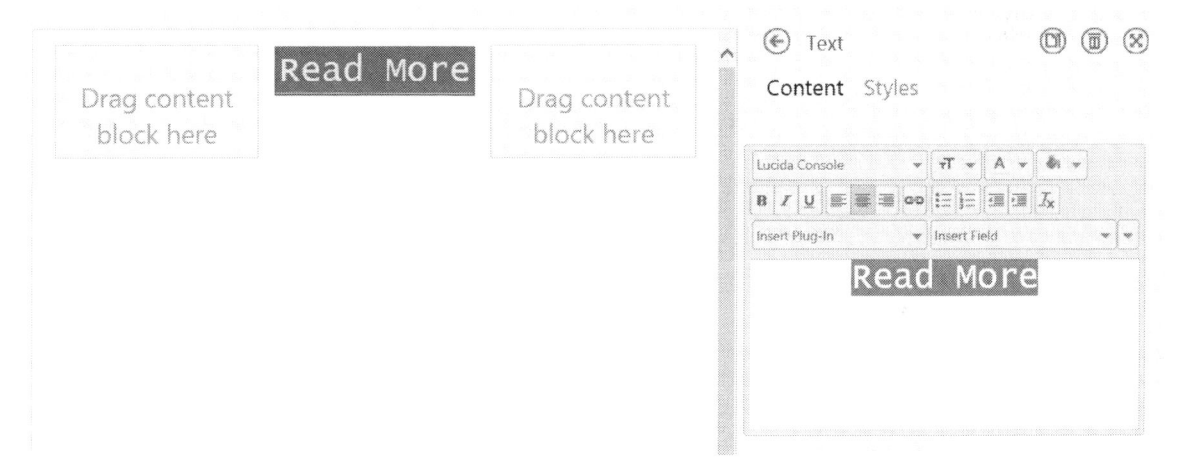

Figure 6.12 –Styling the Text

Note that we could have achieved a similar effect by styling the container's column instead:

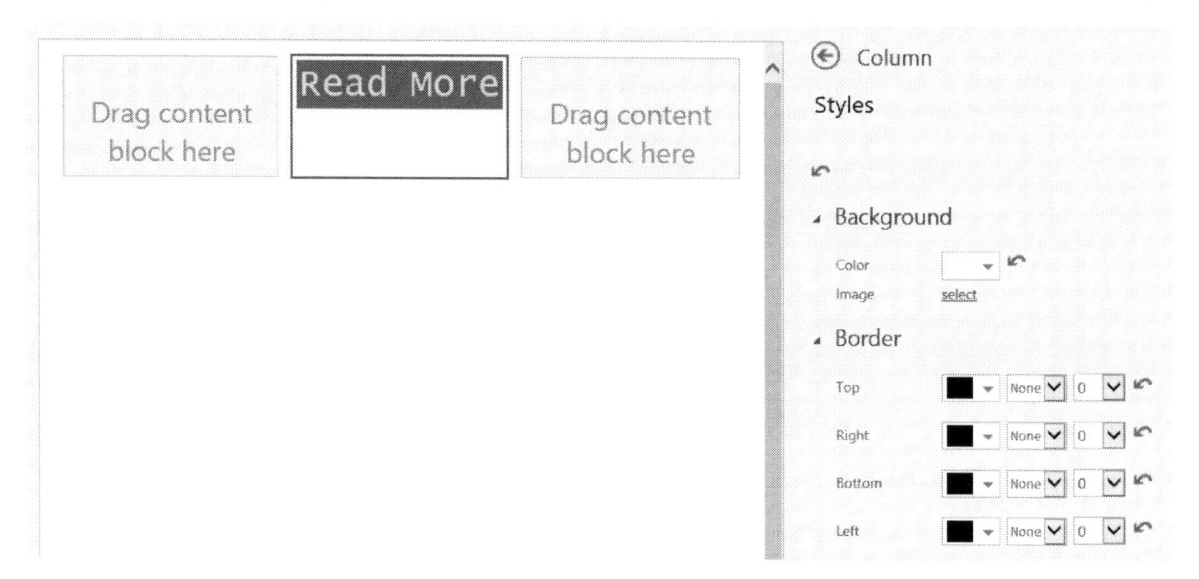

Figure 6.13 –Styling the Text

With the difference that the background color would be applied to the height of the entire column not just the text block.

6.3 A/B Testing

Marketers love to test what works and what doesn't and constantly improve the relevance of their messaging using A/B testing. Dynamics Marketing supports sending out two variants of an email and find the most successful one that will be then sent to all remaining recipients. It is a good practice to keep the two variants very similar and change only a small portion of the email (such as the subject line, for example) otherwise the "experiment" will not really be meaningful and you cannot individuate for sure the "winner" effect.

> **DYNAMICS MARKETING DOESN'T VERIFY WHETHER YOUR A/B TEST RESULTS ARE STATISTICALLY SIGNIFICANT**
>
> Dynamics Marketing does not automatically ensure statistically sound results, so marketers will need to configure their tests using some basic statistical common sense (i.e. adding enough samples to the experiment and waiting enough time before declaring a "winner" variant).

In general a marketer will start from formulating the problem, devising a possible solution and the experiment that will prove it, then implementing it. The implementation is done in Dynamics Marketing: creating the base email and its variant, specify the A/B test parameters, run the experiment and study the results. It is important to get the conceptual phase right and refraining from jumping right away into the implementation without having a clear plan first.

Dynamics Marketing A/B tests can use the following measurements (or weighted combinations of them):

- Opens
- Total clicks
- Unique clicks
- Hard bounces
- Soft bounces
- forwards
- unsubscribes

Here are some examples of possible dilemmas that marketers might attack with some principled A/B testing:

- Our emails have a low open rate (compared to industry average). We should focus on optimize things like the subject, the preview text etc. for higher Opens.
- Open rates are OK but the call to action (the link to a webinar or offer, etc.) just does not seem to work. In this case we could focus on maximizing total clicks (and/or include unique clicks or a combination on both depending upon our content etc.)
- We have completed our all-new revamped layout and visual upgrade after months of work. We want to see how it roughly compares against the old one. Although A/B testing is not very significant here (we have two radically different emails so we risk to compare apples with oranges) we can still leverage the A/B testing machinery to validate that the new version is not a total disaster and how it roughly compares with the current one. We can send it to a limited audience and observe results. (This technique is similar to what most web sites and applications do daily on the Internet when rolling out new functionality.)

Let's illustrate how A/B testing works in Dynamics Marketing by creating and running one. For simplicity we will create the test for a manual email, without a campaign automation model.

6.3.1.1 An Example

We have our monthly newsletter that is still performing under-the-market average open rates, and we want to improve that. We have studied a couple of options that we think would improve the open rates. In order to perform a solid test we choose only one (an improved subject line) leaving the others for next months.

So we want to send a newsletter email and we want to experiment with two different subject lines, with the winning criteria being the open rate.

We have already the base email defined. Now we need to create an A/B test for it and add the variants. We create a new A/B test under:

```
Home > Marketing Execution > A/B Testing→ A/B Testing
```

Here we fill all the details:

- The name of the experiment
- The Designation (that will make the test use emails for campaign automation or manual emails)
- The company (this will filter out companies and)
- From where gather samples (from some list of as a percentage of the total target). In our example we decide to use 20% of all recipients for the test so that the winner email will be sent to the remaining 80%.
- The winning criteria. In our case it is a single criteria, the open rate.
- Finally we choose the candidate versions. If only one is available like in our case we can click on the Copy button in the version B email to make a copy of the base email as the second variant. Note that the candidate emails need to have Designation "A/B testing" in order to be usable for an A/B test.

Inside Microsoft Dynamics Marketing

New A/B Testing

Name	*	Newsletter 2.0
Designation	*	Commercial
Status		Draft
Company	*	Contoso

Test Recipients

○ Use a marketing list

● Use sample from the Lists/Queries   20

Winning Criteria

	Criteria	Weight
☑	Opens	100%
☐	Unique Clicks	0%
☐	Total Clicks	0%
☐	Hard Bounces	0%
☐	Soft Bounces	0%
☐	Forwards	0%
☐	Unsubscribes	0%

Candidate versions

Email

Name	Created By
Monthly Newsletter	Benjamin

Email

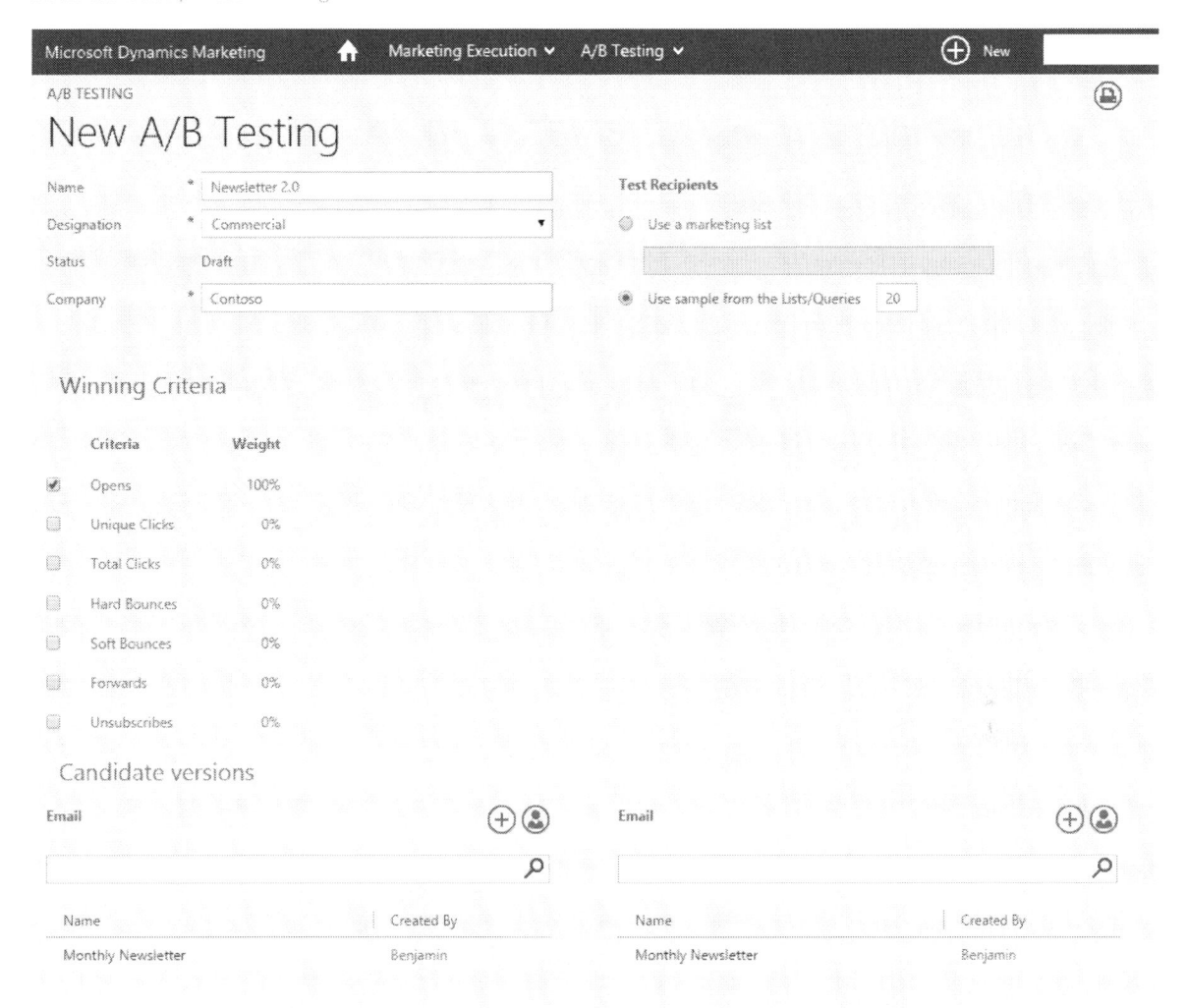

Name	Created By
Monthly Newsletter	Benjamin

Figure 6.14 –Defining an A/B Test

Once the variants are chosen and saved we can enter the scheduling time parameter (when the winner variant will be sent to the remaining recipients). In our example we decide to declare a winner 48 hours after the initial sending. If not specified yet of course we need to add the target lists.

Inside Microsoft Dynamics Marketing

☑	Opens	100%
☐	Unique Clicks	0%
☐	Total Clicks	0%
☐	Hard Bounces	0%
☐	Soft Bounces	0%
☐	Forwards	0%
☐	Unsubscribes	0%

Candidate versions

Version A

Version Name	*	Monthly Newsletter - Variant A
Email Name	*	Monthly Newsletter
Subject	*	My subject A
From	*	Benjamin
From Email		Benjamin [mauro@marinilli.com]
Status		
Recipients		
Send Time		

Version B

Version Name	*	Monthly Newsletter - Variant B
Email Name	*	Monthly Newsletter
Subject	*	My subject B
From	*	Benjamin
From Email		Benjamin [mauro@marinilli.com]
Status		
Recipients		
Send Time		

Send winner

○ No scheduled delivery

● Number of hours after both A/B versions sent

   Hours 48

○ Specified Time And Date

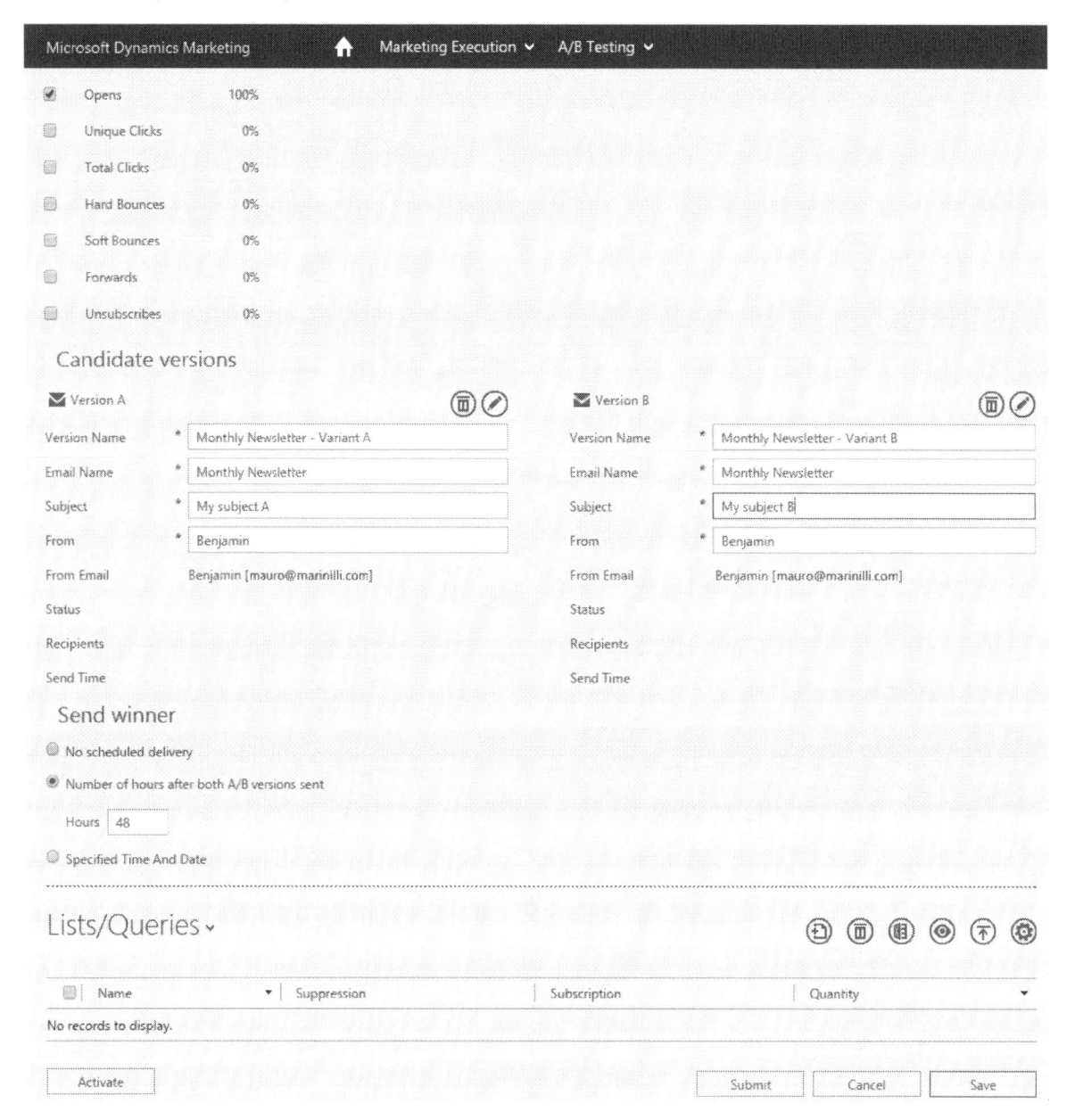

Lists/Queries

	Name	Suppression	Subscription	Quantity
☐				

No records to display.

[Activate]   [Submit] [Cancel] [Save]

Figure 6.15 –Defining the variants

At this point we are ready to activate our test.

Once a test is activated (started) we can observe the results flowing in over time under the Performance panel.

Figure 6.16 – A/B Testing Results

A/B tests results shown in the campaign automation editor

6.4 Adding Dynamic Content to Emails

Dynamic Content is a very powerful functionality available for Traceable Transactional as well as Email Marketing Messages. It is about changing some of the content of email messages based on some values of the Contact at hand.

There are four parts to what we call "dynamic content" in this book:

- Special "tags" that are substituted with the actual values from the current Contact being processed. These tags use the Razor syntax, i.e. are added in the form of @Contact.FirstName
- Content blocks selected based upon the segment (i.e. Marketing List) the Contact is in.
- Special logic executed at sending time using the Contact data and other context. This logic uses the C# syntax and it is contained in "Code Blocks".
- For traceable transactional emails, extra data can be passed to the message. This extra data is passed as an XML file via the API and consumed by the email template thanks to a predefined schema file. This "extended" data is not persisted in the DB, and it is only used for compiling and sending traceable transactional emails in Dynamics Marketing, then is discarded.

In this subsection we will look at the first three types of dynamic content supported in Dynamics Marketing. The last type will be described in the next section of this chapter.

In Dynamics Marketing dynamic content is available both in email marketing messages and in traceable email messages.

6.4.1 Inserting Recipients' Fields

Built-in fields related to the recipient's Contact are available from the "Insert Field" dropdown. User-defined fields and custom fields enabled in the Contact entity will also appear here.

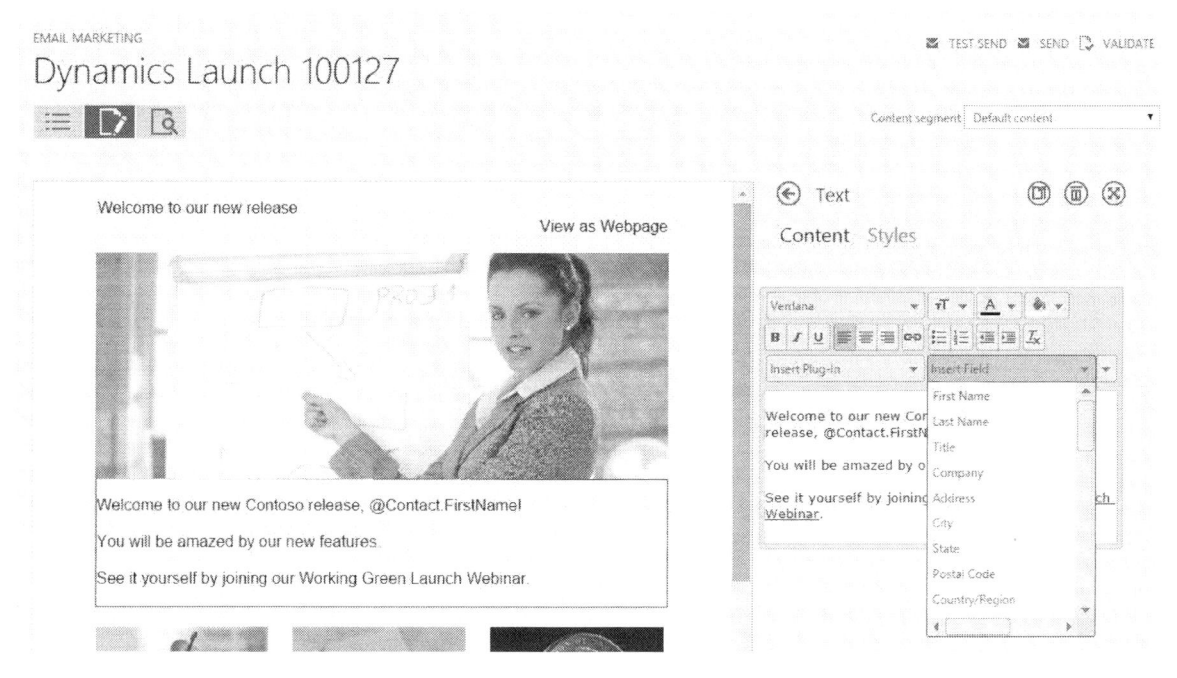

Figure 6.17 –Recipient Contact Fields in Emails

These fields will be added using the @Contact.* syntax. A similar dropdown is available also in the HTML editor.

6.4.1.1   Segment-Based Adaptation

Segment-based adaptation is about providing different version of an email based on the list your recipients are on. This is a simple yet powerful adaptation mechanism that doesn't require any technical knowledge. Note that this type of adaptation is only available in marketing emails sent manually. It is not available in marketing emails sent from the Campaign Automation module or A/B testing emails.

Both the content block editor and the HTML editor provide dropdowns from where you can change the version of an email. Below you can see where the segment-based dropdown is located in the content block editor.

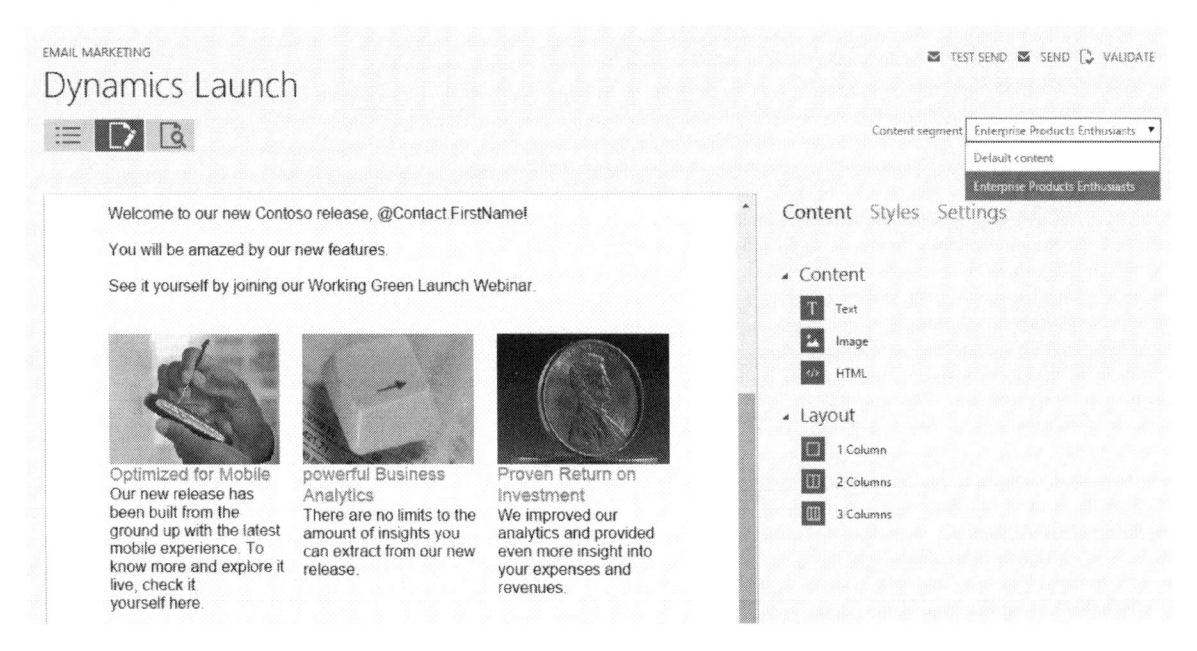

Figure 6.18 –Segment-Based Adaptation in the Content Block Editor

6.4.2 HTML Blocks - Add logic to your emails
It is possible to add HTML blocks in order to add HTML or Razor code to an email.

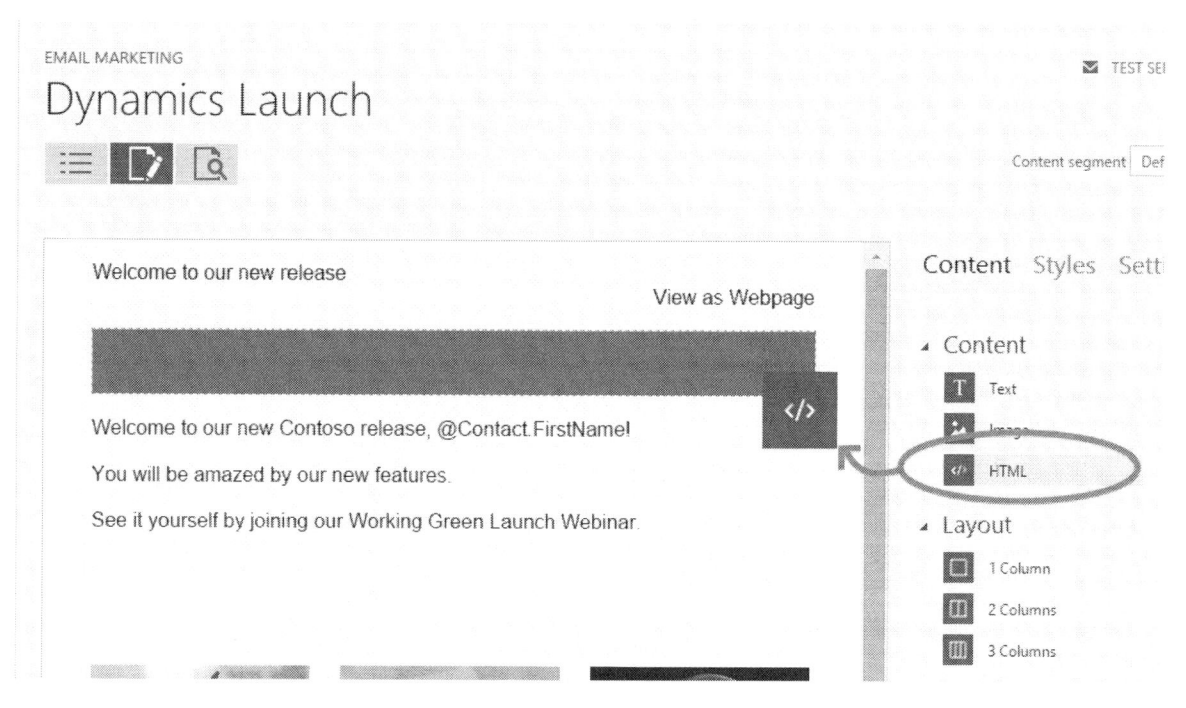

Figure 6.19 –HTML Block

By clicking on the block it is possible to edit the HTML or Razor code, see the example below:

Inside Microsoft Dynamics Marketing

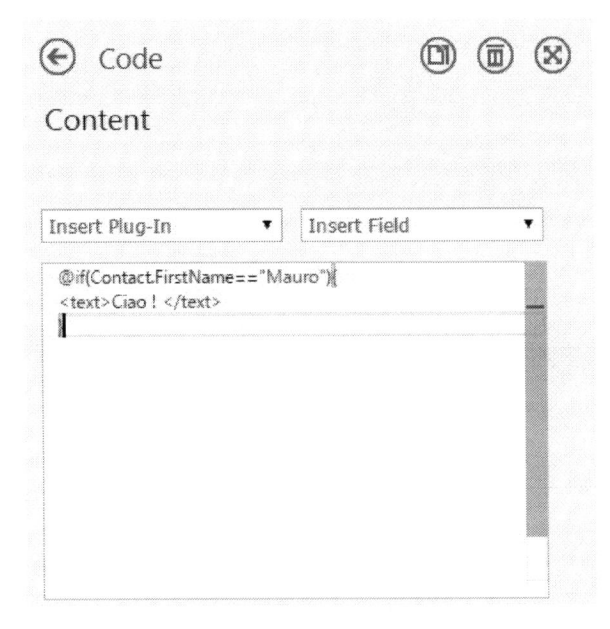

Figure 6.20 –Editing an HTML Block

The following table shows the basic constructs supported in Dynamics Marketing:

Statement	Example

If-then	@if (Contact.FirstName=="Mauro") {
	<text>Ciao!</text>
	}

If-then-else[33]	@if (Contact.FirstName=="Mauro") {
	  @:Ciao!
	}
	else
	{
	  @:Hello!
	}

---

[33] With an alternative syntax for plain text.

loop	@foreach (…) {
	
	 }

Any compliant Razor code can be added to emails, so the list above is only a small subset of what is possible.

> **TEMPLATES BUILT WITH LEGACY SYNTAX ARE STILL SUPPORTED**
>
> Legacy Dynamics Marketing releases used for dynamic content fields the syntax based on "{{}}" characters. While this syntax is still supported in the latest release, customers using old templates should move to the new and more powerful Razor syntax as the old one will become obsolete in future releases.

6.4.3 Dynamic Content in the "From" field

The "From" field (both in the content block and HTML editor) can be specified as a contact (with a valid email address) or as Razor expression, as shown below.

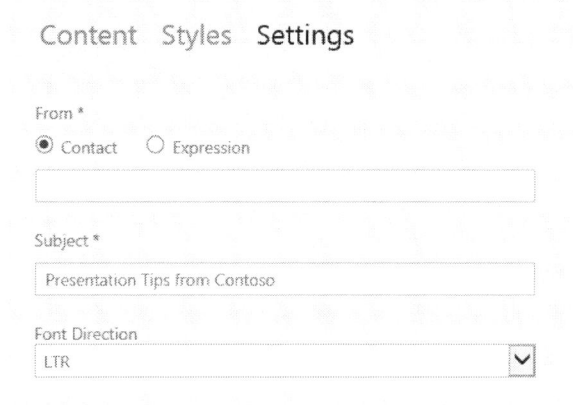

Figure 6.21 –From Field

The format is as follows:

```
FullName [Email]
```

It is possible to enter simple Razor expressions following the format above, usually involving some custom fields that will provide the email address and name of the person that will appear as if sent the email to our target Contacts.

> **EMAILS WITH INCORRECT OR MISSING "FROM" FIELD ARE NOT SENT**
>
> When sending mails to hundreds of thousands (if not millions) of contacts it can happen to have some emails sent with a malformed "From" address. Dynamics Marketing takes a conservative approach and does not send these emails in order to keep high deliverability rates and avoid confusing recipients.
> Marketers can look at the "Invalid Sender Email" line in the Performance Summary and in the Contacts panel for contact with "Invalid Sender Email" type.

Dynamics Marketing already supports the notion of roles for a given Contact, including the role of primary sales representative. You are not required to use this existing functionality, you can use any custom field as wanted.

6.4.3.1 Primary Sales Rep in Dynamics Marketing

This section describes how to leverage the standard Dynamics Marketing way to track primary sales representatives and how to use it to send emails appearing as they were sent from a contact's primary sales rep (so that recipients can reply to the right person).

In Dynamics Marketing the Teams panel shows the contacts that have relationships with a given record. We can assign a primary sales representative to a Contact as shown below.

Inside Microsoft Dynamics Marketing

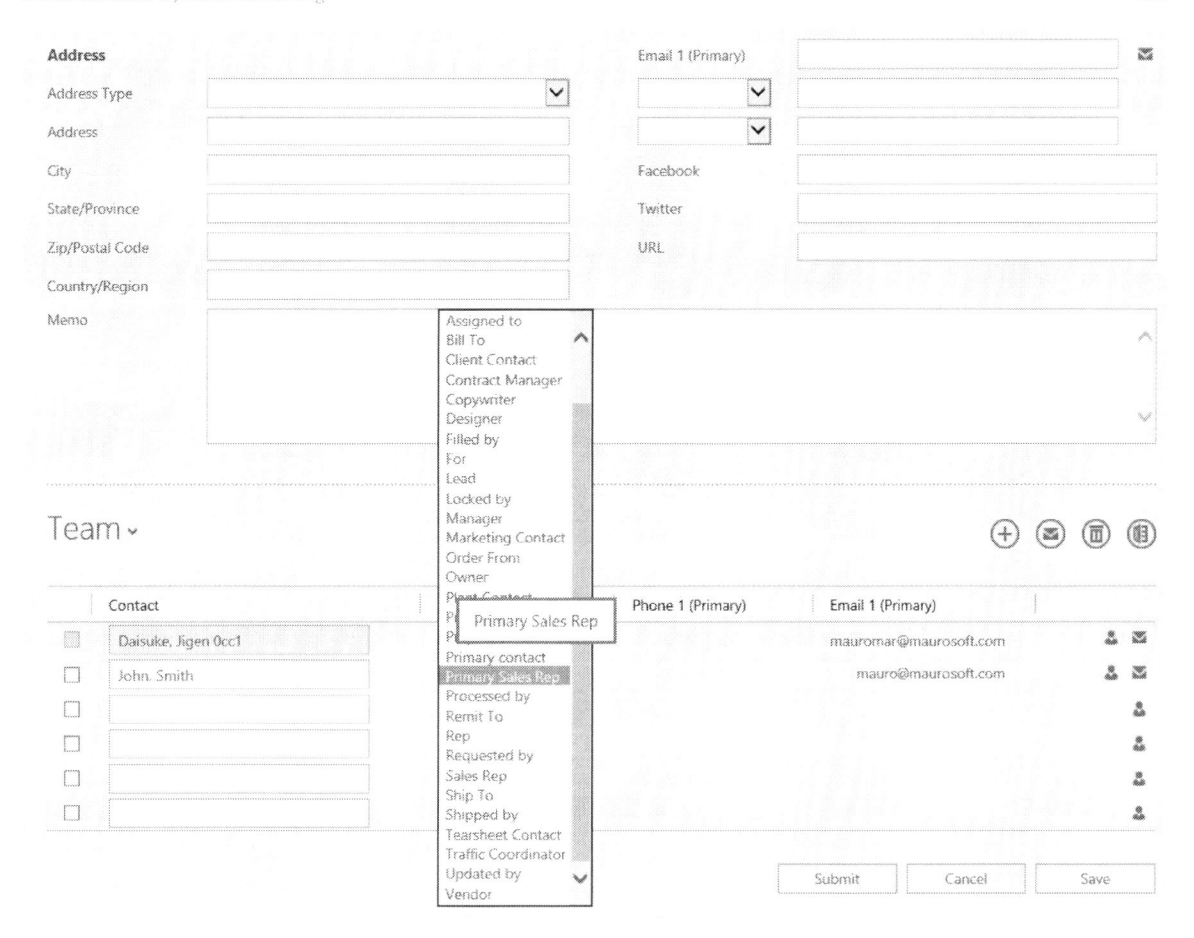

Figure 6.22 –The Primary Sales Rep role in the Team panel

Once we have this data setup in all our recipient contacts we can define the following expression in the "From" field:

@Contact.PrimarySalesRepresentativeFullName [@Contact.PrimarySalesRepresentativeEmail]

This expression will send emails having in the "From" field the primary sales rep contact defined as shown above. This increases the open rates (the email appear as sent from a familiar and relevant person rather than a generic address) and enables recipients to reply directly to the right person.

When integrating with Dynamics CRM the final step is to set up the connector mappings in order to carry the relevant contact from Dynamics CRM.

6.4.4 Entities in Emails

It is possible to add links directly to three type of entities from an email:

- Offers
- Webinars
- Landing Pages

This can be done by expanding the toolbar in the text editor as shown below.

Figure 6.23 –Adding Entities to an Email

In the extended toolbar the first dropdown is used to select the entity type:

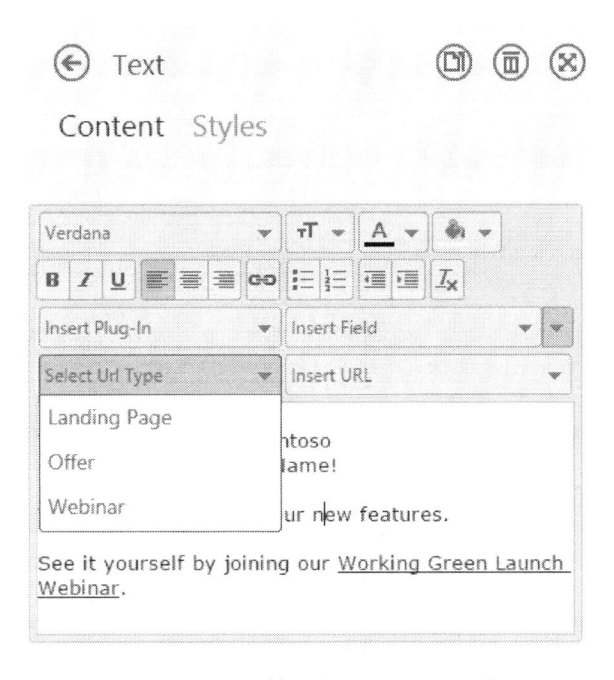

Figure 6.24 –Adding Entities to an Email

Then the second dropdown ("Insert URL") will add one record for that entity into the email. This can be used to add links to offers, webinars or landing pages in the text block. Chapter 2 "Campaign Automation" shows how these entities are made available in campaign automation models.

It is possible to reuse the expressions built with the dropdowns above in the HTML editor.

6.5 Sending Emails via API

Dynamics Marketing allows sending emails (both with Designation traceable transactional and Commercial) via an API call when the "Send Externally" checkbox is ticked:

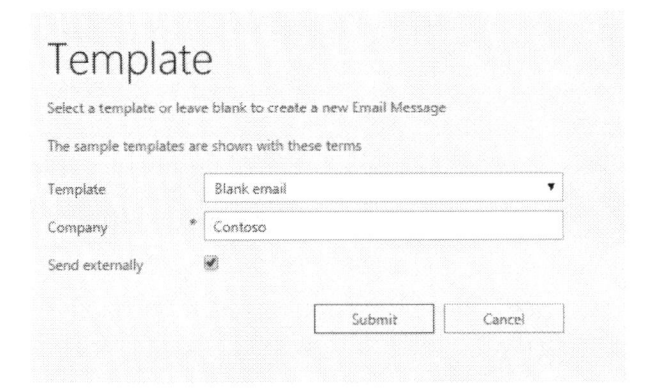

Figure 6.25 –Choosing a Template

Note that once the email message is saved with "Send Externally" ticked this property cannot be changed afterwards. If users don't specify this value at this step (and it is not specified already in the template) they can specify it in the message later. All these controls in the UI ensure that the list of messages that are marked as "Send Externally" remain consistent and can be queried in advance from an external system via our dedicated API.

> ***THE "SEND EXTERNALLY" OPTION***
>
> Conceptually the "Send Externally" option delegates sending the message entirely to the dedicated API. As such all the actions related to sending out the email (manually via the UI) are disabled for this kind of messages.
>
> The "Send Externally" is an option available only after this functionality is made available via a preliminary configuration. If this functionality is not enabled user will not see the "Send Externally" checkbox.

6.6 Creating Traceable Transactional Emails

As we have seen traceable transactional emails are emails that are sent as transactional (i.e. ensuring the highest deliverability) but provide the same power as traditional email marketing messages in terms of content and traceability. The days of boring to read and untraceable notification emails are over with Dynamics Marketing.

Traceable transactional emails are created using the same UI as Email Marketing messages, with the difference

The editing experience is the same as of Email Marketing (although some panels like List / Queries or plug-ins and subscription centers or the Test button are not available).

Let's now have a look at the details of the extra content capabilities that are available when creating traceable transactional emails. Sending them will be the subject of the next section.

6.6.1 Creating Traceable Transactional Emails

A client of an agency using Dynamics Marketing, a flower shop, wants to send email receipts to their customers. Some custom code will call Dynamics Marketing in order to send the receipt email with the actual user data. These emails must be delivered with the highest deliverability level and at the same time they will have all the bells and whistles of state of the art email marketing, both in terms of dynamic content and visual appearance. And thanks to Dynamics Marketing infrastructure, the customer can easily scale to very large volumes of emails, if needed to, effortlessly.

Our task is to prepare the content of the email that will be sent via the API for traceable transactional emails in Dynamics Marketing.

We could create an email template in order to reuse the message multiple times. But before digging into the email content let's look at how we can specify external content sources for traceable transactional emails in Dynamics Marketing. In order to do so we create a new External Content record. The form is available under:

```
Home > Marketing Execution > Email Marketing → External Content
```

Here we fill in the mandatory fields and upload an XSD schema file representing the external content fields.

EXTERNAL CONTENT

FlowerPower Content

Status	*	Active
Name	*	FlowerPower Content
File	*	flowers
Description		

Emails

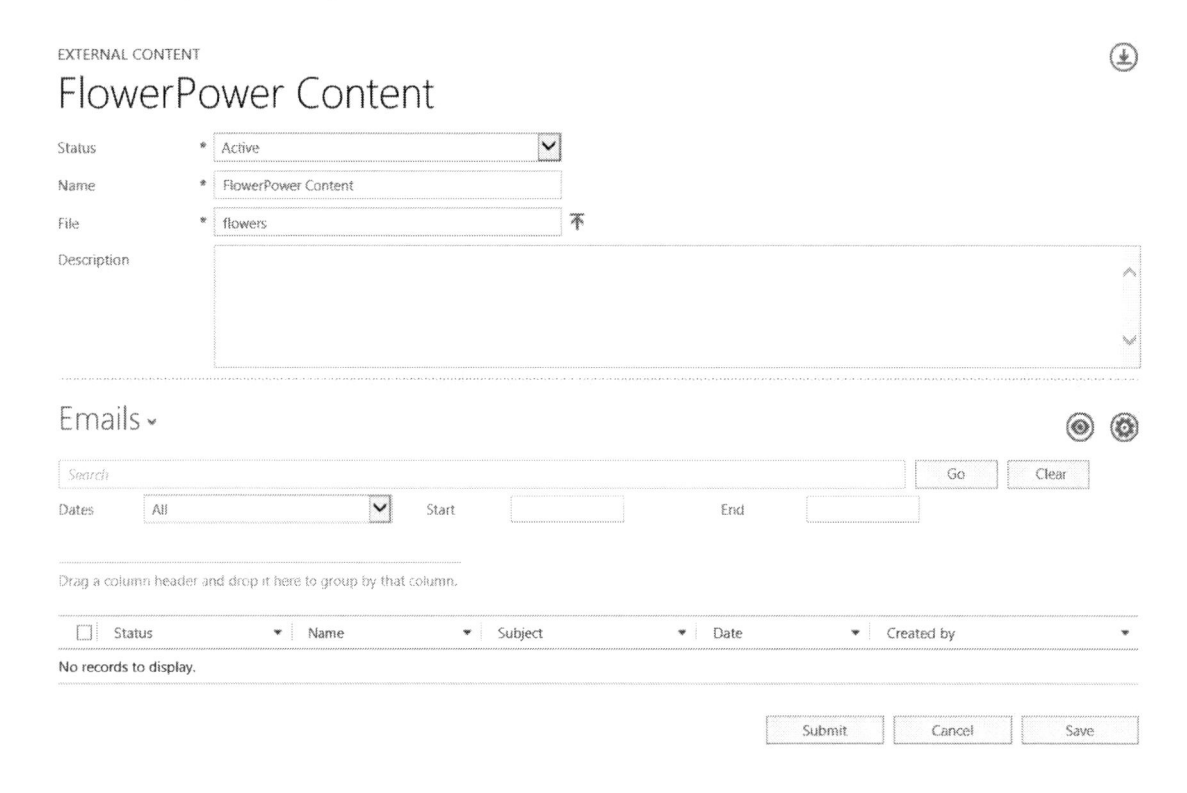

Figure 6.26 –External Content

This is the schema file we upload:

```xml
<?xml version="1.0" encoding="utf-8"?>
<xs:schema xmlns:xsi="http://www.w3.org/2001/XMLSchema-instance"
xmlns:xsd="http://www.w3.org/2001/XMLSchema"
xmlns:xs="http://www.w3.org/2001/XMLSchema" attributeFormDefault="unqualified"
elementFormDefault="qualified">
  <xsd:element name="FlowersReceipt">
    <xsd:complexType>
      <xsd:sequence>
        <xsd:element name="FlowerName" type="xsd:string" />
        <xsd:element name="BouquetStyle" type="xsd:string" />
      </xsd:sequence>
    </xsd:complexType>
  </xsd:element>
</xs:schema>
```

Inside Microsoft Dynamics Marketing

Now we are ready to use the external content we just defined in a traceable transactional email message. We will have our external code pick this message when sending receipts from our flower shop.

When creating the receipt message we tick the "Send externally" option. By marking this message as external a new panel in the related information dropdown is available for specifying the external content we might want to use, as shown below.

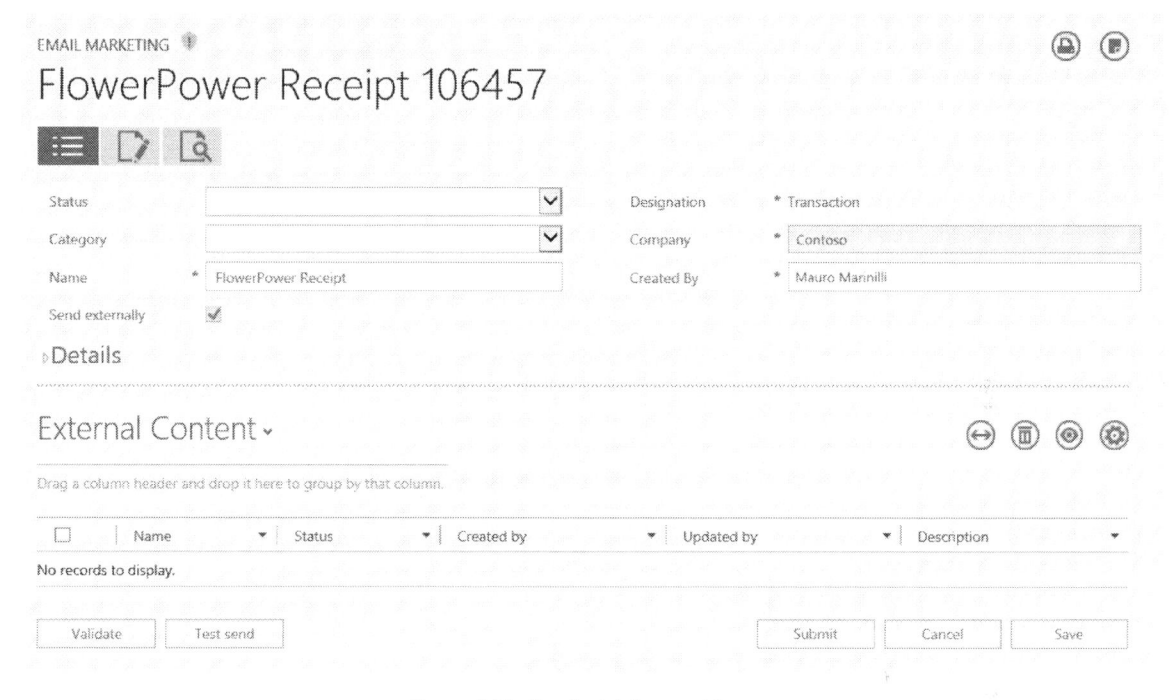

Figure 6.27 –Email with External Content

We assign our external content to this message, so we can use the newly added external content fields to our content.

At this point we are able to use the new fields in our message using the @Ext.* syntax in a codeblock.

For example we can add to the message the two fields defined in the schema

```
You bought a @Ext.BouquetStyle made of @Ext.FlowerName.
```

Inside Microsoft Dynamics Marketing

And when saving the message Dynamics Marketing will verify these fields are part of the namespace for this message, otherwise a validation error will be shown.

So we can put together a transactional email, fully traceable, using these external fields:

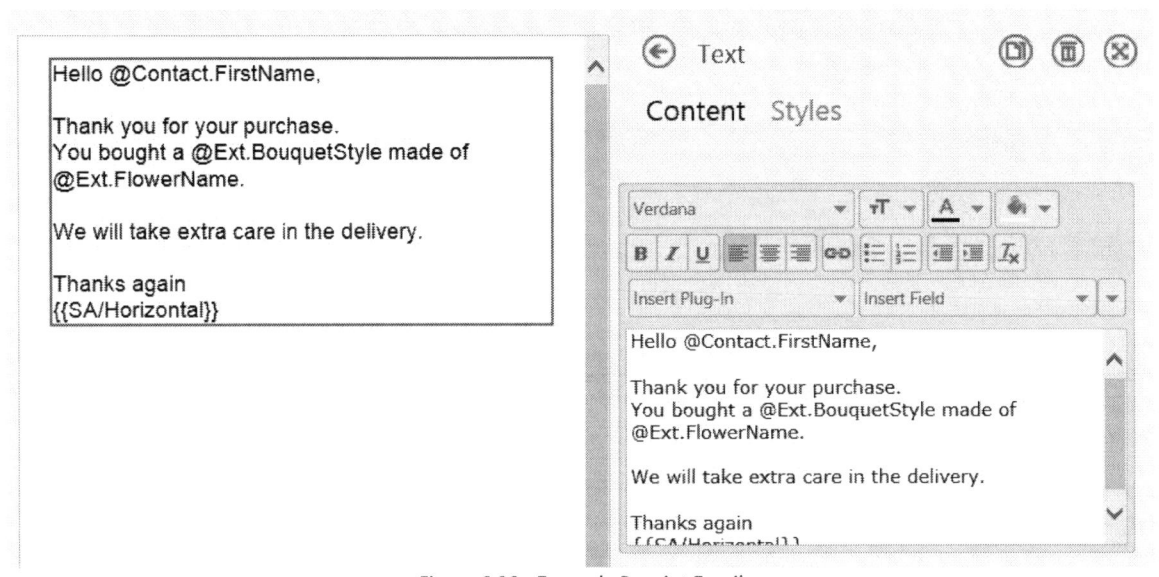

Figure 6.28 –Example Receipt Email

At this point we are ready with our content. We save it and take note of the ID for this message so that we can call it from our API later.

Schemas can be more complex than mere simple fields, and we can iterate over multiple records and include these iterative items in our emails.

Let's change the schema for our external content to the following:

```
<?xml version="1.0" encoding="utf-8"?>
<xs:schema attributeFormDefault="unqualified" elementFormDefault="qualified"
xmlns:xs="http://www.w3.org/2001/XMLSchema">
  <xs:element name="FlowersReceipt">
    <xs:complexType>
      <xs:sequence>
        <xsd:element name="FlowerName" type="xsd:string" />
        <xsd:element name="BouquetStyle" type="xsd:string" />
        <xs:element name="PurchaseItems">
          <xs:complexType>
```

```
            <xs:sequence>
              <xs:element minOccurs="0" maxOccurs="unbounded" name="PurchaseItem">
                <xs:complexType>
                  <xs:sequence>
                    <xs:element name="Quantity" type="xs:unsignedByte" />
                    <xs:element name="ItemName" type="xs:string" />
                    <xs:element name="ItemPrice" type="xs:decimal" />
                  </xs:sequence>
                </xs:complexType>
              </xs:element>
            </xs:sequence>
          </xs:complexType>
        </xs:element>
      </xsd:sequence>
    </xsd:complexType>
  </xsd:element>
</xs:schema>
```

Now we can handle a list of items as part of our receipt.

We now need to extend our email content to handle these items.

The following code block in our traceable transactional email will iterate over the items passed in the external data via the API (providing purchase information) and print them in a table in our email.

```
<table>
@foreach (var purchase in @Ext.PurchaseItems)
{
<tr>
    <td>@purchase.ItemName</td>
    <td>@purchase.ItemPrice</td>
    <td>@purchase.Quantity</td>
</tr>
}
</table>
```

6.6.2   Sending Traceable Transactional Emails

Assuming we have created in Dynamics Marketing the message we want to send as seen previously and have done all the setup required for accessing the external Send API (described in detail in Chapter 12 "Development Scenarios") we are now ready to send our first traceable transactional email.

When we invoke the API to send out a message, we will specify the message ID for this message and an XML file with the proper values for the fields specified in this template.

6.7 EXTERNAL SUBSCRIPTION CENTER

Dynamics Marketing provides an integrated subscription center facility that simplifies the user preferences management and improves legal compliance for our email marketing campaigns. External Subscription centers are used by those customers that employ their own subscription centers and user preferences.

An external subscription center is an advanced functionality that should be used with care, mostly because of legal reasons. When external subscription centers are used marketing managers will have the onus of managing unsubscribes and tracking the related statistics. As such, we suggest to employ external subscription centers only when strictly needed.

Simply put, an external subscription center is just a URL we can embed in our emails that can be constructed with parameters from Dynamics Marketing so that it opens an external web page where recipients can manage their email preferences.

We create a new plug-in by navigating to:

```
Home > Settings > Campaign Management→ Email Marketing Plug-ins
```

And here we create a new plug-in of type "External Subscription Center":

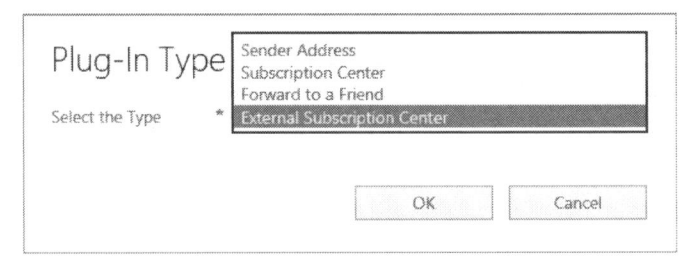

Figure 6.29 –Creating an External Subscription Center

In this form we enter all the information needed to create our external subscription center:

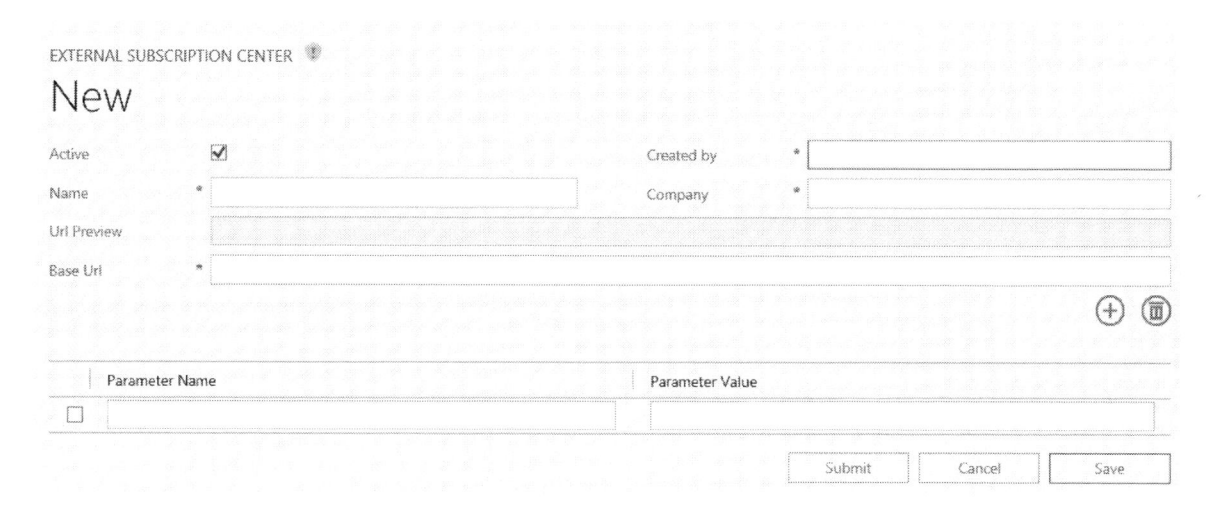

Figure 6.30 –Empty External Subscription Center

We specify the base URL for the service that will generate the preferences page for our recipients. For example our base service is https://maurospreferencecenter.com/.

Now we add the parameters that will be passed to this base URL to create the recipient preference page. The most common parameter used by these services is the email address of the recipient, for our example let's say our service accepts a parameter "email" for this.

We now select the value from Dynamics Marketing used to populate the "email" parameter, as shown below:

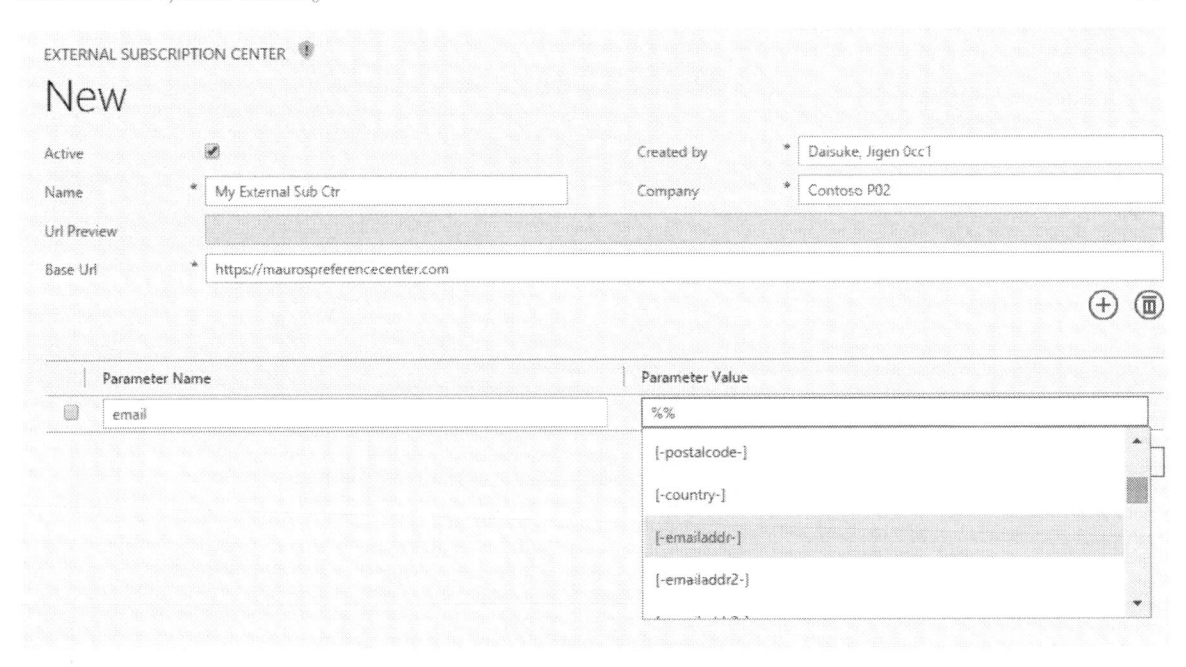

Figure 6.31 –Parameter Values in an Ext. Subscription Center

Dynamics Marketing allows the use of many parameter values, including UDFs and contact fields and fields from the email itself (so that I can have a UDF per email message that can be passed to my external subscription center).

So now I save my new external subscription center and use it in my emails. When a recipient with email address "m@marinilli.com" receives an email and clicks on the subscription center link to manage his email preferences he will be opening the following URL:

```
https://maurospreferencecenter.com:443/?email=m@marinilli.com
```

Dynamics Marketing will not check if there is a valid service at this address or whether the user effectively unsubscribed from the email or just opened the link for curiosity without performing any choice. It is up to the provider of the external preferences service to register the user input and include it in the future mailings to that recipient, for example by means of a suppression list in Dynamics Marketing.

6.8 Contact Permissions Email API

The contact permissions API is used to control email sending from an external system. Similar to the external subscription center is an advanced functionality that might not be required by most customers. You can think of it as an additional filtering based on email addresses.

The contact permissions API allows the control of emails sent by Dynamics Marketing based on email address. Such permissions can be operated (both read and write) only via the API. Contact permissions are assigned per email address, not contact. Two types of permissions can be assigned (or retrieved):

- *Global suppression list*. Dynamics Marketing will never send any email (including traceable transactional emails and excluding plain "1:1" transactional emails) to the addresses in this list.
- *Topics*. These are "tags" that can be associated to a mailing using the Topic category field under the "Details" expandable panel of an email message Summary tab. Via the API you assign the topics a given email address is not allowed to receive and then you can assign topics to emails while creating them and send them to your lists as usual. Dynamics Marketing will automatically filter out those contacts having the email address not registered for that given topic.

When sending emails from Dynamics Marketing and employing this API the emails that are blocked because of these rules will appear in the Performance panel, Summary, in the "Blocked due to Contact Permission Rules" line. If the API is never used, there will be no additional filtering and the "Blocked due to Contact Permission Rules" line will always be empty (zero filtered contacts).

6.9 Identify Duplicate Contacts

Identifying and de-duplicating redundant contacts is a common task in any digital marketing solution. Dynamics Marketing, when coupled with Dynamics CRM can leverage the latter's deduplication capabilities, although in some cases marketers might still want some extra control when sending communications or accepting inbound leads.

Dynamics Marketing can be configured to prevent multiple contacts (having the same "Belongs To" company) from sharing the same email address. These settings define when the system should create a new contact or update an existing one. They are found in the "Duplicate Detection" group under the Contact Options in the Site Settings page:

```
Home > Settings > Administration → Site Settings
```

These settings also affect the duplicate detection algorithm, when a marketing contact is registering on a landing page or contacts are imported in the system.

On top of these global settings, Dynamics Marketing enables yet another level of control, by giving marketers the ability of configuring duplicate per Company, via an option in the Company settings.

This way, for example, all companies in your system will allow for contacts to share the same email address (for example you work with public government offices and they do tend to share the same institutional email addresses although they are routed to different officials). But in some specific cases you might want to send emails only once to such duplicate addresses and keep track of which contact was used, etc.

6.10 TROUBLESHOOTING EMAIL DELIVERY

Understanding why some emails were not sent or were sent but never reached the recipient inbox can be complicated. Dynamics Marketing offers a non-technical, business oriented application on top of the complex and ever-changing world of email marketing deliverability, and offers an extensive reporting facility for troubleshooting such scenarios.

The following section will describe the most common reasons why Dynamics Marketing did not send an email to a given recipient. The second section will touch briefly the more complex topic of what happens to our emails once Dynamics Marketing sends them out. The remaining sections will touch other aspects related to email delivery.

Finally, if despite all your best attempts you still cannot make sense of why some emails didn't get in the inbox then you can consider open a Service Request with the Microsoft email deliverability support team.

6.10.1 Why that email was not sent?

Dynamics Marketing offers many ways to control email sending that can be triggered in unexpected ways. And on top of that, genuine mistakes from busy marketers can happen too. Let's see here all the possibilities and what can go "wrong" with sending our emails for a given recipient.

- **Cross-Campaign rules**. One or more cross-campaign rule can block sending an email to some recipients. Open the Performance panel, Summary and see the "Blocked due to Cross-Campaign Rules" line.
- **Do not Email** flag set for some contact(s). The Do not email checkbox indicates that the contact will not receive any email. See later in this section for a discussion on this field.

- **Invalid "Primary Email"** (used for the "To" field) email address. Attempting to send to an invalid email address will result in a "hard bounce" and the primary address will be removed. You can still see what the invalid email was by opening the Contacts panel and finding the "Email Address" field for that contact.
- **Invalid "Primary Email" of the "From"** contact (used for the "Reply to" and "From") email address. This can happen when an expression is used for the "From" field. Open the Performance panel, Summary and see the "Invalid Sender email" line.
- Because of **Contact Permissions API** rules. Open the Performance panel, Summary and see the "Blocked due to Contact Permission Rules" line. See a complete discussion of this API later in this chapter.
- **Empty dynamic list** at the moment of sending. Dynamic lists can be changing at runtime and you should verify the list had some contacts with a valid email address at the time of sending.
- The recipient email address is recognized as a match in Dynamics Marketing **stop-word list**. Dynamics Marketing maintains an internal list of keywords that are not allowed in email addresses by anti-spam systems. Email addresses such as "abuse"@.. or "postmaster"@.. will be rejected by ISPs so Dynamics Marketing blocks them preemptively. These will appear as "hard bounces" in your statistics.

Performance

▷ Chart
▲ Summary

	Actual		Estimate		Variance	
	%	Qty	%	Qty	%	Qty
Sent	100%	0	100%	0	0.00%	0
Delivered	0.00%	0	0 %	0	0.00%	0
Opened	0.00%	0	0 %	0	0.00%	0
Unique clicks	0.00%	0	0 %	0	0.00%	0
Total clicks	0.00%	0	0 %	0	0.00%	0
Hard bounces	0.00%	0	0 %	0	0.00%	0
Soft bounces	0.00%	0	0 %	0	0.00%	0
Forwards	0.00%	0	0 %	0	0.00%	0
Unsubscribes	0.00%	0	0 %	0	0.00%	0
Unsubscribes per List	0.00%	0	0 %	0	0.00%	0
Leads	0.00%	0	0 %	0	0.00%	0
Blocked due to Cross-Campaign Rules	0.00%	3	0 %	0	0.00%	3
Blocked due to Contact Permission Rules	0.00%	0	0 %	0	0.00%	0
Invalid Sender email	0.00%	0	0 %	0	0.00%	0

Figure 6.32 –Performance panel, Summary

THE "DO NOT EMAIL" FIELD

The "Do not Email" checkbox is located in the Details related information panel of the Contact form. When this checkbox is ticked promotional emails will not be sent to this Contact. This information can be set in three ways:
 - manually by a Dynamics Marketing user in the Contact form
 - via the connector from the connected Dynamics CRM instance
 - by the recipient, when editing his or her subscription center, by clicking on the "unsubscribe all" option.
In the last case, when the recipient unsubscribes all from our communications, even if the checkbox is unselected in the Contact form (by an Dynamics Marketing user for example) the contact will still not receive any email. This might be confusing because

when a recipient "unsubscribes all" and someone then tries to revert the "Do Not Email" in the UI the communications are still not sent but this information is not evident in the product.

In case you are in doubt that some contacts might have an inaccurate "Do Not Email" value, contact Microsoft Support that will provide a list of Contacts that "unsubscribed all".

6.10.2 Email Marketing Deliverability

Every user of Dynamics Marketing email marketing functionality must be aware of email deliverability best practices. The Dynamics Marketing team has published on the Internet a detailed guide discussing the main items to be aware of when crafting email marketing messages.

You can think of sending email marketing messages on the Internet as analogous to driving a car on a public street. There are rules that need to be followed. Incurring in antisocial behavior will lead to your driving license to be suspended. Dynamics Marketing has an entire team devoted to monitoring the usage of email marketing and enforcing such rules. The team can also be contacted for addressing deliverability issues that can always arise despite our best efforts. The team is dedicated to analyzing feedback loops, bounces, back off notices and addressing customers' deliverability issues.

"BAD" URLS IN EMAILS ARE REMOVED AUTOMATICALLY

In order to provide the highest deliverability rates Dynamics Marketing will inspect all URLs in emails being sent and will automatically remove those signaled as Spam by some major anti-spam service, without further notice to the user.

6.10.3 Emails Marked as Spam

Some recipient might mark as spam some of our emails, despite our best efforts to be relevant and engaging in our communications. Dynamics Marketing will track these as part of the "unsubscribes" KPI. If we suspect we are having too many of these we can always open a Service Request to get the actual exact number of "marked as spam".

6.10.4 Blocked Sender IPs

Given that sender IP addressed are pooled some customers fret about the possibility of some Dynamics Marketing sender IP addresses being blocked ("blacklisted") due to spamming by some other (possibly unwary) Dynamics Marketing customer and thus impacting their own traffic. While still technically possible, this can be seen as a rare eventuality. The Dynamics Marketing deliverability team is constantly monitor the sending quality and is able to guarantee extremely high deliverability rates. Even in the case this would happen Dynamics Marketing infrastructure is built in a way that other IPs will absorb the queueing traffic with minimal impact to other customers. Customers might experience some slower processing but no major disruption. Customers sending "offending" mailings (because of content or not respecting anti-Spam laws etc.) will be approached by Microsoft on a case-by-case basis (depending upon frequency and severity of the issues, etc.).

In general Dynamics Marketing will own the sending IPs and will be responsible for interfacing with the various ISPs and address any deliverability issue that might arise.

6.11 Advanced Email Configuration

6.11.1 Customizing Sending Information

As mentioned before, Dynamics Marketing emails appears to be sent from the "From" address field. This email address will show up in the "From" field in the recipient's Inbox. The email server in the email message headers will be a different domain, even though recipients will see the "From" address set in the email message in Dynamics Marketing. The reason why the email message headers will be from a different domain is because this allows sending domain reputation to be clustered among all Dynamics Marketing customers and thus providing higher sending volumes and other email deliverability benefits. For users it is quite straightforward to send emails appearing to be sent from the company's addresses.

One can consult Microsoft documentation to get the IP ranges used for the various regions to add them to their IP whitelist and the SPF and DKIM records that the customer can add to the company DNS. Note that Microsoft has configured already SPF and DKIM for its sending domains so customer DNS configuration is not necessary. Even if not strictly needed, various customers like to configure the DNS for their domain to separate a part of the reputation back to their company domain. If your company requires this configuration, refer to Microsoft documentation for more details.

Finally, few Dynamics Marketing customers might want to send from a private pool of IP addresses (not shared with other Dynamics Marketing customers). They can ask Microsoft on how to configure this functionality although this will require a large and steady delivery volumes and strict deliverability practices.

6.11.2 Custom SMTP Server

Some organizations prefer to use their own SMTP server for "plain transactional" emails (see previous chapter for a discussion of this type of emails).

If this is the case you will need to open a Service Request with Dynamics Marketing Support to get this set up as needed. Note that this option was available in Dynamics Marketing in releases prior to Dynamics Marketing Fall 2014, since this release this configuration is not available anymore in the product UI.

6.12 DOUBLE OPT-IN

The double opt-in feature in Microsoft Dynamics Marketing allows new marketing contacts coming from landing pages to be added to the database only after their email address has been verified. The verification requires contacts to click on an activation link in a confirmation email. This improves the quality of the acquired contacts and makes marketing companies comply with the law in various countries.

In a nutshell this is the supported process:

1. a new potential marketing contact fills out a form built with a Dynamics Marketing landing page, configured for double opt-in.
2. when submitting the form, the prospect contact is instructed to check their email inbox for a confirmation message, and click on the activation link in the message to confirm the email address and provide consent to be added to the marketing database.
3. Dynamics Marketing creates the new contact, with the "Do Not Email" flag set to "true", so that the contact cannot be used in campaigns until it gets fully activated. At the same time Dynamics Marketing sends a confirmation email to the email address of the newly created contact.
4. The user opens confirmation email and clicks on the activation link. The click is registered with Dynamics Marketing and the user is redirected to a welcome page.
5. At this point the user provided consent and acknowledged the email address as valid. So Dynamics Marketing changes the contact's "Do Not Email" flag to "false" and sends a welcome email to the user.
6. At any time a marketer can inspect the process progress for each contact and landing page, as follows:
    a. Open the Contact page and then select the Email opt-in related information panel.

b. Open the Landing Page and then select the Contacts related information panel.

In summary the double opt-in functionality requires:

- A Confirmation email. This is an email message with Designation "Double opt-in".
- A double-opt-in-link plug-in. This plug-in creates the opt-in confirmation link to be included in marketing emails and the redirect URL to open the "thank you" page;
- An optional Welcome email. This is an email message with Designation "Commercial" and the "Send recurring" checkbox enabled. This email will be automatically sent to users that complete the opt-in process.

> **CONFIRMATION AND WELCOME EMAILS ARE COUNTED AS MARKETING EMAILS**
>
> All confirmation and welcome emails sent by the system are calculated against the email marketing sending quota.

The double opt-in is configured per company, so all landing pages created under that company will use the setting. If you don't have multiple companies then you can configure it for the Site Company in

`Home > Settings > My Company → Company Settings`

If you have multiple companies then you can configure double opt-in for each company.

CHAPTER SEVEN
HOME PAGE AND ANALYTICS

7.1 OVERVIEW

Dynamics Marketing provides a rich offering of analytics, in the form of internal reports and KPIs, available for the various functional areas of the product and also from the user home page. On top of this already remarkable offering, Dynamics Marketing also makes available select data as external data sources supplied in a standard format that can be consumed by clients such as Microsoft Excel for additional customizable reporting and analysis.

> **DYNAMICS MARKETING WIDGET PANE**
>
> Dynamics Marketing provides a widget pane in the right hand side of the screen providing similar widgets to the ones available in the home page.

7.2 HOME PAGE

Dynamics Marketing home page is the first page shown when a user opens the product. You can reach it clicking on the home icon in the top navigation area. You can personalize its content by adding removing or configuring a number of components, called "widgets". Your contact's picture in the header in the home page doubles as a handy link to your Contact form.

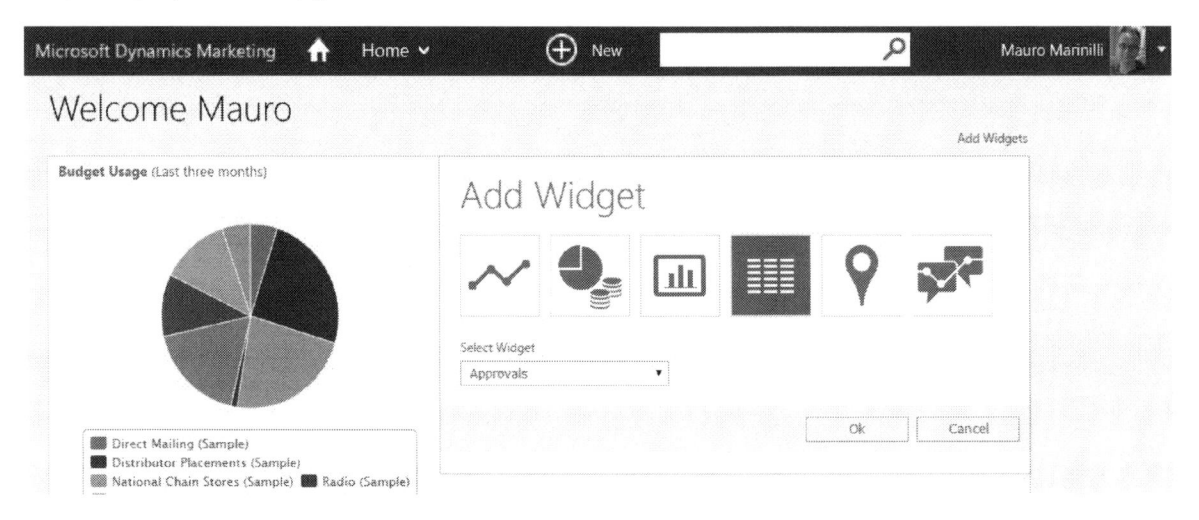

Figure 7.1 – Adding a Widget to your Home Page

By clicking on the "Add Widgets" link is possible to add a new widget to your home page.

The following table describes the various options available:

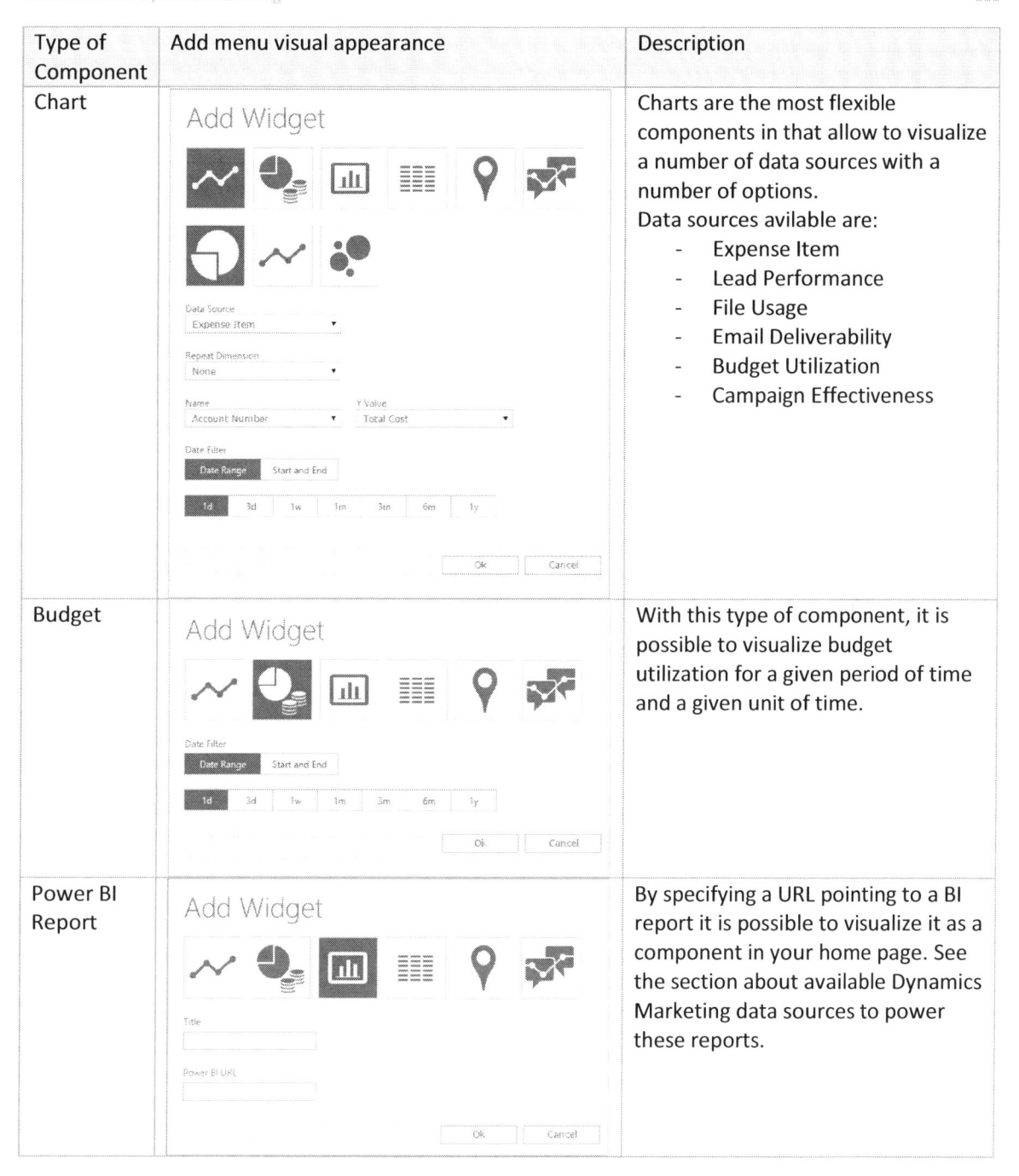

Type of Component	Add menu visual appearance	Description
Chart	*(Add Widget dialog with chart type icons, Data Source: Expense Item, Repeat Dimension: None, Name: Account Number, Y Value: Total Cost, Date Filter with Date Range/Start and End options: 1d, 3d, 1w, 1m, 3m, 6m, 1y)*	Charts are the most flexible components in that allow to visualize a number of data sources with a number of options. Data sources avilable are: - Expense Item - Lead Performance - File Usage - Email Deliverability - Budget Utilization - Campaign Effectiveness
Budget	*(Add Widget dialog with chart type icons, Date Filter with Date Range/Start and End options: 1d, 3d, 1w, 1m, 3m, 6m, 1y)*	With this type of component, it is possible to visualize budget utilization for a given period of time and a given unit of time.
Power BI Report	*(Add Widget dialog with chart type icons, Title field, Power BI URL field)*	By specifying a URL pointing to a BI report it is possible to visualize it as a component in your home page. See the section about available Dynamics Marketing data sources to power these reports.

Inside Microsoft Dynamics Marketing

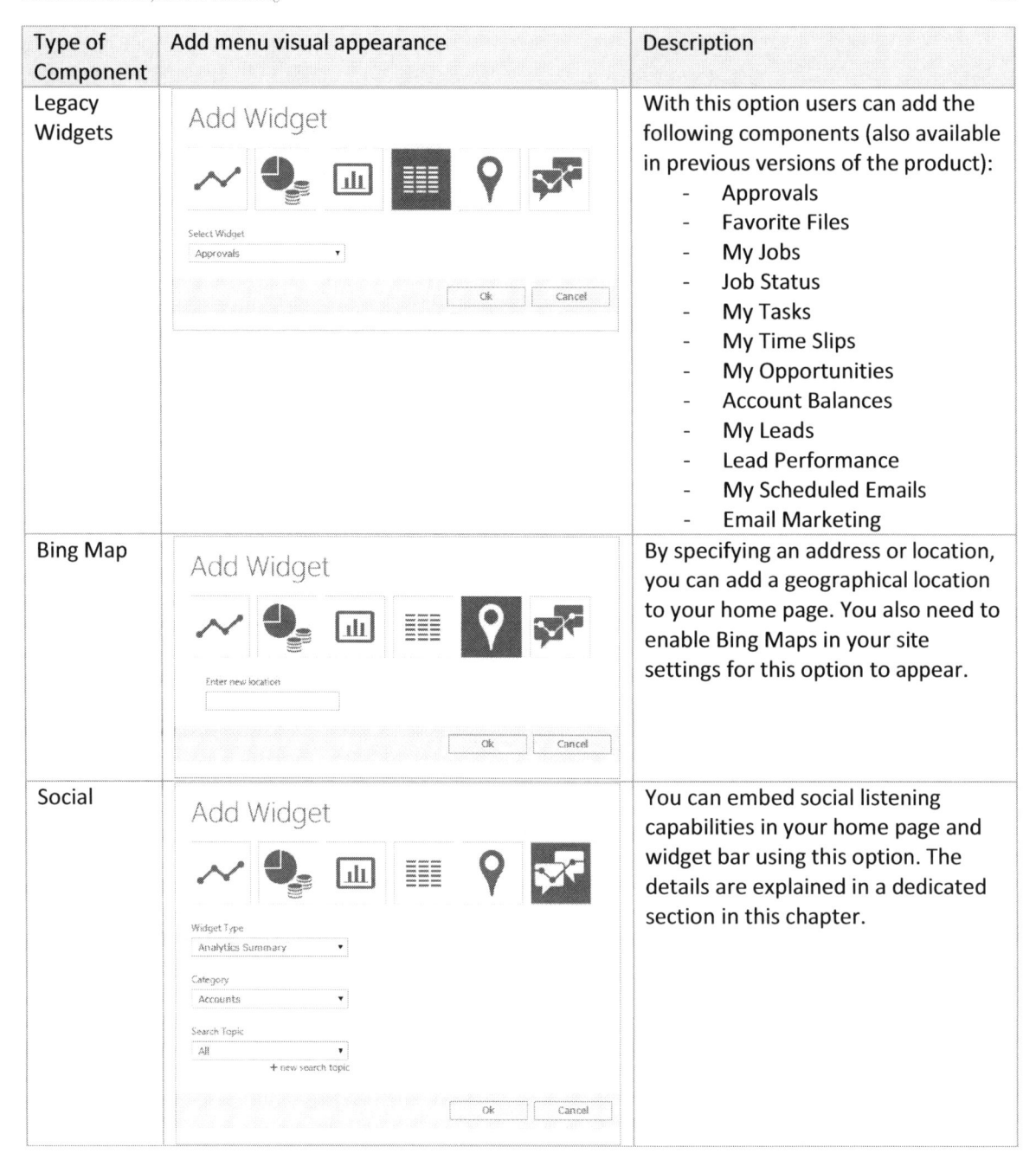

Type of Component	Add menu visual appearance	Description
Legacy Widgets	Add Widget / Select Widget: Approvals / Ok Cancel	With this option users can add the following components (also available in previous versions of the product): - Approvals - Favorite Files - My Jobs - Job Status - My Tasks - My Time Slips - My Opportunities - Account Balances - My Leads - Lead Performance - My Scheduled Emails - Email Marketing
Bing Map	Add Widget / Enter new location / Ok Cancel	By specifying an address or location, you can add a geographical location to your home page. You also need to enable Bing Maps in your site settings for this option to appear.
Social	Add Widget / Widget Type: Analytics Summary / Category: Accounts / Search Topic: All / + new search topic / Ok Cancel	You can embed social listening capabilities in your home page and widget bar using this option. The details are explained in a dedicated section in this chapter.

7.3 Dynamics Marketing Social Analytics

Dynamics Marketing provides a seamless integration with Microsoft Social Listening, enabling a wide range of sophisticated social listening analytics right within Dynamics Marketing.

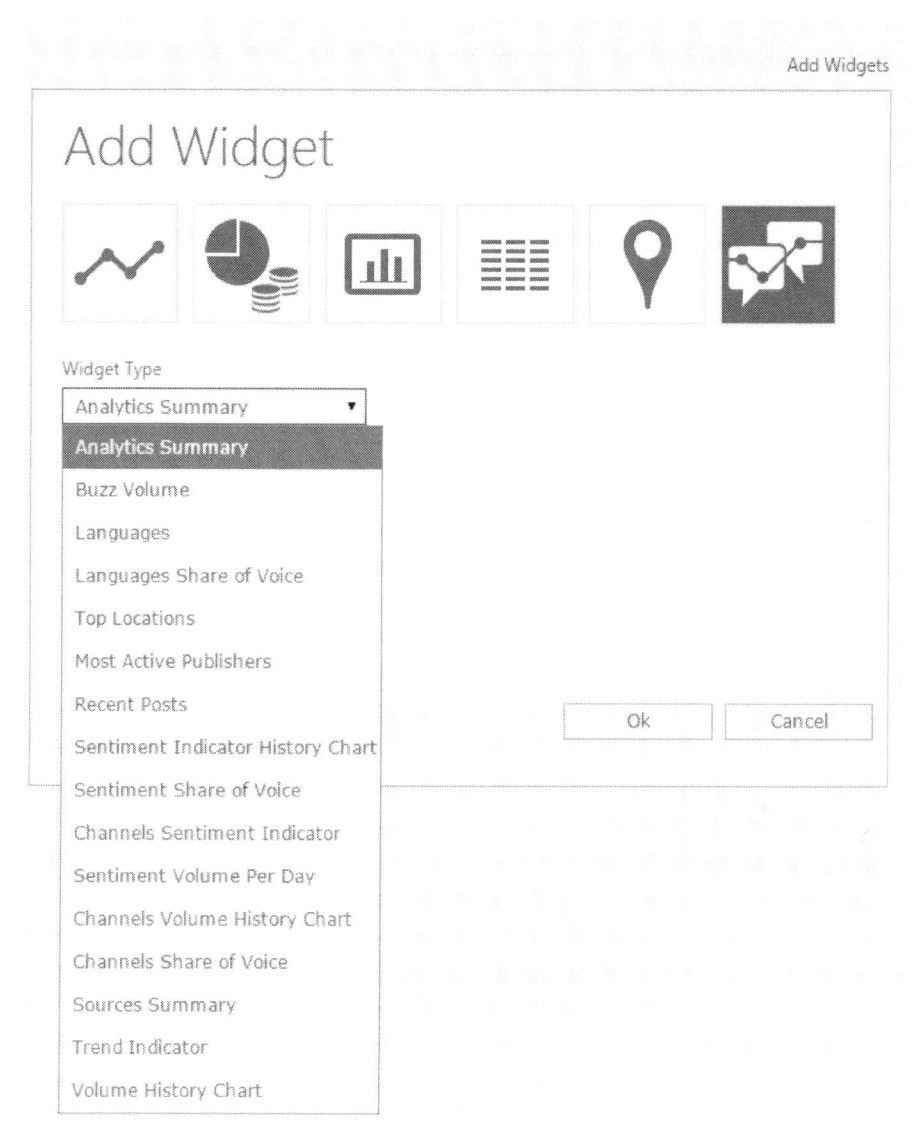

Figure 7.2 – Types of Social Analytics Widgets

To set up queries users can employ the simple UI in Dynamics Marketing or access Microsoft Social Listening and set queries from the main UI.

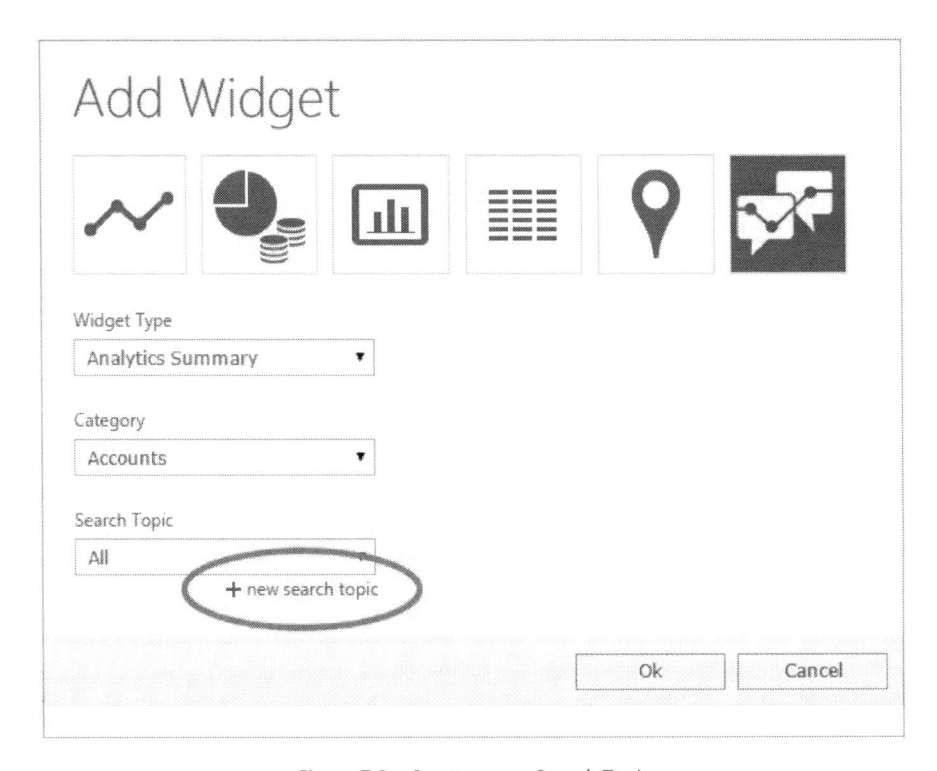

Figure 7.3 – Create a new Search Topic

You would need to enter a name for your new search topic, then choose a category.

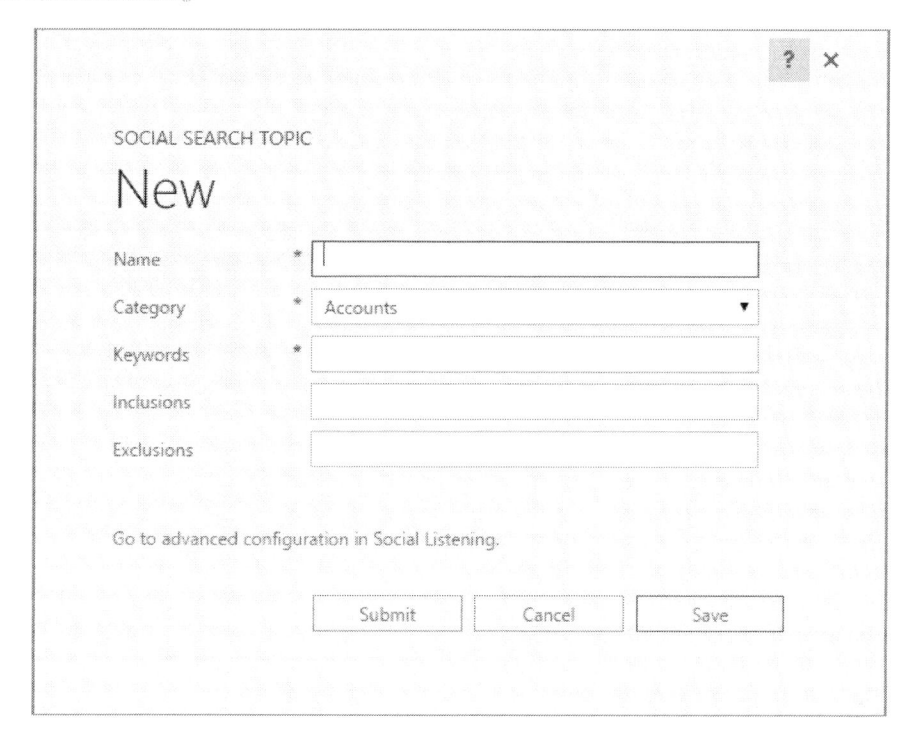

Figure 7.4 – Enter a new Search Topic from Dynamics Marketing

The keywords field is where the actual search keywords are entered, separated by a comma. The inclusion and exclusion fields provide additional flexibility in keywords that should not be present in the text and those that can be there.

When more flexibility is needed users can click on the link at the bottom of the dialog that will open up Microsoft Social Listening for complete configuration, as shown below.

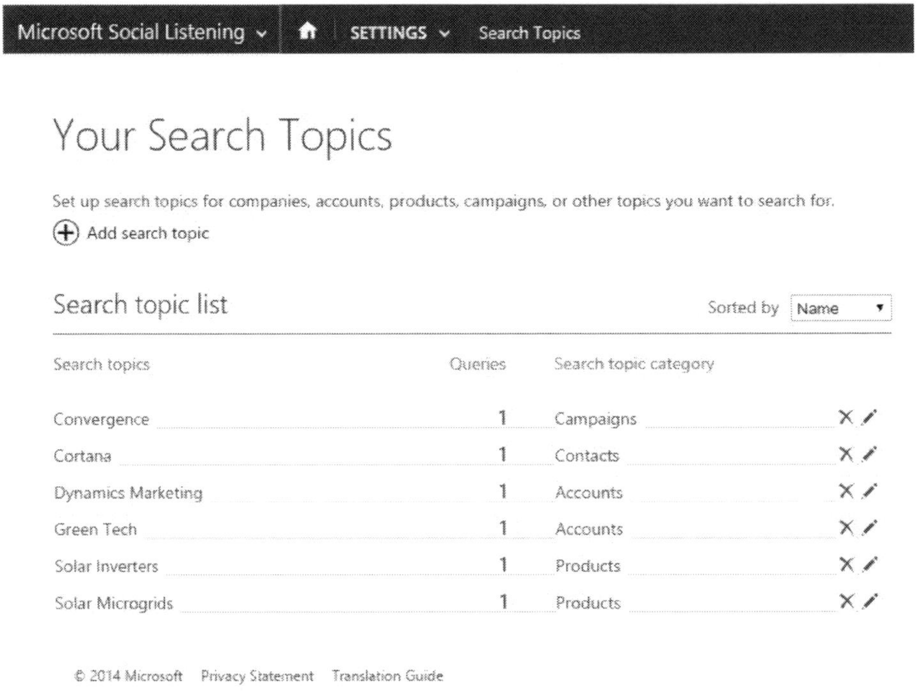

Figure 7.5 –Search Topic Management in Microsoft Social Listening

Now the same users –in Microsoft Social Listening– can add, remove or edit the search topics they have access to.

In particular, creating new search topics using the Microsoft Social Listening UI provides more functionality as shown below:

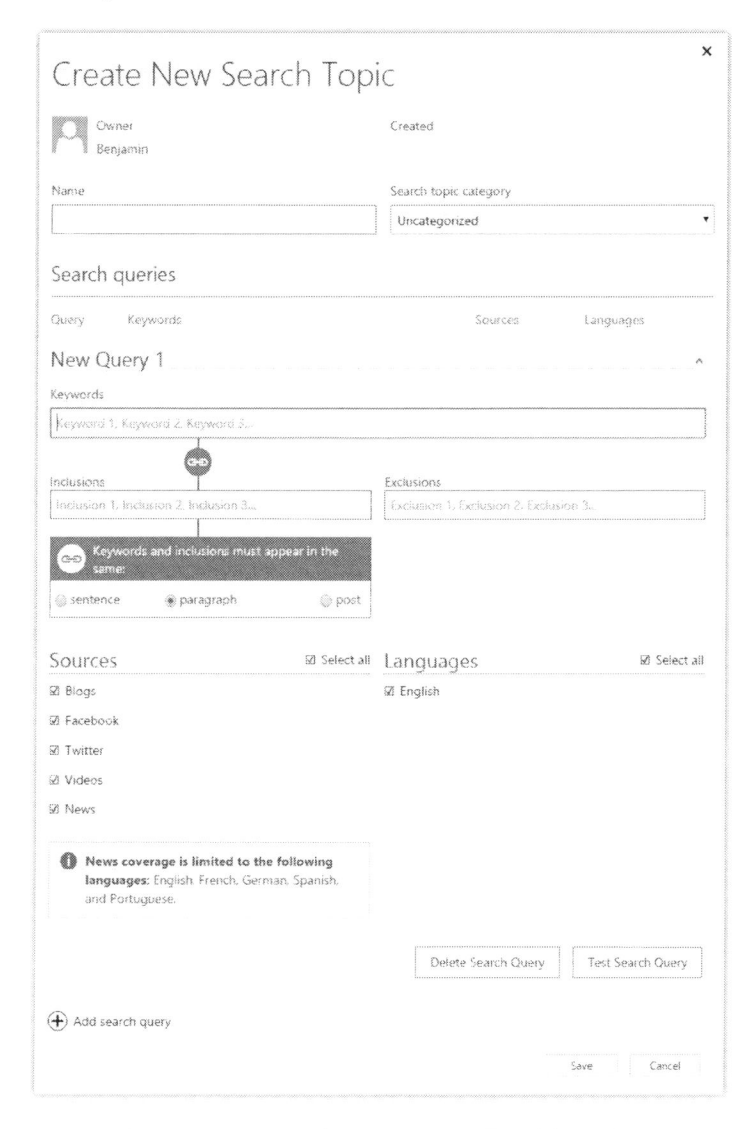

Figure 7.6 –New Search Topic in Microsoft Social Listening

Keywords in Microsoft Social Listening represent a topic of interest. All the wanted variants of the topic should be entered manually. For instance if we want to listen to green technology in English, then we could enter these keywords:

```
Green Tech, Green Technology, Green Technologies
```

You can also enter Twitter hashtags as needed. See for more information the Microsoft Social Listening documentation.

Microsoft Social Listening listens at blogs, videos, news and social (Facebook and Twitter).

7.3.1 Setting Up Microsoft Social Listening Integration

In order to use Microsoft Social Listening analytics a valid Microsoft Social Listening Subscription should be available.

Microsoft Social Listening integration options are available under:

```
Home > Settings > Administration→ Social Listening Options
```

In this page is possible to configure Dynamics Marketing to connect to an Microsoft Social Listening instance, by specifying the URL of the instance, accepting the Microsoft Social Listening license agreement and making user the integration is enabled.

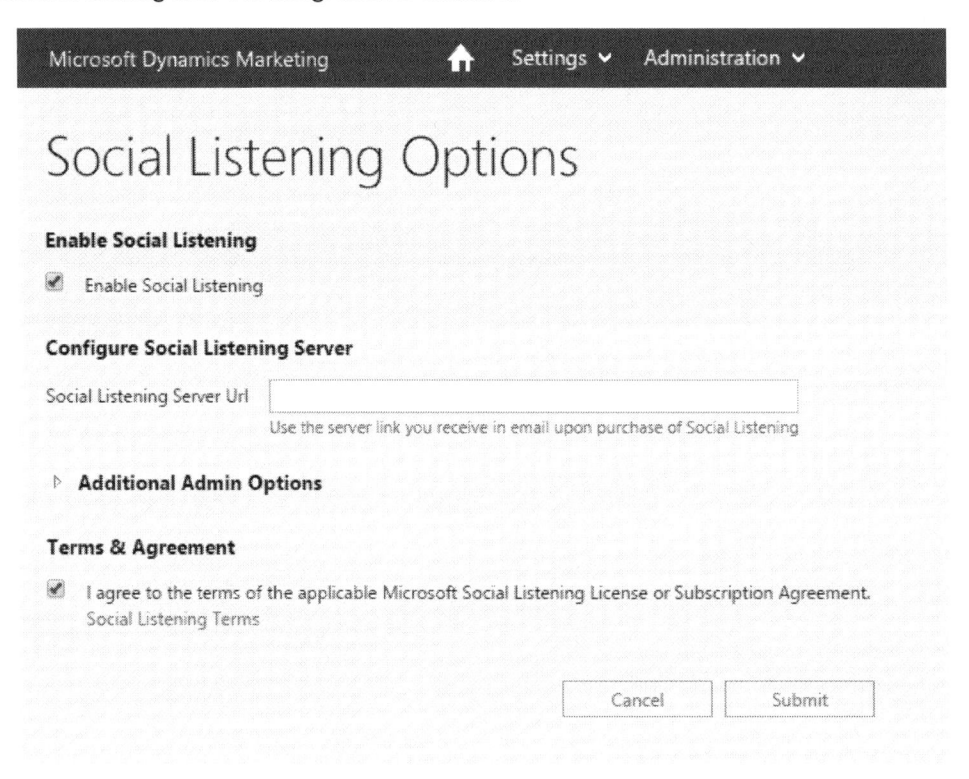

Figure 7.7 – Configuring Microsoft Social Listening Integration

MICROSOFT SOCIAL LISTENING URL

Microsoft Social Listening application URLs have a different structure than Dynamics Marketing or Dynamics CRM ones. The default Microsoft Social Listening URL is identified by a numeric value and it is not related to the tenant organization name, so when specifying the Microsoft Social Listening instance to integrate with it is necessary to use the URL found in the Microsoft Social Listening notification email when the instance is created or the Microsoft Social Listening link available from the Office 365 portal.

7.4 Dynamics Marketing External Analytics

Dynamics Marketing provides a number of data sources (implemented as OData feeds) that can be used as the basis for rich analytics. Such read-only data sources are provided by Dynamics Marketing but are meant to be consumed by external clients such as Microsoft Excel or other software able to consume standard OData feeds.

On a default Dynamics Marketing instance, with OData enabled an extensive list of analytics feeds is available. The main ones are shown in the table below, see the product documentation for the latest list.

Feed Name	Description
Accounts	Lists the financial accounts in the database (by default an empty database comes with three accounts).
AdvertisementApprovals	Advertisement Approvals
AdvertisementBudgetSheets	Advertisement Budget Sheets
AdvertisementCampaigns	Advertisement Campaigns
AdvertisementClientQuoteItems	Advertisement Client Quote Items

Feed Name	Description
AdvertisementClientQuotes	Advertisement Client Quotes
AdvertisementDetails	Advertisement Details
AdvertisementExpenseItems	Advertisement Expense Items
AdvertisementExpenses	Advertisement Expenses
AdvertisementFiles	Files and Advertisements
AdvertisementInvoiceItems	Advertisement Invoice Items
AdvertisementInvoices	Advertisement Invoices
AdvertisementProducts	Advertisement Products
AdvertisementPurchaseOrderItems	Advertisement Purchase Order Items
AdvertisementPurchaseOrders	Advertisement Purchase Orders
AdvertisementResults	Advertisement Results
Advertisements	Advertisements
ApprovalEmails	Approval Emails
ApprovalItems	Approval Items
Approvals	Approvals
Approvers	Approvers
Attendances	Attendances

Feed Name	Description
BudgetItems	A budget workbook is composed of budget sheets, each with budget items (essentially budget amounts over a period of time with an assigned Account).
BudgetKPIs	Provides an aggregated view of all budget items in all the budget worksheets for given a budget workbook.

Feed Name	Description
Budgets	Provides the budget workbooks in the database.
BudgetSheetKPIs	Provides an aggregated view of all budget items in the budget worksheet.
BudgetSheets	Provides the worksheets for a given budget workbook.

Feed Name	Description
CampaignKPIs	Provides a set of KPIs for a Campaign.
CampaignResponses	The Campaign Responses in the system.
Campaigns	Lists all campaigns in the database. Each Campaign includes the ID for the Campaign Response and the Campaign's KPI.
CampaignWithMarketingLists	Campaign With Marketing Lists
CampaignWithMarketingQueries	Campaign With Marketing Queries
ChannelClientQuoteItems	Channel Client Quote Items
ChannelExpenseItems	Channel Expense Items
ChannelInvoiceItems	Channel Invoice Items
ChannelPurchaseOrderItems	Channel Purchase Order Items
Channels	Lists all the channels.
ClientQuoteItems	Client Quote Items
ClientQuotes	Client Quotes
Companies	Companies
ContactCustomFields	"system" feed for custom fields on Contact
ContactCustomFieldsCategory	"system" feed for custom fields on Contact
ContactCustomFieldsCheckbox	"system" feed for custom fields on Contact

Feed Name	Description
ContactCustomFieldsDateTime	"system" feed for custom fields on Contact
ContactCustomFieldsExternalEntity	"system" feed for custom fields on Contact
ContactCustomFieldsFloat	"system" feed for custom fields on Contact
ContactCustomFieldsInteger	"system" feed for custom fields on Contact
ContactCustomFieldsText	"system" feed for custom fields on Contact
Contacts	Contacts
ContactsInMarketingLists	Contacts In Marketing Lists
ContractFiles	Files and Contracts
Contracts	Contracts

Feed Name	Description
DepartmentApprovals	Department Approvals
DepartmentBudgetSheets	Department Budget Sheets
DepartmentClientQuotes	Department Client Quotes
DepartmentEmails	Department Emails
DepartmentExpenses	Department Expenses
DepartmentFiles	Files and Departments
DepartmentInvoices	Department Invoices
DepartmentPurchaseOrders	Department Purchase Orders
Departments	Departments
DepartmentTeamRoles	Department Team Roles
DivisionBudgetSheets	Division Budget Sheets
DivisionClientQuotes	Division Client Quotes

Feed Name	Description
DivisionEmails	Division Emails
DivisionExpenses	Division Expenses
DivisionFiles	Files and Divisions
DivisionInvoices	Division Invoices
DivisionPurchaseOrders	Division Purchase Orders
DivisionResults	Division Results
Divisions	Divisions
DivisionTeamRoles	Division Team Roles

Feed Name	Description
Emails	Email (messages)
EmailTrackingResults	The Email Tracking Results is an important feed as it provides a detailed, "event-based" history of all behavioral events for a mailing. This feed tracks information about a marketing email (opens, forwards, bounces, open links).
EstimateItems	Estimate Items
Estimates	Estimates
EventBudgetSheets	Event Budget Sheets
EventChannels	Event Channels
EventClientQuotes	Event Client Quotes
EventExpenses	Event Expenses
EventInvoices	Event Invoices
EventJobs	Event Jobs
EventKPIs	Event KPIs

Feed Name	Description
EventLeads	Event Leads
EventMarketingEmailMessages	Event Marketing Email Messages
EventPurchaseOrders	Event Purchase Orders
Events	Events
ExpenseItems	Expense Items
Expenses	Expenses

Feed Name	Description
Facilities	Facilities
FileAlertsOrSubscribers	Files alerts or notification subscribers
FileApprovals	Files Approvals
FileEmails	Files Emails
FileInFolders	Files structure
FileRelatedFiles	Related Files
Files	Files
FileUsages	Files Usage
FileVersions	File versions
FolderInFolders	Folders
Folders	Folders
InvoiceItems	Invoice Items
Invoices	Invoices
ItemServices	Item Services

Feed Name	Description
JobAdvertisements	Job Advertisements
JobBudgetSheets	Job Budget Sheets
JobChannels	Job Channels
JobClientQuotes	Job Client Quotes
JobContacts	Job Contacts
JobCurrencies	Job Currencies
JobExpenses	Job Expenses
JobFiles	Job Files
JobInvoices	Job Invoices
JobKPIs	Job KPIs
JobLeads	Job Leads
JobMarketingEmailMessages	Job Marketing Email Messages
JobMarketingLists	Job Marketing Lists
JobMarketingQueries	Job Marketing Queries
JobMilestones	Job Milestones
JobProducts	Job Products
JobPrograms	Job Programs
JobPurchaseOrders	Job Purchase Orders
JobRequestRequirements	Job Request Requirements
JobRequests	Job Request
Jobs	Jobs
JobTasks	Job Tasks
JobTeamRoles	Job Team Roles

Feed Name	Description
LandingPageApprovals	Landing Page Approvals
LandingPageEmails	Landing Page Emails
LandingPageInteractions	Landing Page Interactions
LandingPageLeads	Landing Page Leads
LandingPageResults	Landing Page Results
LandingPages	Landing Page
LeadInteractionCustomFields	"system" feed for custom fields on Lead Interaction
LeadInteractionCustomFieldsCategory	"system" feed for custom fields on Lead Interaction
LeadInteractionCustomFieldsDateTime	"system" feed for custom fields on Lead Interaction
LeadInteractionCustomFieldsFloat	"system" feed for custom fields on Lead Interaction
LeadInteractionCustomFieldsText	"system" feed for custom fields on Lead Interaction
LeadInteractions	Lead Interactions
Leads	Leads
LeadScoringEvents	Lead Scoring Events
LeadScoringModelGrades	Lead Scoring Model Grades
LeadScoringModels	Lead Scoring Models

Feed Name	Description
MarketingContexts	A marketing context is a valid combination of a Company, a Program and a Campaign. An effective marketing context is defined by the lead creation strategy and lead creation scope of the respective Company. Companies here are only Client ones or the Site Company.

Feed Name	Description
MarketingEmailMessageKPIs	Aggregated Marketing Email Message KPIs for a message.
MarketingEmailMessages	Marketing Email Messages
MarketingEmailsForMarketingLists	Marketing Emails For Marketing Lists
MarketingLists	Marketing Lists
MarketingListWithContacts	Use this to find contacts in a given Static Marketing List.
MarketingQueries	Marketing Queries
OfferApprovals	Offers and Approvals
OfferCampaigns	Offers and Campaigns
OfferEmails	Offers Emails
OfferLeads	Offers Leads
OfferPerformances	Offers Performance
OfferResults	Results for Offers
Offers	Offers

PriceRates	Price Rates
ProductApprovals	Product Approvals
ProductBudgetSheets	Product Budget Sheets
ProductCampaigns	Product Campaigns
ProductClientQuotes	Product Client Quotes
ProductExpenses	Product Expenses
ProductFiles	Product Files
ProductInvoices	Product Invoices
ProductJobs	Product Jobs

ProductPrograms	Product Programs
ProductPurchaseOrders	Product Purchase Orders
ProductResults	Product Results
Products	Products
ProductTasks	Product Tasks
ProductTeamRoles	Product Team Roles
ProgramKPIs	Program KPIs
Programs	Programs
ProjectRequestClientQuotes	Project Request Client Quotes
ProjectRequestEmails	Project Request Emails
ProjectRequestEvents	Project Request Events
ProjectRequestExpenses	Project Request Expenses
ProjectRequestFiles	Project Request Files
ProjectRequestInvoices	Project Request Invoices
ProjectRequestPurchaseOrders	Project Request Purchase Orders
ProjectRequests	Project Requests
PurchaseOrderItems	All Items associated to a Purchase Order.
PurchaseOrders	Purchase Orders

Feed Name	Description
RegistrationItems	Registration Items
Registrations	Registrations
RegistrationSetupLanguages	Registration Setup Languages
RegistrationSetups	Registration Setups

Feed Name	Description
Results	Results
SessionRegistrations	Session Registrations
Sessions	Sessions
SessionTasks	Session Tasks
TaskEvents	Task Events
Tasks	Tasks
TimeSlipEvents	Time Slip Events
TimeSlips	Time Slips
Venues	Venues
VisitedWebSites	Visited Web Sites
Visits	Lists all Visits.
WebSites	All Web Sites in the database.

ADDITIONAL SECURITY FOR POWER BI REPORTS

Dynamics Marketing allows Power BI reports to be connected directly to Dynamics Marketing data sources. This might be dangerous if a user is not fully aware of the security implications of his setup. To prevent possible security issues, Dynamics Marketing administrators can specify the domains that are allowed for hosting the Power BI reports in the Site Settings page. If such a "whitelist" is not defined there will be no restriction enforced.

The following section illustrates how to take advantage of the data listed above and create Power BI and Excel workbooks that can consume Dynamics Marketing data.

7.4.1 How to Setup Custom Dynamics Marketing Reports using Power BI

If it is the first time you are connecting or you incur in an access error it's worth checking the Site Settings page (or asking your administrator) to see if the external data access is enabled (it is not by default):

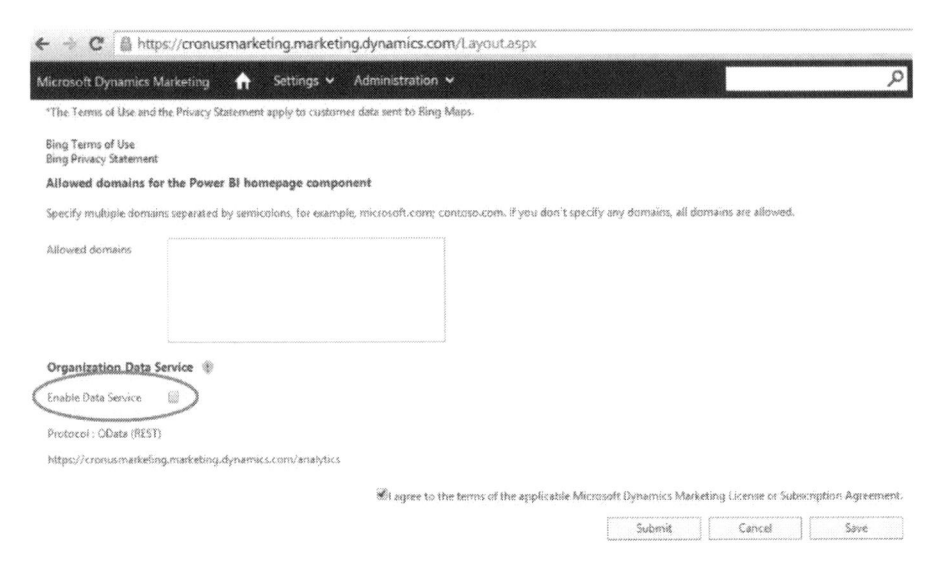

Figure 7.8 – Enabling Data Services

We assume that Power Query (or the other products of the Power BI family such as Power Map etc. all available for download online) is already installed on your copy of Excel.

Now that you made sure the service is enabled and you have Power Bi installed and you have Power BI installed, open Excel, select the Power Query tab, and create a new data source from the OData feed pointing to the analytics URL found in the Site Settings page under the "Enable Data Service" checkbox.

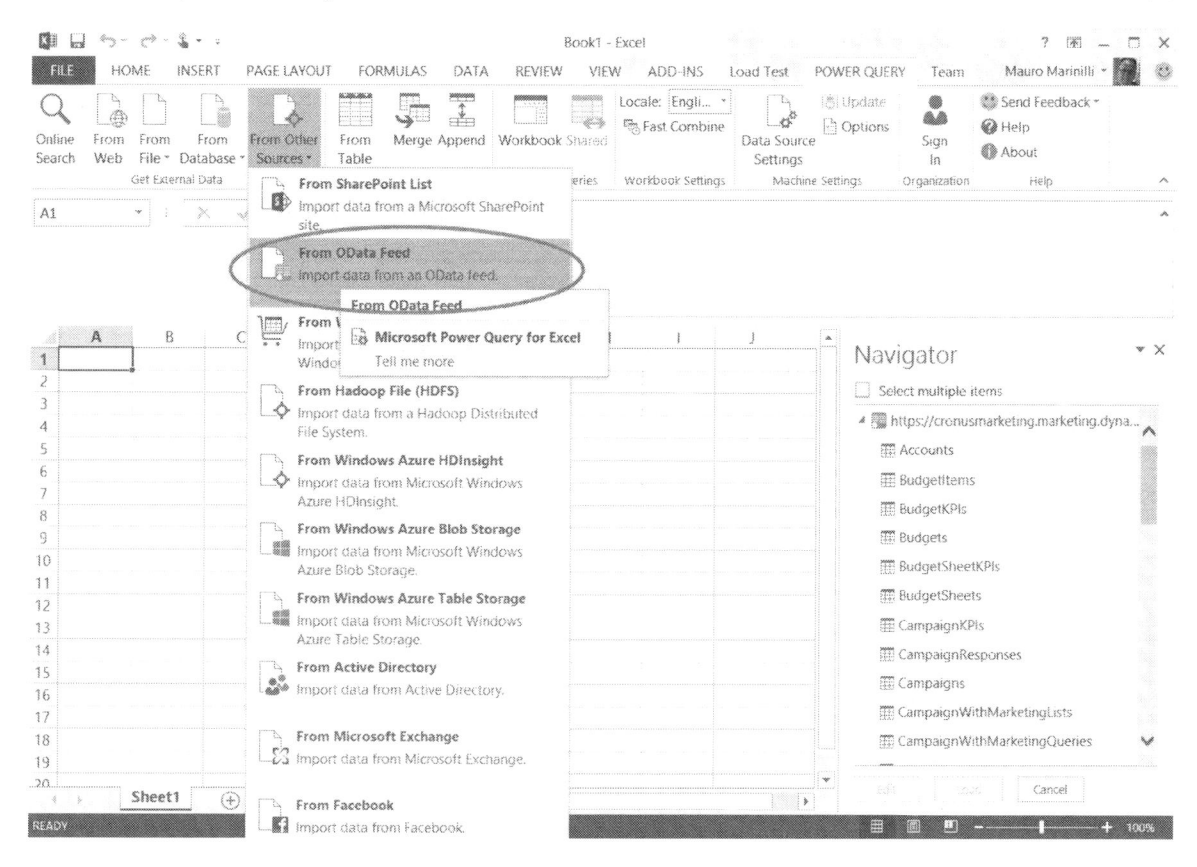

Figure 7.9 – Consuming Dynamics Marketing OData Feed

At this point, once you logged in again with your Office 365 account you should be able to see the list of data sources available in the right hand side of the Excel window.

At this point you are ready to go. All the power of Excel is at your fingertips to tame Dynamics Marketing data.

Inside Microsoft Dynamics Marketing

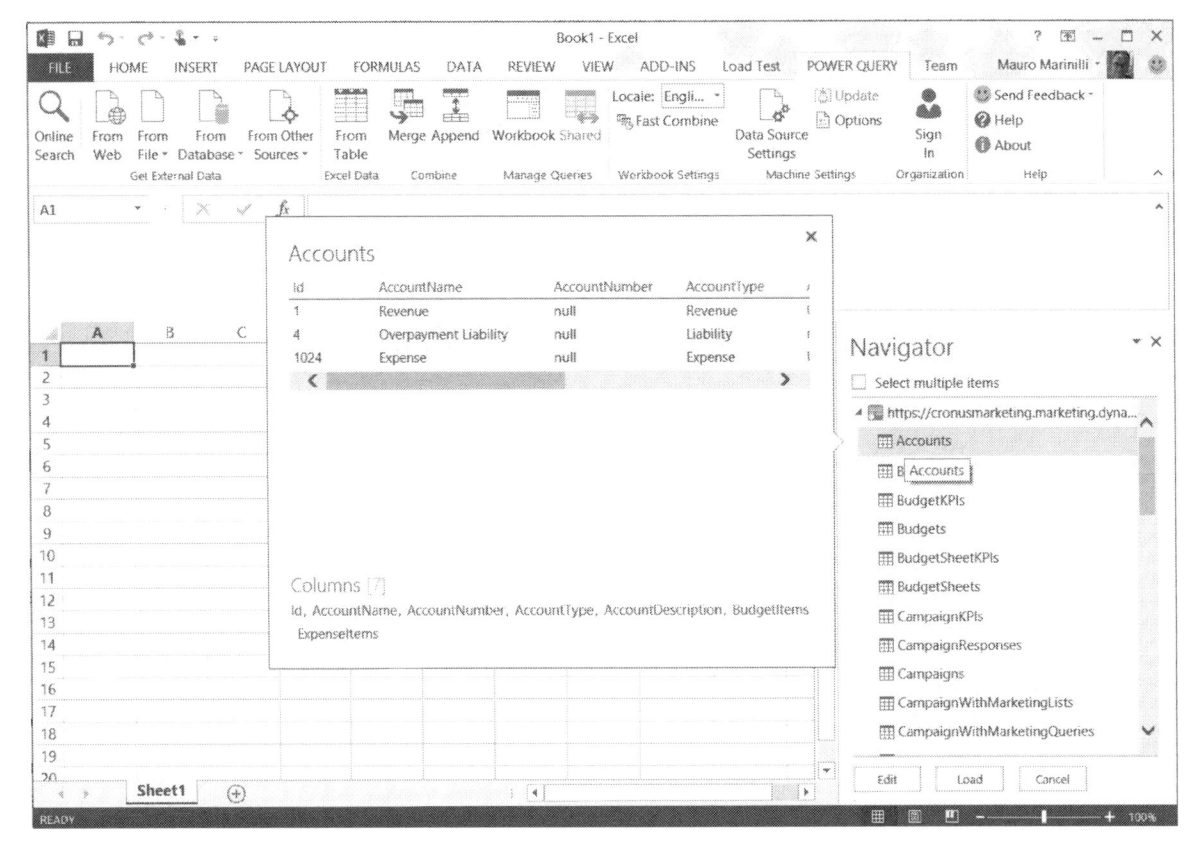

Figure 7.10 – Exploring OData feeds

Consult the Microsoft documentation for the details of how to save a Power BI Excel workbook onto an Office 365 Power BI library so that your custom reports can be shared with other in the organization without the need of specifying additional credentials for authentication.

> **UDF AND CUSTOM FIELDS ARE AVAILABLE IN POWER BI REPORTS**
>
> Dynamics Marketing OData feeds support custom fields and User Defined Fields so users can add them to their Power BI reports.

7.5 DYNAMICS MARKETING BUILT-IN REPORTS

Dynamics Marketing comes with a few hundred "classic" reports built into the product, ready to use. These reports are usually available under the "Reports" section, the last part in each main functional area of the product. See for example the reports available for the "Projects" area:

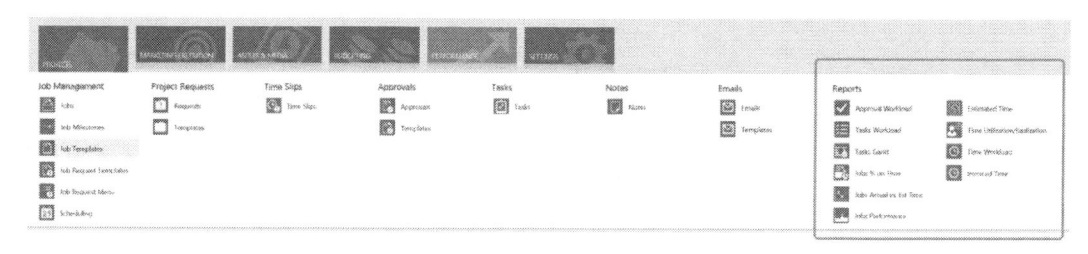

Figure 7.11 – Project's Reports in the Navigation UI

There is also a dedicated functional area, "Performance", entirely dedicated to reporting.

Figure 7.12 – Reports in the Navigation UI

The "Other Reports" option in particular provides a handy centralized hub for a number of useful reports organized per area.

In the following pages we list the various reports available.

Area	Reports	Description
Administration		
	Category Listing	Provide a comprehensive overview of all categories and category values used in the database.
Banking		
	Cash Receipts	Provide a list of payments received from clients.
	Check Details	The details of a Check.
	Deposit Details	The Details of all deposits made in bank accounts within a specified date range.
	Deposit Slip	Deposit Slip.
	Reconciliation Summary	A summary of a Bank Reconciliation.
Campaigns		
	Campaign Listing	A list of all the campaigns in the database.
	Campaign Report	A formatted view of the campaigns in the database.

Area	Reports	Description
Clients and Receivables		
	A/R Aging	All unpaid invoices grouped by due date.
	AR Aging Detail	Balance of each invoice owed. The invoices are grouped by client.
	AR Aging Summary	A summary version of the A/R Aging report.
	Client Balance Report	All receivables for each client.
	Client Quote	A formatted client quote that can be sent to a client for sign-off or approval.
	Client Quote Listing	A list of client quotes.
	Collections Report	Client receivables and contact information.
	Credit Memo / Refund Report	Credit memos and issue credits or refunds.
	Invoice Report	A formatted invoice.
	Item Price Listing	All items and services and their prices.
	Open Invoices	All unpaid invoices grouped by due date.
	Rep Balance	All receivables for each client grouped by representative (Rep).
	Retainer Balance	All unpaid invoices grouped by due date.
	Sales Order Report	Sales orders for a specific date interval or organization. You can also see who ordered these sales orders.
	Statements	Produces a report for each client showing what they owe.
	Unbilled Costs By Client	All unbilled expenses ordered by the client.

Area	Reports	Description
Company and Budgeting		
	Balance Sheet	The site company's assets and liabilities in a typical Balance Sheet format as of a specific date.
	Budget Workbook	A budget workbook.
	Comparative Income Statement	Compare income statements.
	General Ledger	The activity in accounts over a specific period of time.
	General Ledger (Cash)	The activity in accounts over a specific period of time using cash-basis accounting rules.
	Income Statement	The income statement.
	Income Statement (Cash)	An organization's revenue and expenses in a typical Profit & Loss Statement format for a specific date range, using the Cash Method of Accounting.
	Income Statement By Client	The income statement per client.
	Journal	All debits and credits that occurred during a period of time.
	Payroll	Print out a payroll.
	Revenue Trend Chart	See revenue by date in a line chart.
	Statement of Cash Flows	Cash flow statement.
	Trial Balance	Create a trial balance as of a specific date, and shows the balance of each account in debit and credit format.
	Trial Balance (Cash)	Create a trial balance as of a specific date using cash-basis accounting rules, and show the balance of each account in debit and credit format.

Area	Reports	Description
Email		
	Email Report	The contents of an email message.
Estimates		
	Client Estimate	The prices using the information in an estimate in spreadsheet format.
	Cost Estimate	The cost estimate using the information in estimates (not from client quotes).
	Estimate	The estimate and price.
	Estimate - Cost and Price	The estimated cost and estimated price.
Events		
	Event Listing	List the events.
	Event Report	See various important details about each event.
	Staffing	See the staffing details for the events.

Area	Reports	Description
Jobs		
	Component Requests	The component requests.
	Component Usage Summary	Summary for the component usage.
	Expense Listing by Job	Expenses listed by job.
	Job Calendar	List of jobs showing which ones have passed the due date and which are on time.
	Job Listing	List the jobs.
	Job Profitability	Get the job profitability overview.
	Job Report	Details about each Job.
	Job Time Billing By Contact	Job time billing by contact.
	Job Time Billing By Service	Job time billing by service.
	Job Time by Contact	Job time by contact.
	Job Trend Chart	Jobs by start date in a line chart.
	Job/Task Gantt Chart	Jobs and their tasks in a Gantt Chart format.
	Unbilled Costs By Job	Unbilled expenses for each job within a date range.

Area	Reports	Description
Media		
	Broadcast Media Plan	Shows a media plan using a tabular format that is typically used for broadcast media.
	Client Media Purchases	A listing of media purchases by each client.
	Media Outlet Report	Lists of media outlets in spreadsheet format.
	Media Outlets	Media outlet details.
	Media Results Summary	Summary of results for a media outlet and date range.
	Media ROI	Showing the ROI from different media outlets.
	Media Sales	The media sales within a given timespan.
	Media Traffic	A summary of advertisements by media type and vendor, ordered in a certain time frame for a selected Outlet, Media, or Expense Type.
	Print Media Plan	A media plan in a format that is typically used for newspapers, magazines and other print media.
	Radio Expense Report	Information contained in each radio expense.
	Radio Invoice Report	Radio invoices in a tabular format.
	Radio Order Report	Radio orders in a tabular format.
	TV Expense Report	Information about a TV Expense.
	TV Invoice Report	TV invoices in a tabular format.
	TV Order Report	TV orders in a tabular format.

Area	Reports	Description
Programs		
	Program Listing	Listing of Programs.
Results		
	Result Metrics	A summary of results for a project and date range.
	Results Trend Chart	Results by date in a line chart.

Area	Reports	Description
Sales		
	Contact Listing	A list of contacts in spreadsheet format.
	Contact Report	Information about a single contact.
	Lead Listing	See leads in a tabular format that occurred during a period of time.
	Lead Report	Information about a single lead on each page.
	Lead Trend Chart	New leads by date in a line chart.
	New Contacts By Assignment	Overview of new contacts ordered by assignment role.
	New Contacts By Month	Overview of new contacts by month role. You can further filter the report by date interval, group, type, and active status.
	Opportunity Forecast	An opportunity forecast.
	Opportunity Listing	All opportunities in a spreadsheet style grid.
	Opportunity Report	Information about a single opportunity.
	Opportunity Summary	Opportunity summary
	Opportunity Trend Chart	Opportunities by date in a line chart.
	Sales By Client	All sales to each client, except Retainers.
	Sales by Client (Cash)	All sales to each client, except retainers that have been paid for.
	Sales by Item	All sales of each item/service.
	Sales by Item (Cash)	See sales by items. Retainers are not included in this report.
	Sales by Rep	Listing all paid invoices for each client. Retainers are not included in the report.
	Sales By Rep (Cash)	Listing all paid invoices for each client grouped by Rep and by Item. Retainers are not included in the report.
	Sales by Rep by Item Type (Cash)	All invoices for each client. Retainers are not included in the report.
	Sales Rating Trend	Sales ratings (of leads) by date in a line chart.
	Unit Sales By Item	All items/services sold and paid for.
	Unit Sales by Item (Cash)	All items/services that have been invoiced (Accrual-basis).

Area	Reports	Description
Tasks		
	Task Listing	The tasks within a given timespan.
	Task Report	Information contained in a task.
	Task Time Listing	All the time slips associated with a specific task.
	Task Trend Chart	Opportunities by date in a line chart.
Taxes		
	1099 Details	Transaction details for 1099 Vendors tabulated by the 1099 Category.
	1099 Report	Tax report in the format used on the 1099 Tax form.
	1099 Summary	All transactions for 1099 Vendors tabulated by 1099 Category.
	Tax Liability (Accrual)	Total tax owed by tax rate as of a specified date. This is an accrual-basis report.
	Tax Liability (Cash)	The total tax owed by tax rate as of a specified date. This is a cash-basis report.
	Tax Liability Details (Accrual)	See taxable transactions for a general ledger account and date range. This is an accrual-basis report.
	Tax Liability Details (Cash)	See the total tax owed by tax rate as of a specified date. This report is a cash-basis report.
Time Slips		
	Labor Analysis	An overview of the used time spent grouped by department and client for a specific date range.
	Time Slip Audit	Used for controlling whether time keepers have entered all their time slips for a period of time. Canceled time slips are not included in the report.
	Time Slip Billing	A listing of billable and/or non-billable time slips and shows the rate associated with the service specified for each time slip.
	Time Slips	A listing of time slips.

Area	Reports	Description
Vendors and Payables		
	A/P Aging	All A/P (expenses to be paid) grouped by their due date.
	AP Aging Detail	The balance owed on each expense in a tabular format, grouped by vendor.
	AP Aging Summary	An overview the amount owed to each vendor.
	Expense Item Listing	Expenses by period in a bar chart.
	Expense Report	Expense items associated with multiple expenses in a listing.
	Expenses Bar Chart	Details about a single expense.
	Expenses by Vendor	All expenses for each vendor within a date range.
	PO Listing	A list of purchase orders.
	Purchase Order Report	Information about a purchase order.
	Purchases by vendor	An overview of the purchases made on each vendor.
	Unpaid Bills	A list of the expenses that haven't been paid in full.
	Vendor Balance	A summary of the outstanding balances due to each vendor.
	Vendor Open PO Balance	All the outstanding purchase orders and the balance due to each vendor.
	Vendor Quote	Information on each vendor quote.

CHAPTER EIGHT
ASSETS AND MEDIA

8.1 Overview

Marketing departments traditionally devote the largest chunk of their budget to advertisement. Media buying can be very challenging in terms of complexity, sometimes involving large budgets. This complexity requires extensive planning and tracking at various levels (in terms of information granularity and organization layers) in order to justify and report on ads expenditures. On top of that, many media buying plans evolve incrementally, usually from a vague initial plan that gradually matures adding details until a point is reached when you are ready to execute the plan and create buys.

Broadly speaking, Assets and Media in Dynamics Marketing encompass four main areas:

- Media planning
- Media buying
- Tracking Media performance
- Digital asset management

The first three areas are in reality one larger area of functionality related to the management of ads, from the initial budgeting to the detailed planning, the actual purchase and subsequent performance assessment. The last area, digital asset management, is about uploading multimedia files, review and annotate them across multiple organization boundaries and user roles. In terms of security permissions, the Media Buyer user type has the largest number of authorization permissions in Dynamics Marketing.

8.2 Main Entities in this area

The Asset and Media area covers a wide range of functionality, mostly centered on the management of traditional ads and related capabilities. Here's a list of the main concepts and entities for this functional area in Dynamics Marketing.

All these entities are located under the Asset and Media area:

```
Home > Assets and Media
```

Entity	Description
Advertisements	This entity can be used to track a wide array of traditional advertisement types such as direct mail, display and banner advertisements, TV commercials, radio spots, and more.
Broadcast Verification	Broadcast Verification records are used to verify that the ordered TV ads actually ran as expected. This item is not directly available from the navigation UI. Dynamics Marketing achieves this by importing files in the Commercial 2 format provided by Kantar Media.
Components	Components are promotional items that can be bundled in packs. Using components you can track promotional material like ads, brochures, business cards, letters, posters, TV commercials, Radio spots, web pages and more. Dynamics Marketing can track Component requests and their inventory.
Demographics	These are used for creating media plans, buy and analyze advertising effectiveness. They are not available from the navigation UI.
Media Outlets	Media Outlets represent communication outlets for advertisement such as magazines, TV, radio, mailing lists, search engines and more. Media outlets can be organized in folders.
Media Plans	A Media Plan represents an entire media purchase plan in Dynamics Marketing potentially containing advertisements for multiple Media Outlets. Media plans are essentially forecasting and planning tools. Depending upon the role and the phase of the planning process they are in, users will need different information aggregated at different levels from the same Media Plan.
Media Sales and Inventory	Dynamics Marketing allows for managing ad sales for a wide range of advertising sales environments such as traditional media outlets (e.g. magazines, event producers, newsletter publishers, list managers, etc.) and "new media" outlets (e.g. web sites, blogs, email marketing, etc.). You can also handle in Dynamics Marketing event-related sales opportunities such as event producers offering booths, sponsorships etc. Also in-house media sales departments can take advantage of this functionality for managing Cooperative Marketing Funds, Market Development Funds and other similar promotional programs. On top of these, given Dynamics Marketing flexibility,

Entity	Description
	one can imagine managing even more types of promotional opportunities as well.
Markets	The Market entity represents the structure of your audience in the context of the Media area in that you can associate various Media Outlets to Market segments to better represent your customers. Note that this entity is geared towards Media usage and is not representing "actionable" segments such as those used in Marketing Automation (i.e. represented by the List/Query entity). Markets in turn can be broken down in Market Segments to more closely represent the various segments of interest. Markets are different than other entities in this area and are available under `Home > Settings > Media → Markets`
Rate Cards	Rate Cards are meant primarily to be used to store cost information for future reuse, when the same media is bought at the same rates again and again (at least a number of times per year)[34]. Rate Cards can be used also for recording special rates negotiated with Clients. For companies that sell media, Rate Cards can be used to store the price you charge. Once Rate Cards are entered in the system (for example as part of defining the details of a Media Outlet) you can use them to minimize data entry also in other places as well like when creating invoices for instance. Dynamics Marketing allows Rate Cards to be imported from external sources.
Postal/Zip Codes	Some types of media outlets (such as newspapers, mailing lists, email lists, inserts) allow to specify postal codes and divide circulation in order to provide Marketing Managers with a finer granularity of segmentation. This entity is available from the Media section under Settings.

8.3 SCENARIOS

These are some interesting scenarios you can perform with Dynamics Marketing in the Assets and Media area.

8.3.1 Create and Execute a Media Plan

Before looking at a specific scenario let's summarize the typical flow when running a Media Plan in terms of Dynamics Marketing entities and functionality. The main entities involved are Media Orders, Media Invoices, Media Expenses and of course Media Plans.

---

[34] Rate cards are essential for organizations that do a great deal of media buying.

The Marketing Manager handling media buys receives Purchase Orders for media (represented as Media Orders in Dynamics Marketing, also including print ads which are usually known as Insertion Orders in the industry). Such Media Orders are then sent to the proper Media Outlets (Media Outlets are specified per each Media Order item, so you can have multiple Media Outlets in a single Media Order).

When Vendor Invoices are received, the Marketing Manager creates Media Expenses in Dynamics Marketing. Media Expenses should include any adjustments to the original Media Orders due to possible changes such as agreed discounts, price changes and so on.
At this point Media Invoices are created by the Marketing Manager and sent to Clients. Dynamics Marketing will keep track of these transactions for future reference.

> **POSTING MEDIA EXPENSES AND INVOICES TO THE GENERAL LEDGER**
>
> Media Expenses are automatically posted to the General Ledger while Media Orders are not. Likewise Media Invoices as well are automatically posted to the General Ledger.
> The General Ledger is available under
> `Home > Budgeting > Settings → Chart of Accounts`
>
> If you need to create the equivalent of Media Invoices that don't need to be posted on the General Ledger then you can use Media Sales Orders.

Now that we have refreshed at a high-level a typical Media Plan setup let's get back to our scenario of creating and executing a Media Plan in Dynamics Marketing. The scenario details a possible, simple methodology for creating media plans and campaigns, employed for illustrative purposes. Dynamics Marketing is a very flexible tool that can be adapted to a wide range of marketing approaches.

User	Description	User permissions
Marketing Manager	Depending on the size and type of marketing practice this scenario will be carried out by multiple roles such as a marketing manager, senior media buyer, accounting manager etc. In order to illustrate the capabilities of the	Media Buyer user type

	product concisely we will use one single user for all these steps of the scenario.	
Vendors	These are registered as Vendor Contacts in Dynamics Marketing.	None
Client	The client the campaign is run for, represented as a Client Company.	None

So the first step in our journey to buy effective ads is in conceiving campaign(s) and identifying at a high level the resources needed in order to run them. For simplicity we will focus in this scenario exclusively on media campaigns, although it is easy to imagine how Dynamics Marketing can accommodate in the same campaign traditional ads, in-person marketing approaches such as events and other digital marketing techniques described elsewhere in this book.

The Marketing Manager studies the data from previous media campaigns run in Dynamics Marketing especially in terms of ROI, in order to shape the new campaign.

The Marketing Manager creates a new Campaign record and uses the Brief panel to start documenting the campaign overview and to capture informally goals, objectives, strategies and creative approach. If her company has a more structured approach involving formal documents and high-level specifications the Marketing Manager will attach these to the Campaign as Files instead of using the Brief panel.

When the ideation phase is completed, she can finally move on start creating the ads. In Dynamics Marketing Jobs are used to manage the ads. Optionally, the Brief panel in Jobs can be used to track high level documentation while the Jobs are being defined, similarly for what has been done for Campaigns.

Depending on the level of formality needed or the scale of the media campaign, Components can be created and bundled together to represent various parts of each advertisement.

At this point vendors start entering into the picture. The Marketing Manager works on contracts, negotiating rates and striking deals against the allocated budget with the various vendors. All of this is tracked in Dynamics Marketing to the needed level of detail. When everything is ready, the plan enters in execution. Orders are placed (purchase orders approved internally, then generated, communicated externally, etc.) and verified (using Ad Traffic, Broadcast Verification and other functionality) all using Dynamics Marketing.

The Marketing Manager can optionally ask for prepayments by sending Client Advance Invoices to the Client. The prepayment is received against the Advance Invoice and posted to Unearned Income.

Then the Marketing Manager typically can invoice clients then receive payment from them then pay vendors. Media agencies will also verify that the ads run appropriately before paying the invoices for the ads.

All these expenses can be posted to Prepaid Expenses. She also receives the Vendor Invoices signing off on orders as needed.

Now we're ready for perhaps the tensest moment in every campaign, when the ads are finally run and the money gets spent, without any feedback on the results yet.

At the same time or earlier, the Marketing Manager starts processing the incoming vendors' bills represented in Dynamics Marketing as Marketing Expenses, generated from the Media Orders. Dynamics Marketing provides a reconciliation function to simplify this task. When vendor invoices are verified they can be posted.

At one point the results from purchased ads start rolling in. Dynamics Marketing captures them as Results records. Usually an intense analysis phase is conducted at this point in order to adjust the aim as the campaign is progressing.

If prepayments were used, the Marketing Manager applies Vendor Prepayment to the Marketing Expenses. The money is moved from Prepaid Expenses to Expenses. Similarly, if advanced was agreed upon, the money is applied to invoices and moves from Unearned Income to Income.

If the Marketing Manager works in an agency, she needs to bill the client in turn. She creates client invoices and sends them to the clients. When they pay, she posts the payments to the appropriate accounts.

8.3.2 Buy Media Associated to a Campaign and Track Results

The marketing team has devised the strategy for a campaign for a customer about the launch of a new product that revolves around media buying. The Marketing Manager on charge of executing it starts creating the data in Dynamics Marketing. An empty Product Launch campaign is created:

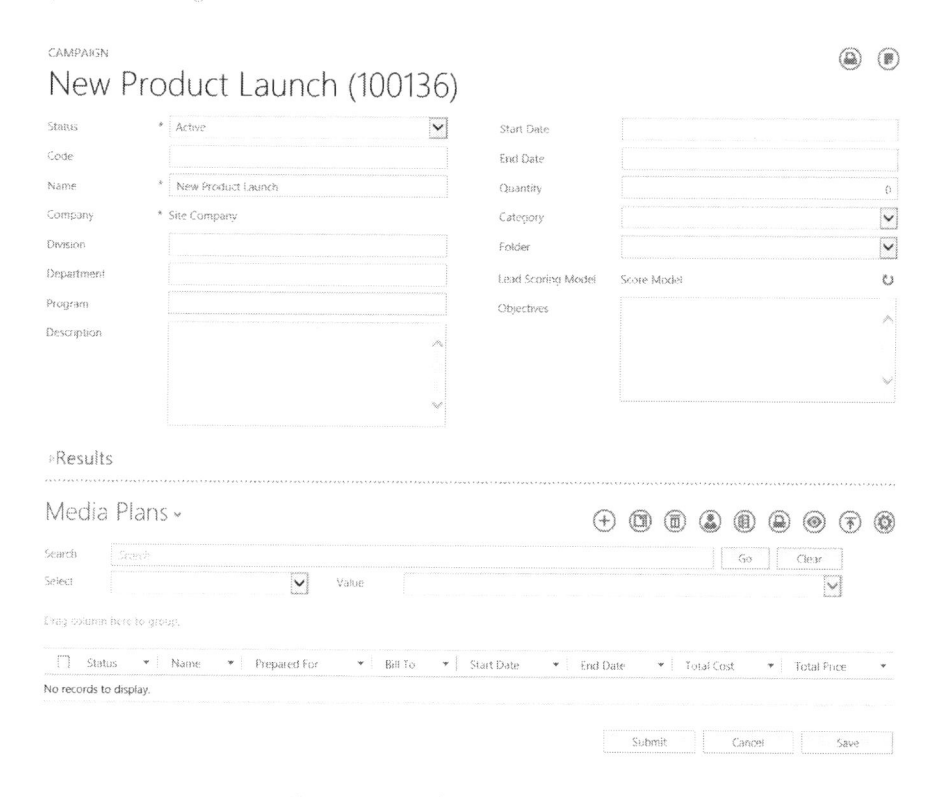

Figure 8.1 – Media Plans for a Campaign

A Media Plan can be created on the fly and associated to the Campaign by means of the "Add" action in the Media Plans panel.

As stated before media buying is a sensitive area as it might involve large chunks of the marketing budget. For this reason as special User type, the "Media Buyer" is required. If you do not see media buying entities and functionality in your instance of Dynamics Marketing see Chapter 11 "Configuration" for more details on how to configure this area for your Users.

Inside Microsoft Dynamics Marketing

Figure 8.2 – Media Plan

"PREPARED FOR" IN MEDIA PLANS

Some organizations prefer to track directly in each Media Plan the contact person on the client side. This makes communication more streamlined and allows tracking in a more flexible way.

The "prepared for" contact is used to automate defaulting on invoices from Media Plans so that the buyer can track on multiple Contacts. This might be useful for agencies and other organizations that do media buying for multiple entities/organizations.

An important field in the Media Plan header that requires a bit more explanation is "Interval". Intervals define the way data is shown and the level of detail used. If a plan is simple (few ads on few Media Outlets) a simpler visualization will do, but complex Media Plans will require a greater level of detail. This mandatory field represents the basic format of the Plan and it has six possible options:

- "Details" will show all the ads (media, print insertions, spots) for one date on one row. This type of visualization suits better the nature of printed media such Newspapers and Insert Programs.
- "Day" will show an editable grid for each row that enables entering the quantity of ads for each day from the Start Date to the End Date. This approach usually fits best Network TV and Radio buys.
- "Week" will show an editable grid for entering the quantity of ads for each week from the Start Date to the End Date. Also this organization suits Network TV and Radio Plans.
- "Month" will show an editable grid for entering the quantity of ads for each month from the Start Date to the End Date. This organization is usually used for Magazines Plans.
- "Quarter" will show an editable grid for entering the quantity of ads for each quarter from the Start Date to the End Date. This and the next are usually used as an overview.
- "Year" Same as above but for ads entered for each year from the Start Date to the End Date.

Dynamics Marketing supports integrating your media buying efforts and related campaign execution with the budget initially allocated for these activities, bringing results into the picture as well. For more details on this see Chapter 10 "Budgeting".

Similarly to other marketing software Dynamics Marketing provides redirecting URLs as a tool for tracking online media results. When a customer clicks on one of these links Dynamics Marketing gets notified while the navigation to the original link is performed so that Dynamics Marketing can keep track of customers' behavior. When your online media buys include media such as online banner ads, content on Twitter, Facebook, Yammer, LinkedIn, blog posts, other external web sites, etc., you can insert Redirect URLs created by using the Redirect URL entity at:

```
Home > Marketing Execution > Internet Marketing → Redirecting URLs
```

This way Dynamics Marketing tracks accurately customer behavior on these links across all your online media content. Needless to say, Redirecting URLs can be used in other circumstance too. One thing to keep in mind is that in the following cases Dynamics Marketing will automatically add redirecting URLs:

- Traceable Email messages
- Landing pages
- Google, Yahoo or Bing Search Results

Note that redirect URLs can be shortened even further by using Dynamics Marketing URL shortening service. This shortening is performed automatically on links made available on Twitter.

8.3.3 Associate Market and Demographics with Media Buys

A somewhat frequent misconception when buying media is to think primarily in terms of niches when formulating the media buying strategy for your needs. A more effective approach is to include more about the target demographics, and make them explicit parts of your plan. Dynamics Marketing encourages this approach by allowing the tracking of detailed demographic data to support your media buys.

In Dynamics Marketing it is possible to associate Demographic information to a single Media Order item line using the "Demo" field:

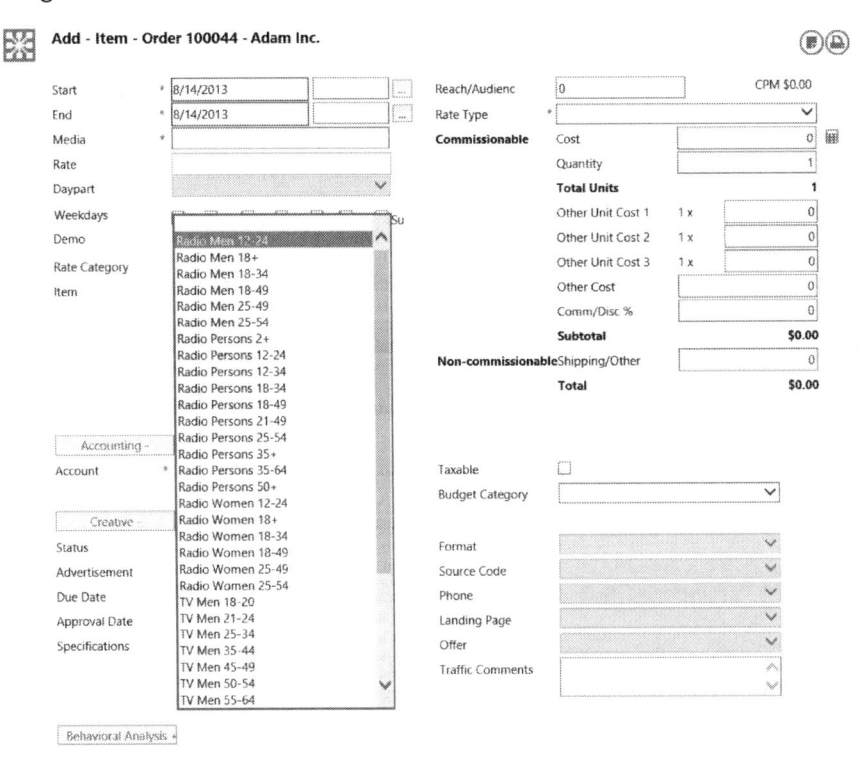

Figure 8.3 – Item on an Order

In turn, Markets can be managed from

```
Home > Settings > Media → Markets
```

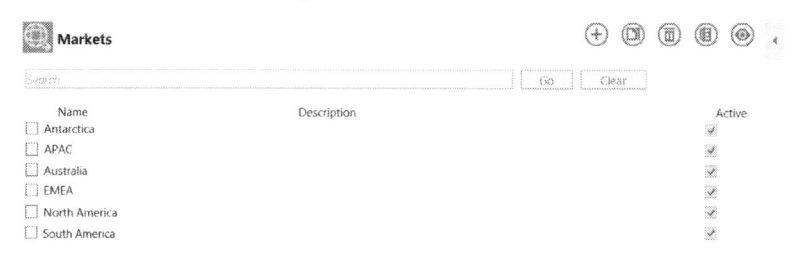

Figure 8.4 – Markets

Markets can be broken down into Market Segments:

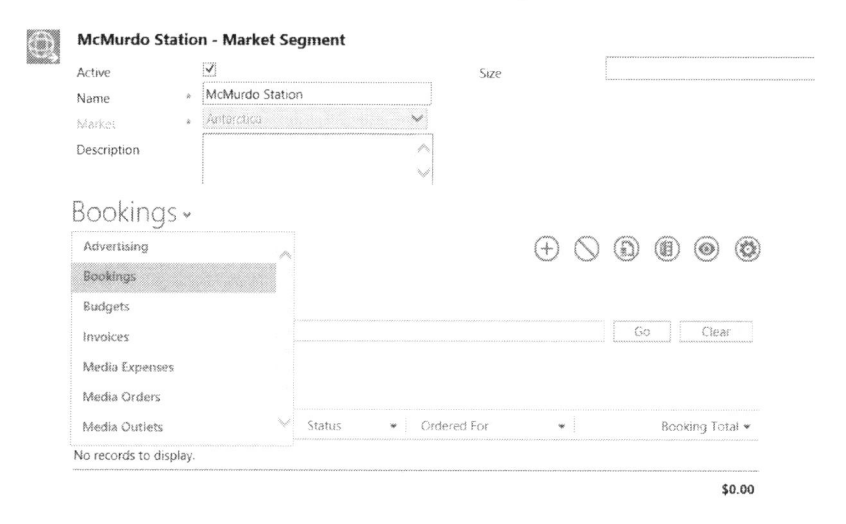

Figure 8.5 – Market Segment

Market Segments can be associated to Media Outlets.

8.3.3.1   Media Calendar
A useful overview of all the media activity going on with a given clients or even across clients is given by the Media Calendar, available at:

```
Home > Assets and Media > Media Planning → Media Calendar
```

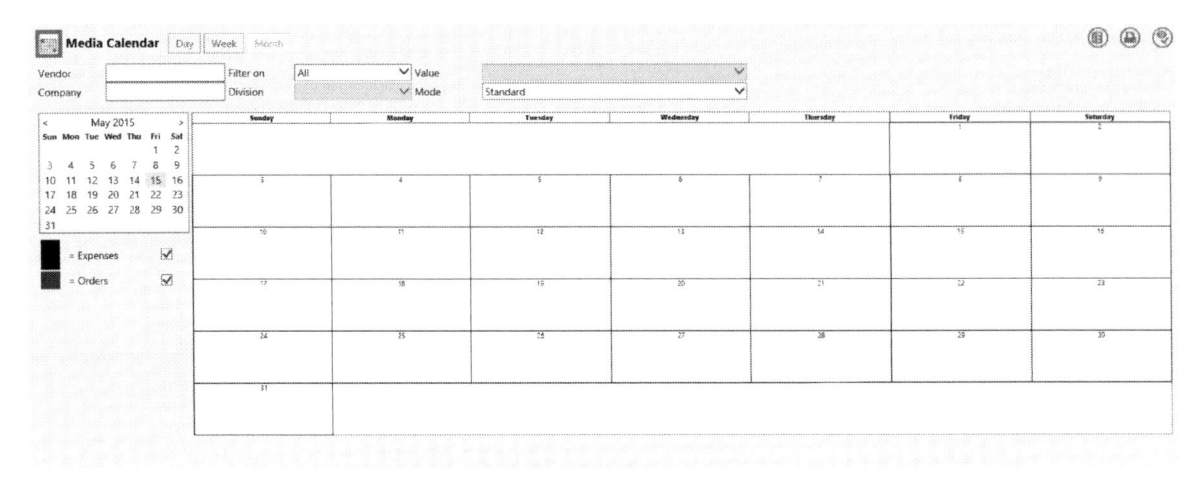

Figure 8.6 – Media Calendar

8.3.4 Use digital asset management to create media content

In this scenario we will use Dynamics Marketing Files functionality in order to collaborate with external vendors and internal employees to create reviewed creative multimedia content using the legacy approval system[35].

User	Description	User permissions
Marketing Manager	Manages the execution and approves minor versions	Files User Role[36]
Senior Marketing Manager	Is in charge of the final approval of the creative content	Files User Role
Creative Vendor	An agency hired to provide creative content for a campaign	Web Portal use with Files User Role

The Marketing Manager coordinates the work of various vendors for the creative material needed in a number of campaigns. Vendors have been given access to upload of Files and a few other operations in Dynamics Marketing. When a draft is ready for review the Marketing Manager is notified.

Notifications can be configured using the Alerts/Subscriber panel on the File form once you have a File open. The File form is available at:

---

[35] We will see the graphical approval support in Chapter 9 "Projects".
[36] This is a built-in security role as described in Chapter 11 "Configuration".

Home > Assets & Media > Files → Files

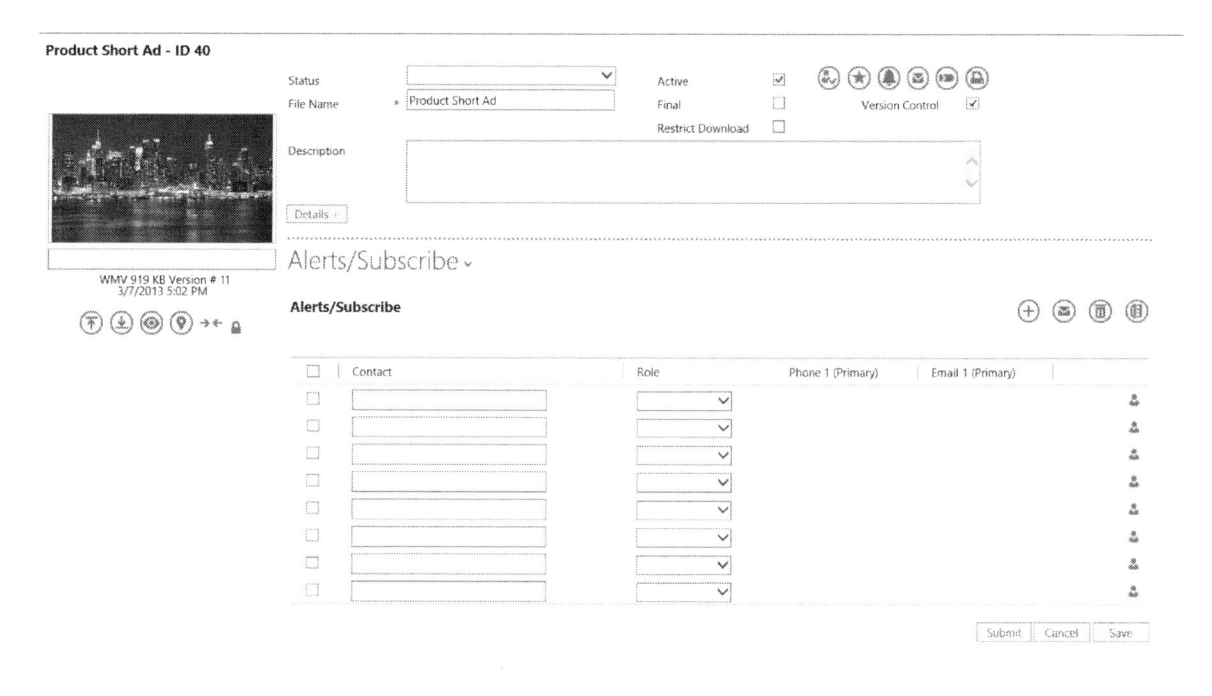

Figure 8.7 – File Alerts

It is possible to subscribe to Files notifications for the current user also using the "Subscribe" action at the top of the File form.

Let's have a look at the actions available for the given file (available in the UI under the file thumbnail):

- "Upload" will upload a new version if the "Version Control" checkbox is selected, otherwise will overwrite the current file.
- "Download" will download the (latest version of the) file.
- "Preview will show a preview of the multimedia file.
- "Markup" will open the
- "FPO" will download a small (full size, low-resolution) version of the original multimedia file, a version called in the industry "For position only" (FPO).
- "Click to Lock" will check out the file to the current user so that other users cannot edit it until is checked in.

Inside Microsoft Dynamics Marketing

RESTRICT DOWNLOADS

By selecting the Restrict Download option (assuming the user has the privileges to do so) of a selected file in

`Home > Assets and Media > Files→ Files`

one can disable downloads and only enable in-browser previews for reviewers and approvers to better control the distribution of the content.
If a reviewer or approver has the Can Read permission for a file, they can still preview the file, but cannot download it. If they have the Can Update permission for a file, you can also download it.

Figure 8.8 – Video Annotation

It is possible to add comments to various file types, including videos, as shown below.

This functionality provides a great deal of flexibility in modeling review and content creation processes. Note that external parties involved in this process need to have an Office 365 account.

Inside Microsoft Dynamics Marketing

The Marketing Manager will review the work done by the vendors at given milestones until it is ready for the final approval. An Approval Request is created from a predefined template following the company process:

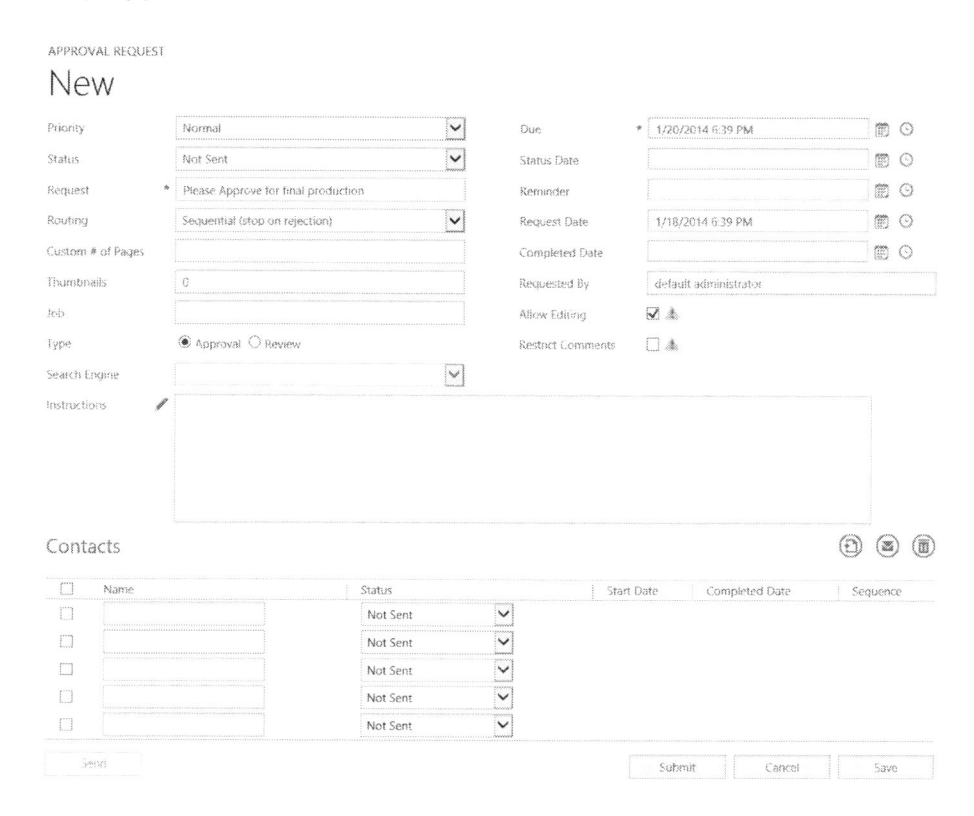

Figure 8.9 – Approval Request

At this point the file is routed to the senior manager (or other Contacts entered in the fields above) pending her final approval.

FILES DO NOT REQUIRE SILVERLIGHT ANYMORE

The Files functionality can work using the legacy Silverlight UI or with the new HTML 5 UI.

Chapter Nine
Projects

9.1 Overview

The Projects functional area is all about getting things done, and tracking them via Dynamics Marketing.

The heart of this area is the Job entity:

    Home > Projects > Job Management → Jobs

Within Dynamics Marketing, Jobs are collections of tasks that can be used for managing nearly any activity in an organization.

Jobs and Tasks are so flexible that they were used to manage work execution in developing and supporting the pre-acquisition version of the software. Closer to the marketing domain, Jobs are typically used for tracking the building of creative work and digital assets.

9.2 Main Entities in this area

Although there are more entities in this area we focus first on the most important ones, in order to give a succinct overview of the capabilities of the product before moving on with more details.

All these entities are located under the Projects area:

    Home > Projects

Entity	Description
Activities	Activities are simple calendar items like appointments, placeholders for trade show exhibits, conferences and so on. Although not a critical part of this area, it is useful to call out the difference in Dynamics Marketing between Activities (lightweight calendar items), Tasks (items tracked and assigned to people for completion) and Events (complex entities representing all the information related to a physical marketing event, from collateral, to participant scheduling, financials, and more).
Jobs	This entity is the heart of this area, gathering in one place all the information tracked in Dynamics Marketing regarding the execution of a project. Jobs are optimized for marketing organizations, covering the entire production process from ideation, request design, copywriting and printing. They can be used for generic work tracking as such work on new campaigns, development of collateral materials and more. Milestones and completion progress can be measured, and Job status can be updated when the related tasks are complete. Jobs can be used to track a project's progress.
Requests	These entities track requests for projects potentially coming from product management, merchandising, branches, stores, remote locations and offices, etc. The Job Request menu page allows internal and external users to submit Job Requests. We will discuss this more in detail in the rest of the chapter. For now keep in mind that there are two types of Job requests in Dynamics Marketing: Project Requests (which require a preliminary approval before a Job is created) and Job Requests (Job Request Templates are created to populate the Job Request Menu and when a request is created via the menu a Job is created in the system right away).
Locations	Locations organize marketing activities related to a specific geographical location. For example, tracking marketing activities in retail stores. Locations can be assigned to Companies and can be grouped into Regions.
Scheduling	This list shows how much work is assigned to each person in the system in a given period of time.
Tasks	Tasks track work assigned to people (Contacts). Dynamics Marketing provides notifications when tasks gets assigned, key information is changed, and reminders in various other occasions. You can track the actual duration of tasks versus the original estimate. Tasks synchronize both ways with CRM tasks (when the CRM connector is setup).
Time Slips	Dynamics Marketing can track time spent while working on Jobs or services including the generation of invoices and expenses. It provides a practical editing experience for quick data entry ("Worksheet" view).

9.3 SCENARIOS

9.3.1 Set up External Job requests and track them until completion.

A digital agency uses Dynamics Marketing for their daily work. They want to enable their premium customers to place frequent requests directly into the system to streamline execution and provide a higher level of service.

These are the users for this scenario.

User	Description	User permissions
Marketing Manager	Overseeing the execution of Jobs as requested by clients.	Regular User
Designer	Agency contractor creating the requested marketing material.	Regular User
Client	The client requesting the marketing collateral.	Web Portal user

New users are added in Office 365[37] and then their permissions are assigned in Dynamics Marketing, making sure to select only the functionality they are supposed to access and not enabling more than needed.

Now it is time to create the Job Request Template entry that will define the details of the work. The Marketing Manager navigates to:

```
Home > Projects > Job Management → Job Request Templates
```

Here the Marketing Manager defines all the fields available to the Client when specifying the work request:

---

[37] If you only have an Dynamics Marketing subscription new users will get assigned a paid license seat. See Chapter 11 "Configuration" for more details.

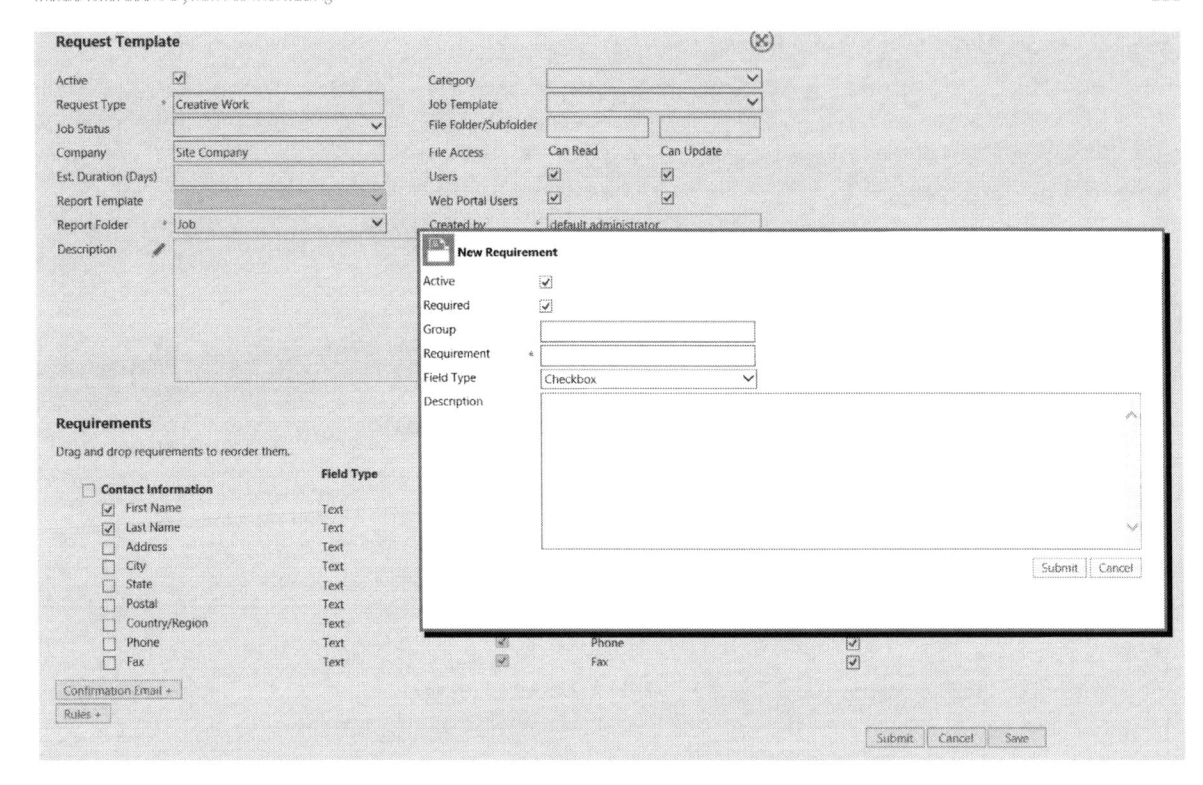

Figure 9.1 – New Requirement in a Job

The "Web Portal Users" checkbox is ticked so that the Job Request Template is available to Web Portal users as well (this page is not available anonymously).

Once the details are saved it is possible to preview them by using the Preview action. When done with the configuration of the Job Request Template they are already available in the Job Request Menu page. Note that this page is meant to be hosted in an external portal to follow the branding and look and feel of the hosting site. Such a page is available at:

```
https://[site]/JobRequests/ViewJobRequestMenu.aspx
```

or alternatively navigating to

```
Home > Projects > Job Management → Job Request Menu
```

This is the page Web Portal users will be able to access when wrapped in an iframe in the hosting portal.

Clients will submit Job Requests via the Job Request Menu and this will create Job records in Dynamics Marketing.

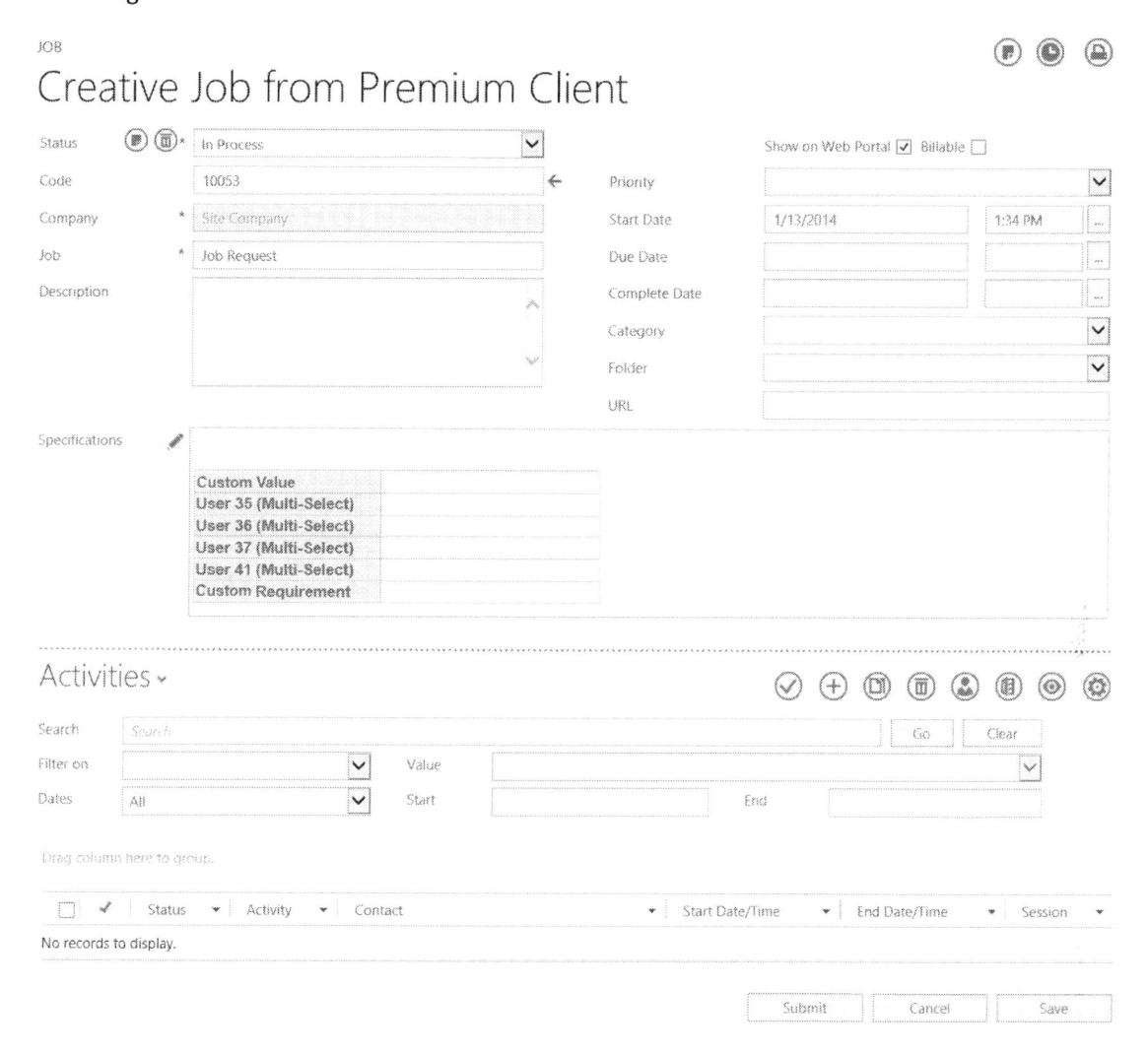

Figure 9.2 – Specifications of a Job

Similarly to what happens when leads are created from landing pages, the details of the data entered by clients is available in the rich text field "Specifications" in a table.

At this point the Job entered the system and according to what has been defined in the template it gets assigned to the Designer for execution. The Marketing Manager can monitor progress by using

Dynamics Marketing in various ways, for example he can add a widget to his home page to closely monitor the Jobs he is overseeing.

During its progress a Job can be monitored in various ways:

- Using the Job Actual Versus Estimated Time report to measure completion against original estimates
- Using the Job % on time to inspect the amount of time jobs take (the time that passes from the beginning to the end of the Job, also known as cycle time) and the variance between the estimated and actual cycle time
- By setting milestone for all Job's tasks and using the Milestone action in the Jobs list, it is possible to inspect all the Jobs along with the status of each Milestone's task.
- Using the Tasks Gantt page under Reports to see a Gantt chart showing all tasks with their status (On time, Completed and Overdue).
- See more reports available under
  `Home > Projects > Reports`

SHIPMENTS

It is possible to define and track the distribution and shipments of Packs and Components related to a Job. For example when shipping printed material to a conference or to a client.

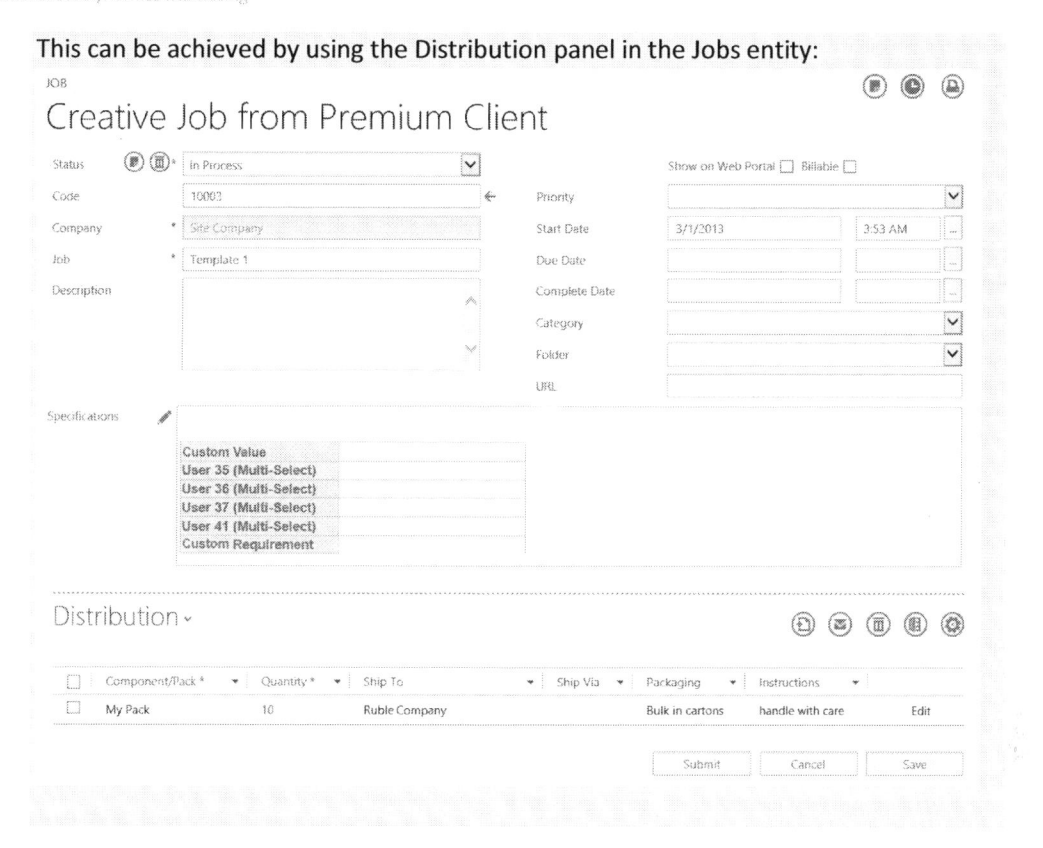

This can be achieved by using the Distribution panel in the Jobs entity:

9.3.2 Define a Process with Job Templates

Let's continue the previous scenario to zoom into the details of how Tasks were set up in the requested Jobs. A Media Agency wants to capture their production process in Dynamics Marketing so that it can be used across all their projects.

In order to define their process in Dynamics Marketing the Marketing Manager will enter all the details in a Job Template, including the needed Tasks.

By means of using the "Next Task" field in the Task entity she chains tasks together to represent the company execution procedure. By linking these tasks to a Job Template she will capture such a process in a reusable and actionable way by anyone involved.

She will add other values as well to each Task, if the process prescribes them. Things like the person and role to whom the tasks are assigned to, the typical duration, whether the containing Job should change status with the completion of this Task etc.

Of course Status values and other Category values can be configured too (as with other entities), but we'll discuss these general configurations in Chapter 11 "Configuration".

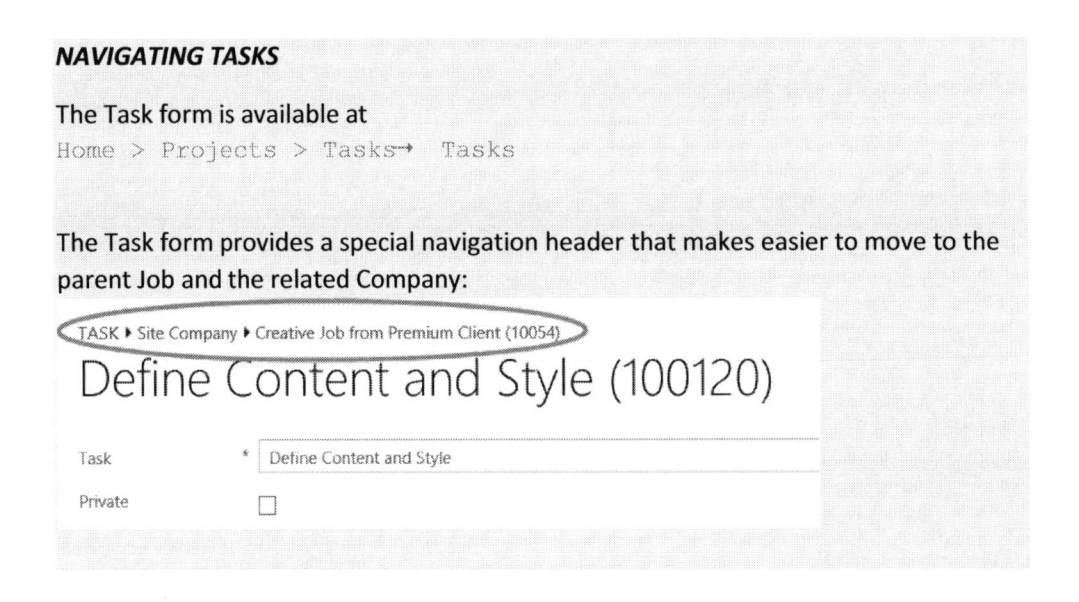

NAVIGATING TASKS

The Task form is available at

    Home > Projects > Tasks→ Tasks

The Task form provides a special navigation header that makes easier to move to the parent Job and the related Company:

TASK ▶ Site Company ▶ Creative Job from Premium Client (10054)

Define Content and Style (100120)

Task	* Define Content and Style
Private	☐

Regarding the assignment of Tasks to people in the company, the Marketing Manager has some flexibility provided by Dynamics Marketing.

If the Task is typically performed by a given person (say a senior executive providing approval) then it is enough to enter that person's Contact in the Assigned To field of the Task Template.

If the Task in the Job Template can be assigned to a pool of people (covering the same job role) you can define a Role and assign the Task to that Role instead of a single Contact. When a new Job is created based on the Template the user will need to reassign it to the right Contact.

Roles can be found at:

    Home > Settings > Administration → Roles

"ONE-CLICK" TASKS

In the Task panel for both Jobs and Contacts there is a special dropdown for quickly creating some predefined Tasks, called "One-Click tasks". These are mostly used to log activities, such as phone calls made, and other actions taken.

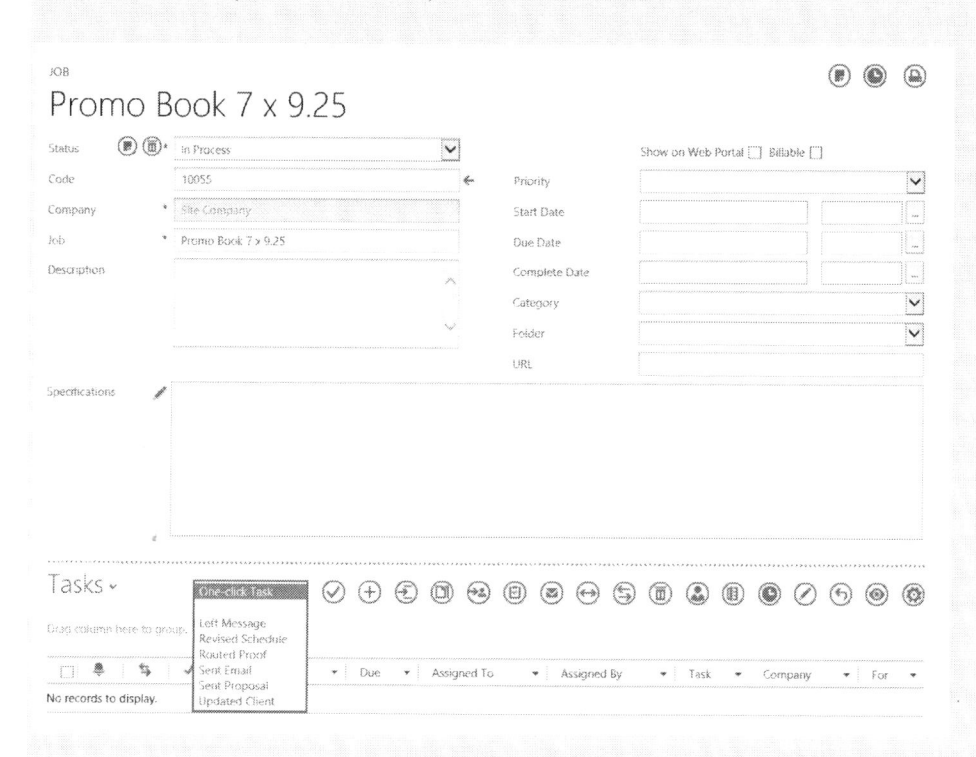

These options and the corresponding Task Template they invoke are fully configurable by changing the One-Click Task Categories in:

Home > Settings > Business Administration → Categories

And select the "One-Click Task (Jobs)" or "One-Click Task (Contacts)" category to change or add / remove new entries. The value of the Category name will be used as the name of the new Task and in the details.

9.4 EMAIL ALERTS

Although Alerts are not strictly related to the Jobs area, alerts are an important functionality in Dynamics Marketing typically used for organizing work. Non-Marketing Contacts have an additional panel for Alerts. This shows the list of email alerts a given Contact is registered to.

In the following screenshot we can see that this Contact is registered for tracking task status changes[38].

---

[38] Remember that Contacts must have one or more email addresses defined in order to set alerts.

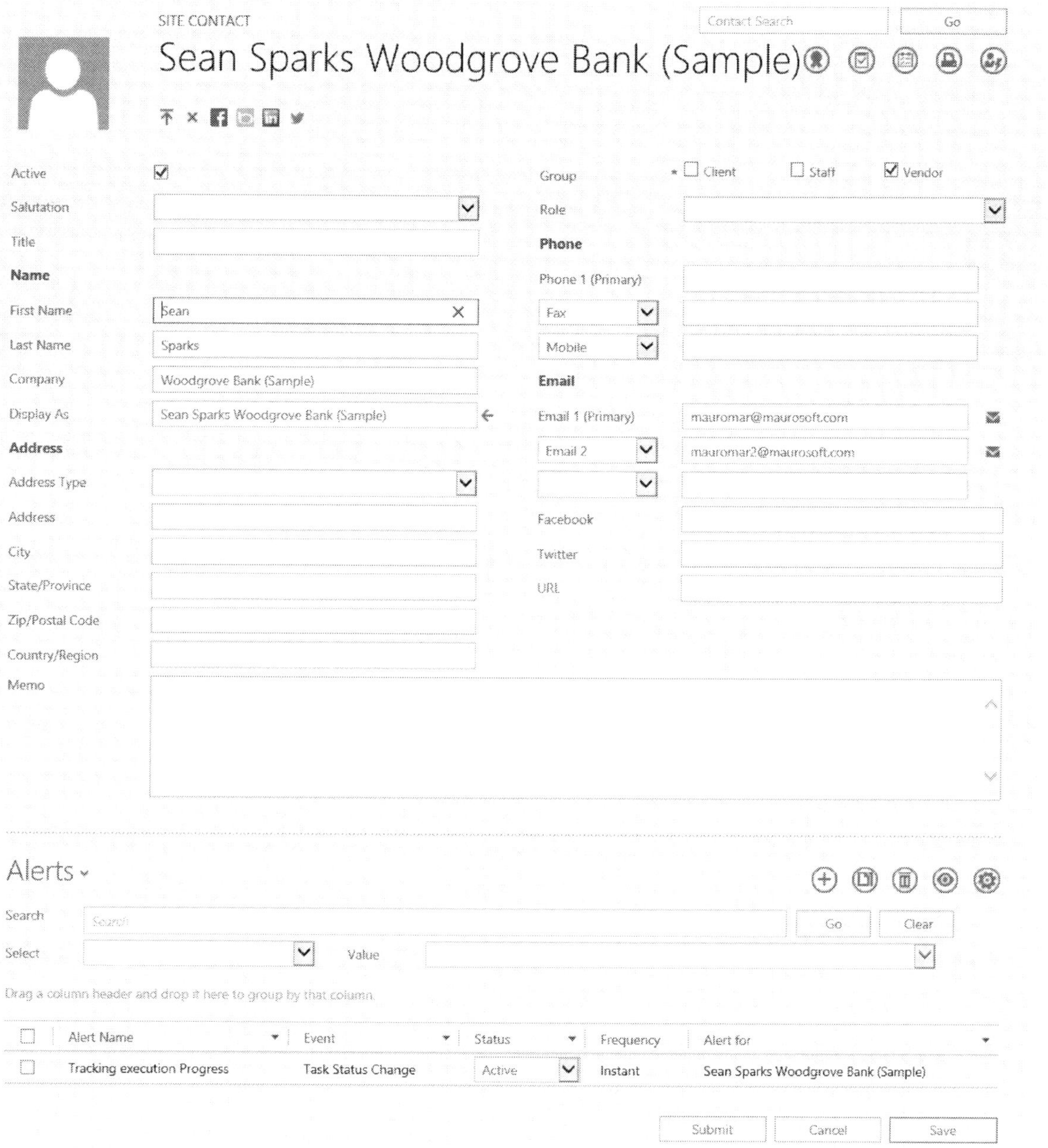

Figure 9.3 – Alerts for a Contact

An alternative way to see all the alerts in the system, for all Contacts (if security settings allow) is to use the Alert Settings list.

The Alert Settings list is available from the options menu, in the top-right corner of the screen (the "gear" menu), as shown below.

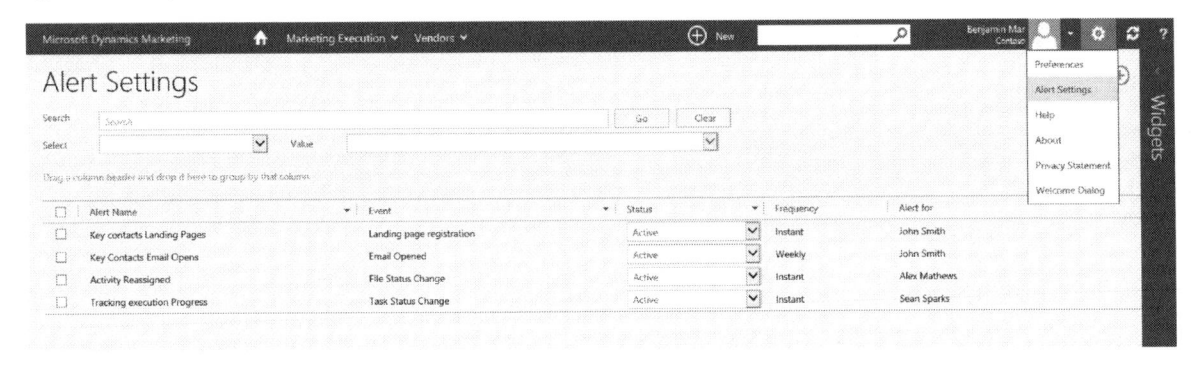

Figure 9.4 – Alerts Settings List

This list provides a centralized overview of all the alerts registered in the system. It is also possible to manage them (create from scratch or copy an existing one etc.).

9.4.1 Creating alerts

A new alert can be created by clicking on the add button in the Alert panel for the chosen contact or from the Alert Settings list.

The alert frequency can be defined as Instant, Daily and Weekly. The email address that will receive the alert email can also be chosen among those available in the Primary email address and the other addresses for the given Contact[39].

It is possible to define alerts on a number of events, as follows.

Website Visit:

- Notifications are triggered when some given Contacts visits some Websites

---

[39] See Figure 9.3 for an example of a Contact with multiple email addresses.

Email Opened:

- Define triggers for when some given Contacts open some emails

Email link clicked:

- Notifications are triggered when some given Contacts clicks some links in some emails

Landing page registration:

- Notifications are triggered when some given Contacts registers to some given landing page

Other:

- Trigger notification based on criteria based on the following Entities: Activity, Approval, Campaign, Component, Contact, Contract, Email Marketing, Equipment, Event, File, Financial, Job, Lead Management, Media, Note, Program, Project Request, Task, Travel —each of these "types" provides a number of possible triggers.

For instance the screenshot in the following page shows an alert that sends a digest of notifications spanning a week regarding when the specified contacts opened a specified set of emails. For example a marketing manager or a sales rep might be watching closely the behavior of some key customers now that a sale is finally getting closed.

ALERT
Key Contacts Opening Campaign emails

Alert Name	*	Key Contacts Opening Campaign emails
Status	*	Active

- ○ Website Visit
- ● Email Opened
- ○ Email link clicked
- ○ Landing page registration
- ○ Other

Emails on watch list
- Working General Template ✗

Start typing or press the Down Arrow key

Contacts on watch list
- Aaron Fernandez ✗
- Lewis Carroll ✗

Fields to be included: *Start typing or press the Down Arrow key*

Alert Frequency * Weekly

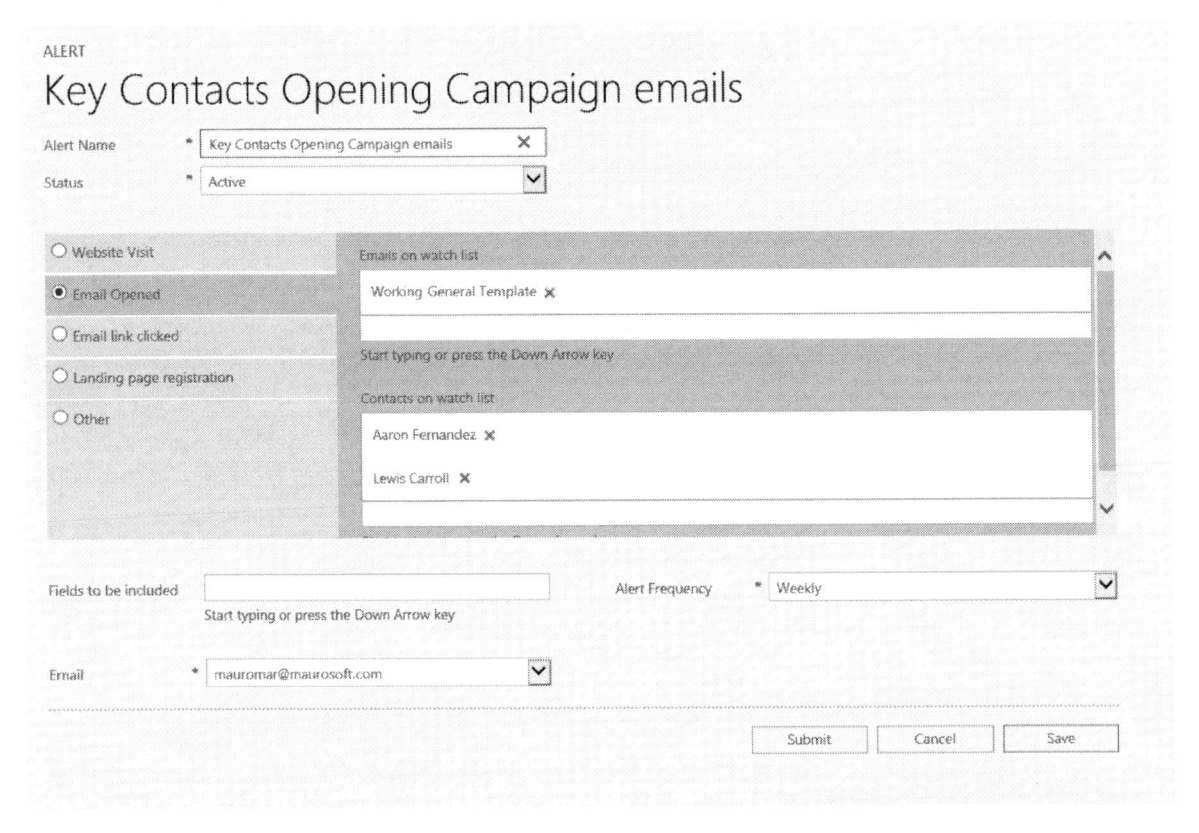

Email * mauromar@maurosoft.com

[Submit] [Cancel] [Save]

Figure 9.5 – Example of Alert

If wanted some additional fields can be added to the content of the notification email in order to provide more context about the notification.

As another B2B example, imagine we want to closely monitor some key decision makers from a customer's purchasing department visiting our product's price pages. We want to be notified instantly with details about their visit (the time they spent, the pages they visited together with the pricing table, etc.).

The following alert implements these requirements.

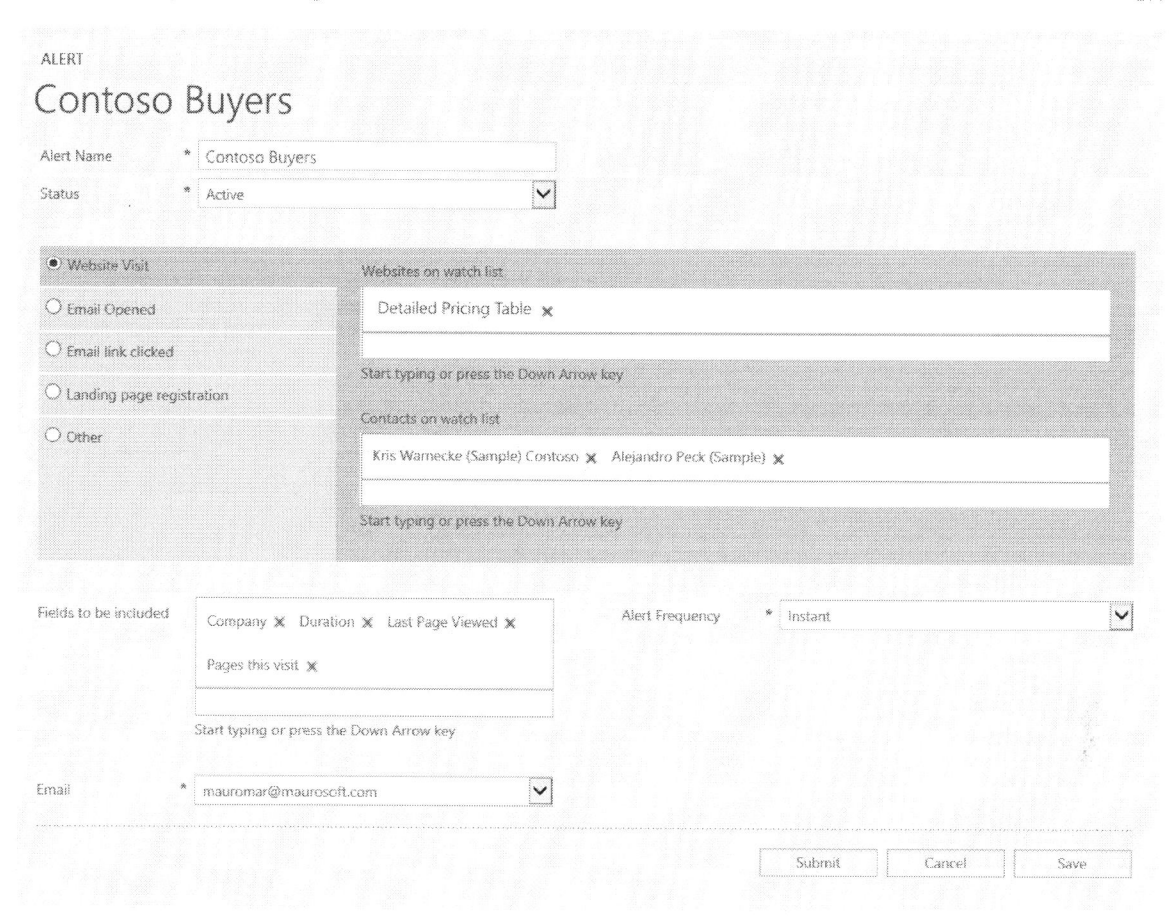

Figure 9.6 – Another example of alert

9.5 APPROVALS

Although not strictly related to Projects – Approvals are possible for most meaningful entities in Dynamics Marketing (documents, email messages, videos and many more)–we discuss them here because they are usually used as part of projects.

9.5.1 Some Terminology

Dynamics Marketing traditionally uses a dedicated terminology for the approvals area. Let's see the main concepts used in the product.

Concept	Description	Available from:
Approval Request	This is the definition of an approval "workflow", a schema that defines what should happen and the rules for completing the approval of a given record.	Home > Projects > Approvals → Approvals
Approval Response	These are the responses single actors in the approval or review workflow provide back to the system.	Home > Projects > Approvals → Approvals With "Show Inactive/Deleted" to see the completed ones.
Approval Request Template	It is equivalent to an approval request but it is used as a template.	Home > Projects > Approvals → Templates

9.5.2 Creating an Approval or Review

To create a new Approval or Review request:

```
Home > Projects > Approvals → Approvals
```

An example of the Approvals Request form is shown in the following page.

Inside Microsoft Dynamics Marketing

APPROVAL REQUEST
New

Priority	Normal	Due	* 11/17/2014 10:30 AM
Status	Not Sent	Status Date	
Request	*	Reminder	
Routing	Concurrent	Request Date	11/16/2014 10:30 AM
Custom # of Pages		Completed Date	
Thumbnails	0	Requested By	Mauro Moreno Litware (Sample)
Job		Allow Editing	☑
Type	● Approval ○ Review	Restrict Comments	☐
Instructions			

Users

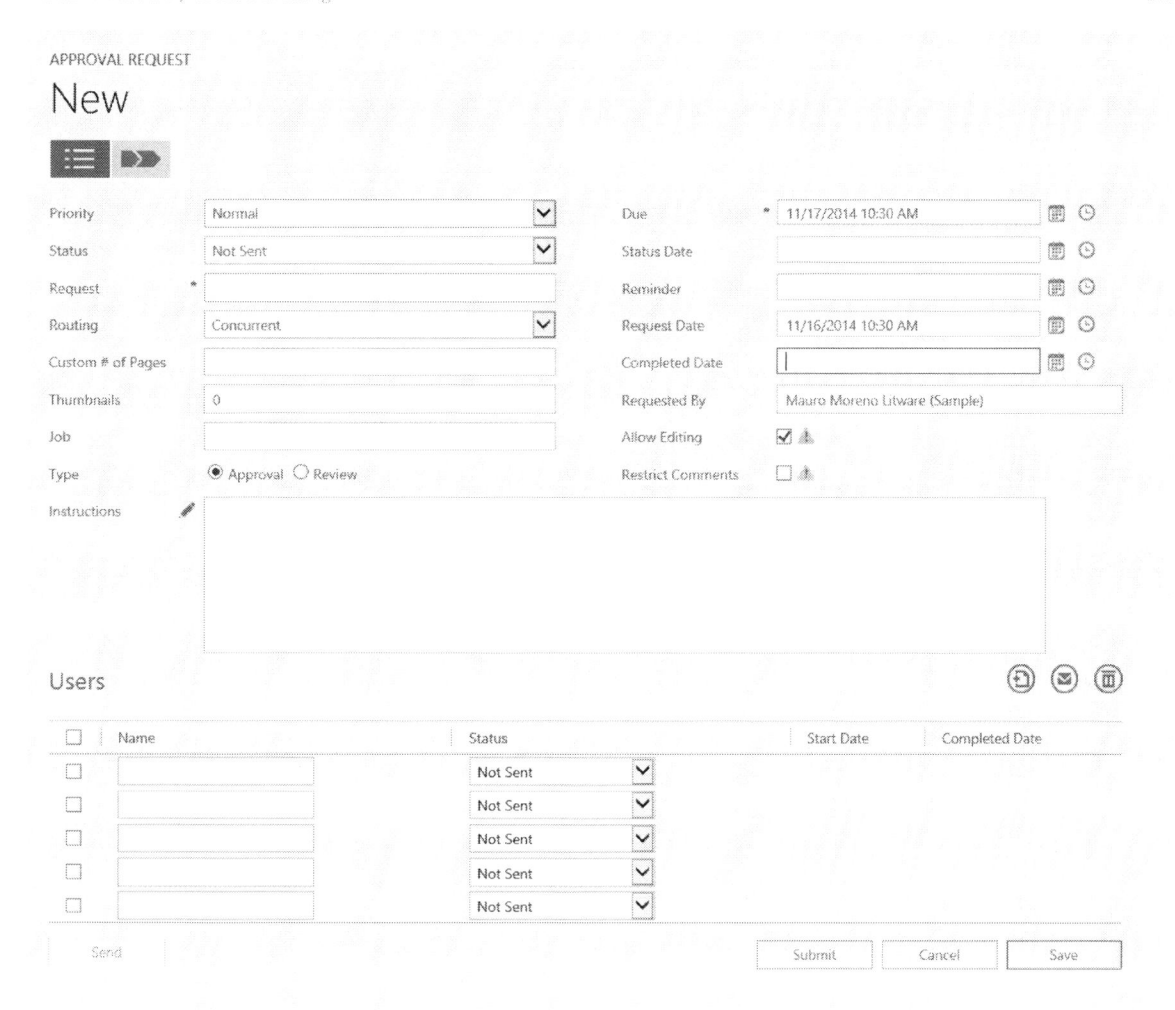

	Name	Status	Start Date	Completed Date
☐		Not Sent		
☐		Not Sent		
☐		Not Sent		
☐		Not Sent		
☐		Not Sent		

Send   Submit Cancel Save

Figure 9.7 – New Approval Request

From here we need to enter a name for the request, and we can specify whether we want an approval or a review, or the due date, etc. When entered all the mandatory information we save.

When clicking on the "Workflow" button the Workflow Tab of our Approval Request is open. Here we can define visually all the details of the approval (or review) process we want to implement in Dynamics Marketing:

Inside Microsoft Dynamics Marketing

APPROVAL REQUEST
Newsletter (Approval)

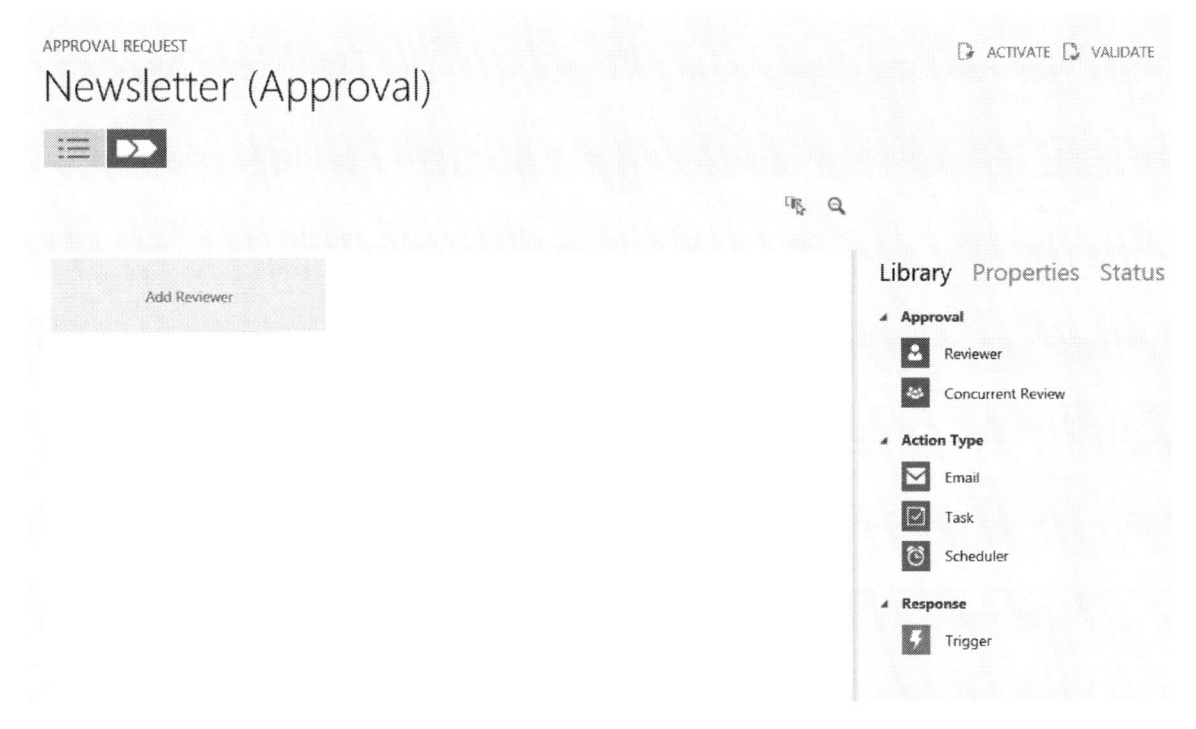

Figure 9.8 – Approval Editor

Let us look at the palette available for designing approval requests in Dynamics Marketing.

Activity (Model Block)	Icon	Description
Reviewer		Route the approval to a given User
Concurrent Review Group		Routes the approval to a group of Users. The approvals are routed in parallel to all the Users in the group.
Email action		Sends a an email (with simple content formatting but complete traceability) to a Contact
Task action		Creates a Task assigned to a specified Contact.
Scheduler action		Waits for a given amount of time before carrying on an action.
Trigger		Defines conditional triggers based on the preceding activity in the model.

These are the simple triggers options for each activity block, i.e. the trigger options in the "Simple" tab when the following activity is preceding the trigger block[40]:

- Reviewer
    - Approve, Rejected
- Concurrent Review Group
    - Approve, Rejected
- Email action
    - Email Delivered, Email Opened, Email Link Clicked, Email Bounced
- Task action
    - Approved, Cancelled, Completed, In Process, Not Approved, Not Ready To Start, Not Started, On Hold, Waiting for Reply
- Scheduler action, Trigger
    - No options available

To see how all of these activities work in practice, let's start with a simple example (some more elaborated examples will come in a following section). Let's assume we want to model the approval of a Newsletter by Nancy, a manager. We also want to react to the approval remaining unaddressed for more than 5 days, by sending her a reminder email. When the newsletter is approved we assign a Task to John to make the approved file available for the marketing operator working with the newsletter. This will complete the approval (i.e. when this final step is completed the Approval Request Status will become "Completed").

This is how we can represent this simple workflow in Dynamics Marketing:

---

[40] Note that the capabilities in the "Advanced" tab (similar to those described in Chapter 2 "Campaign Automation" for Campaign Automation models) are also derived from these options.

APPROVAL REQUEST

Newsletter (Approval)

| Nancy | Approved | Publish Newsletter | Drag activity here |
| Not Ready To Start | 0 | 0 | |

| | Wait 5 days | Approval Reminder |

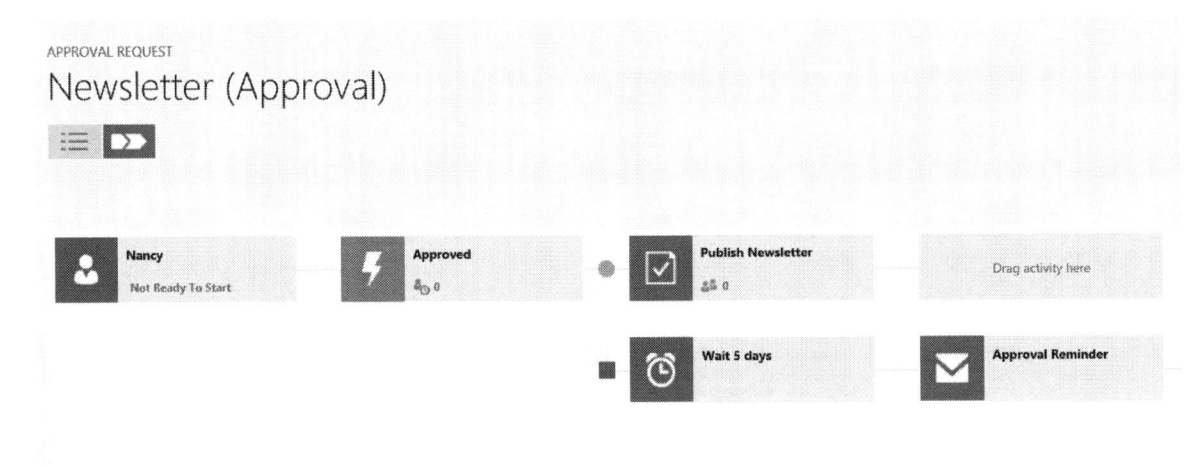

Figure 9.9 – An Example Approval Request

Note that we still didn't started the workflow (by activating it) so the numbers and the status in the blocks is not updated. Once a workflow is activated (i.e. started) most of the fields in the Summary tabs become read-only.

> **WORKFLOW DETAILS**
>
> Note that it is possible to specify the details of an approval / review workflow both from the visual editor and from the Summary tab. Given that the latter was the only option available in older releases of Dynamics Marketing we refer to these workflows as "legacy" approval requests (see an example in Chapter 8 "Assets and Media"). Such approval requests are superseded by the new visual workflow functionality described here, which provides more flexibility and capabilities.
>
> Legacy workflows are activated via the "Send" button in the Summary tab and have only three routing options possible (defined in the "Routing" field): Concurrent, Sequential (waiting for all steps to complete) or Sequential –stop and complete on first rejection.
>
> Once a workflow is defined using the visual editor the "Send" action in the Summary tab for legacy workflows is not available anymore.

Chapter Ten
Budgeting

10.1 Overview

Dynamics Marketing provide extensive functionality for the accounting of marketing financial transactions. Dynamics Marketing supports both Accrual Accounting and Cash Accounting. Depending upon the size and complexity of your organization you might want to use one or the other method, although the primary method in Dynamics Marketing is Accrual Accounting.

> **ACCRUAL VS. CASH ACCOUNTING**
>
> Here's a brief refresher.
>
> With Accrual Accounting income and expenses are considered incurred at the time they are realized (rather than when the payment is actually made). The time when a user enters a transaction and the time when the user actually pays or receives cash may be two separate events."
>
> Cash Accounting considers income and expenses incurred at the time payment is made or received. This approach is simpler than Accrual Accounting and usually used by smaller organizations.

It is important to remember that the budgeting functionality in Dynamics Marketing is not meant to replace the traditional, company-wide accounting functionality available for instance in ERP software such as Microsoft Dynamics ERP. The Budgeting functionality in Dynamics Marketing is meant to complement your accounting software for the specifics of your organization's marketing operations only.

10.2 Main Entities

These are the main entities available in this area of the product[41]:

Entity	Description
Accounts Payable	Used to pay your expenses with Dynamics Marketing.
Accounts Receivable	Used to receive Client's payments.
Budget Workbooks	Dynamics Marketing provides an articulate representation of budgeting for you marketing operations.
Chart of Accounts	For every transaction Dynamics Marketing automatically creates two corresponding entries (a debit and credit line in the General Ledger). The list of the Account names available in the General Ledger is called the Chart of Accounts.
Client Quotes	Dynamics Marketing provides support for capturing Client's Quotes in the system and provide invoices and various other operations as needed.
Closing	This functionality is about handling your Fiscal Year Closing process. Remember that Dynamics Marketing is not meant to replace a specialized accounting software, but only complement it for marketing-specific flows. Having said that, this is the workflow implemented in Dynamics Marketing for the Fiscal year Closing. 1. Reconcile all bank and payment accounts to ensure that their balances are correct. 2. Pay any year end payroll liabilities. 3. Review open Purchase Orders and Open Sales Orders and create appropriate accruals. 4. If needed, correct and adjust the information in the system. 5. Prepare depreciation and amortization entries for all new fixed assets purchased during the year and for all other asset you purchased in prior fiscal years. 6. Adjust Retained Earnings. 7. Print Income Statement and Balance Sheet. 8. Close the books. 9. Prepare your tax return and other tax related forms.

---

[41] If you cannot see some of these entities in your navigation you will need to configure your User for accessing budgeting functionality as described in Chapter 11 "Configuration".

Entity	Description
	Dynamics Marketing provides some elasticity in this process by allowing some changes in the steps above and also to enter transactions that occur prior to the closing date, if wished so.
Estimates	Dynamics Marketing supports the process of preparing detailed price, cost and time estimates. You can: - Associate Estimates to a Job, Campaign, Event or Program. - Compare Estimates' costs, revenue and time against actual values for the Estimates associated to Projects.
Expense & Expense Reconciliation	Dynamics Marketing allows users to track expenses and to reconcile them as described in more detail later in this chapter.
Invoices	Invoices are automatically posted to the General Ledger.
Items/Services	Items and Services are used to track items you buy, sell and use and are tracked as financial transactions. Dynamics Marketing distinguishes between two types of Items: - Standard Items that can be used to track the things that your organization buys, sells or uses. - Inventory Items can be tracked using additional inventory management functionality. These latter items are available only in the Enterprise Edition.
Journal Entries	In a company most accounting transactions are usually handled via invoices, posting expenses and paying bills. In some cases though, your General Ledger might not balance. You can then enter accounting transaction as Journal Entries to post them directly against your accounts and balance your general ledger.
Payroll	Dynamics Marketing can manage basic payroll transactions for your employees.
Purchase Orders	When you purchase items, media and services from Vendors you can issue a Purchase Order using Dynamics Marketing.
Record Deposits	Dynamics Marketing allows tracking bank deposits created from a payment account, for example on a weekly basis all the week's checks can be deposited in the bank account.
RFQ Requests	Dynamics Marketing provides support for the processes revolving around Requests For Quote, handling quotes for vendors for Jobs, Campaigns and Events. When an RFQ Request is 'sent' Vendors receive a notification email and can securely use the RFQ Response page in Dynamics Marketing to respond to the RFQ.

Entity	Description
	Automatic email alerts notify Vendors and Requestors of various other events in this process (when a new RFQ is issued, when all Responses have been received, when a Vendor is selected and the RFQ is awarded). Other functionality helps handling the rest of the process as well, such as the "Award" function used to specify the selected Vendor and to create a PO. The Vendor receives an automatic notification.
Sales Orders	Dynamics Marketing allows for tracking Clients' orders before being invoiced (i.e. when the given Items / Services have been provided) as Sales Orders. Differently than Invoices, Dynamics Marketing does not post Sales Orders to the General Ledger.
Tax Rates	Dynamics Marketing calculates and tracks the following taxes: Sales Tax, Value Added Tax and Withholding Tax.
Transfer Funds	Dynamics Marketing allows transferring funds from one account to another.
Vendor Quotes	Dynamics Marketing provides support for the basic vendor quoting process as follows. (We assume here the Users working for the Vendor have been created as Web Portal Users in order to get email alerts and access the Dynamics Marketing Web Portal.) 1. Selection of one or more Vendors for a quote request, and creation of a Vendor Quote with the needed Requirements. If more than one Vendor is selected, use the Copy function to send copies of the quote to multiple Vendors 2. An automatic alert email can be generated to all the Vendors when the Vendor Quote is 'Open for Tender'. 3. Each Vendor User can login to the Web Portal and access the Vendor Quote. Here they can submit a quote (using the "Tender" action). At this point the Quote is locked and cannot be changed further by the User Vendor.
Write & Write Check	Dynamics Marketing allows for entering and printing checks. Printing follows standard US formats.

10.2.1 Create and Work with Marketing Budgets

Dynamics Marketing organizes the data in a Budget in a set of Worksheets. A collection of Worksheets is called a Workbook. So the information for a given Budget is represented as a Budget Workbook in the system.

Budgets are available under:

Home > Budgeting > Settings → Budget Workbooks

Marketing Budgets in Dynamics Marketing can be associated with the following entities:

- Brands
- Campaigns
- Channels
- Components
- Companies/Clients
- Contacts
- Departments
- Events
- Jobs
- Locations
- Markets
- Media Outlets
- Products
- Programs

Marketing Budgets can be posted against Expense, Cost of Goods Sold and the Revenue accounts.

In the next page is shown an example of a Budget Worksheet (i.e. a "line" in a Budget Workbook).

Inside Microsoft Dynamics Marketing

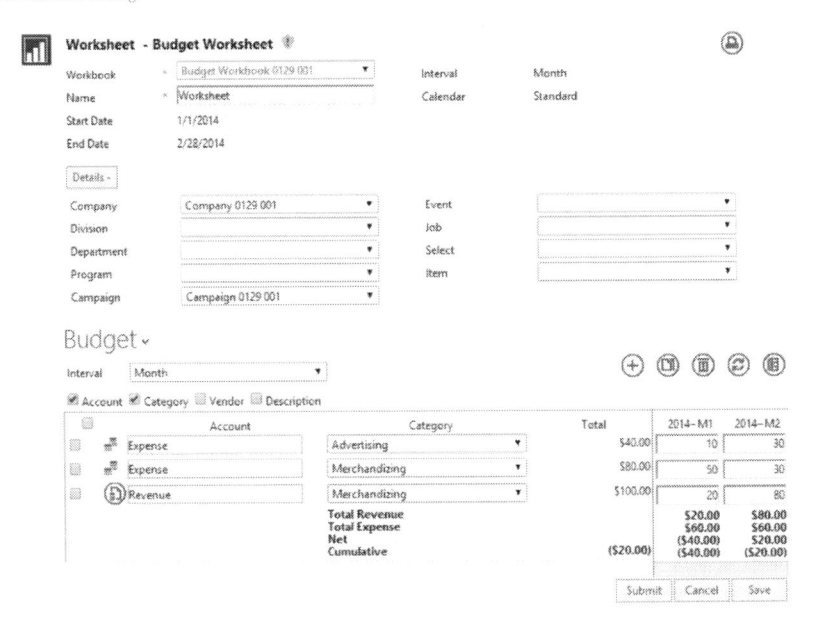

Figure 10.1 –Budget Worksheet

10.2.2 Account Types
Dynamics Marketing provides the following standard account types:

- Asset Accounts track the value of depreciable assets purchased and owned that aren't likely to be converted into cash within a year (equipment, furniture etc.).
- Bank Accounts are Asset Accounts used for paying bills via bank transactions.
- Cost of Goods Sold (COGS) Accounts track the value of the cost of goods and materials held in inventory and then sold.
- Expense Accounts track marketing expenses such as advertising, supplies, etc.
- Liability Accounts track the value of Liabilities that are scheduled to be paid within one year, such as sales, purchases, and short-term loans.
- Revenue Accounts represent revenue from services such as design, copywriting, etc.
- Tax Accounts track sales tax, withholding taxes, value added taxes and other tax payments.
- Payment Holding Accounts are used to temporarily hold cash receipts.

10.2.3 Expense Reconciliation

In Dynamics Marketing, Reconciliation consists of matching Purchase Orders and Media Orders with Vendor Invoices.

When a Vendor Invoice is received the reconciliation process starts:

1. Find the original Purchase order(s) and/or Media Order(s).
2. Compare the Purchase Order(s)/Media Order(s) with the Vendor Invoice.
3. Create Expenses including adjustments for any differences (this posts the Expense to the General Ledger and creates an entry in the Accounts Payable register).
4. Finally, the related Purchase Order(s)/Media Order(s) can be closed.

The following screenshot shows the Expense Reconciliation form. These are available under:

Home > Budgeting > Reconciliation → Expense Reconciliation

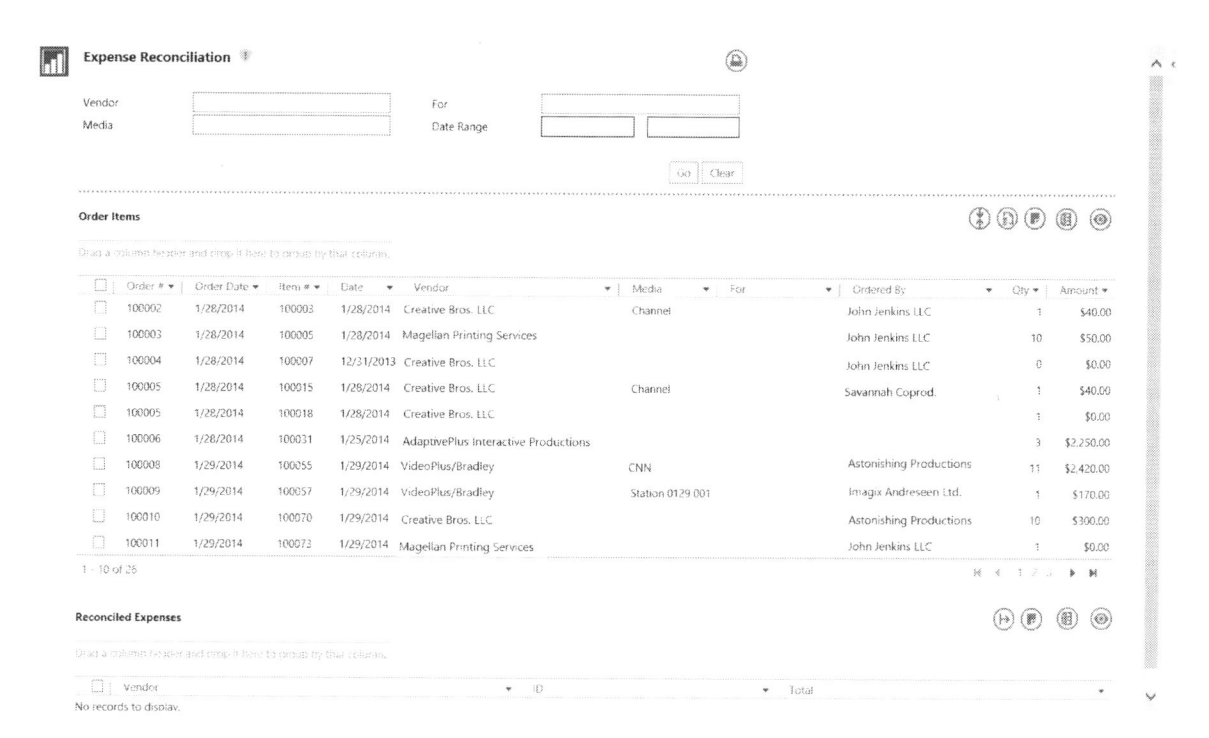

Figure 10.2 – Expense Reconciliation

FINANCIAL TRANSACTIONS WITH MULTIPLE CURRENCIES

Dynamics Marketing allows organizations to handle multiple currencies and their exchange rates, as described in Chapter 11 "Configuration".

CHAPTER ELEVEN
CONFIGURING DYNAMICS MARKETING

11.1 OVERVIEW

While Dynamics Marketing lacks the flexible development platform of a product like Dynamics CRM, it still provide a number of powerful configuration options. This chapter is for power users and system administrators learning how to take advantage of the flexibility built in Dynamics Marketing. All the functionality described in this chapter doesn't require coding or special setup.

Configuring Dynamics Marketing can be divided into two main areas:

- Business configuration. Tweaking Dynamics Marketing to fit your business processes. These are the most common configurations.
- System configuration. Setting up technical and extra-functional capabilities. Most of these options are available under the area:

    ```
    Home > Settings > Administration
    ```

> **DYNAMICS MARKETING DOESN'T REQUIRE "IT SUPPORT"**
>
> Dynamics Marketing has been designed in a way that it does not require technical, dedicated "IT" personnel to configure and operate. The software is built using high-level, business-oriented abstractions and concepts. There are a few configuration settings that require some limited technical expertise, though. These will be called out explicitly in this chapter.

11.2 USERS AND SECURITY

A critical task that needs to be performed carefully is the registration of new users in the system.

Dynamics Marketing is part of the Office 365 Suite and as such users and their license details are specified in the Office 365 portal. The security permissions and other Dynamics Marketing-specific setup are performed in Dynamics Marketing. Although this might seem confusing at first, the line of separation is quite clear: domain user and license-related tasks (e.g., administration impacting licenses - the money spent on the subscription) are performed in the Office 365 portal. Other administration tasks that are specific only to Dynamics Marketing (e.g., setting up security permissions for an already assigned Office 365 user, Dynamics Marketing Site Settings, etc.) are performed in Dynamics Marketing. Thanks to the common Office 365 user accounts, the same users are obviously shared across the Office 365 portal, enabling single sign on with other subscriptions such as Dynamics CRM, Microsoft Social Listening, Power BI etc. Dynamics Marketing encourages a separation between business administrative roles and software administration ones.

11.2.1 First-time setup

In a nutshell these are the main steps involved in configuring the product for your users from scratch:

1. A Dynamics Marketing subscription is acquired in Office 365. The subscription could be a Trial (free of charge) or a paid one. The Office 365 administrator login used for acquiring the subscription will become administrator in Dynamics Marketing.
2. At this point we have license administrators configured in Office 365 but only one user, the initial administrator that is enabled to log into Dynamics Marketing as an administrator. So the next critical step for the administrator is to add additional users in Office 365 that she will then register as administrators in Dynamics Marketing. Typically[42] she will add a non-administrator user in Office 365 and assign to him administrator rights only in Dynamics Marketing.
3. From this point on the role of the administrator the initially provisioned the subscription is not critical anymore, because all her functions (both impacting licenses in Office 365 and administering the product in Dynamics Marketing) can be performed by the other users she registered in the previous steps. At this point the one-time initial setup is concluded.

   Let's summarize the steps we have been through with a small example. Let's assume the administrator created another user, "John" as an Office 365 administrator[43] and assigned him an Dynamics Marketing license in the Office 365 portal.

---

[42] In small companies or if she is a "power user" she will perform all the users setup herself also in Dynamics Marketing.
[43] To replace her in all her functions she would create him as a "Global administrator". John will then automatically become an administrator in Dynamics Marketing. If she wanted John only to be administrator in

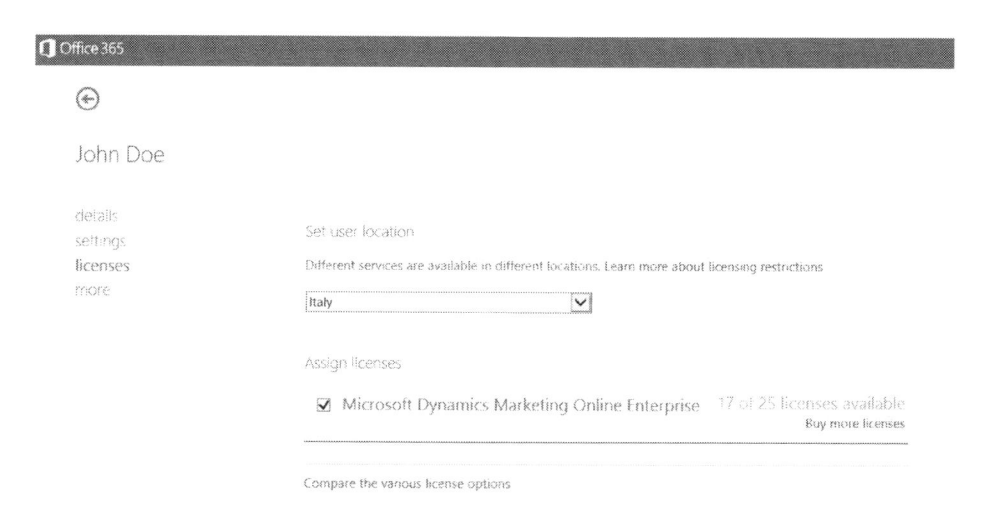

Figure 11.1 –User License Details in the Office 365 Portal

As a good habit, it is a good idea to create other administrators in Office 365 or Dynamics Marketing. So that if the administrator that initially created the subscription is on vacation or sick and something is required from her user account (say buy additional disk storage) the entire company doesn't grind to a halt.
Note that (similar to Dynamics CRM) administrators of type "Service" and "Global" in Office 365 automatically become administrators in Dynamics Marketing, although the administrator option in Dynamics Marketing can be changed independently then the user type in Office 365.

The administrator also logged into Dynamics Marketing and gave John administrator rights so that he could complete the detailed setup of all the Dynamics Marketing users. She opened Dynamics Marketing from the top-right navigation bar, and once in Dynamics Marketing she navigated to the list of Users:

```
Home > Settings > Administration → Users
```

She opened John (added users are synced automatically from Office 365 into Dynamics Marketing[44]) and assigned him additional privileges as needed.

Dynamics Marketing but not in Office 365 she will create a normal non-administrator Office 365 user and then grant him administrator rights only in Dynamics Marketing.
[44] The sync usually takes few minutes to complete.

From now on, John can log into the Office 365 portal and setup users and their license seats as needed, and set them up in Dynamics Marketing. This will be the subject of our next subsection.

Note that if the organization was already on Office 365 (for example they already have a subscription of Dynamics CRM Online and Office 365 Enterprise E3) then an Administrator would simply have to assign that user the Dynamics Marketing subscription and assign license seats to the users as needed.

> **ALWAYS PROVIDE BACK-UP ADMINISTRATORS**
>
> Although a power user can purchase an Dynamics Marketing subscription and set up all the users using her own account, it is always a good idea to spend five minutes more to set up other administrators right away. Just remember to assign Dynamics Marketing security settings to these new admins as well or they will only able to access the "Settings" menu.

11.2.2 User setup

Once an Office 365 administrator has prepared the essential subscription details and setup the key administrator users both in Office 365 and Dynamics Marketing it is time to add the rest of the users to the system, by her or another administrator.

Such an administrator will perform the following steps for each user to add:

1. Add the user in the Office 365 portal.
2. If the user needs to be a Web Portal User then do not assign him an Dynamics Marketing license seat.
   Otherwise, if the user needs to be an Dynamics Marketing paid user (i.e. a Dynamics Marketing User that is *not* a Web Portal User) then assign a license seat to the user.
3. After some time to let the system sync the users from Office 365, in the Dynamics Marketing Users list available at

   ```
   Home > Settings > Administration → Users
   ```

   The newly added users should be visible. Note that the users that don't have a license assigned in the Office 365 portal can only be given the Web Portal user type in Dynamics Marketing.

4. Select the user at hand and assign the wanted security privileges in Dynamics Marketing. We will dig more into the details of this important step in the next section.

11.2.2.1 User Permissions in Dynamics Marketing

Once the users are created and / or assigned in the Office 365 Portal to a Dynamics Marketing subscription and they are propagated into Dynamics Marketing[45] they are available in the Users list available at

> Home > Settings > Administration → Users

This is how a User form looks like in Dynamics Marketing:

---

[45] The first time a new Dynamics Marketing subscription is added to a tenant with thousands or more of existing users it might take some more time to do the initial synchronization of all the users.

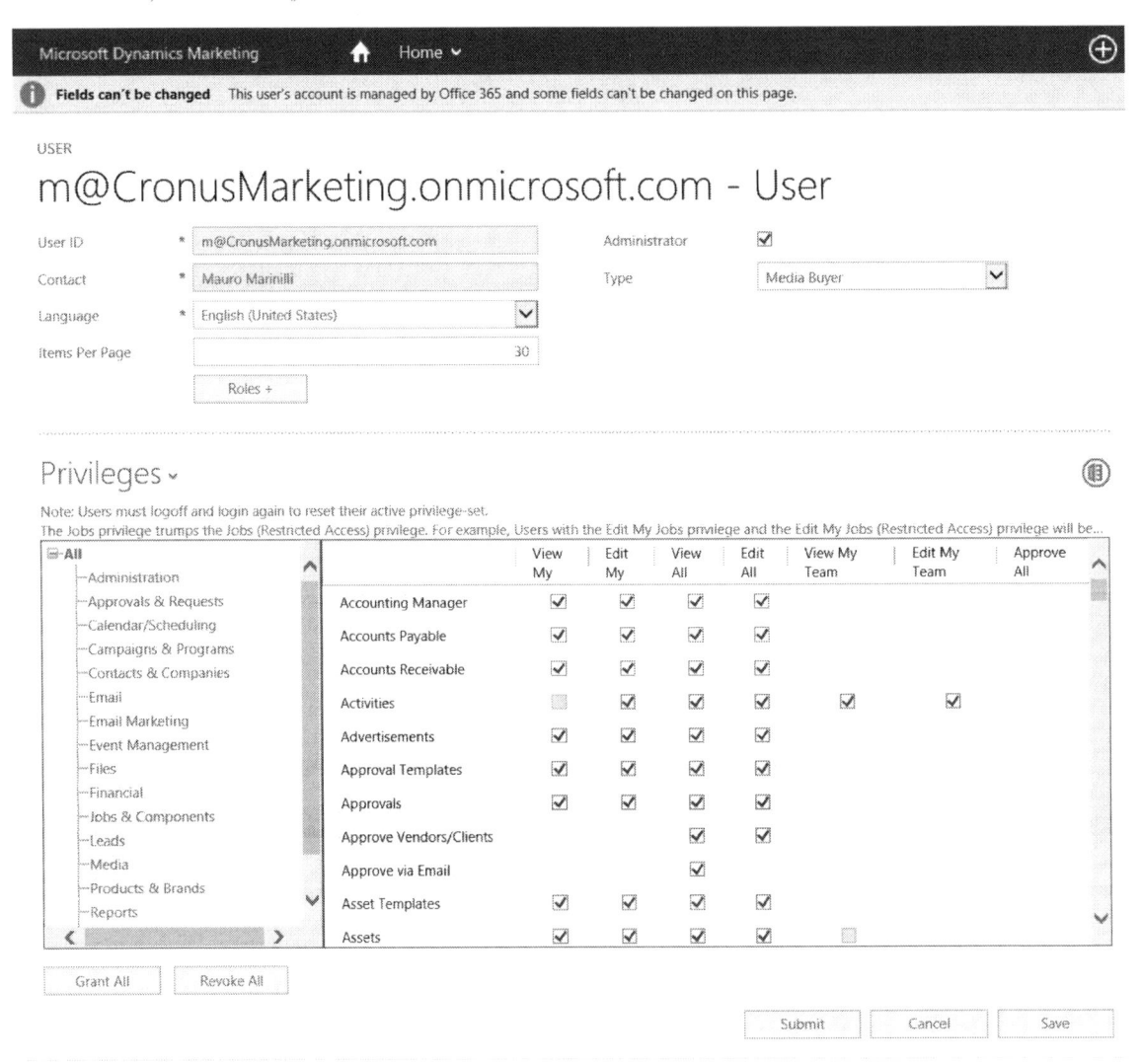

Figure 11.2 –User Form in Dynamics Marketing

The "User Type" field defines the main capabilities of a User in terms of privileges (functionality and data that User can access) and filters out Privileges accordingly.

There are three types of users in Dynamics Marketing, in order of number of privileges they can be assigned:

User Type	Description
Media Buyer	These users are the most powerful as they can potentially perform all functions in the system, including media buying.
Regular User	These users can potentially perform all functions apart from media buying.
Web Portal	These users have fewer privileges to choose from. You can add an unlimited number of these, and they are free of charge. We will dig more into the details of this user type in a separate subsection.

When assigning security permissions to users in Dynamics Marketing, always keep in mind to assign the lowest set of permissions to minimize security risks and perform the following steps:

1. Set the user type
2. Add some Security Roles for the user and / or remove or add privileges as needed directly from the Privileges Matrix

IT IS NOT SAFE TO ALWAYS USE "GRANT ALL" PRIVILEGES OR THE "MEDIA BUYER" USER TYPE

Needless to say, do not use the highest levels of security or the "Grant All" button as a blanket practice to shortcut user setup time as this might create security holes in your organization and unintended employees and / or external users can gain access to your confidential information.

11.2.2.1.1 The Privileges Matrix

The Privileges Matrix is the list of capabilities per functional area. It is filtered by the chosen User Type. Privileges can be exported to a CSV file. For ease of use, users can select a portion by clicking on the tree on the right hand side of the control. In the example below, one can see the Privileges available for the Leads area in the Enterprise Edition of the product.

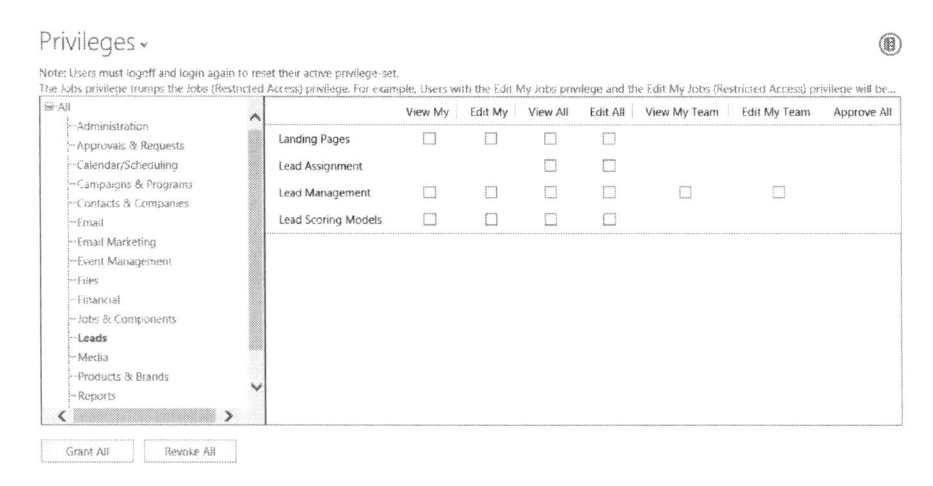

Figure 11.3 – Dynamics Marketing Security Privileges

The following table describes the type of Privileges available (i.e. the columns of the matrix):

Privilege	Description
View My	Allow the user to view the owned records.
Edit My	Allow the user to edit the owned records (created by). Note that this option alone does not imply "View My" capabilities.
View All	Allow the user to view records owned by other users too (by means of the "View All / Mine" action).
Edit All	Allow the user to edit all records. Note that selecting this option only does not imply "View All" capabilities.
View My Team	Allow the user to view the records that have been assigned via the Team Panel for that entity.
Edit My Team	Allow the user to edit the records that have been assigned via the Team Panel for that entity. Selecting only this option does not imply "View My Team" capabilities.
Approve All	Allow the user to approve records for that entity Approval / Review functionality.

Note that when assigning few partial permissions the user might not be able to navigate to the entity so extra care should be taken in testing out the final result.

11.2.2.1.2 User Roles in Dynamics Marketing

The User page enables administrators to assign Roles to Users.

Roles are prepopulated set of Privileges that can be reused for many Users, similarly to Dynamics CRM Security Roles.

User Roles can be found at:

```
Home > Settings > Administration → Roles
```

Note that trial instances have also a handful of trial roles (having "Sample" in the name) that are used to change the user role for demo purposes. These trial roles have less capabilities because they are meant to show a limited version of the product to ease the learning curve for new users.

11.2.2.2 Web Portal Users

Web Portal Users are Dynamics Marketing fully authenticated Office 365 users that are free of charge. An organization can add as many Web Portal Users as wanted. As mentioned before Web Portal Users are just like any other Dynamics Marketing user, only they can do fewer things, if enabled to by the administrator.

This type of user can be useful because it provides an additional level of flexibility at no cost to the Marketing organization. They are usually employed to give access to users external to the organization such as reviewers, approvers, contributors etc.

Given that these users are free of charge and can be added with no limitation on their number they do not consume a license seat in the Office 365 Portal, so administrator don't have to assign them a paid license. The steps to add Web Portal Users to an instance of Dynamics Marketing is as follows:

1. Add the users in the Office 365 Portal, but *do not* assign them a (paid) license seat.
2. Wait a couple of minutes as usual for user synchronization then open Dynamics Marketing and assign to these users the wanted privileges from those available to Web Portal Users.

11.2.2.3 The "Administrator" Option

The Administrator checkbox is a shortcut equivalent to assign administrator privileges -view and edit and admin functionality on the Administration, Business Administration and Campaign Management areas under Settings. It is enabled automatically for Office 365 Global and Service administrators, but it can be changed afterwards as needed in Dynamics Marketing.

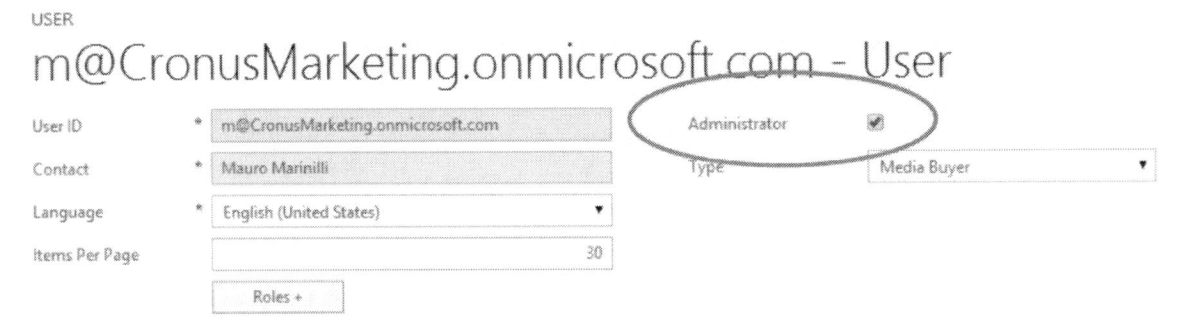

Figure 11.4 – Dynamics Marketing Administrator Checkbox

There is no need to assign Privileges to users that only have administrative responsibilities in Dynamics Marketing. It is enough to click the "Administrator" checkbox only, and they get access to the following pages in order to perform configuration and administration of the system:

- (Administration)
    - Site Settings
    - Users
    - User Groups
    - File Options
    - Languages
    - Integration Options
- (Business Administration)
    - Dashboards
    - Email
    - Marketing Automation
    - Media Buying
    - Budgeting
    - Jobs & Components
- (Campaign Management)
    - Marketing Automation

11.2.2.4 Minimal Privileges Users

What happens when an administrator doesn't assign any privilege to a User and doesn't select the "Administrator" checkbox? Every User will always have access to a few "anonymous access" pages in Dynamics Marketing such as Landing Pages or Subscription Center.

Of course you will never assign "zero" Privileges to a paid User, and the same applies to free-of-charge Web Portal Users. So it makes little sense to have no Privileges at all for your non-Administrator Users.

> **ALL USERS ON A TENANT ARE COPIED INTO DYNAMICS MARKETING**
>
> Some customer might be confused by the fact that all Office 365 assigned to a tenant organization, even if they don't have assigned an Dynamics Marketing license, are automatically copied over to Dynamics Marketing as *potential* Web Portal users. This behavior does not enables all users in a tenant to get access to Dynamics Marketing. In fact, without Dynamics Marketing user permissions set for each of them, these users cannot do much in Dynamics Marketing, so they can be ignored.

11.3 Integration Settings

Dynamics Marketing allows the integration with external systems via a CRM Connector and a number of dedicated APIs. Using the latter will be discussed in the next chapter. Here we focus on the configuration aspects in order to enable the integration services.

All the configurations described here are available at:

```
Home > Settings > Administration → Integration Options
```

11.3.1 The Azure Service Bus

Before we start digging into the details of the various integration options we will need to discuss how Dynamics Marketing integrates with external systems.

The Azure Service Bus is a messaging infrastructure managed and operated by Microsoft with a 99.9% monthly SLA that provides message delivery both for on-premises and cloud applications.

Dynamics Marketing uses the Azure Service Bus both for connecting to Dynamics CRM and also for accepting requests for its integration APIs.

> **ALWAYS CONNECT ONE INSTANCE OF DYNAMICS MARKETING TO ONE INSTANCE OF DYNAMICS CRM**
>
> The Connector only supports 1:1 connections between Dynamics Marketing and

Dynamics CRM instances. It is not possible to connect one instance of Dynamics Marketing to multiple instances of Dynamics CRM, and vice versa.

Luckily Dynamics Marketing provides a convenient user interface for setting up the details of the Service Bus account for our site.

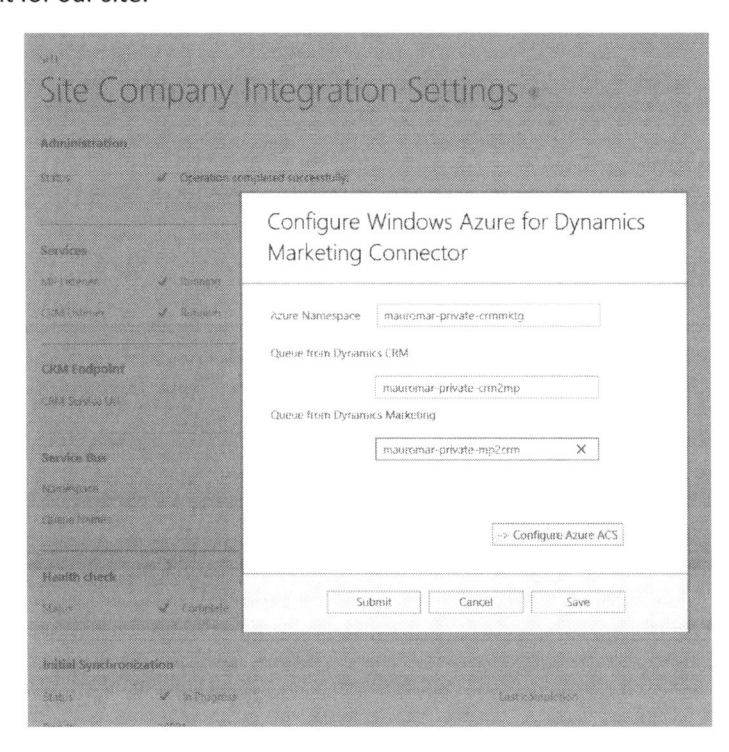

Figure 11.5 – Dynamics Marketing Configure Azure Queues

By clicking on the "Configure Azure ACS" button users can enter the details of how the Azure Service Bus should connect to the Dynamics CRM instance as shown below.

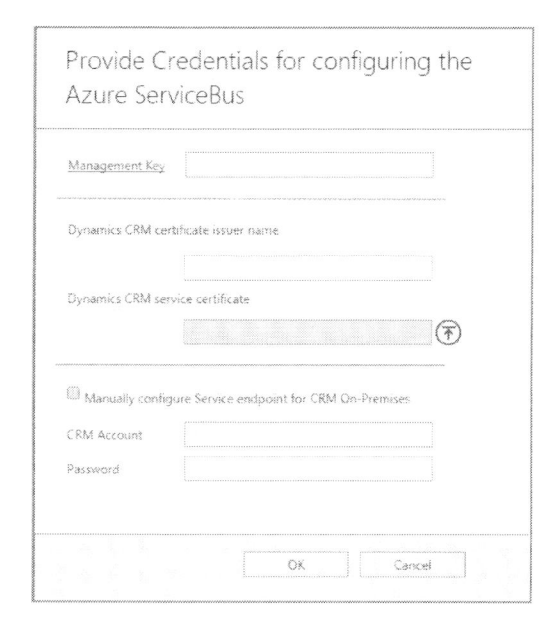

Figure 11.6 – Dynamics Marketing Configure the Azure Service Bus

Note how the Management Key used for your account can be accessed directly from the link on the field caption.

11.3.2 Configuring the CRM Connector

The CRM connector configuration and administration is operated via the Integration Options page:

```
Home > Settings > Administration → Integration Options
```

> **YOU DON'T NEED A MICROSOFT AZURE ACCOUNT AND SERVICE BUS NAMESPACE FOR CRM ONLINE INTEGRATION**
>
> You can use Microsoft-owned Azure queues for CRM Online integration. Note that this option is not available for CRM on-Premises integration.

In a nutshell these are the main steps needed to setup the CRM Connector:

1. Prepare an Azure account
2. Create the Windows Azure Message Queues
3. Configure Dynamics CRM for integration with Windows Azure
4. Setup Dynamics Marketing CRM Connector
5. Configure Windows Azure integration with Dynamics CRM
6. Configure the Windows Azure Service Bus for X.509 certificate authentication
7. Configure Dynamics Marketing CRM Connector
8. Run post-Installation tasks and first-time data synchronization between Dynamics Marketing and Dynamics CRM
9. (Optional) Configure data mapping between Dynamics Marketing and Dynamics CRM

Administrators setting up the connector will need to click on "Enable Connector Services" button in the "Services" sections in the Integration Options page in order to have the CRM Connector enabled and start the setup process described above.

In reality you will not need to perform all these steps yourself, as the connector configuration experience provides a number of simplified setup:

- For on-premises CRM installations you can run a wizard that will walk you through the entire configuration.
- For online CRM installations you can use managed queues without the need of setting up your own Azure account, unless you want to.

The Integration Options page is available under:

    Home > Settings > Administration → Integration Options

This is an example of this page with all services configured and running correctly:

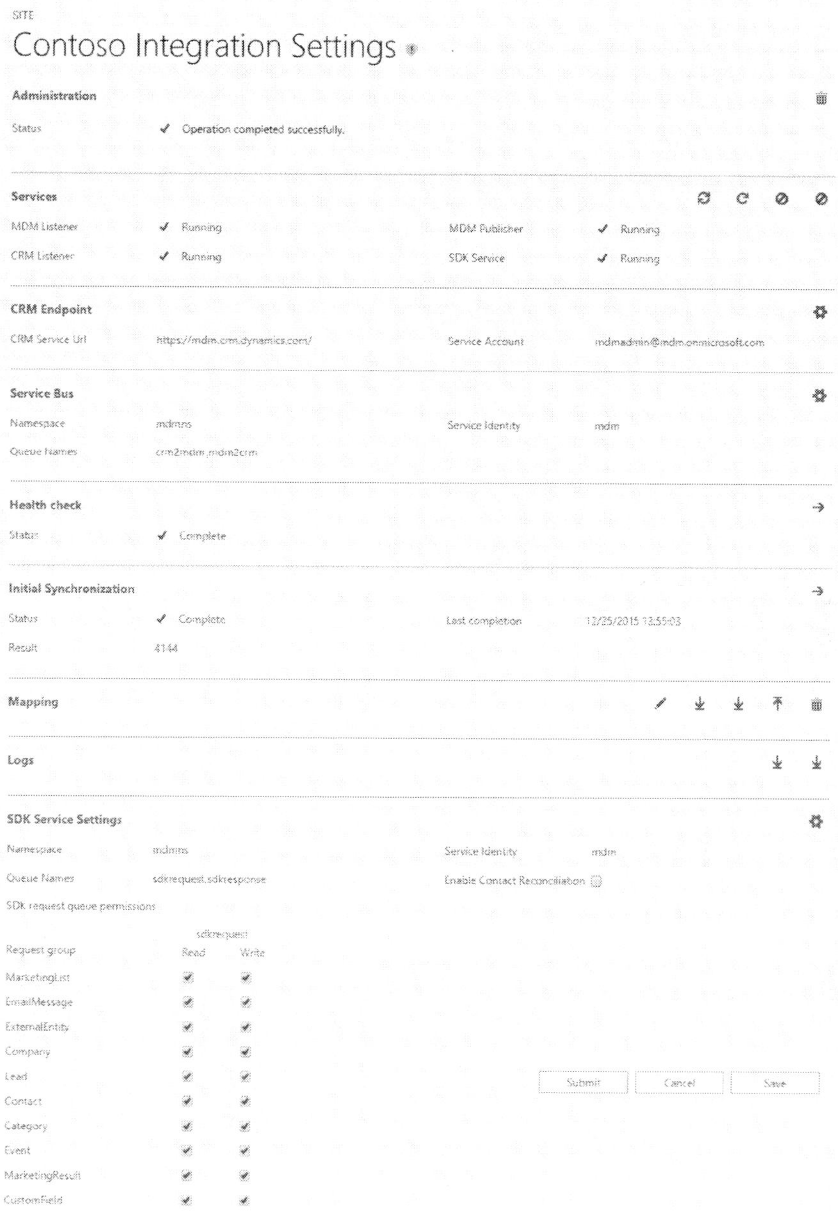

SITE
Contoso Integration Settings

Administration

Status ✓ Operation completed successfully.

Services

MDM Listener	✓ Running	MDM Publisher	✓ Running
CRM Listener	✓ Running	SDK Service	✓ Running

CRM Endpoint

CRM Service Url	https://mdm.crm.dynamics.com/	Service Account	mdmadmin@mdm.onmicrosoft.com

Service Bus

Namespace	mdmns	Service Identity	mdm
Queue Names	crm2mdm,mdm2crm		

Health check

Status ✓ Complete

Initial Synchronization

Status	✓ Complete	Last completion	12/25/2015 13:55:03
Result	4144		

Mapping

Logs

SDK Service Settings

Namespace	mdmns	Service Identity	mdm
Queue Names	sdkrequest,sdkresponse	Enable Contact Reconciliation	

SDK request queue permissions

Request group	sdkrequest Read	sdkrequest Write
MarketingList	✓	✓
EmailMessage	✓	✓
ExternalEntity	✓	✓
Company	✓	✓
Lead	✓	✓
Contact	✓	✓
Category	✓	✓
Event	✓	✓
MarketingResult	✓	✓
CustomField	✓	✓

Submit Cancel Save

Figure 11.7 – Dynamics Marketing Integration Options

11.4 Adapting Dynamics Marketing to your Business

Dynamics Marketing provides a number of options to configure functionality based on business requirements. This section describes generic functionality to expand the fields and values available out of the box in default instances.

User Defined Fields (UDF) and Custom Contact Fields are additional fields that can be added to entities to capture custom information. Categories are customizable values for some of the fields and parameters available in the system.

11.4.1 Custom Contact Fields

Custom Contact fields are dynamically created fields that can be used in the product UI, OData, landing pages, email marketing dynamic content and API. They can also be mapped to custom fields in Dynamics CRM if the connector is used, and they can be localized to various languages.

Custom Contact fields are available only for the Contact entity. They are different than UDFs because UDFs are existing fields that are just renamed while custom contact fields are entirely dynamic and you can create as many as you, of any supported data type.

To set up these fields open the Custom Contact Field related information panel in the Site Company:

```
Home > Settings > My Company > Company Settings
```

The example below shows a number of Custom Contact Fields created for registering book readers on a landing page. We have also created three custom categories values used by one of our new Custom Contact Fields (Dynamics CRM readers can think of these as option values).

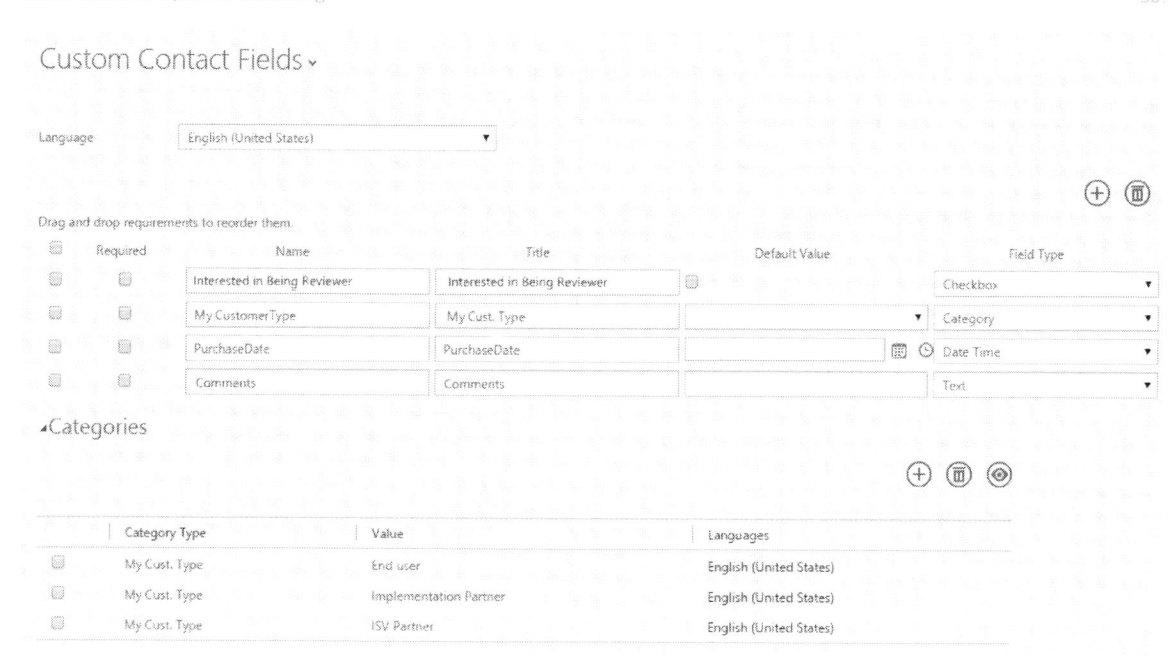

Figure 11.8 – Custom Contact Fields

11.4.2 User Defined Fields

Most entities have a handful of fields for each data type that are hidden by default and can be added as needed. In order to "show" these fields we will need to change their default label.

User Defined Fields are available from the Language labels as any other field:

`Home > Settings > Administration > Languages`

We then need to choose a language, for instance "English (United States)".

Because there are so many labels the easiest way to find UDFs for a given area is to search for "User Defined" or even just "User"[46].

As soon as you edit the default label string for one User-Defined Field they will become visible in the UI, if they were not before. To remove them from the UI you will need to restore the original name using the related button by the field.

---

[46] Remember that once you rename them you will not find them anymore with this trick as you will need to search for the name you assigned them.

Inside Microsoft Dynamics Marketing

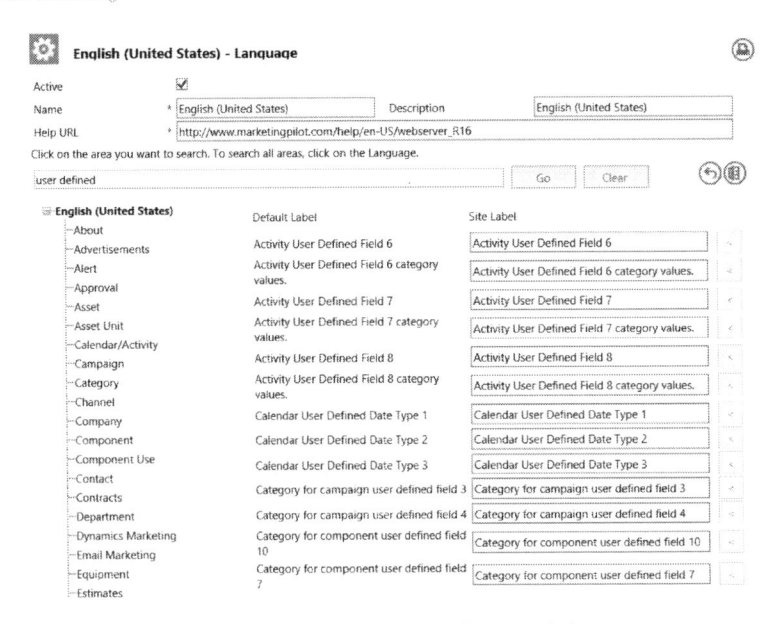

Figure 11.9 – Dynamics Marketing Labels

UDFs are a simple and flexible way to account for your custom business requirements with Dynamics Marketing.

WHEN TO USE UDFS VS. CUSTOM CONTACT FIELDS

It is preferable to use Custom Contact Fields when possible. It is expected in future releases that custom fields will be extended to other key entities apart from Contact (and eventually to all entities). UDFs will be maintained as a legacy functionality but they will not be extended moving forward.

11.4.3 Categories

As mentioned in other chapters, Categories (user-renamed values) are an important extensibility mechanism in Dynamics Marketing. Administrators setting up and editing Categories will need the Categories' Privileges defined accordingly (under the "Administration" Privileges group in the User or Role entity).

Categories are available from:

Home > Settings > Business Administration → Languages

Most entities use Category fields. A typical example is the "Type" field in many entities, which is empty by default but can be configured as described above to provide values useful to track records based on your customized values. We will see an example of use later in the chapter.

Categories are translated according to the chosen Language[47].

DELETING CATEGORIES

Some Categories values are built into the system and cannot be deleted (these are also called System Categories). As for non-system Categories values, similarly to other data in Dynamics Marketing, they are always soft-deleted (i.e. marked as deleted but never removed from the database).

As an example the following screenshot shows the Categories available as default for the "Component Storage Location" field.

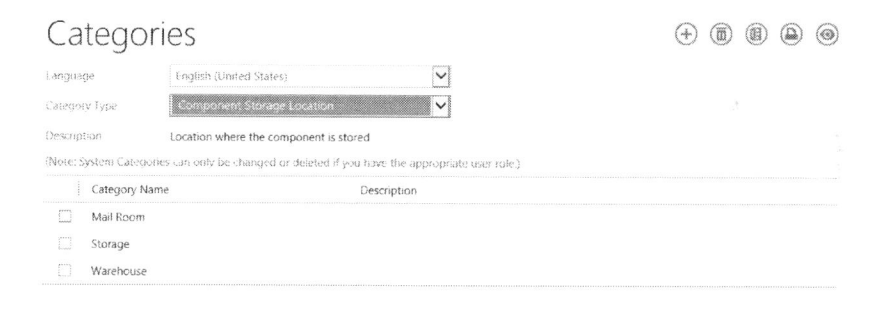

Figure 11.10 – Categories

---

[47] You can also specify an "Account" value that is used on few Categories to provide more functionality in some built-in uses.

Such values are used in the Storage field in the Component form:

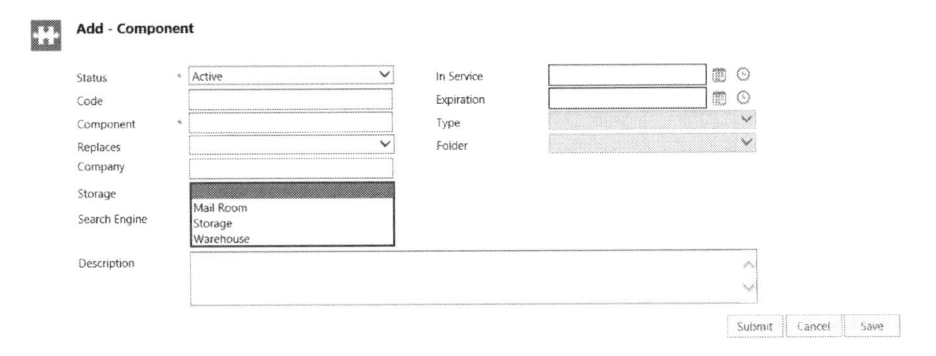

Figure 11.11 – Using Category Values

11.5 MAKING YOUR APPLICATION INTERNATIONAL

Dynamics Marketing supports international business environments and provides a very flexible infrastructure for customizing any text available from the UI, regardless of the language used. Text is encoded as Unicode, both in the UI and in the Database.

11.5.1 Languages

In Dynamics Marketing labels (i.e. UI text) are organized in Languages. Even if you wish to use the default language and just want to tweak a few labels you will need to do so from the Language entity.

To get to the list of Languages installed on your application:

```
Home > Settings > Administration → Languages
```

You can create new Languages or edit existing ones, thus changing virtually any label available in the system. You can export and import them too[48].

---

[48] Typically you will also provide customized values for Categories too, as part of a new language.

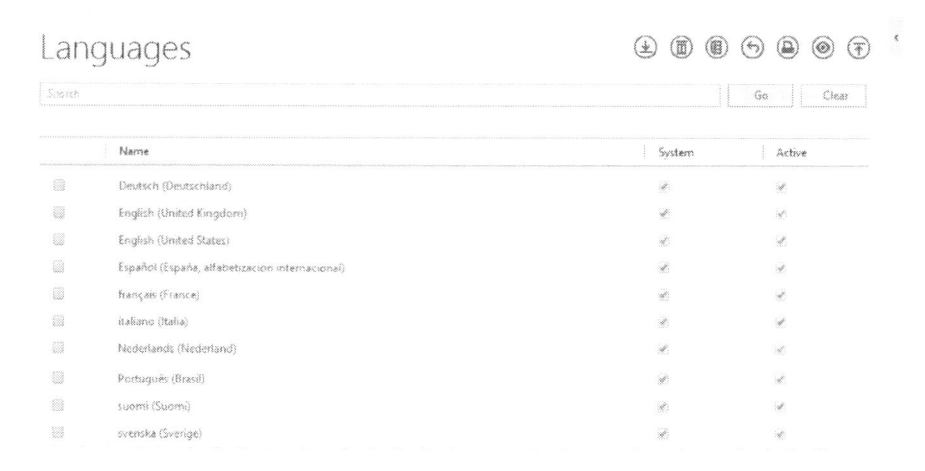

Figure 11.12 – Languages

Of course you don't have to create a new Language, if all you need is to customize some labels on an existing one.

In order to change a label you will need to select the Language first, then edit the labels you want to change. Usually there are so many labels that you need to apply a filter to restrict the choices. Note that search searches the label not the area name on the left-hand side. Keep this in mind when working with foreign languages.

Figure 11.13 – Example of a Language

You can use languages also for creating new terminologies for the same language, if needed to. The following scenario shows how to set this up.

Note that with a language we are just changing the Unicode strings used in the UI, so custom Languages don't affect product functionality and can be created also for languages not supported by the product.

11.5.1.1 Creating a new terminology (Language)

The Languages list provides two important actions: import and export of languages as XML files. We can leverage this functionality to create custom Languages based on existing ones.

We start from downloading the base language we want to use for our new Language. For example we would like to change the English language and customize it for non-profit organizations. So we would like to change labels of entities like Company that will become "Organization" in our new Language, still based on the "EN-US" language.

Once the base language is exported in XML we edit it to tweak some of its values. We could perform all the editing in the XML format if we wish to (in our scenario that will be handy as we will need to replace all occurrences of the string "Company" with "Organization"). Of course we could edit the labels in the Dynamics Marketing UI and export them to XML again (if we wish to distribute it to other customers or have it as a backup).

We rename the system name of the Language:

Figure 11.14 – Example of a Language

When done with the editing we import the file back and given that we want to override the default English labels with these new ones, we check that related option in the upload dialog:

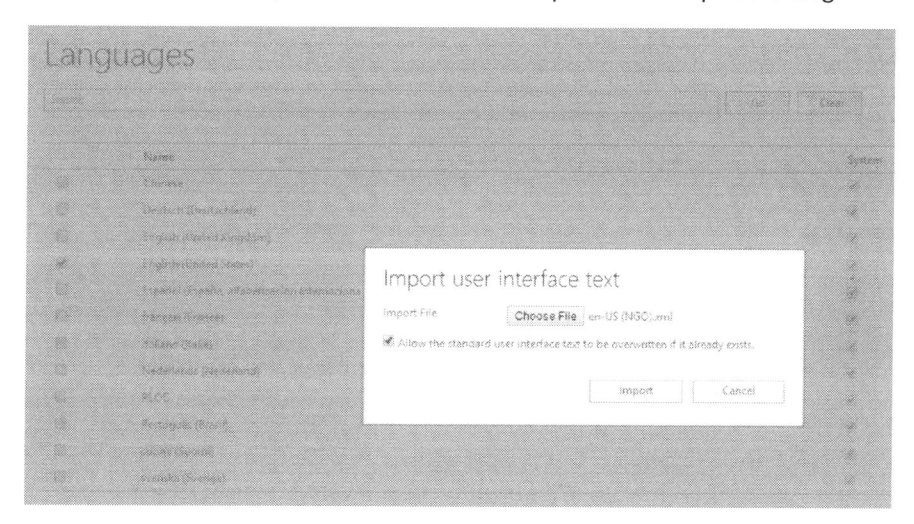

Figure 11.15 – Import a Language

At this point we are good to go with our new custom Language.

11.5.2 Locales and Formats

Dynamics Marketing stores default values for International settings in the Site Preferences page, available from:

```
Home > Settings > Administration → Site Settings
```

In this page the "Regional Options" group provides localization settings global to the entire instance.

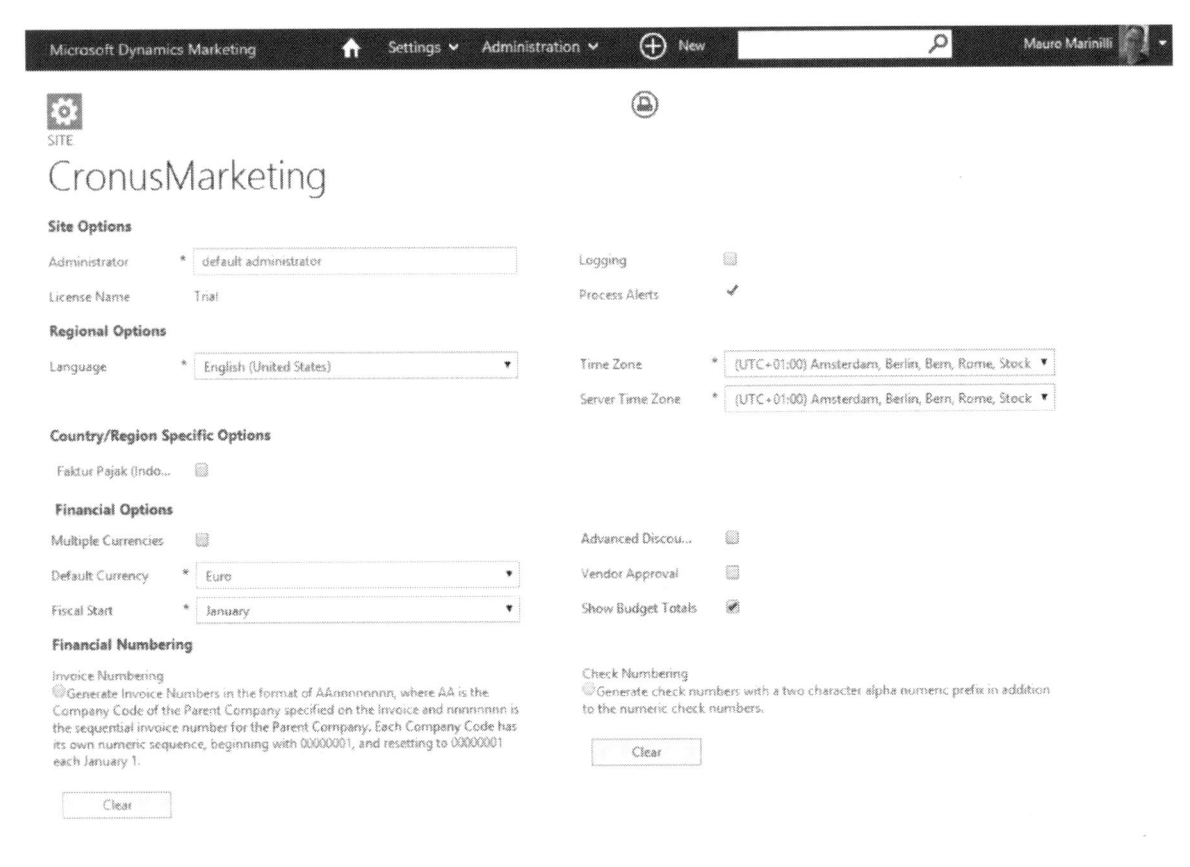

Figure 11.16 – Site Settings Regional Options

11.5.2.1 User Preferences

Dynamics Marketing allows end users to personalize the language, time zone and locale from the User Preferences page (accessible from the user preferences dropdown menu, the one with a "gear" icon on the top-right corner of the screen).

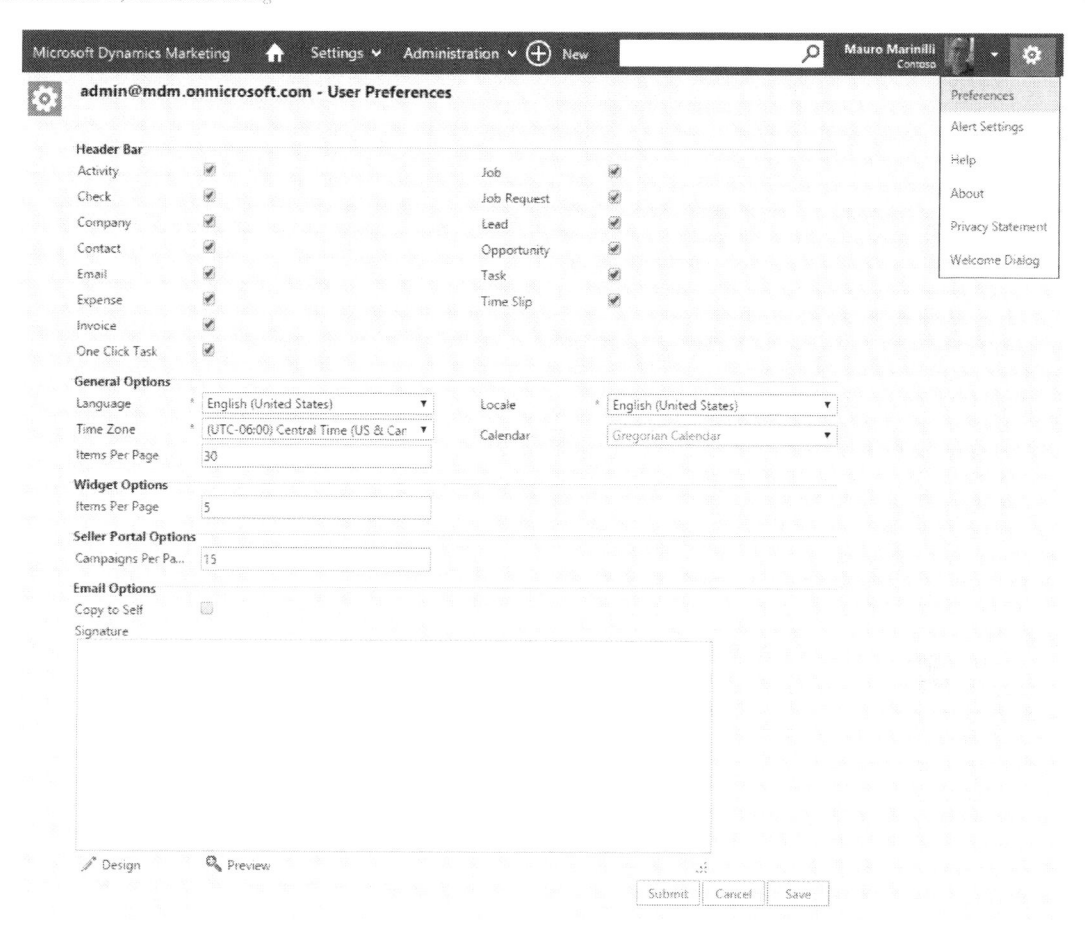

Figure 11.17 – User Preferences

THE OFFICE 365 LANGUAGE IS NOT USED IN DYNAMICS MARKETING

Dynamics Marketing uses the language set by the user in the Preferences menu. Other languages used in Office 365 do not necessarily apply. Dynamics Marketing will set the default language to the one specified when the instance is being provisioned the first time (i.e. when the instance is being created from Office 365). Users can always change the language from their Preferences page afterwards. Note also that users can choose Dynamics Marketing custom Languages as well as built-in Languages.

11.5.2.2 Currencies

The Enterprise Edition of Dynamics Marketing supports working with multiple currencies, if your organization regularly does business in countries with different currencies.

Multiple Currencies are enabled in Site Settings (under "Financial Options"):

```
Home > Settings > Administration → Site Settings
```

When working in an international environment you might need to add additional currencies to the default ones provided in Dynamics Marketing.

Currencies are represented as Categories with Category Type "Currency":

```
Home > Settings > Business Administration → Categories
```

The default Currencies are (e.g. used in the "Analysis" pane for a Campaign):

- USD
- AUD
- CAD
- EUR
- MEX NP
- GBP

Dynamics Marketing also supports the notion of a default currency that is handy in minimizing data entry, although is not mandatory to specify one. The default currency in your application is specified in the Site Settings page available at:

```
Home > Settings > Administration → Site Settings
```

> **MULTIPLE CURRENCIES ARE NOT "ON" BY DEFAULT**
>
> Note that enabling multiple currencies in Dynamics Marketing will turn on complex functionality in various parts of the system. Unless you need such functionality for business reasons, do not turn Multiple Currencies on.

11.5.3 Time Zones

Dynamics Marketing stores internally all dates as UTC. In order for time zones to work correctly you will need to set up your server time zone in the Site Settings page. The default value is set up at site provisioning (when the instance is created the first time).

11.6 Technical Setup

Dynamics Marketing provides a wide range of functionality that can be configured from the Site Settings page.

```
Home > Settings > Administration -> Site Settings
```

11.6.1 Communication Options

It is also possible to enable one-click calls to Contact phone numbers using either Lync or Skype, by configuring the "Provider" field under Communication Options.

Figure 11.18 – One-Click Calls Setup

Note that the Webinar Provider field is used for setting up Lync webinars (see Chapter 2 "Campaign Automation"). Note that only on-prem Lync servers are supported as Webinar Providers.

Chapter Twelve
Developer Scenarios

This chapter provides a succinct overview of the possibilities offered by Dynamics Marketing in terms of integrating into third-party external systems. The chapter is concluded by a discussion of the main scenarios enabled with the Dynamics Marketing SDK.

12.1 Overview for the Developer

These are the main integration points available in Dynamics Marketing.

Integration Point	Implementation Technology	Scenarios
CRM Connector	Azure Queue Based Service	Dynamics Marketing data integration with Dynamics CRM
Traceable Transactional or Commercial Email APIs	Azure Queue Based API	Send either traceable transactional emails (e.g. notifications, receipts, invoices, possibly with additional promotional content) or commercial marketing emails.
Marketing List Management API	Azure Queue Based API	Create, read, update and delete Dynamics Marketing Marketing Lists from external systems
Other entities API	Azure Queue Based API	Manage the following entities: - Company - Lead - Contact and Custom Contact Fields - Category - Event - Etc.
Analytics Data Sources	OData Feed	Consume read-only data sources from Dynamics Marketing mostly for reporting scenarios

This is the list of the main namespaces available from the SDK library.

Microsoft.Dynamics.Marketing.SDK.Common
Microsoft.Dynamics.Marketing.SDK.Messages
Microsoft.Dynamics.Marketing.SDK.Messages.Category
Microsoft.Dynamics.Marketing.SDK.Messages.Company
Microsoft.Dynamics.Marketing.SDK.Messages.Contact
Microsoft.Dynamics.Marketing.SDK.Messages.CustomField
Microsoft.Dynamics.Marketing.SDK.Messages.EmailMessage
Microsoft.Dynamics.Marketing.SDK.Messages.Event
Microsoft.Dynamics.Marketing.SDK.Messages.ExternalEntity
Microsoft.Dynamics.Marketing.SDK.Messages.Lead
Microsoft.Dynamics.Marketing.SDK.Messages.MarketingList
Microsoft.Dynamics.Marketing.SDK.Messages.MarketingResult
Microsoft.Dynamics.Marketing.SDK.Model

In this chapter we will not cover the CRM Connector, which has been described in Chapter 11 "Configuration".

12.1.1 SDK Services Configuration

In order to use the APIs connecting to the Microsoft Azure Service Bus queues you will need to set these up in the Integration Option page in your Dynamics Marketing instance.

The page is avilable from:

```
Home > Settings > Administration → Integration Options
```

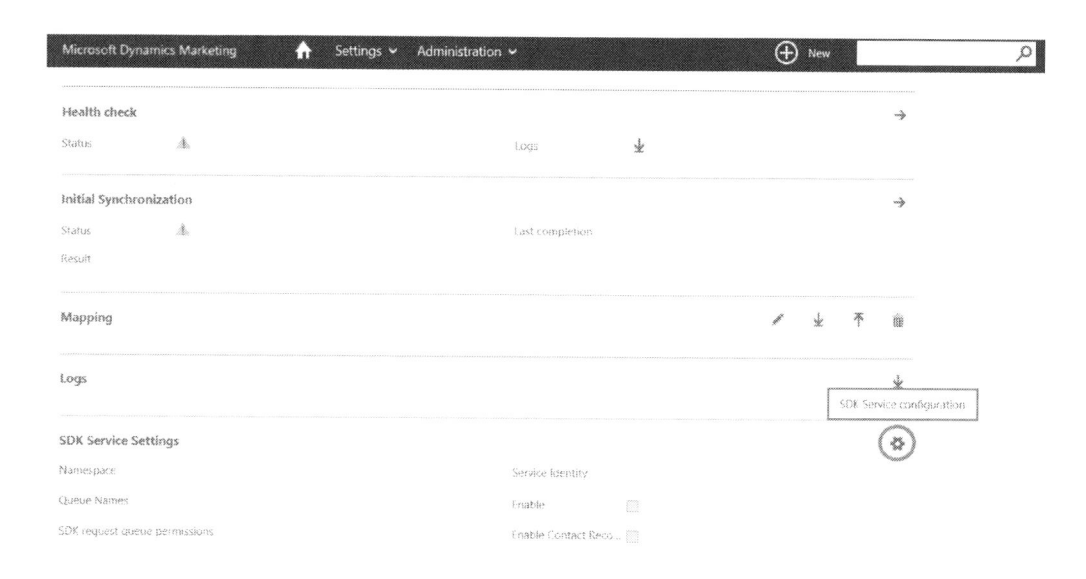

Figure 12.1 –Integration Options

This information is needed for configuring the Azure queues to be used.

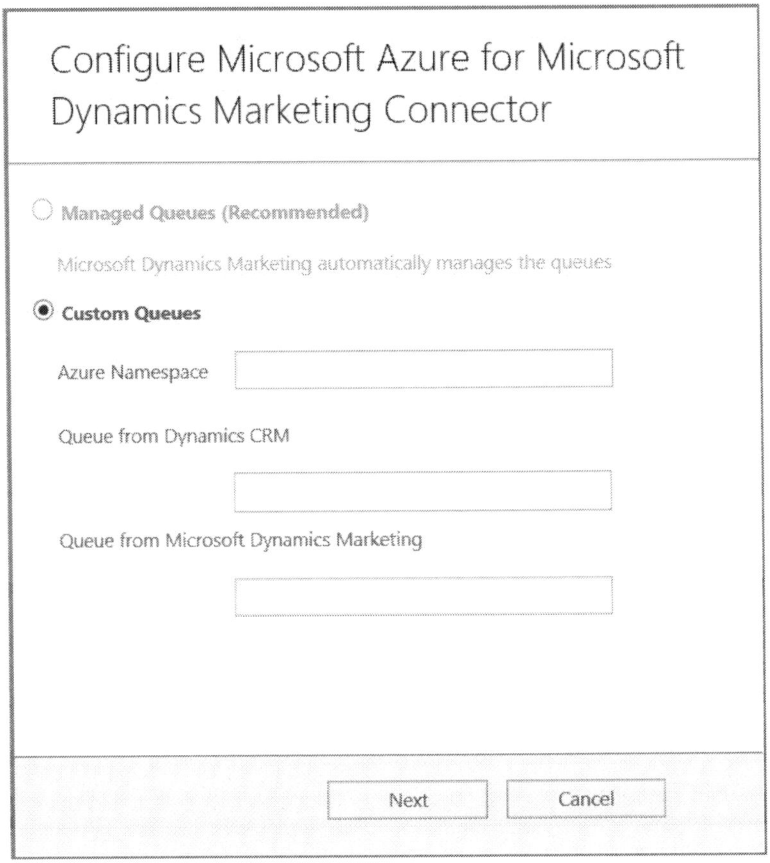

Figure 12.2 – Configuring Azure Queues

Below you can see the information available once the setup has been completed successfully:

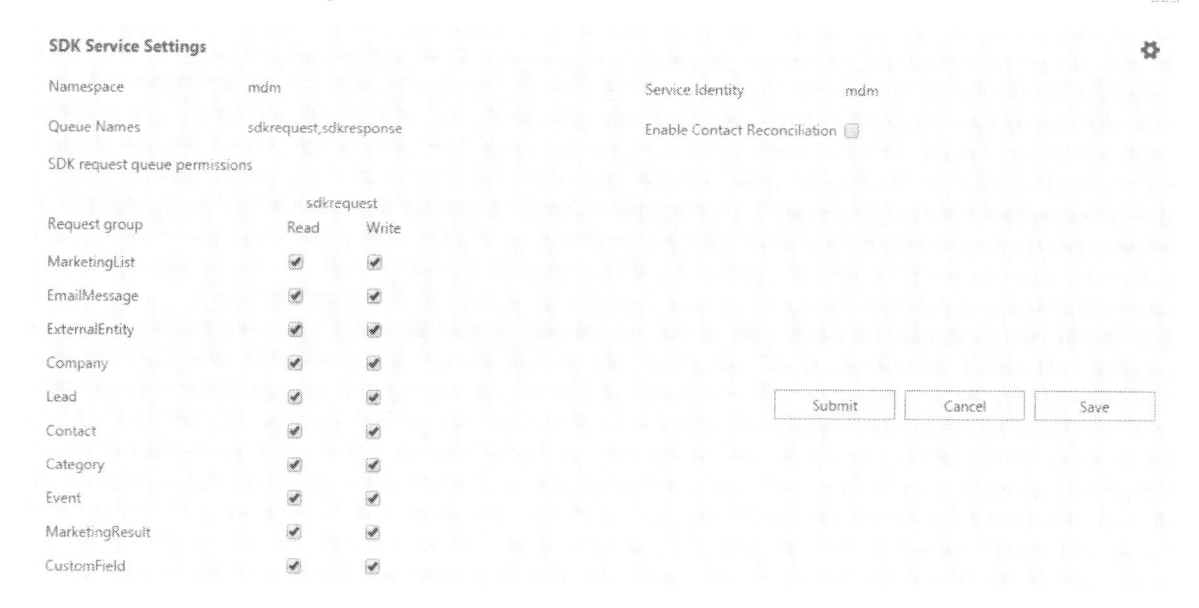

Figure 12.3 – Configuring Services

The SDK Services can be disabled if needed.

The **Namespace** field defines the unique ID these queues will be referenced with. You will always have two queues, one for requests and one for responses, with names based on the chosen Namespace.

Administrators can further enable read and / or write capabilities (on the request queue) for the following APIs:

- Marketing List
- Email Message
- External Entities
- Company
- Lead
- Contact
- Category
- Event
- Marketing Result
- Custom Contact Fields

So an admin can configure Dynamics Marketing to provide only read access to the Marketing List API. Then it will only possible to query existing lists from an external system but not modify or add new ones from an external system.

> **CONTACT PERMISSION API IS PART OF THE EMAIL MESSAGE API**
>
> The Contact Permission API described in Chapter 6 "Advanced Email Marketing" enabling the integration of external systems in filtering email sending is part of the Email Message API.

12.2 Commercial Emails API

Dynamics Marketing provides an API for sending commercial marketing emails. These are the marketing emails sent by campaign automation. Even when sent via the API these emails still require unsubscribe links (provided by the subscription center plug-in) and sender address (provided by the sender address plug-in).

12.3 Traceable Transactional Emails API

Dynamics Marketing provides an API for handling traceable transactional emails. As described in Chapter 5 "Email Marketing" an email message can be marked with the "Send Externally" option. This will transfer the exclusive control of sending that message to the Traceable Transactional API. In Dynamics Marketing it is not possible to send (commercial) marketing messages via an API. This scenario though can be achieved with a combination of external lists and Campaign Automation as described later in this chapter.

Via the API you can see all of the available traceable transactional emails in the system. You can also send one of these emails to a particular contact.

12.3.1 Sending Transactional Emails via API

These are the main usages available from the SDK and their purpose:

SDK Usage Scenario
Send an email using either an email address or a contact identifier.
Identify the email marketing message to use for promotion.
Set the priority of an email message.
Specify external data (for example, order, product, or pricing information) to be embedded in the email.
Track queuing and response status.
Retrieve a list of email marketing messages that can be used in a transaction.

12.4 Marketing List Management API

Dynamics Marketing provides an API for handling Marketing Lists from external systems. The main usage is to provide contact segmentation into Dynamics Marketing from an external system to support external marketing lists operated in Dynamics Marketing.

12.4.1 Managing Marketing Lists via API

API Method	Description
List Management	
	Create a new Marketing List
	Update an existing Marketing List
	Retrieve an existing Marketing List
	Delete an existing Marketing List
	Copy a Dynamic Marketing List into a Static one
Members Management	
	Add one member
	Add multiple members
	Remove a member (given the ID)
	Remove a member (given the email address)
	Remove all
	Copy members

12.5 Scenarios

Now that we have seen the basics of the SDK available to developers, let's have a look at the options this technology enables for customers.

12.5.1 Sending marketing emails from external systems.

We have seen how Dynamics Marketing provides an API to directly send traceable transactional emails created and managed in Dynamics Marketing. It is also possible to send commercial emails from external systems by leveraging the external Marketing List API and Campaign Automation.

For instance, it is possible to synchronize a Marketing List from external system (excluding Dynamics CRM which has a native integration via the CRM Connector) into Dynamics Marketing.

Such lists can be used like any other list in Dynamics Marketing and are accessible in the Campaign Automation console. Marketers can then define the right content and campaign automation details based on these "external" lists, therefore enabling sending of commercial email marketing from external systems.

Conclusions

The journey of Dynamics Marketing, as a product, is just at the beginning.

Looking at the roadmap for the product as shown in various public conferences and events one cannot avoid to be amazed by the breakneck pace of innovation and the amount of investment that Microsoft is bringing into the market with Dynamics Marketing and the Dynamics CRM Suite.

Just to name a few, multiple new communication channels (such as mobile) are joining the fray plus radical improvements in the user interface of many existing functionality to improve marketers' effectiveness and productivity.

By its unique mix of breadth of functionality, down-to-earth usability, seamless integration with other systems and competitive pricing Dynamics Marketing is posed to be an important player in the market.

So it makes sense, as a marketing professional or manager or just even as a Microsoft partner to invest time in understanding its capabilities. For your time and attention in reading this book I wholeheartedly thank you.

Appendix
Dynamics Marketing History in Pictures

This appendix cover the evolution of the product UI over the main releases.

Dynamics Marketing Fall 2015
(Released December 2015, Codename Capella, v.19)

In Microsoft Dynamics Marketing 2016 Update, various improvements were added to the product, the most notable being the channel for outbound mobile text messages, or "short message service" (SMS).

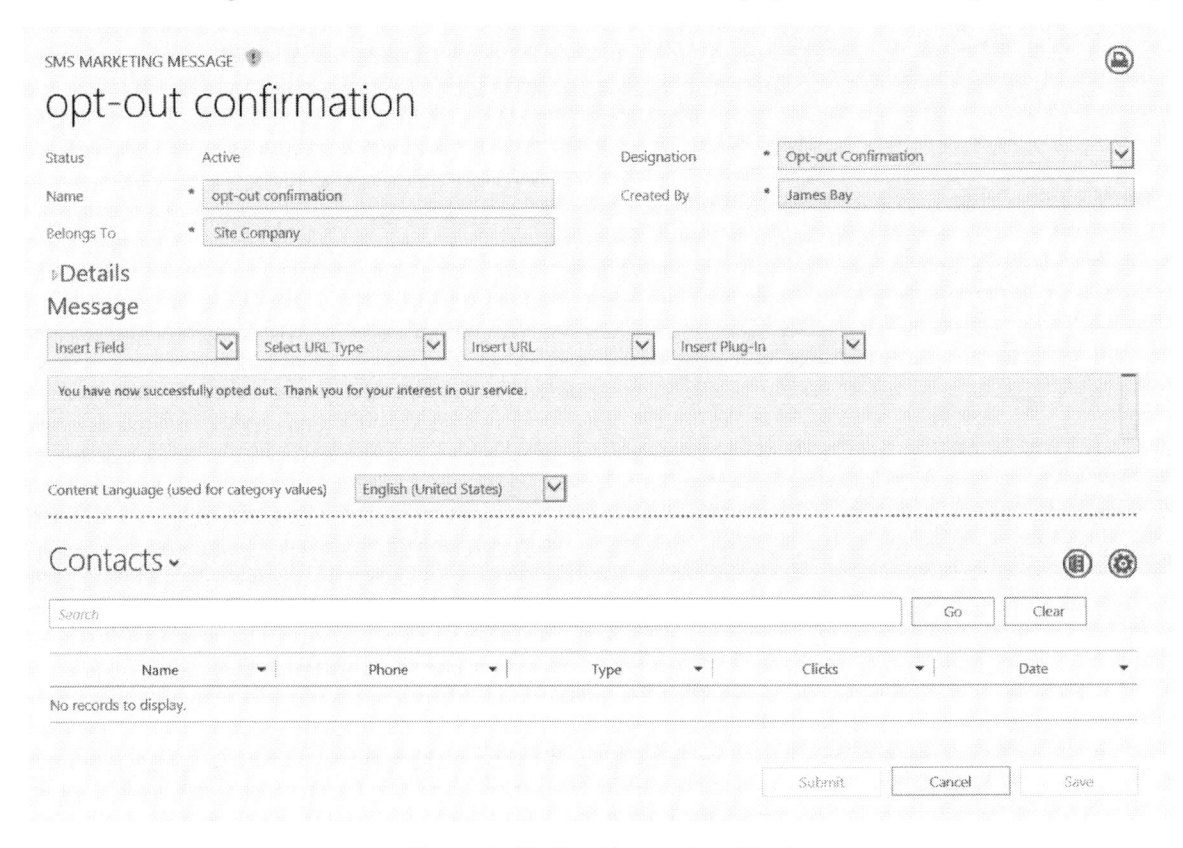

Figure A.1 –The Text Message Form (New)

DYNAMICS MARKETING SPRING 2014
(RELEASED APRIL 2015, CODENAME SPICA, V.18)

For Microsoft Dynamics Marketing 2015 Update 1 there were various functional improvements, perhaps the most notable one from a UI point of view was the introduction of an HTML 5 UI for Digital Asset Management.

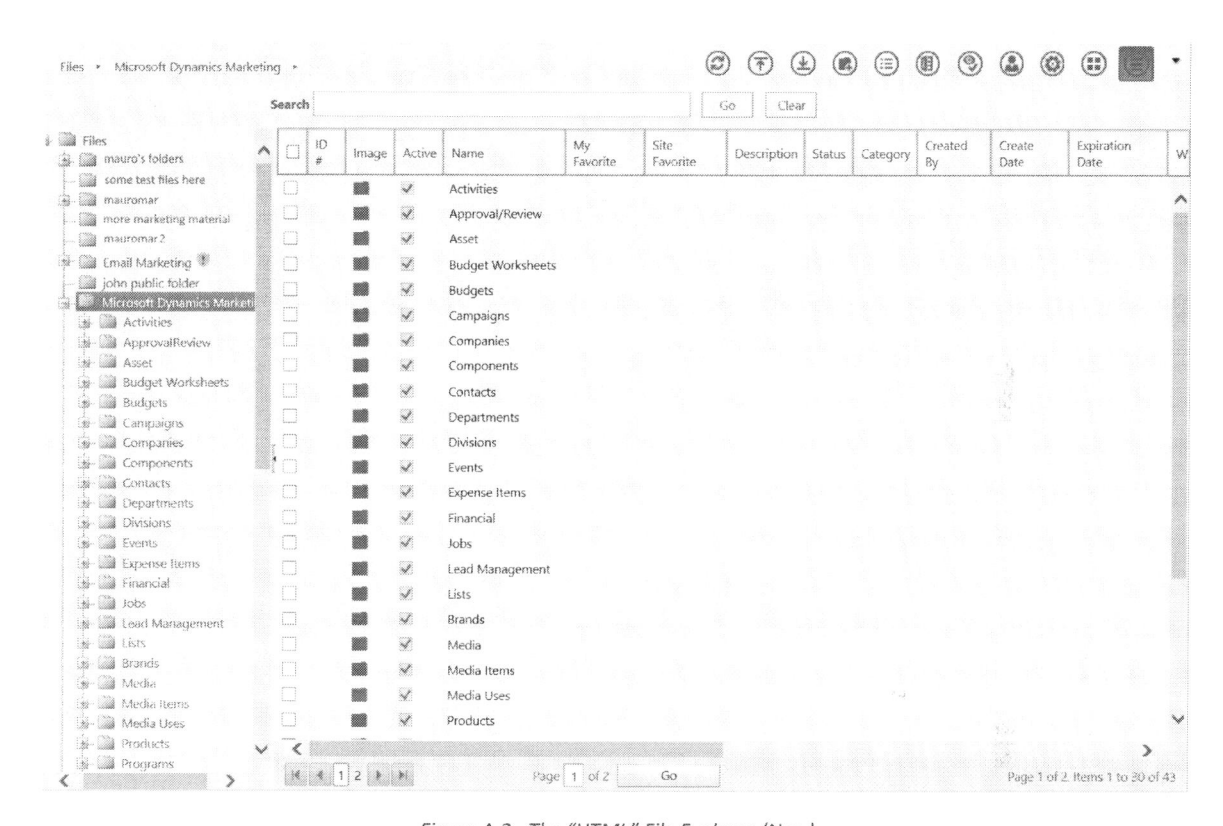

Figure A.2 – The "HTML" File Explorer (New)

DYNAMICS MARKETING FALL 2014
(RELEASED DECEMBER 2014, CODENAME ELECTRA, V.17)

For Microsoft Dynamics Marketing 2015 Update there were many improvements to the UI and main functional areas, such as a new email editor, new approval canvas, improved automation, main screen improved visuals, etc.

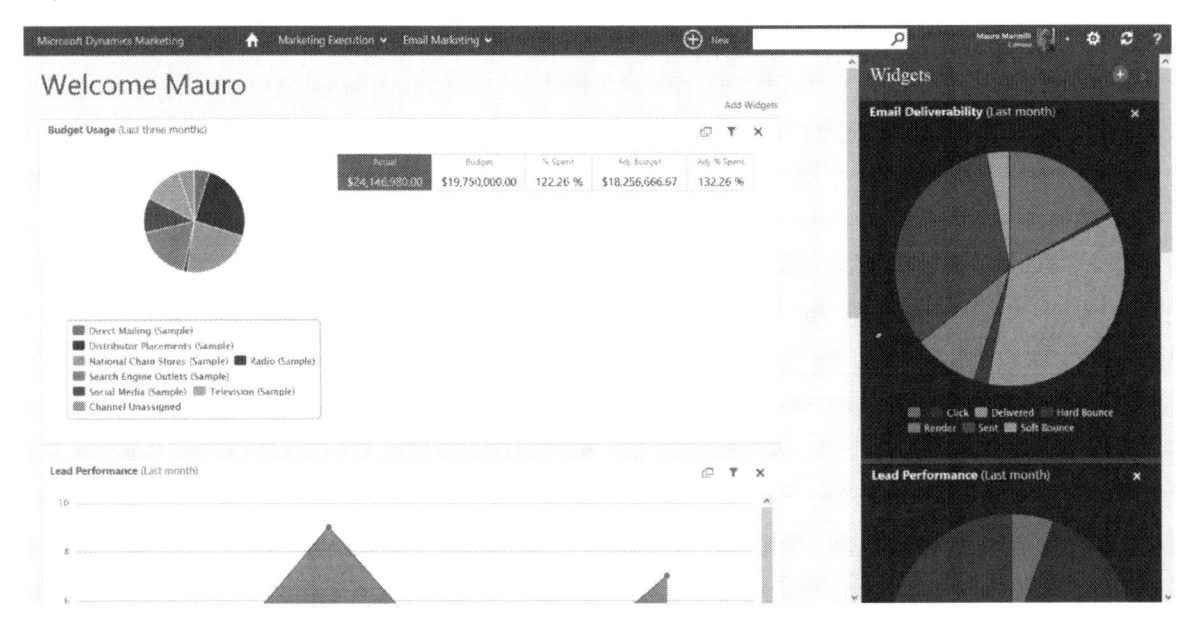

Figure A.3 – "Electra" Home Page

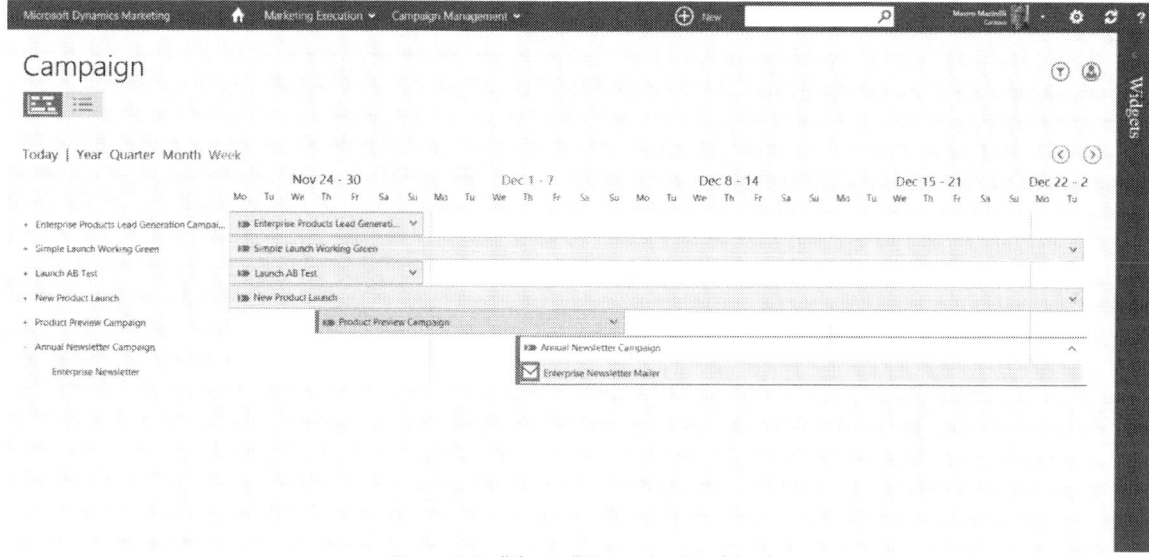

Figure A.4 – "Electra" Campaign List (New)

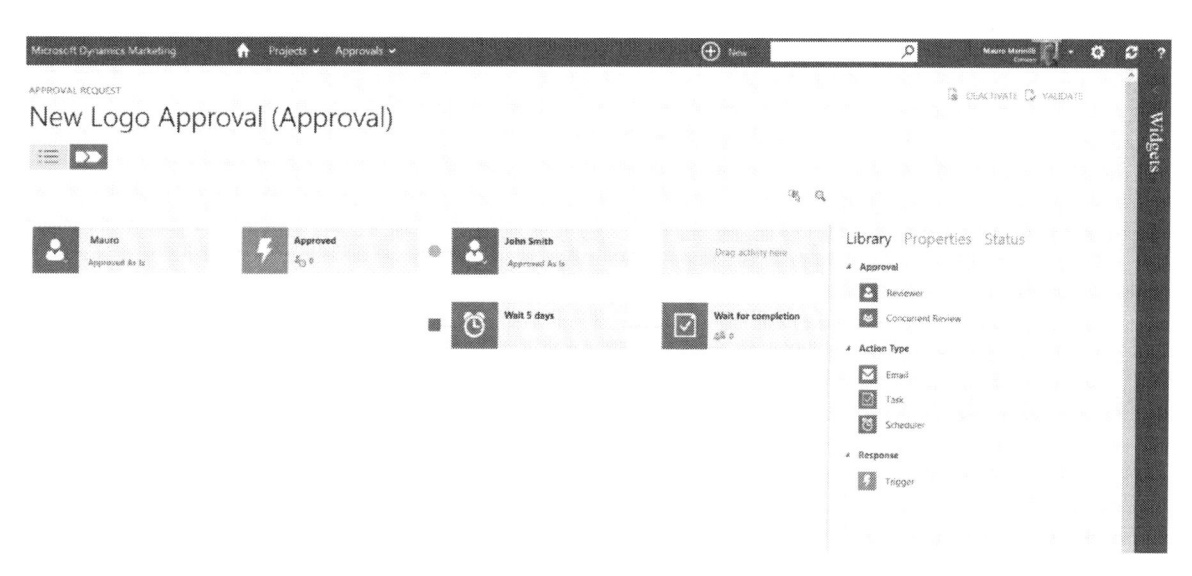

Figure A.5 – "Electra" Approval Editor (New)

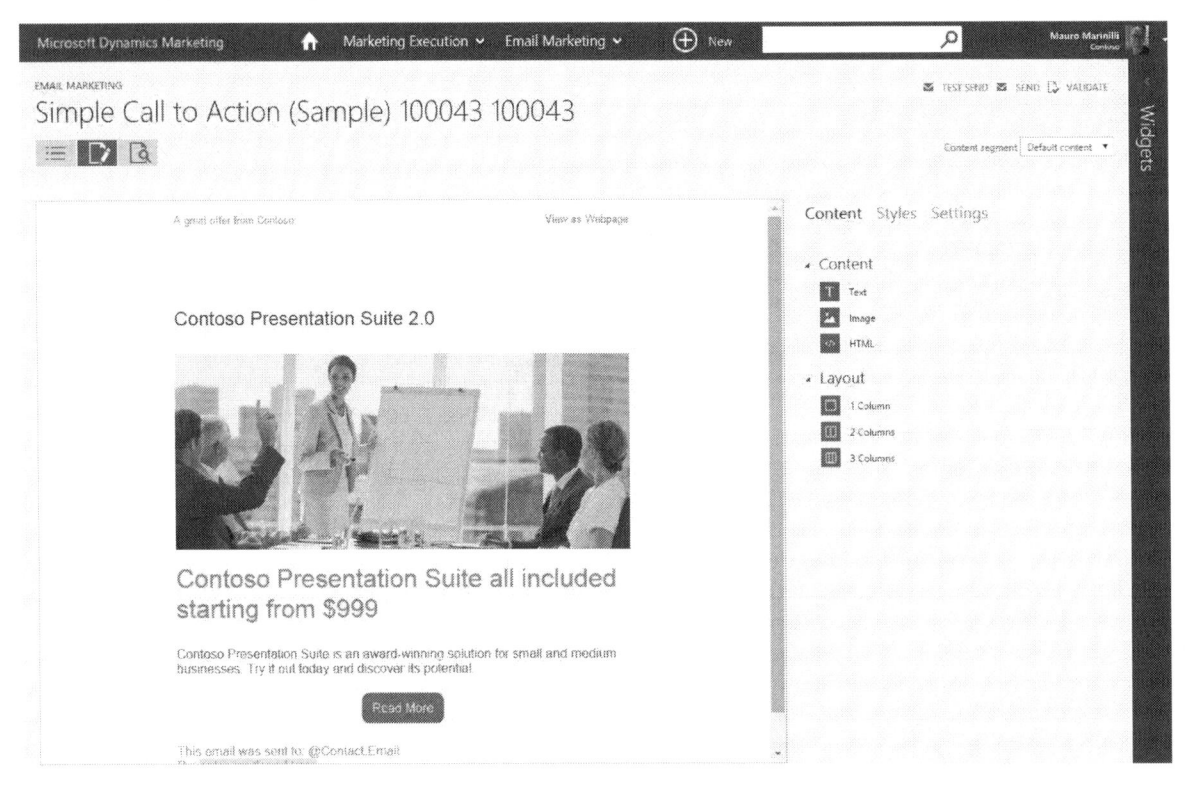

Figure A.6 – "Electra" Email Editor (New)

DYNAMICS MARKETING SPRING 2014 (RELEASED APRIL 2014, CODENAME MIRA, V.16)

Improved navigation, new campaign automation editor and more.

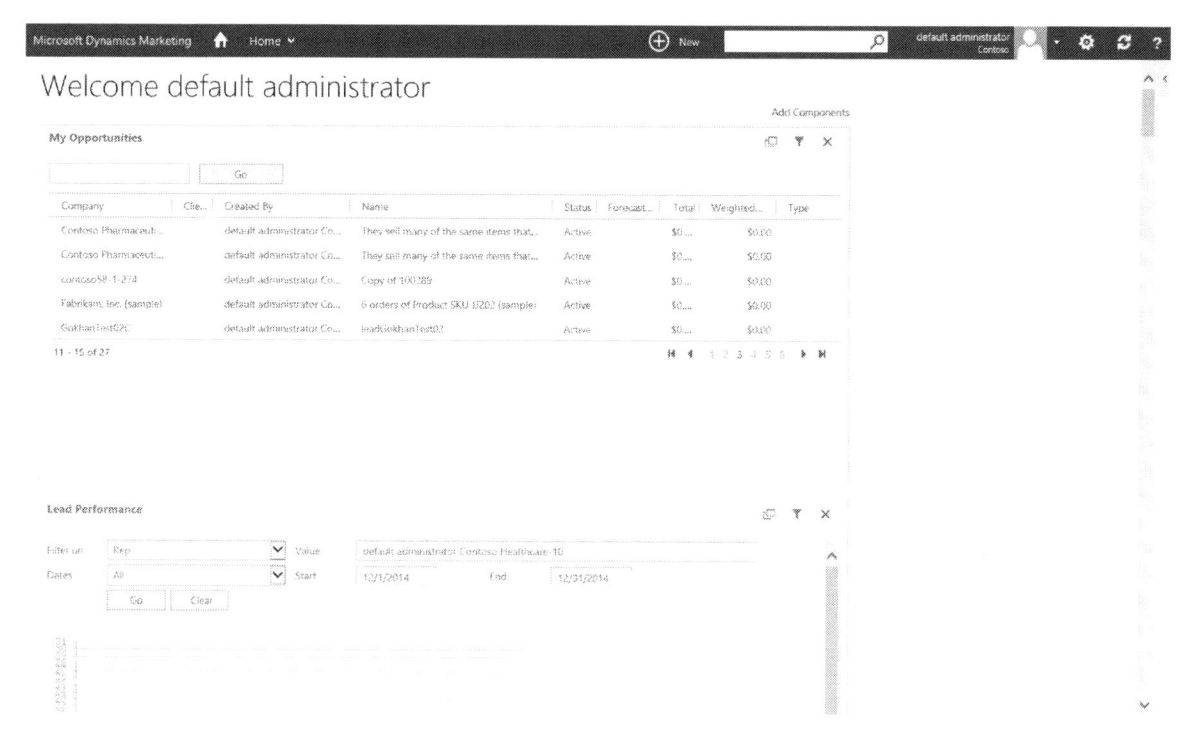

Figure A.7 – "Mira" Home Page

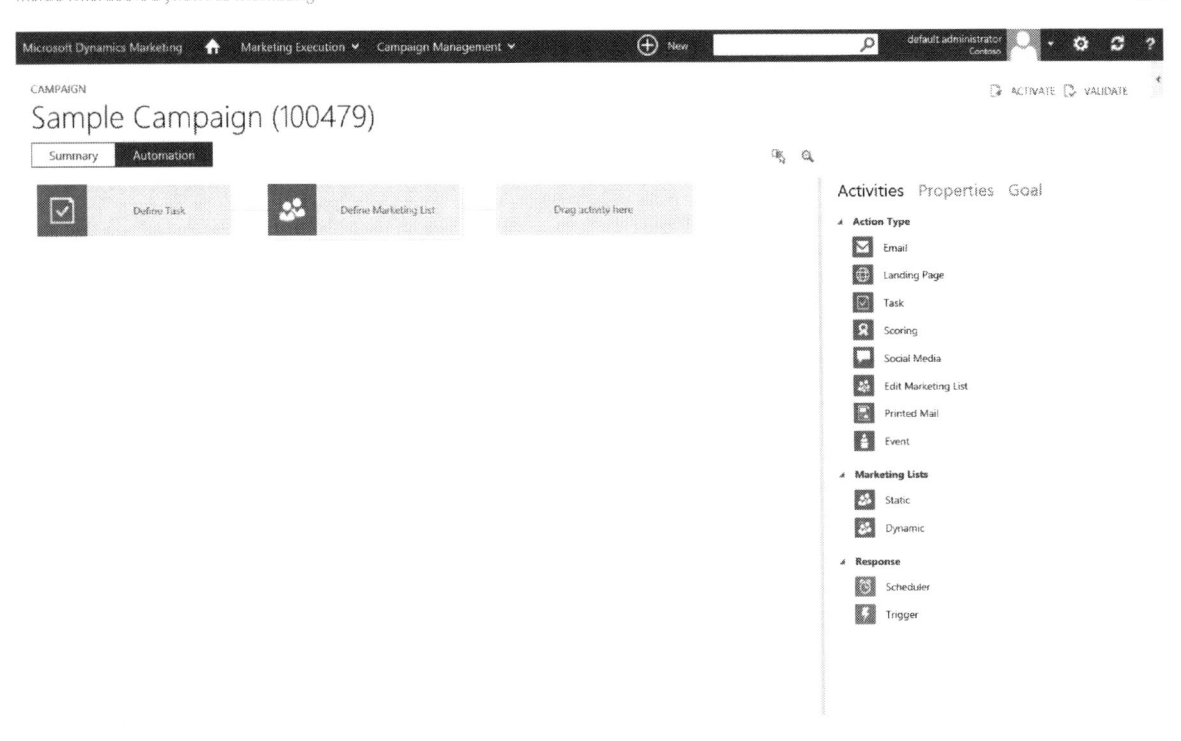

Figure A.8 –"Mira" Campaign Automation Editor (New)

Inside Microsoft Dynamics Marketing

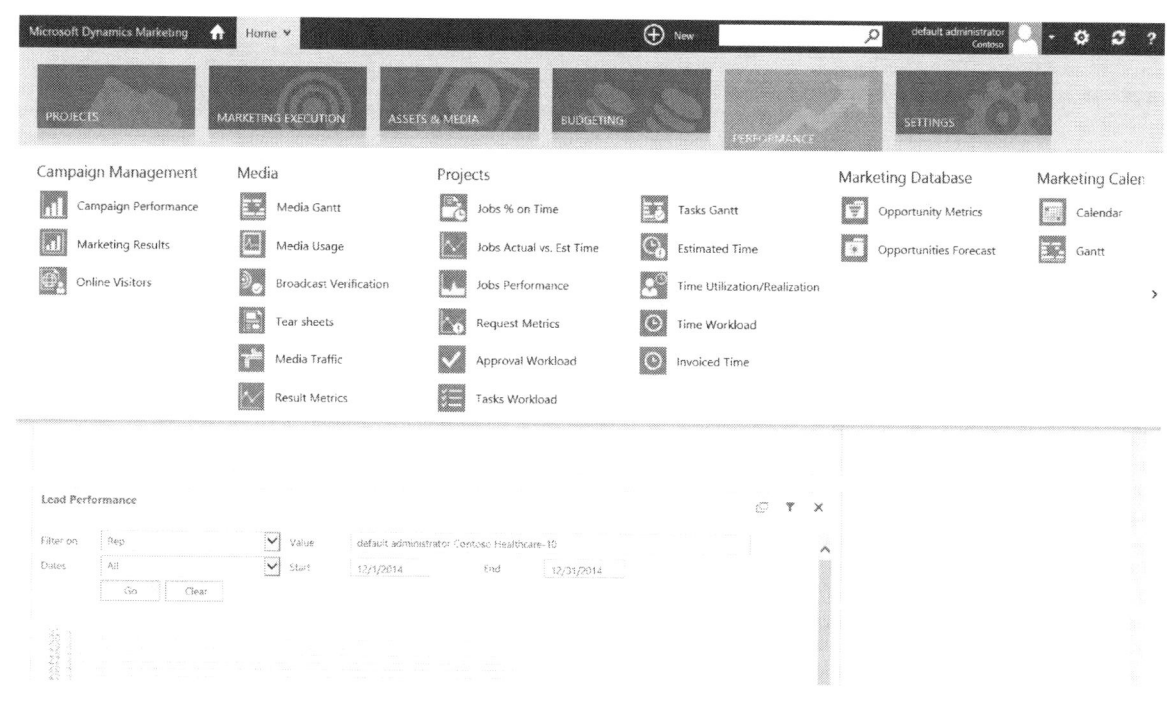

Figure A.9 – "Mira" Navigation (Improved)

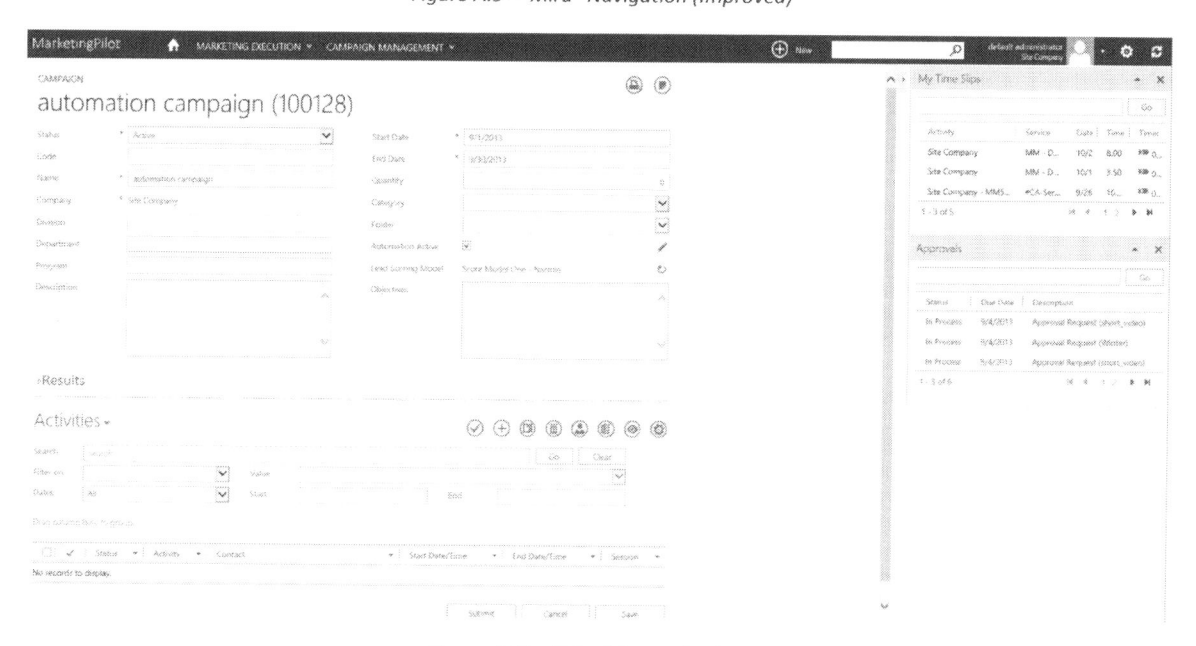

Figure A.10 – "Mira" Campaign Form

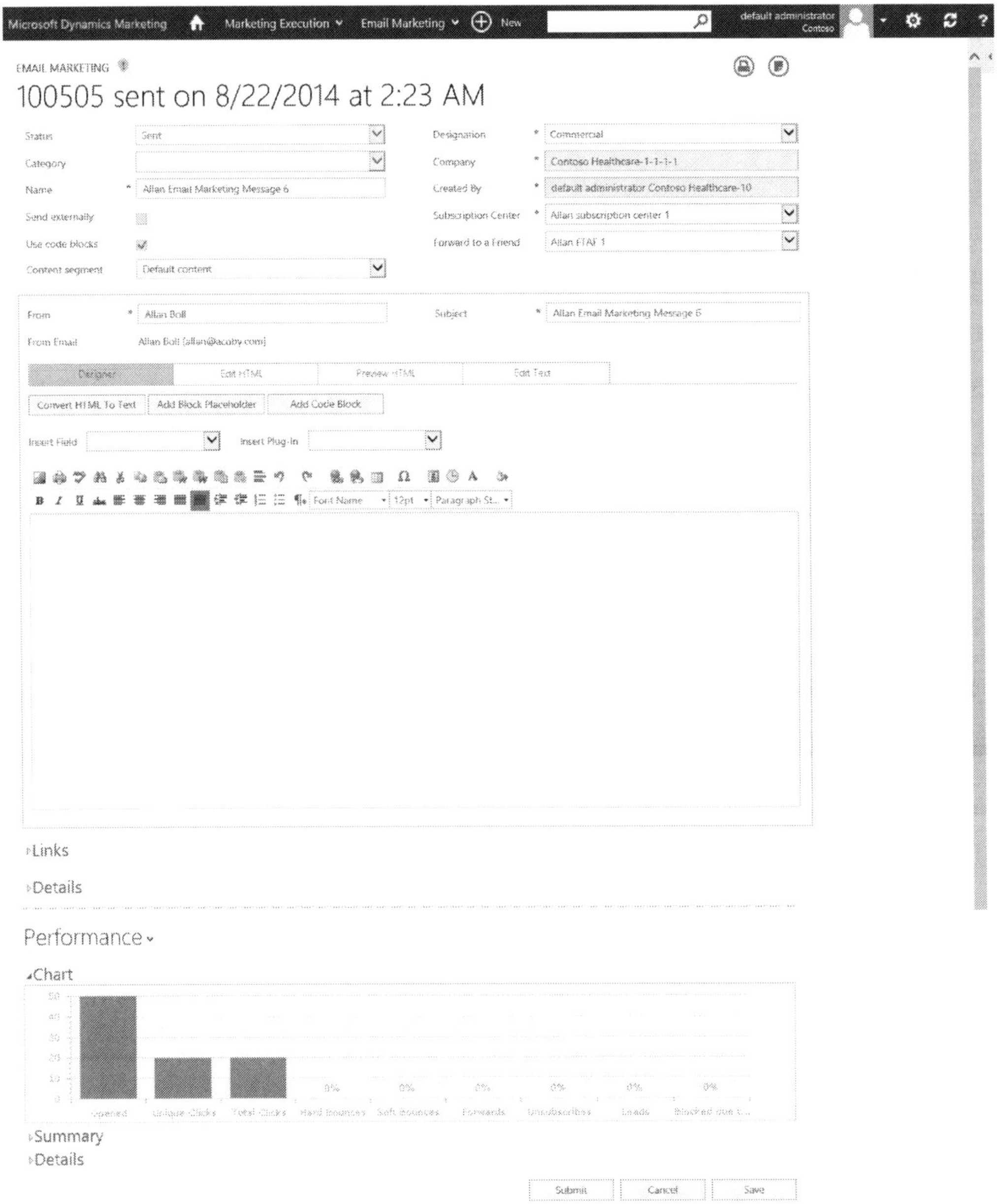

Inside Microsoft Dynamics Marketing

Figure A.11 – "Mira" Email Message

DYNAMICS MARKETING SPRING 2013
(RELEASED MARCH 2013, CODENAME GEMINI, V.15)

A new UX for the entire product, including a new navigation control.

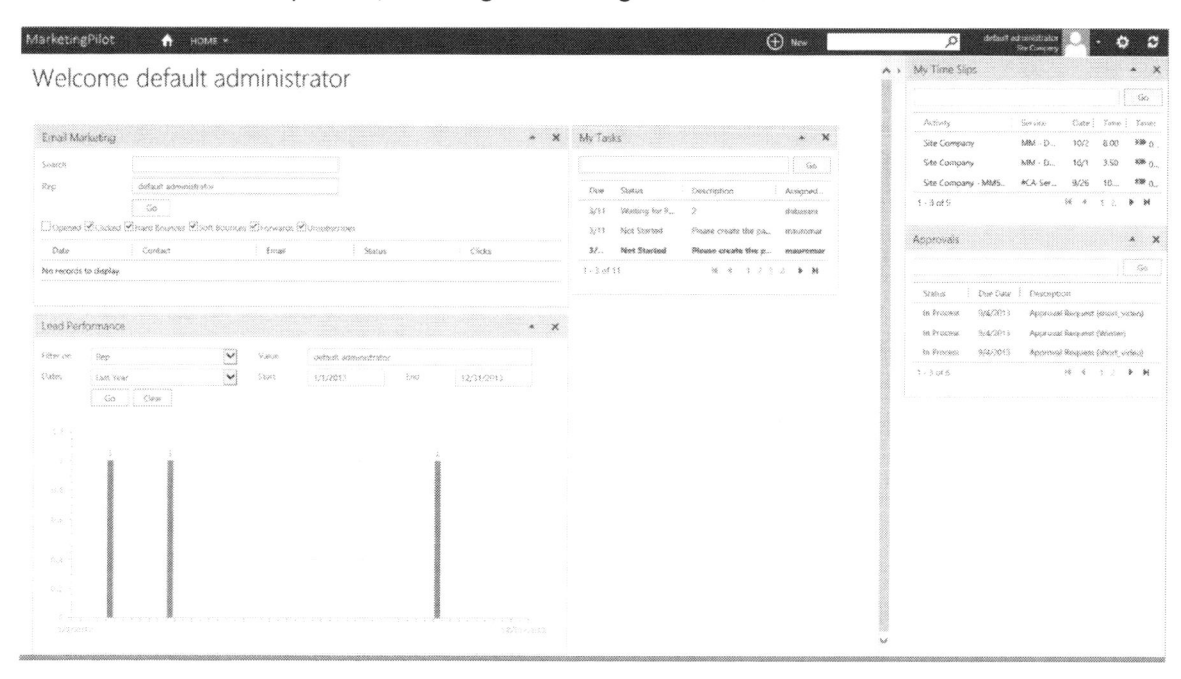

Figure A.12 – "Gemini" Home Page

Inside Microsoft Dynamics Marketing

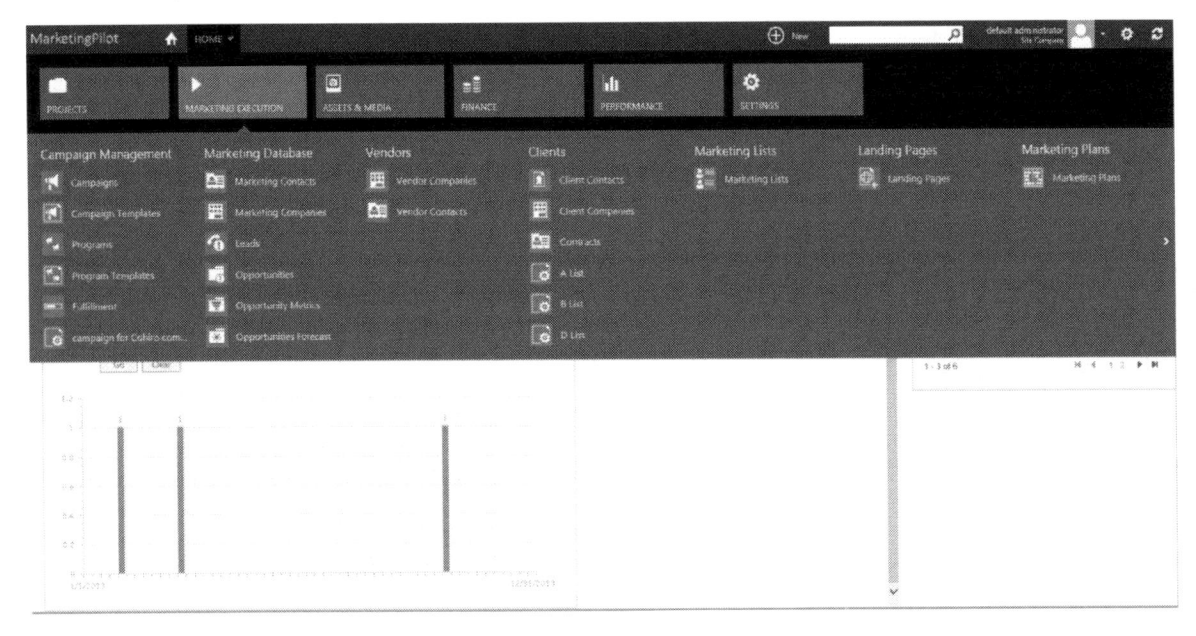

Figure A.13 – "Gemini" Navigation (New)

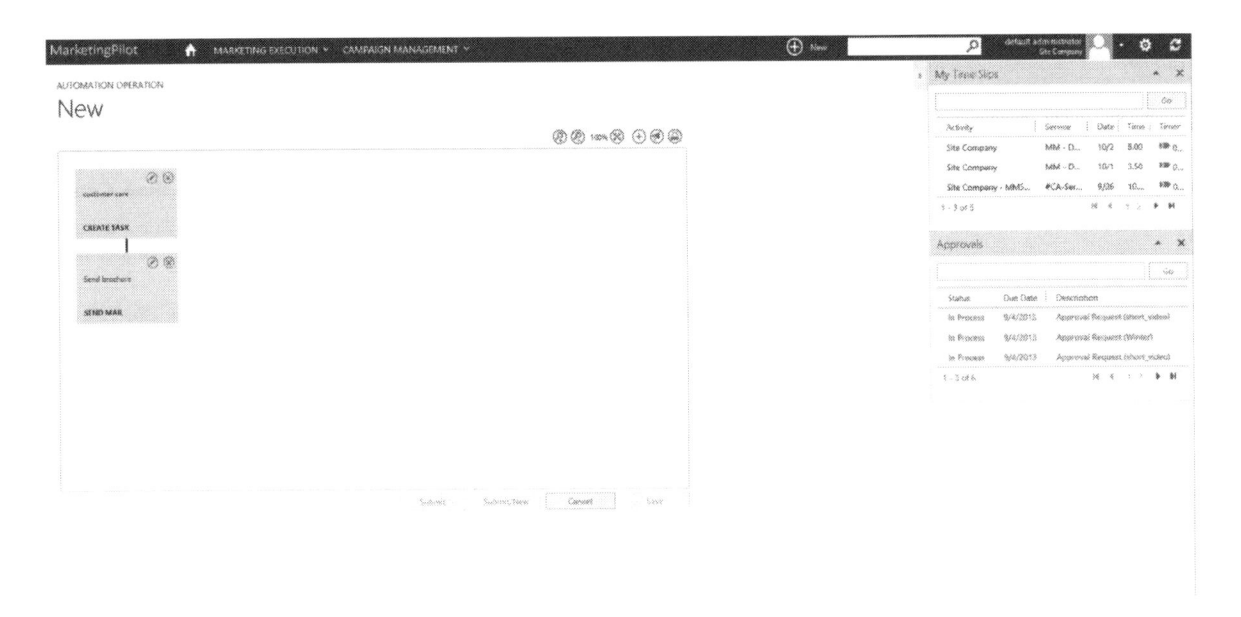

Figure A.14 – "Gemini" Campaign Automation Editor

Inside Microsoft Dynamics Marketing

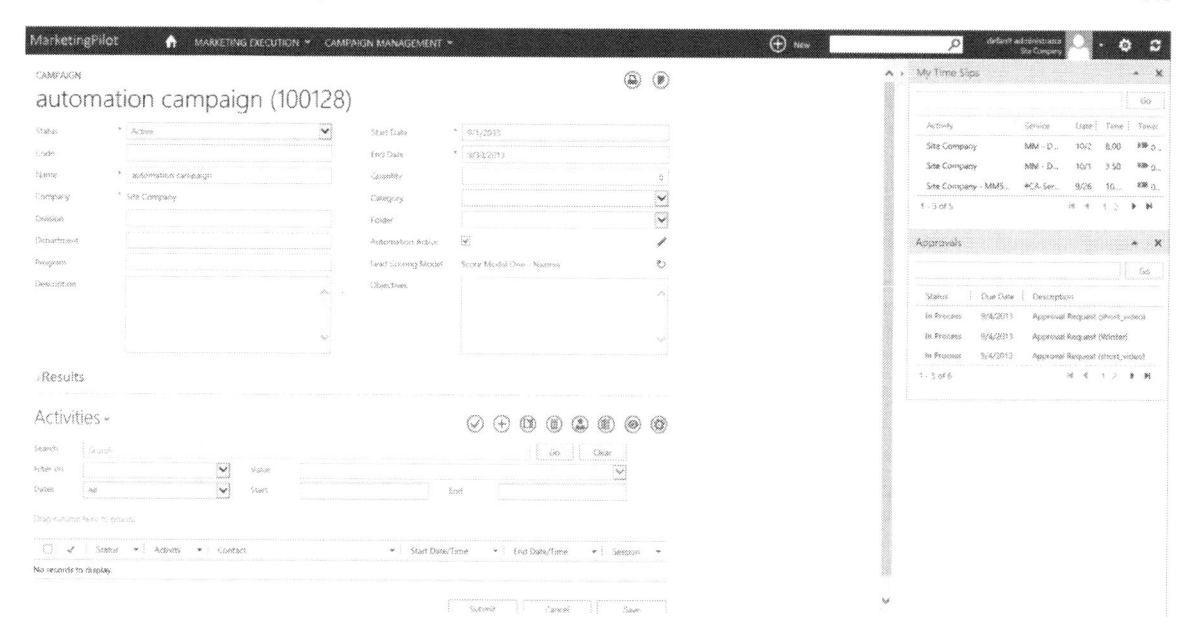

Figure A.15 – "Gemini" Campaign Form

Inside Microsoft Dynamics Marketing

MARKETINGPILOT – AFTER MICROSOFT ACQUISITION (FALL 2012, V.14.3)

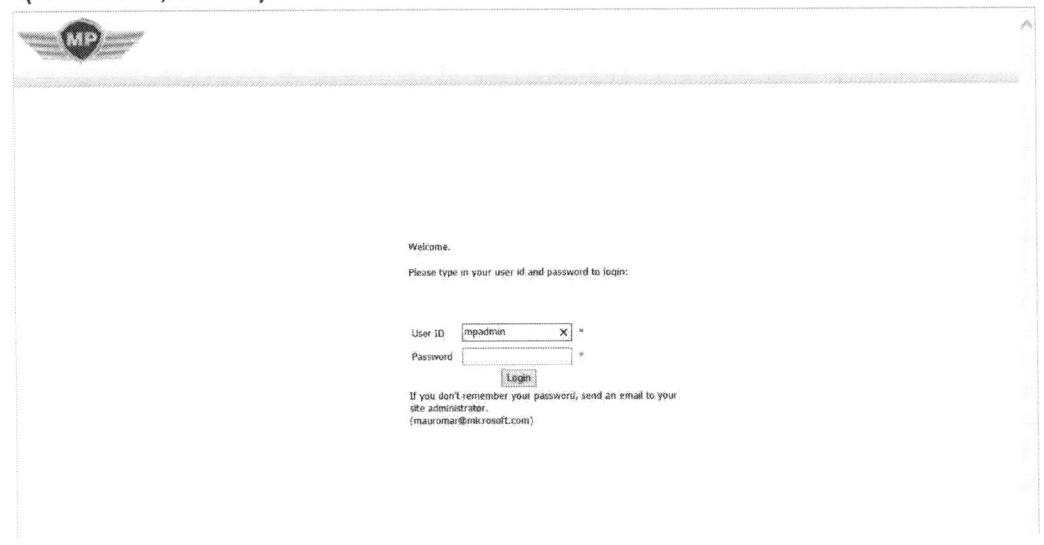

Figure A.16 – MarketingPilot Login Page

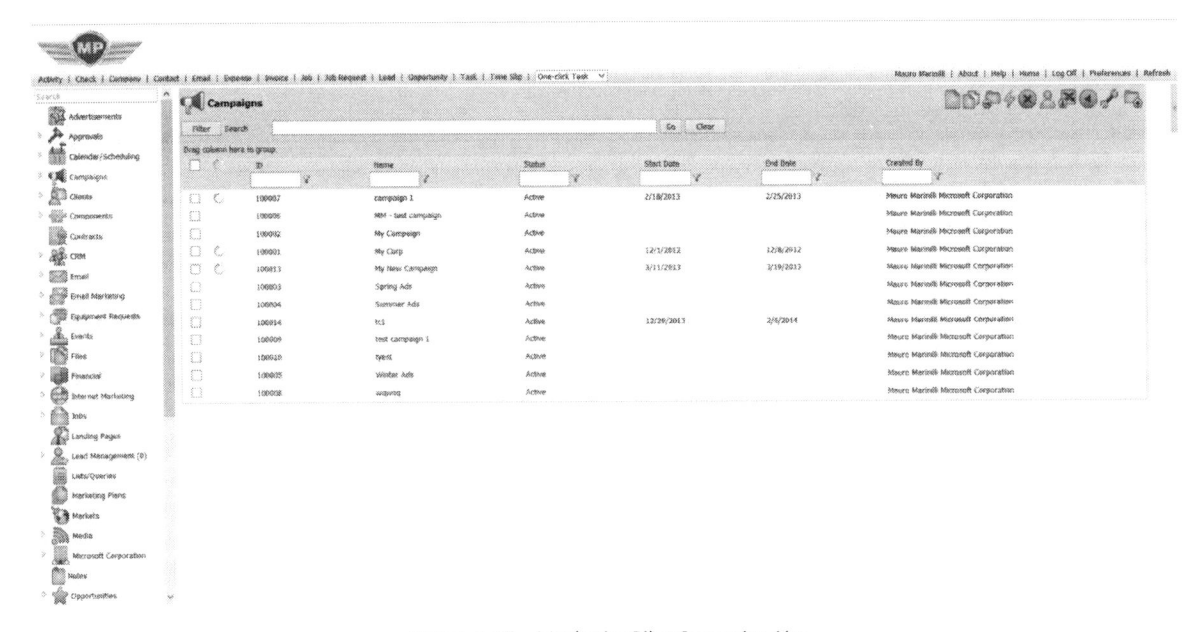

Figure A.17 – MarketingPilot Campaign List

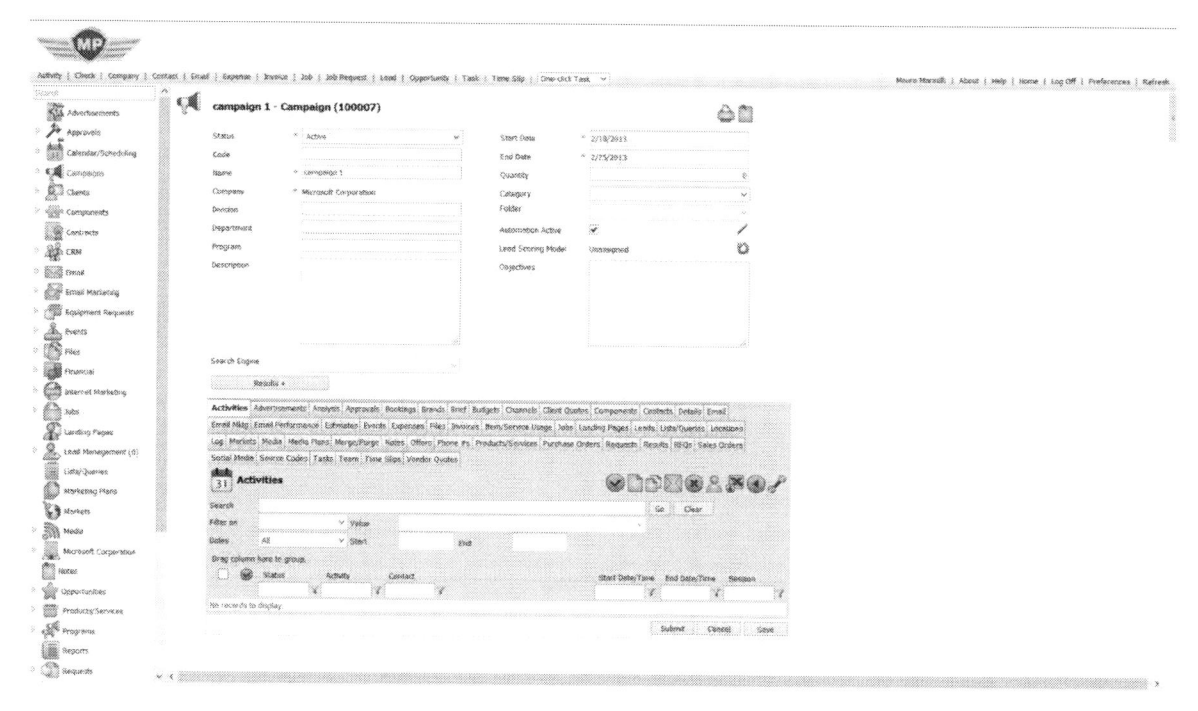

Figure A.18 – MarketingPilot Campaign Form

Figure A.19 – MarketingPilot Campaign Automation Editor

Inside Microsoft Dynamics Marketing 345

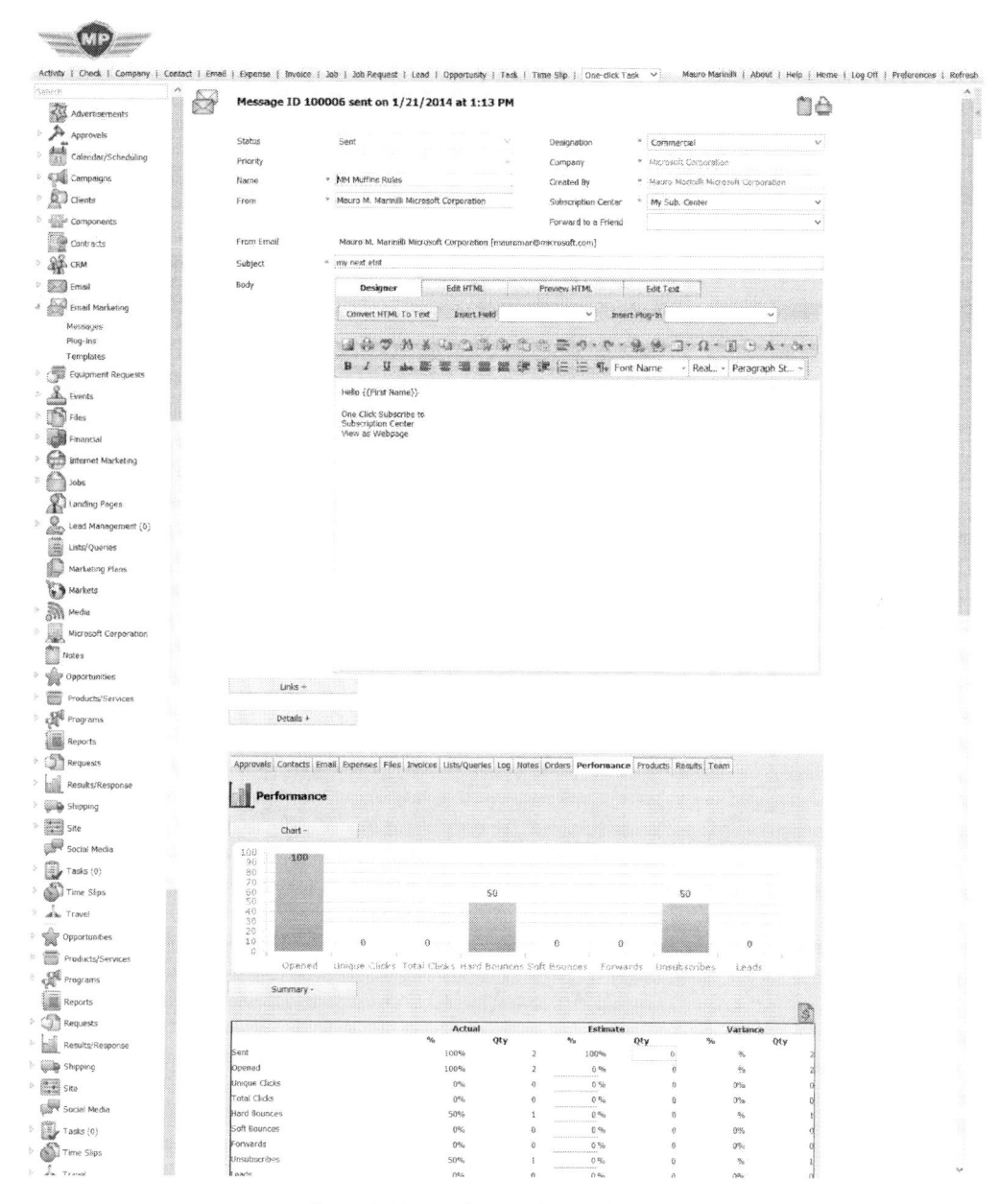

Figure A.20 – MarketingPilot Email Message

This page intentionally left blank

INDEX

A

Account types	288
Accounts Payable	284
Accounts Receivable	284
Accrual Accounting	283
Activities	264
Activities in Campaigns	47
Adaptive layout in emails	170
Administration Reports	236
Advertisements	248
Alert Settings, Page	274
Alerts	272
Alerts, Overview	27
Analytics in Dynamics Marketing	211
Anonymous access pages	31
Approval	
Legacy Approval	261
Approval Request	278
Approval Response	278
Approvals	277
Approvals, Overview	27

B

Banking Reports	236
Blacklisted IPs, Email Marketing	208
Broadcast Verification	248
Budget	287
Budget widget	213
Budget Workbooks	284

C

Calendar, Marketing	93
Campaign Automation Engine, Overview	46
Campaign, Marketing Automation	37
Campaign, Marketing Resource Management	69
Campaigns Reports	236
Cash Accounting	283
Chart of Accounts	284
Chart widgets	213
Clients and Receivables Reports	237
Commercial Emails API	324
Companies	77
Company and Budgeting Reports	238
Components	248
Contact Group Field	75
contact permissions API	203
Content block editor	
Email Marketing editor	170
Cross-Campaign Rules	64
Cross-Campaign Rules, blocked emails	66
Cross-Campaign Rules, Overview	54
Custom Fields in Odata feeds	234
Customer Driven Updates	33
Customers, Vendors and Clients, working with	74

D

Deliverability, Email Marketing	207
Demographics - Media Plans	248
Digital Asset Management - Files	258

Double Opt-In 37
Drip Campaign Example 57
Dynamic Content in emails 184

E

Email Address used for technical notifications 31
Email Marketing advanced configuration 207
Email Marketing Billing 133
Email Marketing Editor types 141
Email Marketing Message Status Field 149
Email Marketing Messages Results 150
Email marketing sample templates 119
email Marketing templates 128
Email Marketing terminology 128
Email Marketing Test Send 126
Email Marketing validation 145
Email Performance, Contacts panel - Type column 161
Email Reports 239
Email Types 129
Entities, Main 22
Estimates 285
Estimates Reports 239
Events 85
Events Reports 239
Expense, Expense Reconciliation 285

F

Fiscal Year Closing 284
Forms, Related Information Area 9
Forms, UI Overview 7
From field, dynamic content 189

H

home page 211
HTML code in emails 186

I

Information Architecture 4
Instances and Application URL 3

J

Job Requests 264
Job Templates 269
Jobs 264
Jobs Reports 240
Journal Entries 285

L

Landing Page, Creation 112
Landing Page, iFrame Hosting 116
Landing Page, Lead creation confirmation email 117
Landing Pages in Campaigns 53
Lead Assignment 117
Lead Interactions 110
Lead Scoring Model, Rules of Use 107
Lead, Automatic Scoring 102
Leads Scoring Rules 108
Leads Strategy 105
Leads, Management 101
Leads, Manual Import 102
Leads, Marked As Read 112
List, Marketing Entity 83
Lists , Configuring 20
Lists, Filtering 19
Lists, UI 19
Locations - Jobs 264
lookup fields, searching 17

M

Map Widgets 214
Market Segments 257
Marketing Budgets - Budgeting 287
Marketing Calendar 93
Marketing Lists 83
Marketing Portal 87
Markets 249
Media Buyer user type - Media Planning 253
Media Buys, Market and Demographics, Associating ... 256
Media Calendar 257
Media Expenses and Invoices 250
Media Outlets 248
Media Plan 250
Media Queries in emails 170
Media Reports 241
Media Sales and Inventory 248
Microsoft Social Listening 215
Microsoft Social Listening Integration options 220

Microsoft Social Listening keywords 217

O

OData feeds 221
OData feeds and Power BI 231
OData feeds, custom fields and UDFs 234
Office 365 Add-ons 1
Office 365 User Setup, Overview 29

P

Payroll 285
Postal/Zip Codes 249
Power BI Report Widget 213
Primary sales representative in "From" field 190
Programs Reports 242
Projects - Overview 263

R

Rate Cards 249
Razor code in emails 186
Razor code in emails, basic constructs 188
Reconciliation 289
Record-based Security 24
Reports 235
Response model for a Campaign 61
Results Reports 242

S

Sales Collaboration with Marketing 87
Sales Ready Leads 111
Sales Reports 243
Sample Double Opt-In Example Campaign Model 35
Scheduling - Jobs 264
Security Overview 26
Segment-based adaptation in emails 185
Seller Portal 87
Send Externally option in emails 194
Services Configuration 321
Shipments - Jobs 268
Silverlight not required for Files functionality 261
Social Analytics 215
Social widgets 214
Soft Delete 23

Soft-Deleted File, permanent removal 24
Spam, Email Marketing 207
Staff Contacts from Office 365 79

T

Tabs in Campaign, Email Messages, Approvals etc. 18
Tasks 264
Tasks Reports 244
Tasks, One-Click Creation 271
Tax Rates 286
Taxes Reports 244
Templates, General Concepts 25
Test Instance 2
Time Slips 264
Time Slips Reports 244
TODAY operator in Queries 60
Traceable transactional emails 194
Traceable Transactional Emails API 324
Tracking User Behavior 38
Transfer Funds 286
Trial Experience 32
Trigger events in Campaigns 50
Triggers in Campaigns, Advanced 55
Troubleshooting email sending 204

U

UI Simplified for large DBs 74
User Defined Fields in Odata feeds 234
User Preferences, Configuration 314
User Preferences, Menu 314

V

Vendors and Payables Reports 245
Version Send Time in AB Testing 56

W

Web Portal Users, Overview 26
widgets 211
Widgets, others 214

Z

Zoom, Campaign Editor 52

thank you!

Made in the USA
Lexington, KY
07 June 2016